Contending Approaches to the Political Economy of

TAIWAN

Studies of the East Asian Institute—Columbia University

The East Asian Institute of Columbia University

The East Asian Institute is Columbia University's center for research, publication, and teaching on modern East Asia. The Studies of the East Asian Institute were inaugurated in 1962 to bring to a wider public the results of significant new research on Japan, China, and Korea.

Contending Approaches to the Political Economy of
TAIWAN

Edwin A. Winckler and Susan Greenhalgh
Editors

An East Gate Book

M. E. SHARPE, INC.
ARMONK, NEW YORK
LONDON, ENGLAND

An East Gate Book

Copyright © 1988 by M. E. Sharpe, Inc.

Available in the United Kingdom and Europe from M. E. Sharpe, Publishers, 3 Henrietta Street, London WC2E 8LU.

Library of Congress Cataloging-in-Publication Data

Contending approaches to the political economy of Taiwan.

    Bibliography: p.
    Includes index.
    1. Taiwan—Economic conditions.
I. Winckler, Edwin A. II. Greenhalgh, Susan.
HC430.5.C75   1988   338.951′249   87-16413
ISBN 0-87332-440-4

Printed in the United States of America

CONTENTS

Introduction

Prewar Background

Postwar Formation

LIST OF FIGURES

LIST OF TABLES

ACKNOWLEDGMENTS

The editors thank the following organizations and individuals for their indispensable assistance.

The Joint Committee on Contemporary China of the Social Science Research Council and the American Council of Learned Societies, particularly Jason Parker, for funding the December 1980 workshop that launched this project.

The East Asian Institute of Columbia University for hosting the workshop and providing office space and secretarial support to Winckler during his organizing and writing.

The other authors—Richard Barrett, Bruce Cumings, Thomas Gold, and Denis Simon—for sharing our purpose and completing the task.

The other Asian specialists who contributed to the workshop—Emily Ahern, Ralph Clough, Myron Cohen, Hill Gates, Bruce Jacobs, Johanna Meskill, James Seymour, and Ezra Vogel.

The distinguished comparativists who contributed to the workshop—Alice Amsden, Christopher Chase-Dunn, Mrini Datta Chaudhuri, Peter Evans, Robert Kaufman, James Kurth, Juan Linz, Richard Rubinson, and Theda Skocpol.

The Publications Committee of the China Committee of SSRC-ACLS, including their two anonymous reviewers, for raising useful questions.

The Center for Chinese Studies at the University of California, Berkeley, for supporting Greenhalgh during part of her writing and editing.

The Department of Sociology of Harvard University for support of Winckler during much of his writing and editing.

The Center for Policy Studies of the Population Council, for supporting Greenhalgh in a project begun before she joined that organization. Particularly Doreen Totaram, for superb secretarial support and for consolidating the bibliography and compiling the index.

M. E. Sharpe, especially Anita O'Brien, for expeditious and expert editing and publishing.

Edwin Winckler and Susan Greenhalgh

CONTRIBUTORS

Richard E. Barrett is an associate professor of sociology at the University of Illinois at Chicago. He researches East Asian political economy and historical demography and has a book forthcoming on *Population Processes in China since the Nineteenth Century*.

Bruce Cumings, a political scientist, is professor of history at the University of Chicago. His forthcoming work includes volume 2 of *The Origins of the Korean War* (Princeton) and *Industrial Behemoth: The Northeast Asian Political Economy in the Twentieth Century* (Cornell).

Thomas B. Gold teaches sociology at the University of California, Berkeley. His publications include *State and Society in the Taiwan Miracle* (M. E. Sharpe, 1986). He is currently working on a book-length study of the reemergence of the private sector in the People's Republic of China.

Susan Greenhalgh, an anthropologist, is an associate of the Center for Policy Studies of The Population Council in New York City. She researches population policy, family entrepreneurialism, and socioeconomic change in East Asia and is currently doing field research on demographic change in a village in Shaanxi, North China.

Denis Fred Simon is an associate professor of international business and technology at the Fletcher School of Law and Diplomacy in Medford, Massachusetts. A political scientist, he studies international technology transfer and business strategy, comparative government-business relations, and East Asian technological development.

Edwin A. Winckler, a political scientist, is a research associate of the East Asian Institute at Columbia University in New York. He studies Chinese political and economic development and is currently writing a book on the role of Taiwan in the future of China.

Contending Approaches
to the Political
Economy of
TAIWAN

INTRODUCTION

1

Edwin A. Winckler and Susan Greenhalgh

ANALYTICAL ISSUES AND HISTORICAL EPISODES

East Asian societies continue to become more important, both as practical participants in the global economy and as comparative cases for theorists of economic and political development. Developed countries wonder where their industries have gone, developing countries wonder whence their industries will come. Among developed countries, Japan threatens to assume the lead in technology-intensive industries. Among developing economies, China threatens to appropriate a large share of labor-intensive industries. Development economists wonder whether there is room in the global economy for more ''newly industrialized countries.'' Political economists debate the relationship between economic development and authoritarian politics.

Aside from Japan, the ''capitalist'' East Asian cases remain underresearched, relative both to their intrinsic interest and to the extensive literature on comparable societies in other regions. As the dramatic successes of the 1960s and 1970s, they caught the attention of development planners and development economists. This attention, however, revealed how little is known about the actual political economy of their development. Much of what we know about Taiwan and Korea comes from economists, and much of their data comes from governments. The governments of both states have ably documented their remarkable macroeconomic performance, and they have even solicited searching examination of macroeconomic policies by foreign experts. In the past few years, social scientists have produced a first round of comparisons of the East Asian countries, both with each other and with other regions. Yet what those studies gain in breadth they lose in depth. Most of the historical-economic background and microeconomic detail of the Taiwan and Korean experiences remain unsketched. Work on political and social processes, and how they related to economic processes, has hardly begun. Consequently, one of the objectives of this volume is to improve the descriptive treatment of key episodes in Taiwan's development, and of the political-economic and sociocultural processes that underlie them. All the authors in this volume are area specialists who speak one or more of the region's languages and have done field research in the societies they write about, primarily Taiwan but also South Korea.

The other purpose of the volume is to confront these historical episodes with the analytical issues on which they bear. The comparative literature about late-developing, non-Western countries involves a dialogue between the three basic reactions to the experience of the earlier-developing Western countries—conservatism, liberalism, and radicalism. The existing literature about Taiwan is for the most part liberal in portraying Taiwan's rapid postwar development as largely the result of successful adjustment to market processes. This volume examines the applicability to Taiwan of radical models emphasizing conflicts of interest between early- and late-developing countries and between elites and masses within developing countries. In particular, the chapters focus on recent "radical globalist" models critical of "dependency" and the capitalist "world system," and recent "radical statist" models critical of "bureaucratic authoritarianism" and "state autonomy." Most conclude that both liberal and radical literatures require supplement from the conservative orientation, particularly its emphasis on the positive contributions of strong states and strong societies.

Thus, classically, liberalism has emphasized the benefits of free competition by individuals in economic markets and political elections. Most of the literature about Taiwan is by liberal economists who have documented the benefits to Taiwan of market mechanisms, and who regard Taiwan's experience as confirming that externally oriented capitalist development can benefit other countries as well. Less has been written about political development on Taiwan, but that literature, too, is largely liberal in expecting socioeconomic modernization to produce the modernization of administration and the democratization of representation.

Radicalism, classically, has argued that society and politics are organized around the requirements of economic development and has emphasized the unfavorable terms presented by capitalist markets to mass workers and backward countries. In the 1970s a new tide of radical literature argued that participation in global capitalism stunts or distorts both economic and political development. Economic dependence on foreign aid, trade, and investment would result in slow economic growth and unequal income distribution. Political dependence on foreign states and foreign firms would result in domestic states that served the interests of capitalist development, either by remaining abjectly weak or by acting strongly on behalf of capitalist elites against proletarian masses. Much of this still-evolving radical literature has been based on changing Latin American experiences—first the slow growth and relaxed politics of the 1950s, then the fast growth and repressive politics of the 1960s and 1970s, and most recently the slower growth and more democratic politics of the 1980s.

The radical literature continues to hold both promise and problems as applied to newly industrializing capitalist countries of East Asia such as Taiwan. On the one hand, for both economic and political processes, radical analysis promises to deepen our appreciation of domestic costs, foreign causes, and future problems. On the other hand, much of the East Asian experience appears to contradict radical expectations. Economically, participation in global capitalism has been accompanied by some of the most rapid growth rates and most equal income distributions in the world. Politically, East Asian states were quite authoritarian before they became capitalist, and they have remained quite autonomous since they became capitalist.

Intrigued by radical claims but puzzled by their inapplicability to Taiwan, the authors in this volume met with a group of prominent comparative political economists at Columbia University in December 1980 to discuss the relevance of radical models to East Asia. In retrospect, what emerged from those discussions and from the authors' collective and individual rethinking of the Taiwan experience since then is the importance of a third set of processes—historical, geopolitical, and sociocultural. These processes are "conservative" both in the sense that they persist from the past and in the sense that they correspond to political theories stressing the benefits of strong states and strong societies. Often it is these conservative factors that help explain why on Taiwan the liberal processes have worked so well and why the ill effects that radicals fear from liberal processes have not occurred.

Thus, taken as a whole, this volume gropes toward a synthesis of the liberal, radical, and conservative orientations. The authors accept many of the findings of the existing liberal literature about Taiwan, summarized in the second chapter of this volume. The authors attempt to sort out what is and is not applicable to East Asia from the radical comparative literature, summarized below in the first half of this introduction. They draw heavily on, and add considerably to, the existing conservative literature about Taiwan, also summarized in the second chapter.

The papers published here include nine that were first presented at the workshop and then rewritten or substantially revised in the mid-1980s (chapters 3–11), a Korea comparison solicited by the editors (chapter 12), and introductory and concluding chapters prepared by the editors. The second half of this introduction briefly reports the main descriptive topic and main interpretive theme of each chapter. The volume's concluding chapter compares the authors' interpretations and suggests their implications for further research.

Radical Globalism: Dependency and World System Theories

At the supranational level, the "globalist" paradigm emphasizes worldwide processes that, it is argued, strongly condition national development and subnational outcomes. By now there are radical, conservative, and even liberal versions of this paradigm, each giving different accounts of political-economic, geopolitical, and sociocultural processes and the relationships between them (e.g., Wallerstein 1974; 1979; 1980; Gilpin 1975; 1981; Keohane and Nye 1972; 1977; Keohane 1984). In general, globalism should be applicable to Taiwan, which has always been a part of some larger political unit heavily influenced by external political and economic events. Though refuting some radical-globalist claims, all the authors in this volume emphasize the strength of external impacts on Taiwan.

Since midcentury, radical analysis of the supranational level has evolved toward some synthesis with conservative and liberal globalism. There have been two major stages, the earlier "dependency" and later "world system" perspectives. Both of these have early and late versions. Functionally, the progression has been from predominant preoccupation with radical political economy toward a comprehensive account giving explicit attention to military-political and socio-cultural processes as well. Spatially, the progression has been from a focus on unequal relations between particular countries toward a comprehensive account of global capitalism (and communism) as a whole, and the differentiation of subglobal regions within them. Temporally, the progression has been from episodic case studies toward a systematic history of the trends, cycles, and transformations in global capitalism over the past five hundred years.

Dependency Theory

Dependency theory was originally formulated in the 1950s and 1960s by Latin American authors arguing that U.S. hegemony had inhibited Latin American development. Relative to previous liberal literature, it shifted attention from internal to external causes of underdevelopment. Relative to previous radical literature, however, it shifted attention from the origins of imperialism in advanced countries to the mechanisms through which imperialism affected backward countries. Most dependency literature is not truly global, but rather usually looks upward from a particular segment of the less developed world at its relationship with a particular segment of the more developed world.

Classical Marxism had seen internal "feudalism" as the source of domestic economic backwardness, eventually to be overcome in country after country by capitalist development. In contrast, early dependency theory saw global capitalism itself as the source of underdevelopment, arguing that external economic involvement prevents internal economic development (e.g., Baran 1957; Frank 1969b; 1969c). The reasons were both economic and political. The basic economic reason was the existing unequal international division of labor. Early-developing countries had already achieved an overwhelming competitive advantage in high-productivity industries, allowing them to reap high profits from both sales and investments in late developers. This left late developers to specialize in primary exports, the markets for which were unreliable and the prices for which were unstable. The basic political reason why external involvement prevented internal development was the unequal distribution of political power, both external and internal. Advanced countries backstopped economic advantages with military force when necessary. Backward countries themselves adopted policies reinforcing rather than overcoming backwardness, partly under pressure from the states and firms of advanced countries, but mostly because the states of backward countries were themselves dominated by local economic elites engaged in primary exports. These patterns of economic specialization and power distribution also produced poor income distribution within underdeveloped countries.

The later version of dependency theory was formulated in the 1960s and 1970s in response to the obvious fact that, despite the pessimism of early dependency theory, some Latin American countries were rapidly industrializing. Consequently, theories of "dependent development" conceded that external economic involvement may produce internal economic growth but argued that such involvement distorts that growth in favor of external rather than internal needs (e.g., Bonilla and Girling 1973; Cardoso and Faletto 1979). Thus the kinds of products produced were those demanded by affluent consumers in developed (or developing) countries, rather than those appropriate to the basic needs of the masses of the developing countries themselves. The kinds of technologies employed were capital-intensive ones transferred from developed countries, rather than labor-intensive ones that would maximize employment and equalize income in developing countries. High-productivity economic activities tended to concentrate in spatial enclaves under the control of foreign firms, government bureaucracies, and economic elites, inaccessible to most of the population, and therefore aggravating the maldistribution of income.

Most of the existing literature, and most of the chapters in this volume, emphasize the inadequacies of both early and late dependency literature as applied to Taiwan (e.g., chapters 4, 9; Barrett and Whyte 1982). Before 1945, though the colonial Japanese state did force Taiwan to specialize in primary products, it also guaranteed a market for them. Moreover, the development program implemented by the Japanese was much more comprehensive than that of other colonial powers, resulting not only in the modernization of agriculture and industry, but also in the exposure of Taiwanese to some light, and even heavy, industry. After 1945, the Nationalist Chinese state on Taiwan destroyed any indigenous elites attached to primary exports, unleased domestic industrial entrepreneurs, and used the Japanese legacy to develop agriculture, light industry, and heavy industry. Having few natural resources other than its dense population, Taiwan specialized in labor-intensive agriculture and industry for meeting domestic needs, thus increasing employment and equalizing income. Labor- and skill-intensive industries also provided Taiwan's burgeoning exports, with similarly beneficent domestic effects. Taiwan is sufficiently small in both area and population that industrialization soon penetrated the entire island, further contributing to equality of income distribution.

These happy outcomes are well known. What remains to be explained, however, is why Japanese, American, and Chinese states and firms adopted policies so beneficial to Taiwan. Another strand of radical globalism, world system theory, suggests some answers to these questions.

World System Theory

Building on the work of Braudel, Frank, and others, world system theory was formulated in the 1970s by the radical American scholar Immanuel Wallerstein as a broad framework for analyzing global development over the past five hundred years. It includes the struggles of both advanced and backward countries and emphasizes the connections between these struggles. Wallerstein's formulation posits both political conflict between states and economic competition between firms, evidently regarding technological capacity and market advantage as fundamental to both economic and political success (Wallerstein 1974; 1979).

Wallerstein distinguishes three main "zones" in the global stratification system: an advanced core, an exploited periphery, and an intermediate "semiperiphery." Countries rise and fall through these zones to the extent that they succeed or fail in meeting the structural imperatives of their zonal starting position. Wallerstein's global core contains a disproportionate share of high-productivity, well-paid economic activities. This strong economic base both supports and is supported by strong states that also promote national cultural integration and cultural modernization. The periphery contains a disproportionate share of low-productivity, low-paid economic activities. This weak economic base both permits and is permitted by weak states unable to maintain national independence and national integration in the face of external penetration. The semiperiphery contains a mix of high-productivity and low-productivity economic activities. Semiperipheral states usually are either losing a past effectiveness or gaining a future effectiveness, often drawing on national cultural traditions to mobilize domestic support for economic modernization. This middle zone acts partly as a buffer against direct political conflict between core and periphery, and partly as a bridge for upward and downward mobility between them (1974, 346–57; 1979, 95–118).

Thus radical globalists view the world as a mobility struggle. Accordingly, the two key processes whose interaction defines Wallerstein's "modern world system" are global political conflict between national states and global economic competition between capitalist firms. The supranational scale of markets permits capitalist firms to escape the regulation of any particular nation-state, enabling them to operate in the interstices of the international system, and providing much of the dynamism to the global economy. To extract as much profit as possible, firms exploit both their domestic lower classes and the populations of peripheral countries. To achieve as much power as possible, states support their own firms and base their military power on the resulting economic capacity. Changing struggles of firms and states in the core cause the changing impacts of the core on the periphery (Wallerstein 1974, 346–57; Bergesen 1980; Friedman 1982). In particular, competition between core states and core firms may lead them to "invite" peripheral states and firms to develop as "associated dependent" allies.

In the 1980s, "later" world system theory continues to be elaborated by both supporters and critics. Supporters have added more explicit treatments of political-military and sociocultural processes (e.g., Meyer and Hannan 1979; Wallerstein 1983; Bergesen 1980; 1983). Supporters have also explored reasons for change over time and variation between regions (e.g., Meyer and Hannan 1979; Hopkins and Wallerstein 1980; Wallerstein 1980; Bergesen 1983; Arrighi 1985b). Critics have questioned the tightness with which Wallerstein ties military-political and sociocultural processes to political-economic ones (e.g., Modelski 1978), denied his claim that the core and periphery were already strongly interacting before the mid-nineteenth century (Stinchcombe 1982), and challenged the existence and utility of his concept of a semiperiphery (e.g., Brieger 1981; Snyder and Kick 1979).

The Taiwan case illustrates the usefulness of both early and late world system theory for explaining national development. On the one hand, early world system theory, by restoring rivalries between core states and core firms to global radicalism, helps explain why first Japan and later the United States "invited" Taiwan to develop (e.g., chapters 4 and 12). By identifying some of the structural characteristics and strategic dilemmas of countries trying to achieve mobility up into and up through the semiperiphery, world system theory helps explain some of the structural tensions within Taiwan's economy (e.g., chapters 9 and 11) and some of the economic policies adopted by the Nationalist state (e.g., chapters 7 and 10). By emphasizing the interpenetration of the supranational level with the national and subnational levels, world system theory helps explain how external arrangements affect internal outcomes (chapters 3 and 5).

On the other hand, the improvements incorporated in later versions are essential for realizing the full potential of world system theory as applied to the Taiwan case. Functionally, military-political and sociocultural processes play roles that are partially independent of political-economic ones (e.g., chapters 3 and 10). Spatially, explanation must include interactions within and between core and semiperiphery, as well as the impact of core and semiperiphery on periphery (chapters 6 and 12). Temporally, only a long-term treatment of cumulative history and historical conjuncture can fully explain the distinctiveness of the East Asian region and the timing of particular events within it (chapters 3, 5, and 12).

Radical Statism: Authoritarianism and Autonomy

At the national level, the "statist" paradigm emphasizes the partial autonomy of the state from both its supranational environment and its subnational constituencies, both in the objectives the state pursues and in its role as a mediator between supranational and subnational actors. Although statism is basically a conservative idea (Weber 1925/1968; Hintze 1906/1975), by now there are radical and even liberal versions of this paradigm as well (e.g., Skocpol 1979; Nordlinger 1981). Statism, particularly versions dealing with "authoritarian regimes," is applicable to the imperial Chinese, colonial Japanese, and Nationalist Chinese states that have governed Taiwan. All the authors in this volume emphasize the active role of the Japanese and Nationalist states in Taiwan's development. The strong role of the Nationalist state is a theme that also emerges from comparative studies of the East Asian NICs (Deyo 1987b; Haggard and Cheng 1987) and from published and forthcoming work of Wade (1984; 1985; 1988).

Since midcentury, radical models of the national political state and its relationship to national economic elites also have evolved toward some synthesis with conservative and even liberal orientations. Again there have been two major stages, each with two phases. The first stage examined postwar states in Third World countries, in the earlier phase finding peripheral states weak, and in the later phase finding semiperipheral states strong, in both cases because of largely economic processes. The second stage, more broadly theoretical and comparative, is exploring the partial autonomy of political states from economic processes, first emphasizing the extent of that autonomy, then examining limitations on it, in a wide range of historical situations. Thus, again, the progression has been to distinguish functional processes, broaden spatial comprehensiveness, and deepen historical treatment. Conceptually, authors have distinguished political autonomy from administrative capacity and actual policy intervention and argued that "state strength" may be uneven across different external and internal policy areas.

Authoritarianism, Weak and Strong

The first two phases of radical statism's treatment of peripheral states largely correspond to the first two phases of radical globalism's treatment of peripheral economies. Early dependency theory itself included a political component arguing that external economic involvement prevented not only internal economic development but also internal political development. Weak peripheral states remained subject to capitalist elites—foreign, domestic, or both. Weak peripheral polities alternated between representative institutions dominated by economic elites and military suspension of even this "bourgeois" democracy, whenever populist forces advanced. Though thus excluding the masses, these polities remained ineffectual, particularly at advancing economic development.

The later "bureaucratic authoritarian" literature provided the political counterpart to the later dependency literature. Intermediate stages of capitalist economic development—domestic, foreign, or both—"required" the state to play a larger role (O'Donnell 1973; Evans 1979). Thus both O'Donnell and his critics (Collier 1979) searched for economic crises that may have provoked the appearance of authoritarian regimes in Latin America. For O'Donnell, this crisis was the transition from light to heavy industry, requiring the state to mobilize capital, concentrate income, and demobilize labor. For some of his critics, the crisis was the transition from domestic to export orientation, requiring the state to change both the external terms of trade and the internal composition of the economy, despite the political opposition of both elites and masses in the losing sectors. In either case, as Evans elaborated, the state helped run the economy, in both collaboration and competition with foreign and domestic economic elites. Nevertheless, radical analysts of bureaucratic authoritarianism searched for possible sources of change in, and variation between, such regimes. O'Donnell argued, essentially, that the narrower the interests represented, and the greater the use of repression, the greater the likelihood of regime transformation. Conversely, authoritarian regimes adopting policies that benefited many segments of society could succeed in institutionalizing partial mass participation through a dominant party, corporatist associations, or both.

The Taiwan case does not fully conform to either the "weak peripheral state" or "strong semiperipheral state" phases of radical statism. On the one hand, states on Taiwan have always been stronger than early dependency theory expected. Until 1895, the imperial Chinese state remained stronger than indigenous states in most other peripheral areas. From 1895 to 1945 the colonial Japanese state became much stronger than most Western colonial regimes in other peripheral areas. The postwar Nationalist state on Taiwan combined the administrative apparatus inherited from Japanese colonialism with the military-administrative resources transported from the Chinese mainland. Despite extensive accommodation to core states and core firms, the Nationalist state maintained control of its own armed forces and national budget and used them to pursue its own objectives.

On the other hand, the postwar Nationalist state on Taiwan only partially resembles Latin American bureaucratic authoritarian regimes, though for reasons that bureaucratic authoritarian theory can accommodate. The intensity of political authoritarianism has not varied noticeably in conjunction with economic transitions, either from light to heavy industry, or from domestic to export orientation. Postwar Taiwan does display the decline of elites based on primary exports and the predominance of an "internationalized, oligopolized bourgeoisie" found in Latin America. It has not, however, experienced open political intervention by the military as an institution. The military has not had to intervene, partly because Taiwan has no effective respresentative institutions to suspend, and partly because Taiwan's broadly distributed prosperity means that there is little mass discontent to repress.

Autonomy, Extent and Limits

In the late 1970s and early 1980s, North American scholars began revising and extending radical theories of the state and integrating them with conservative and even liberal ideas. An early phase emphasized the autonomy of the state, particularly during revolutions (Trimberger 1978; Skocpol 1979). This phase sketched some main features of contemporary radical statism. First, states are actors pursuing their own institutional interests, not just arenas registering other social forces. Second, national states typically mediate between the supranational environment and subnational society, deriving some support from each. Third, a national state can achieve considerable autonomy from social forces. Fourth, autonomy from social forces, capacity to implement policies, and actual intervention in social affairs may, to some extent, reinforce each other. Fifth, in addition to intended policy impacts, the pattern of state activities may unintentionally set the pattern for the state-focused activities of political parties, interest groups, social classes, political culture, and other broad social phenomena.

A later phase, still under way, has explored limitations on state autonomy, qualifying each of the above propositions (e.g., Evans, Rueschemeyer, and Skocpol 1985). First, states do also remain arenas for conflicting social interests and have significant difficulty acting coherently in pursuit of the state's own overall interest. Second, states derive constraints as well as support from the external and internal social forces between whom they mediate. Third, the circumstances under which states can achieve political autonomy, administrative capacity, or policy intervention need to be carefully specified, may be limited to particular problems, and may be hard to maintain. Fourth, autonomy, capacity, and intervention may, to some extent, undermine each other. Fifth, changes in external or internal environments, many of them partly caused by the state, can eventually transform elements of the state itself.

The Taiwan case provides support for both the autonomy-emphasizing and autonomy-limiting phases of this recent synthesizing literature. On the one hand, the Japanese and Nationalist states on Taiwan have exemplified the autonomy that the earlier phase emphasized (e.g., Amsden 1979). External and internal legacies gave the early postwar Nationalist state exceptional political autonomy and administrative capacity (chapter 8). Political autonomy and administrative capacity have been preconditions for policy effectiveness, and the three have reinforced each other (chapter 9). The pattern of state activities has set the pattern of both elite collaboration and mass acquiescence (chapters 3 and 5).

On the other hand, the Taiwan case also reveals many of the qualifications to autonomy that the later phase is exploring. The autonomy of states on Taiwan— Japanese, American, and Nationalist—has resulted from particular circumstances, which require clear specification (chapters 4 and 6). The success of Nationalist state intervention varies by problem (chapter 10) and the Nationalist state has husbanded its autonomy by limiting its interventions. Much of Nationalist state policy has been constrained by anticipation of external elite and domestic mass reaction (chapter 3), and the Nationalist state itself has gradually been transformed by changes in its external and internal environments (Amsden 1985).

Descriptive Topics and Analytical Themes

Each chapter in this volume makes some contribution both to describing Taiwan's (or Korea's) history and to analyzing the implications for comparative theory.

Prewar Background

Three chapters provide an overview of Taiwan's history to 1945. Winckler's chapter on mass incorporation (chapter 3) argues that the changing terms on which the general public has been incorporated into the political system on Taiwan have reflected the changing terms on which Taiwan has been incorporated into global and regional politics. On the one hand, he describes Taiwan's external political status during the three major political eras in Taiwan's history—local administration by imperial China until 1895, colonial rule by imperialist Japan from 1895 to 1945, and de facto independence under the Nationalist state since 1945. On the other hand, he describes the accompanying internal political conditions—initial pacification under the Chinese empire, administrative modernization under the Japanese empire, and gradual evolution from "hard" to "soft" authoritarianism under the Nationalist state and American influence. During the imperial, colonial, and Nationalist eras Taiwan has always remained half incorporated into an external political entity and half independent as an internal political entity. Consequently, its population has never achieved full political rights in either external or internal polities. Nevertheless, fear of mass reaction has always influenced both external and internal political arrangements. Winckler's argument synthesizes elements of conservative and radical orientations to provide the supranational and national context for liberal theories of political development focused on subnational modernization.

Greenhalgh's chapter on supranational processes (chapter 4) emphasizes the need to place Taiwan's postwar economic development, and particularly the unusually equal distribution resulting from that development, in the context of external global and regional economic history. Her main argument is that exactly because radical-globalists are correct in saying that external economic involvement strongly affects internal development, they should distinguish more carefully between different types of external transactions and their effects. On Taiwan, the mix of external transactions has varied over time—primarily trade during the imperial period, colonialism during the Japanese period, and aid, trade, and technology during the Nationalist period. She finds that none of them had the effects on Taiwan that radical-globalists emphasize. In demonstrating the failure of dependency and world system hypotheses to explain inequality on Taiwan, in the 1980s liberal economists and radical-turned-neoliberal political economists have converged on a "new statist" interpretation emphasizing specific policies of Taiwan's strong developmentalist state, especially land reform and labor-intensive export expansion. Greenhalgh argues that the new statist view oversimplifies the processes involved and minimizes the influence of supranational economic and political factors on land reform and export expansion policies. Reaffirming the fundamental insight of radical globalism, she sketches the outlines of a new globalist synthesis containing elements from the liberal, radical, and conservative orientations.

Gold's chapter about Taiwan's colonial origins (chapter 5) argues that the prewar experience of Japanese colonialism was crucial to Taiwan's postwar development. On the one hand, he details Japanese political and economic controls and the opportunities they left the Taiwanese. On the other hand, he describes the Taiwanese response, particularly that of the five leading business families. Originally gentry and merchants, through collaboration with the Japanese they organized diverse enterprises, only some of which survived the transition to the Nationalist era. Gold agrees with Greenhalgh that Japanese colonialism produced much more economic growth than radical-globalists would predict, though with some of the restrictions on mass economic and political opportunities that radical-globalists and radical-statists would expect. Gold's main point, however, concerns the effect of Japanese colonialism on the post-Japanese period. The Japanese had demonstrated to the Taiwanese how to produce economic growth. With the Japanese no longer around to prevent them, the Taiwanese began producing it. Both Gold chapters also give much weight to "conservative" elements—historical legacies, strong states, and strong social organization. For both the Japanese and Nationalist periods, he argues that it was the high internal political autonomy of the state, partly deriving from external political and economic support, that enabled the state to be so effective at its internal and external economic roles. National businessmen have remained dependent on the state throughout, though decreasingly so in the later Nationalist period. Again for both the Japanese and Nationalist periods, he argues that putting traditional social structures to modern economic use was a deliberate state strategy.

Postwar Formation

The next three chapters examine the formative period of Taiwan's postwar development. Barrett (chapter 6) argues that it is important to understand the origins of America's involvement with Taiwan because they set important parameters for Taiwan's postwar development. He argues that if radical-globalists make the impact of the core on the periphery so central to their accounts of national development, then they require a full account of what determines the nature of core intervention. This in turn requires examining radical-statist claims, to see under what circumstances core firms constrain core states, and under what circumstances they do not. Using both existing historical analyses and his own research in recently released documents, Barrett examines these questions for American policy toward Taiwan in the late 1940s. He describes the relative autonomy from American domestic economic pressure with which the American state was able to decide its strategy in the Western Pacific, including Taiwan. He argues that this autonomy was possible because American business had no preexisting stake in Taiwan. Examining different bureaucracies within the American state, he describes the diversity of views about what to do with Taiwan that was permitted by that autonomy. He argues that reformist aid administrators prevailed in American policy toward Taiwan because, until the outbreak of the Korean War, neither the rest of the State Department nor the American military cared. Thus Barrett, too, synthesizes radical and conservative processes, arguing that where radical processes left off, conservative processes took over, allowing aid officials to implement their liberal program.

Simon's chapter on internal reform (chapter 7) continues the story of American intervention and its internal effects. Picking up where Barrett leaves off, he examines the content of aid's liberal policies. The main argument is that incorporating Taiwan into American defense required endowing Taiwan with "free world" attributes, particularly a private sector with a broad distribution of economic assets and economic opportunity. He focuses on negotiations between the American and Nationalist states over the last stage of land reform. In so doing, he deepens the meaning of land reform, showing that it involved such fundamental issues as the size of the private industrial sector, the degree of concentration of industrial capital, and the extent of Taiwanese participation in industrialization. The episode that Simon tackles has been crucial to liberal claims that it was liberalizing reforms that unleashed Taiwan's developmental potential, but it is crucial to radical claims that external incorporation into capitalist markets entails establishment of internal markets as well. However, Simon also notes many "conservative" processes, emphasizing the strength and success with which conservative elements within the Nationalist state resisted both diverting resources from defense to development and reducing state control of the economy.

Winckler's chapter on elite struggle (chapter 8) continues the transition from global to regional external influences, and from external to internal affairs. On the one hand, he describes the military-political factions within the Nationalist state deriving from Republican-period mainland China. On the other hand, he describes the political-economic "fractions" of the Taiwanese economic elite deriving from colonial Japanese Taiwan. Although the relations between them were difficult at first, the two elites gradually merged to form the large-scale postwar political-economic establishment, whose basic structure persists into the 1980s. The main argument is that, contrary to what radical statists might expect, for a surprisingly long time the struggles within the Nationalist state remained basically political ones between factions surviving from the Republican and civil war periods. Only gradually have these power struggles within the state become linked to economic conflicts within the bourgeoisie. Moreover, economic elites remain more dependent on the Nationalist state than the reverse. Winckler argues that elite social networks were central to the organization of both state and class in the early postwar period. The state was segmented into rival networks and coordinated through the Leader's own personal network. The economic elite was segmented into rival networks, with little cooperation between them. The few individuals with networks bridging between mainlander state and Taiwanese elite played key roles. Thus, Winckler delineates both the partial independence and the partial interdependence of "conservative" power struggles within the state and "radical" conflicts within the economy, while emphasizing the conservative social organization of both.

Later Development

The final three chapters about Taiwan focus on the development that ensued after the switch around 1960 from internally oriented to externally oriented development. Gold's overview of Nationalist development (chapter 9) sketches the triangular relationship among foreign companies, the Nationalist state, and domestic businessmen. He describes the differences between American, Japanese, and Overseas Chinese foreign partners; the key role of the Nationalist state in attracting foreign trade and investment; and the different external circumstances under which successive cohorts of Taiwanese capitalists emerged. These differences resulted in different mixes of self-reliance versus collaboration in production and marketing in different sectors, and different amounts of leverage by local businessmen vis à vis the state and foreigners. Overall, however, domestic businessmen remain the weakest corner of this triangle. Thus, Gold provides a detailed description of successive variants of Greenhalgh's trade and technology dependency and their effects on local business. External sources of variation include the changing purposes for which the core wanted to use Taiwan, the differing strategies of foreign businessmen of different nationalities, and the technological and organizational differences between different industries. The internal consequences for local businessmen have been mixed, with some continuing dependence on somewhat unfavorable technological agreements with Japanese companies. Thus Gold documents for Taiwan many of the processes that radical globalists have found in Latin America, but he finds that the mix of these processes, and their outcome, are somewhat different on Taiwan, largely because of "conservative" historical factors, particularly the exceptional autonomy of the Nationalist state.

Simon's chapter on technology transfer (chapter 10) traces the evolution of a particular kind of external-internal transaction. In the 1950s external public aid laid the foundation. In the 1960s external private investors helped launch light industrial exports. In the 1970s internal public actors—government agencies and state firms—remained major agents of technology transfer, particularly for heavy industry. In the 1980s internal private firms remain the weakest link, as Taiwan seeks high technology. Like Gold, Simon finds differences in internal effects by period, nationality, and industry. His main argument, however, is that Taiwan has already acquired much technology, that this acquisition has aided growth, and that the Nationalist state is leading an active effort to overcome remaining technological dependence. As in chapter 7, the process that Simon examines is again crucial to liberal, radical, and conservative claims. Liberals might see confirmation of their theories in the positive role played by foreign firms and the need to modernize domestic firms. Radicals might see evidence of their concerns in the obvious difficulties that both the Nationalist state and Chinese firms face. The theme that Simon chooses to emphasize, however, is basically a conservative one, namely, the indispensable role of the Nationalist state, including public enterprises.

Greenhalgh's chapter on families and networks (chapter 11) emphasizes the independent impact of subnational social factors on development, in this case the influence of Chinese family enterprises on external ties and growth rate. She describes the family form of business organization that Taiwan has inherited and shows that this form has not just persisted but even flourished in the postwar period. Only in the 1970s and 1980s did Taiwan enter a more capital- and technology-intensive stage of development in which the family firm may prove partially maladaptive. Greenhalgh constructs a model of exactly what it is about the familial organization of business enterprise that makes family firms so effective in Taiwan's postwar development. Not only do they make money for themselves, they also contribute to rapid growth, social integration, and supranational affiliation. She argues that although liberal processes do not fully explain these outcomes, radical processes explain them even less. Therefore both need to be supplemented by conservative processes, particularly family mobility strategies and inheritance patterns distinctive to the East Asian cultural region. However, familism is not simply a passive persistence of traditional cultural forms, but rather an active adaptation to modern circumstance. Greenhalgh emphasizes initiative from the subnational level, noting instances in which Taiwanese family firms have outmaneuvered both the Nationalist state and multinational corporations.

Korean Comparison

Finally, Cumings's Korean comparison (chapter 12) provides an overview of many of the same aspects of Korean development that the previous chapters describe for Taiwan. He advances the radical-globalist argument that it is common external influences—before 1945 Japan, after 1945 America and Japan—that have caused the similarities in their histories. The main outcome variable on which he focuses is increase in the internal economic and political role of the national state. He argues that prewar Korea experienced a transition from the weak, traditional, indigenous Yi state to the strong, modernizing, externally imposed Japanese colonial state. Postwar Korea has experienced an analogous transition from the traditionalist and weak Rhee regime to the strong and developmentalist Park regime. The Park regime gradually became more authoritarian, particularly after 1970. Cumings agrees with radical-statists that economic transitions from light to heavy industry and from domestic to export production contributed to this intensification, but he finds the immediate cause for its particular timing in a ''conservative'' factor, the incipient contraction of the geopolitical role of the United States in Northeast Asia. Korea concluded that it would have to rely more on itself, both militarily and industrially. Korea's leaders believed this required restricting mass political participation and postponing mass economic consumption.

Cumings's chapter provides a valuable foil for the Taiwan case, helping identify the similarities and differences between these two societies. Since he emphasizes the similarities, we conclude this introduction by noting some of the differences that emerge from the papers below. Cumings himself notes many differences, including the greater rebelliousness of Korean society, the greater prewar exploitation of Korea by Japan, the greater postwar disruption of Korean economy and society by civil war, and the greater postwar instability of Korean political elites.

Some additional differences pertinent to the theoretical issues of this volume deserve note. Taiwan faces a less dire military threat, enjoyed an earlier postwar industrial start, and has a higher per capita income than Korea. Taiwan's political leadership has had a longer continuous experience of economic management and, as a result of its economic difficulties on the mainland, is more cautious in making and implementing economy policy. On the other hand, the distinction between mainlanders and Taiwanese makes the relationship between the Nationalist state and both business and public more delicate than in Korea. Partly because of the fissiparous nature of Chinese family firms, and partly because of the Nationalist state's reluctance to foster Taiwanese industrial empires, most firms on Taiwan remain smaller than the industrial conglomerates in Korea.

In the early 1970s both countries faced a decline in American support and an increase in external economic challenge. The leadership of both countries responded with programs of economic self-strengthening through government construction of infrastructure and government encouragement of both state and private investment in heavy industry. However, mostly as a result of the characteristics listed above, Korea proceeded more precipitously, more actively forced the merger of private industries into a few large groups, relied more heavily on foreign borrowing, and anticipated larger exports. When global markets for steel, ships and chemicals deteriorated in the 1970s and 1980s, Korea was much more vulnerable to debt-service and balance-of-payments problems. On the other hand, the Nationalist state on Taiwan still found it politically inexpedient to force companies to modernize their management and technology, and to merge their production and marketing, in order to become more competitive internationally.

This introduction should enable readers to proceed directly to the historical-analytical papers if they wish. However, for those wishing more background, the following chapter provides a fuller characterization of the liberal, radical, and conservative orientations in the comparative literature and the findings of each of these orientations in the existing literature about Taiwan. As noted, the concluding chapter returns with a roundup of the findings of the papers in this volume about the radical-globalist and radical-statist models, and the implications of these findings for further research. The index provides a conceptual guide to the main discussions of the central themes of the volume.

2

Edwin A. Winckler

CONTENDING APPROACHES TO EAST ASIAN DEVELOPMENT

Analyzing the reasons for the success or failure of national development requires two things. On the one hand, it requires distinguishing the many different kinds of outcomes involved. On the other hand, it requires distinguishing the many different kinds of influences involved. In short, national development involves many distinct processes. Although related processes can be bundled into "models" or "paradigms," evaluating such larger constructs still involves testing each of the individual propositions they entail. The task of comparative analysis is to examine each proposition in a variety of contexts, to see whether the hypothesized relationship between cause and effect remains the same (Przeworski and Teune 1970/1982).

This chapter makes some elementary distinctions between different kinds of processes involved in national development, in order both to summarize some issues in the comparative literature on national development and to report the findings on these issues in the existing literature about Taiwan. First a fuller definition is given of the liberal, radical, and conservative orientations in social theory than the characterizations in the introduction. Then the argument between these orientations about processes at the supranational, national, and subnational levels is described. In particular, the discussion notes the differing assumptions of these three orientations about the relationship between these levels and about the role of political, economic, and sociocultural processes.

As noted in the first chapter, liberalism, radicalism, and conservatism are the three broad reactions in Western social thought to the political and economic revolutions of the eighteenth and nineteenth centuries. Though revised in response to twentieth-century developments, and elaborated by different individual theorists, they continue to provide alternative analyses that correspond to the contradictory processes within development itself. Here are brief definitions of each.

Classical liberalism emphasized the positive benefits of market mechanisms freed from traditional state regulation (e.g., Adam Smith). What I shall call neoliberalism recognizes the role of the modern state in creating and maintaining markets—national and global (e.g., Keynes). In both versions, the most general underlying proposition is that competition produces development, both economic and political. The degree of competitiveness of contemporary institutions explains most contemporary outcomes. At the supranational level, global economic markets provide national economic opportunities; war is an avoidable aberration retarding economic progress. National economic modernization leads to national political democratization. At the subnational level, industrialization, urbanization, and education dissolve traditional social networks. Traditional culture obstructs capitalist economic and political progress until overcome through the modernization of individual values. As noted, most of the existing academic literature about Taiwan (and Korea) derives most of its explanatory mechanisms from the liberal orientation, particularly neoliberalism.

Classical radicalism emphasized the negative exploitation that can occur through production for the market (e.g., Marx). Neoradicalism has emphasized the malign role of the state, not only in enforcing an exploitative market, but also in distorting development to serve state ends (e.g., Skocpol). In both, the most general underlying proposition is that exploitation impairs development, both economic and political. The degree of exploitativeness of contemporary institutions explains most of contemporary outcomes. Global economic markets create national economic dependence; war is endemic to the capitalist world system. The requirements of late national economic development constrain political choice, and authoritarian rule facilitates some phases of economic development. Economic growth may aggravate rather than ameliorate inequalities and group conflict at the subnational level. Precapitalist social networks constitute obstacles to capitalist relationships, and capitalist relationships constitute obstacles to socialist revolution. Some recent academic literature uses Taiwan (or Korea) either to support or to refute radical mechanisms, including neoradical ones.

Classical conservatism emphasized the positive benefits of the strong traditional state and of strong traditional social networks (e.g., Burke). What I shall call neoconservatism reaffirms the positive benefits of a strong modern state and the positive modern functions of traditional social relations. (Though no one contemporary comparative social scientist reflects all of this emerging position, the classical reference for the positive role of the strong state in late development is Gerschenkron [1962], and for the positive role of tradition in modernization, Bendix [1964/1977].) In both, the most general underlying proposition is that it is political and social discipline that produces economic and political development. Unique traditional and modern histories explain much of contemporary outcomes. War and economic nationalism are endemic features of any supranational system, capitalist or otherwise. A strong state guarantees traditional values, promotes national interests abroad, and guides development at home. At the subnational level, traditional social forms support contemporary economic growth and political stability. Some of the existing academic literature about Taiwan (and Korea) derives some of its causal mechanisms from the conservative orientation, mostly from neoconservatism.

With the general definitions of these orientations established, it is possible to examine their competing accounts of the supranational, national, and subnational levels of development.

Supranational Processes

As noted in the introduction, the globalist paradigm argues that one cannot understand national or subnational development without first modeling the supranational context of national development and the penetration of supranational influences to the subnational level. A global approach is appropriate to East Asian societies, most of which have long been heavily involved in foreign trade and now are located on the frontlines of the global military-political confrontation between capitalism and communism. In both regards they differ significantly from Latin American societies, whose lack of development provided the initial models for radical globalist thinking. Consequently, these American models need modification to account for Asian experiences.

Taiwan (and Korea) provide distinctive opportunities for reexamining the impact of supranational processes on national development. Few cases have such an ambiguous diplomatic status in the international system, or such difficulty maintaining their external political autonomy. Few cases have achieved such rapid economic growth, but how much upward mobility Taiwan has achieved relative to the most developed nations remains debatable. Taiwan's formal external affiliations with international sociocultural organizations remain fragile, but its informal ties to other societies remain robust.

This section considers the contending approaches of the three ideological orientations to interpreting this supranational record. These alternatives may be called liberal internationalism, radical globalism, and conservative regionalism. (For similar distinctions about the supranational literature see Gilpin 1975; Hollist and Rosenau 1981; Strange and Tooze 1981.)

The liberal approach to the supranational level is "internationalist" in regarding it as emerging from relations between nations. Neither the global nor the regional level is strongly organized. Liberals emphasize the opportunities, not the constraints, with which the supranational environment confronts national development. Attention shifts to the extent to which individuals seize these opportunities. Liberals consider the East Asian cases strong support for the developmental potential of these liberal processes.

The radical approach to the supranational level is more truly globalist in viewing worldwide structures as playing a more active role in shaping national destinies. The supranational level itself is more strongly organized by powerful states and multinational corporations. Consequently, radicals stress the constraints that the supranational context places on national development, arguing either that it prevents development altogether or that it distorts development to serve foreign rather than domestic needs. Simpler radical models of exploitation by foreigners cannot explain East Asian success, but more complex models that include global competition between states and firms can.

Most conservative accounts of the supranational environment are regionalist in emphasizing the concrete historical interaction between neighboring countries in a subglobal region rather than some abstract model of global dynamics as a whole. Such a focus on regional history is particularly true of historical and area studies about East Asia. (There are some important abstract conservative models of global power structure, but these have been little applied to East Asia.) Conservatives stress the potential dangers of the supranational environment, but they argue that a strong state and strong society can cope with these dangers and seize opportunities.

In fact, by the mid–1980s, despite continuing disputes, these three orientations are converging toward a globalist synthesis including all of them. Many liberals concede the conservative point that states play an increasingly large role in the global economy, and they also concede the radical point that capitalist development does not always automatically produce rapid growth or good distribution. Conversely, many radicals concede that under some circumstances global capitalism can produce good national development, and the conservative point that geopolitics and cultural history are partly independent of political economy. Meanwhile many conservatives concede the increasing role of international trade in interstate relations, and the radical point that international order requires improving distribution both between and within nations.

Most of the chapters in this volume too pursue such a globalist synthesis, emphasizing the impact of the supranational environment on national development. Most attempt to clarify exactly what the impact has been by carefully distinguishing the different kinds of external transactions involved. Most are conservative-regionalist in emphasizing the East Asian military-political and sociocultural background. The papers attempt, however, to give theoretical significance to this historical background, some by linking it to the dynamics that radical globalists explore.

Liberal Internationalism

Liberal academic disciplines study supranational political, economic, and sociocultural processes separately.

The supranational political processes on which liberalism focuses are "international relations." Global politics consists of interactions between nation-states, and the way to understand those interactions is to study the national and subnational determinants of the foreign policies of each state (e.g., Rosenau 1967; 1969). Most of the large journalistic and academic literature about the practical problem of Taiwan's international status has been written from this point of view. However, little of this literature is consciously theoretical. The few systematic studies too are liberal-internationalist in focusing on confrontations between nations, mostly during the two Taiwan Straits crises in the 1950s. In sum:

> *Autonomy*. Taiwan's main problem is maintaining its political independence in the face of PRC claims to sovereignty over it. This external imperative has retarded internal political development and distorted domestic resource allocation. (Riggs 1952; Tsou 1959; Mancall 1963a; J. Cohen 1970; Clough 1978; Borg and Heinrichs 1980; Tucker 1983)

The supranational economic process on which liberalism focuses is international trade. The global economy is a neutral market in which countries can maximize their benefits by exchanging what they are good at producing for what they are not good at producing. This comparative advantage may change over time (e.g., Balassa 1967; H. Johnson 1967; Krueger 1983). By far the largest body of academic literature about Taiwan derives from liberal international trade theory, for which Taiwan provides an exemplar. This literature gives due attention to the role of supranational aid and the Nationalist state in engineering Taiwan's development, but it regards them as necessary only for making the transition from an abnormal wartime to normal peacetime situation. Thus:

> *Mobility*. The adoption around 1960 of externally market-conforming policies created the opportunity for Taiwan's 1960–1980 export-led growth spurt. Flexible adjustment to changing foreign markets helped sustain that growth. (Hsing 1971; Ho 1971; Scott 1979; Balassa 1981; 1982; Galenson 1985)

The supranational sociocultural process on which liberalism focuses is the international diffusion of Western cultural modernity through communications, media, and migration. Liberalism tends to regard these as neutral channels to which all countries have equal access. (Supranational sociocultural processes are left largely implicit in such liberal classics as Pye 1963; Pye and Verba 1965; Lerner and Schram 1967; 1976; but see Inkeles 1975). Although the exposure to and absorption of sociocultural modernity have been very extensive on Taiwan, there is little literature about these processes, perhaps because they are so obvious.

> *Affiliation*. Despite some external constraints and internal restrictions, Taiwan has maintained high volumes of communication and interaction with foreigners, and experienced extensive education and migration abroad. These have maintained Taiwan's external connections and influenced its internal institutions. However, these processes have not been much studied.

Most of the chapters in this volume regard these liberal supranational processes as well documented by the existing literature, and supplement them with radical or conservative insights. Nevertheless, some do contribute to liberal supranational analysis. In terms of politics, Barrett (chapter 6) illuminates the foreign policy conflicts within the American state, and Simon (chapter 7) illuminates the conflicts between the American and Nationalist states, in the early postwar period. In terms of economics, several chapters (4, 9, and 10) emphasize the need to go beyond radical generalities to liberal specifics about the many kinds of supranational transactions in which Taiwan is involved. Combining political, economic, and sociocultural considerations, Simon (chapter 10) emphasizes the success of the Nationalist state in promoting Taiwan's technological upward mobility.

Radical Globalism

Radicals emphasize the interpenetration of economics and politics. Some emphasize that global markets can themselves be means of political control; others emphasize the intervention in global markets by national states. Because the first chapter has already described the postwar evolution of the comparative radical-globalist literature, this section proceeds directly to the treatment of radical-globalist processes in the existing literature about Taiwan.

The literature about Taiwan contains some analysis of radical mechanisms of economic, political, and cultural dependency under prewar Japanese colonial rule (Yanaihara 1929/1956; E. Ch'en 1968; Ch'en 1973; Tsurumi 1977; 1980). However, there has been little radical-globalist analysis, from either dependency or world system perspectives, of Taiwan's postwar development. (The principal examples are Griffin 1973; Halliday 1980; Huang 1981; Cumings 1984.) Liberal or conservative scholars have used Taiwan (and Korea) to refute the universality of dependency effects posited by the radical literature about Latin America. (The most systematic of these critiques are Barrett and Whyte 1982 and Gold 1986b, but see also Gregor and Chang 1982). Also, conservatives have provided fine accounts of mechanisms such as colonial state entrepreneurship that radicals would regard as examples of dependency (see, for example, the many important contributions of Ramon H. Myers, including Myers and Peattie 1984). On balance, the existing literature has established the following observations about dependency mechanisms during different periods on Taiwan.

Colonial processing. Japanese colonialism was an extreme form of political, economic and cultural involvement, even relative to other colonialisms. In all domains, it greatly accelerated previously incipient development, but it produced development distorted to meet Japanese needs. Postcolonial Taiwan inherited the development and corrected many of the distortions. (Ho 1978a; Myers and Peattie 1984)

Import substitution. Until about 1960 Taiwan developed relatively independently of external trade or investment, though externally stabilized by U.S. aid. This moderate dependence produced substantial development and little distortion. Development combined further modernization of owner-cultivated agriculture, mixed public and private import-substituting industrialization, and vigorous small-scale commerce. (Jacoby 1966; Ho 1978a; Ranis 1979)

Export promotion. After 1960, Taiwan achieved increasingly high levels of external trade and investment but experienced rapid development and little distortion. Export-led development was pulled by the strong global demand in this period, but it expanded faster than global demand. It contracted drastically during the two oil shocks (1974–75 and 1980–81) but recovered faster than global demand. (Balassa 1981; 1982; Galenson 1985)

Conservative Regionalism

Conservative regionalism emphasizes the historical unity of politics, economics, society, and culture (e.g., Bozeman 1960; Aron 1966). As regards Taiwan, Eastern and Western historians explicitly stress past regional processes, while policy analyses and journalistic accounts implicitly stress current regional history. These moderatively large literatures document the following conservative observations.

Historical. East Asian countries share a unique common cultural heritage from classical China, of which each developed its own unique traditional variant. Moreover, much of this uniqueness has persisted into contemporary history because each country preserved some independence from western penetration. (Fairbank, Reischauer, and Craig 1965; Hofheinz and Calder 1982)

Modern. Modern civil, regional and global wars militarized traditional East Asian states and mobilized their societies. In particular, Japanese colonialism was uniquely authoritarian and developmentalist, with unique developmental effects on Taiwan and Korea. Though involving much conflict, these commonalities have persisted and facilitated cooperation in postwar economic development. (Myers 1973; Chang and Myers 1963; E. Ch'en 1968; Myers and Peattie 1984)

Contemporary. External military and internal security concerns remain central to contemporary political institutions and economic development. Lack of capital sources and natural resources has oriented development toward capital-efficient and labor-intensive manufacturing for export. Interdependent expansion within the Japan-centered Northeast Asian region remains partly self-reinforcing. (Little 1979)

Most of the chapters in this volume emphasize the distinctiveness of East Asia. Most agree that common cultural background and mutual military interactions have been important. Most would agree that Taiwan's prewar and postwar development were both in significant part a regional extension of Japan's drive for development. Some chapters go beyond this, however, to explain the uniqueness of Japan's role in Northeast Asia as a result of the particular location and timing of Japan's entry into the modern world system (chapters 3, 4, and 12). Taiwan and Korea jumped through a window of opportunity in the mid-twentieth century, and few other developing countries may be able to follow.

National Processes

In the 1960s liberal modernization theory focused on national societies. In the 1970s radical-globalist theories shifted the focus to the world economy. In the 1980s, however, a statist paradigm basically deriving from the conservative orientation has reasserted the importance of the national level. Historians of East Asia have long recognized the power of political states and economic elites.

On Taiwan (and the Korean peninsula) strong traditional states, Japanese colonial administration, and endemic modern wars have produced the strong state institutions. On Taiwan the resulting political stability and policy continuity have provided the political foundation for sustained and rapid economic growth. Despite some political distinctions between mainlanders and Taiwanese, the integration of groups, classes, and regions into one culturally homogeneous society also remains extremely strong.

This section considers processes surrounding the national state and national elites, particularly the type of state-elite relationship called an authoritarian regime. Variants of this type have appeared frequently in East Asia and have dominated on Taiwan. Again, each ideological orientation has its own accounts of the national level in general, and of authoritarian regimes in particular. These contending approaches may be called liberal pluralism, radical functionalism, and conservative statism. (For similar distinctions about the literature on national development see Alford and Friedland 1985).

The liberal approach to the national level is pluralist in regarding it as emerging from interaction between many contending social forces. The national level itself is not strongly organized by a political state, business class, or cultural elite. Liberals regard power, class, and status as significantly independent of each other and study them separately. The liberal theory of the state is polarized between a theory of the democratic state that assumes no autonomy and total constraint (the state is just an arena for contending social forces) and a theory of the totalitarian state that assumes total autonomy and no constraint (the society is just an arena for implementing state policies). Liberals regard authoritarian regimes as imperfect forms of either democracy or totalitarianism.

The radical approach to the national level is functionalist in regarding national processes as serving the interests of the dominant economic class or meeting the needs of the evolving economic system. Radicals regard power and status as reflections of class, and they fuse the study of politics, society, and culture with the study of the economy. The radical theory of the state assumes no autonomy and total constraint (the state does what the economy requires) in any kind of system—democratic, totalitarian, or authoritarian.

The conservative approach to the national level is statist in regarding the state as rising above contending social forces to pursue its own objectives. Conservatives regard culture as shaping both politics and economics, and they emphasize ideology as a determinant of state policy. Conservatives regard authoritarian regimes as a distinctive type of state with its own logic, different from either democracy or totalitarianism.

At the national level, too, by the mid–1980s the three orientations are converging toward a statist consensus. Fewer liberals believe that markets and states are incompatible, having seen them work together in most countries of the world. Conservatives increasingly recognize that sophisticated management of economic markets and political participation can put them to use for conservative purposes. More radicals concede that the connection between state and class is complex and sometimes tenuous.

The chapters in this volume, too, are working toward such a statist synthesis. Most are basically conservative-statist, emphasizing both the activism (contra liberals) and the autonomy (contra radicals) of the Nationalist state. Nevertheless, some retain some radical processes (particularly chapters 8, 9, and 12). Although the Nationalist state started out on Taiwan independent of local businessmen, after four decades of promoting capitalist development it is increasingly enmeshed in the interests and accomplishments of domestic industrialists. Moreover, to promote trade and attract investment, the Nationalist state has increasingly aligned itself with the requirements of foreign businessmen as well.

Liberal Pluralism

The national political process on which liberalism focuses in developed democratic societies is the tug of war among interest groups outside the state over national policy. In less developed societies, particularly in authoritarian regimes, interest groups outside the state tend to be much weaker, and attention shifts to struggle between competing policy tendencies within the state itself. Liberalism often summarizes these as polarized between traditional forces retarding development and modernizing forces promoting it (Lowi 1979; Packenham 1973). As regards Taiwan, the large journalistic literature is mostly liberal in applauding the modernization of policy and administration that has occurred, but deploring the lack of change within the Nationalist leadership and ideology itself. There are few detailed studies of the formulation or implementation of policy within the Nationalist state, mostly because these processes remain quite confidential. Nevertheless, this literature has documented the following observations.

Institutionalization. Politics within the Nationalist state is basically a struggle between politically reactionary, mainland-oriented security personnel and politically progressive, Taiwan-oriented economic modernizers. The progressives are gradually prevailing over the reactionaries through generational succession (Israel 1963; Gurtov 1967; Jacobs 1971; Tien 1975; Winckler 1984)

The national economic process on which liberalism focuses is market competition. In neoliberal theory the benign minimal state aligns the domestic economy with international markets and guarantees the competitiveness of domestic markets (Balassa 1964; Meier 1964; Chenery et al. 1974). As regards Taiwan, most of the large academic literature about the economy is liberal in praising the Nationalist state for establishing a domestic private sector and encouraging it to compete in foreign markets. It is also liberal in deploring Taiwan's protection of domestic markets from foreign competition and the monopolization of some domestic markets by state firms. This literature has documented the following observations.

Growth. Creation of a private sector of independent farmers and small-scale private industrial firms was the main precondition for import-substituting industrialization of the 1950s. ISI made Taiwan economically viable and laid the foundations for subsequent export-led growth. (Ho 1978a; Ranis 1979)

The national sociocultural process on which liberalism focuses in developed societies is the modernization resulting from internal industrialization. Developing societies also absorb modernizing influences externally from already developed societies. For both internal and external reasons, as societies modernize, they converge from diverse traditional forms toward similar modern forms with high urbanization, high education, and low population growth (Levy 1966). Most research about society and culture on Taiwan has assumed this liberal model, with anthropologists studying the disappearing traditional forms and sociologists studying the spreading modern ones. These literatures have documented the following observations.

Integration. Economic development has both benefited from and contributed to a rapid increase in urbanization and education. Population growth first rose as medical modernization lowered death rates, then fell as education-intensive economic opportunities lowered birth rates. (Barclay 1954; Speare 1969; Freedman and Takeshita 1969; Coombs and Sun 1981; Liu 1983; Freedman and Casterline 1982)

Most of the chapters in this volume accept the national-level processes that have been identified by the existing liberal literature. Moreover, most of the authors would agree that these liberal processes deserve more study, particularly political and sociocultural ones. Nevertheless, most chapters move on to exploring the potential contribution of radical and conservative analysis of the national level.

Radical Functionalism

Again, radicals argue that politics and economics interpenetrate. The key process on which radical functionalism focuses at the national level in developing countries is the relationship between the requirements of capitalist economic development and the difficulties of democratic political development, a process usually labeled authoritarianism. Again, because the introduction has already described the postwar evolution of radical analysis of developing states, this section proceeds directly to the treatment of radical processes in the existing literature about states on Taiwan.

So far, in fact, there is little radical-functionalist analysis of authoritarianism on Taiwan. Both the Japanese and Nationalist states pursued their objectives relatively unconstrained by Taiwanese economic elites. These objectives, however, reflected Japanese or American interests, or Nationalist response to such supranational constraints. In any case, the gist of a radical analysis of the economic role of the state on Taiwan would be as follows. (Citations are to the existing, mostly liberal or conservative literatures.)

> *Colonial.* The authoritarian Japanese colonial state kept Taiwanese political organization weak and political obligations strong, particularly during World War II. Together, the colonial Japanese state and large private Japanese capitalists used a combination of administrative and market means to extract labor, crops, land and other resources from Taiwan. (Barclay 1954; E. Ch'en 1968; Ch'en 1973; Tsurumi 1977)

> *Postwar.* The authoritarian Nationalist state basically continued the Japanese pattern, denying Taiwanese political organization independent of the Nationalist party, and developing the economy as a political and economic base for the Nationalist military machine and mainlander exiles. Benefits to Taiwanese were a means to, or byproduct of, these ends. (Ho 1971; Amsden 1979; 1985)

> *Contemporary.* Dependent capitalist development has facilitated democratization in some ways but facilitated authoritarianism in others. The Nationalist regime might democratize, but it is more likely to shift from more to less coercive authoritarianism as its capacity to win partly free, partly constrained elections increases. (Ch'en 1982; Kagan 1982; Winckler 1984)

Conservative Statism

Conservatives stress politics and culture rather than economics. At the national level this translates into a focus on the autonomy of the state and the ideology of the elite (e.g., Hintze 1906/1975; Holt and Turner 1966; Huntington 1968). East Asians themselves have long stressed both the strength of their states and the importance of ideology; some recent American scholars agree. Though small, this academic literature documents the following conservative observations for Taiwan.

> *Historical.* Confucian ideology motivated Chinese elites to modernize China through the high standards for good governance it raised for them. These high social ideals continue to motivate and orchestrate both public and private actors in the postwar world, facilitating elite cooperation both between and within public institutions and private organizations. (Metzger 1977; Silin 1976)

> *Modern.* Sun Yat-sen's ideology endorsed economic growth as a national objective, including foreign economic involvement and a mixture of public and private ownership, as a means to that end. The Nationalist elite on Taiwan adhered to these ideas, facilitating both adaptation to supranational opportunities and compromise of intra-elite differences. (Gregor, Chang, and Zimmerman 1981)

> *Contemporary.* Common experience of political shocks and economic crisis, particularly in the 1970s, has forced considerable convergence in the originally somewhat divergent ideologies and interests of the Nationalist political elite and Taiwanese political and economic entrepreneurs. Synthesis of traditional and modern philosophies of political and economic organization facilitates constructive cooperation between political and economic managers but also raises new issues (Tien 1975; Winckler 1984)

Most of the chapters in this volume agree that the Japanese and Nationalist states on Taiwan have played an exceptionally strong and, on balance, relatively beneficial role in Taiwan's development. Some (particularly chapter 6) emphasize the importance of ideology in setting policy in such highly autonomous states.

Subnational Processes

In turning to the subnational level, it may be useful to recall the distinction between outcomes and explanations. On the one hand, it is natural to be interested in the impact of development on the population at large—the degree of political participation, the equality of income distribution, and the resilience of sociocultural organization. Identifying issues regarding these outcomes on Taiwan is one of the purposes of this section. On the other hand, it is also natural to assume a top-down model in which the supranational level constrains the national level, and the national level constrains the subnational level, leaving the subnational level with little independent causal influence. Nevertheless, another purpose of this section is to highlight processes that originate at the subnational level. Such processes can be either the result of unconscious cumulative historical processes or the result of conscious contemporary efforts.

In fact, Taiwan (and Korea) provide strong evidence for subnational influence of both the cumulative and current kinds. On the one hand, Taiwan's Chinese social heritage has made a strong independent contribution to its political stability, economic performance, and social solidarity. On the other hand, in the postwar period the possible reactions of the Taiwanese public have been a significant preoccupation behind both the advice of the American state and the actions of the Nationalist state.

Once again the three orientations have different accounts of the subnational level, which may be referred to as liberal individualism, radical collectivism, and conservative culturalism. (For relevant distinctions about the literature on subnational development see again Alford and Friedland 1985.)

The liberal approach to the subnational level is individualist in regarding free choices by individuals as the best means to national development, and increasing individualism as a beneficial result of development. Liberalism emphasizes the opportunities open to individuals in more developed societies and deplores any constraints posed by tradition in less developed societies. Subnational individualism provides the initiative, not only for national, but also indirectly for supranational development. The East Asian cases provide much support but also some challenge to these expectations.

The radical approach to the subnational level is collectivist in regarding group mobilization, particularly organization by the working class, as necessary for effective political participation, equitable economic distribution, and solidary sociocultural organization. Radicals would like such collective mobilization to provide the impetus for national and supranational development, but they emphasize the institutional constraints imposed by capitalist states and capitalist economies. Precapitalist societies had their own institutional constraints, which may remain obstacles to progress in less developed societies. The East Asian cases provide examples of such obstacles.

The conservative approach to the subnational level is culturalist in regarding stably patterned social behavior as beneficial to development. Tradition places strong constraints on individuals, and this is good because it contributes to political order and economic discipline. Consequently, conservatives deplore the weakening of traditional virtues in developed societies, and welcome the persistence of tradition in developing societies. The East Asian cases exemplify both the persistence of tradition and the benefits of that persistence.

By the 1980s liberals and radicals have conceded many conservative points about the subnational level. Liberal development literature now recognizes that tradition can contribute to modernization. Radical development literature has formulated its own concepts for recognizing the persistence of tradition (e.g., "articulation of modes of production" and "combination of stages of development"). In the 1970s and 1980s the area studies literature about East Asia, too, has increasingly emphasized the positive contribution of the traditional heritage to modern development (e.g., Perkins 1975). Most of the chapters in this volume share these conservative themes, and a few emphasize them (particularly chapters 4, 5, 9, and 11).

Liberal Individualism

The subnational political process on which liberalism focuses is individual political participation. Political development involves transition from high levels of uncritical "mobilized" participation to lower levels of more critical "autonomous" participation. Liberals tend to assume that undemocratic, underdeveloped societies will become more democratic as they develop, and they regard authoritarian regimes as traditional anachronisms or personalistic anomalies likely to be transformed into democracies in the course of economic development and sociocultural modernization (Lipset 1960/1981; Cnudde and Neubauer 1969; Huntington and Nelson 1976). As regards Taiwan, until the 1980s there was little literature on politics in general or on participation in particular, no doubt because there was little public evidence of either. In the late 1970s, however, opposition politicians emerged who won some victories and attributed them to socioeconomic modernization. In the early 1980s several local political scientists began analyzing this experience but found no simple correlation between occupation or education and attitude toward the ruling Nationalist party. The literature to date might be summarized as follows.

> *Participation.* Socioeconomic modernization has begun to produce some critical political participation, and some revision of Nationalist party electoral strategies. Eventually it may produce reform of Nationalist representative institutions. (P'eng 1972; Huang 1975; Lerman 1978; Winckler 1984)

The subnational economic processes on which liberalism focuses are individual entrepreneurship and employment in competitive markets. Individuals maximize their welfare by participating in competitive markets, and competitive markets distribute income equitably. Liberal theory now recognizes a conservative qualification to this: In the course of economic development, distribution will get worse before it gets better because it takes time for liberal processes to penetrate the whole society and incorporate the whole population (Kuznets 1955; Paukert 1973). Liberal development economists show great interest in Taiwan's income distribution, which not only is exceptionally equal but also has significantly improved. The liberal explanation for this is that the island is so small that once economic growth began it quickly penetrated everywhere, and that the population is so small that growth quickly absorbed the entire labor force. More elaborate liberal analyses distinguish the markets and returns for rural and urban labor. Thus:

> *Distribution.* A unified competitive labor market mobilized manpower and transferred it from low productivity agriculture to high productivity industry and commerce, improving income distribution. After 1968 competition for labor increased wages, maintaining income equality. (Fei, Ranis, and Kuo 1979; Kuo 1983)

The sociocultural process on which liberalism focuses at the subnational level is the transition from traditional to modern values and behavior. Traditional networks and prolonged exposure to modern influences, particularly educational and occupational organizations, convert individuals from traditional to modern values (Lerner 1958; Inkeles and Smith 1974). As regards Taiwan, there has been relatively little research on sociocultural modernization.

> *Organization.* In response to industrialization and urbanization, families dispersed into small, residentially separate households. Individuals became more independent in their economic, political, and social behavior. (Parish 1970; Yin 1975; Tang 1978; Wong 1981)

Again, most of the chapters in this volume accept much of the liberal analysis of the subnational level, but again they attempt to supplement it. In political development the question is why socioeconomic modernization has not so far produced as much demand for dissenting political participation as liberals anticipate, and the answer is that liberal processes at the subnational level are offset by other processes. In particular, a security-minded state facing military challenge requires citizen discipline, and a growth-oriented state facing economic competition requires worker discipline. In economic development there has been better distribution than even liberal analysis might predict. The explanation involves, among other processes, supranational pressure for internal reforms (chapter 4) and the redistributive organization of subnational society itself.

Radical Collectivism

Radicalism emphasizes the unity of subnational processes, with the formation of political-economic classes structuring society and culture. In a rapidly industrializing society like Taiwan the key process should be proletarianization. This includes first increasing dependence of the labor force on market wages, whether blue collar or white collar; then an accompanying realization of the vulnerabilities of such dependence; and finally collective organization to demand more participation and better distribution (Lenin 1896/1972; Thompson 1963; Hobsbawm 1985). The question is how far this process has progressed on Taiwan. The answer is that there has been a substantial shift from agricultural to industrial and commercial employment, but that much of the latter remains family self-employment rather than employment by large firms. Even employees of large firms have displayed little militancy.

The explanation for this lack of collectivism may in part be state constraints on labor organization, but it may also be that most individuals on Taiwan consider themselves middle class, not working class. Most male employees hope eventually to start their own companies; most female employees plan to work only briefly before getting married; neither has much interest in labor organization. In any case, except for some research on women factory workers, there has been little radical analysis of subnational processes on Taiwan. Consequently, the summary of the existing literature about class formation on Taiwan includes liberal (market) and conservative (family) reasons why class formation remains so rudimentary.

Historical baseline. In late traditional Chinese society the family was the principal unit for organizing economic activity. To maximize income the family allocated investment between production for subsistence and production for markets as opportunities and constraints dictated. All family members worked hard and pooled returns. However, men owned most assets and earned most income; women had low market value and low social status. (Myers 1972a; 1972b; Cohen 1976)

Modern trends. Economic development on Japanese and Nationalist Taiwan has involved a drastic shift from agricultural or commercial family employment to industrial or commercial wage labor. Most families have diversified out of agriculture, but many retain their farms as a hedge against urban-industrial recession. Many women have entered the labor force. (Cohen 1976; Ch'en 1977; Gates 1979; Sando 1981; Greenhalgh 1984)

Gender differentiation. Both men and women work in both export-oriented and domestic-oriented industrial sectors. However, on average men remain out of the labor force longer for military service and higher education, and many prefer jobs in small enterprises where they can learn how to start their own firm. Women go to work earlier, at lower pay, in dead-end jobs in large factories, which they leave to marry. (Diamond 1979; Arrigo 1980; Stites 1982b; Kung 1983; Gallin 1984; Greenhalgh 1985)

Most of the chapters in this volume take radical analysis of the subnational level seriously but find it inadequate. Most accept the radical point that the constraints that the Nationalist state has placed on political participation have some economic function in enforcing labor discipline and muting labor demands. Most, however, consider the main reason for those constraints to be political, the protection of the Nationalists' own tenure in office. Subnational economic distribution is much better than classical radical collectivism would expect, though, as noted above, recent radical globalist theories can help explain this equality. Finally and perhaps most important, radicalism's own key subnational process, proletarianization, is much less further advanced than radical analysis would predict: society and culture on Taiwan are not organized along class lines. To understand these departures from radical expectations, the authors in this volume turn mostly to conservative processes.

Conservative Culturalism

The conservative approach to the subnational level also emphasizes their unity, but with culture informing politics and economics. Traditional social organization and traditional cultural values provide the foundation for modern political stability and modern economic growth. Even for developed societies, Western research deriving from the conservative anthropological literature has recently begun modeling the extent to which even Western individuals require social networks for pursuing their interests, even in markets. For example, sociologists have distinguished "strong" ties within organized clusters that handle a large volume of routine tasks (such as the family) and "weak" ties (such as friendship) between clusters that provide crucial access to strategic resources when needed (Nadel 1957; White 1970; White, Boorman, and Breiger 1976; Boorman and White 1976; Granovetter 1974; Burt 1982; 1983).

East Asian states have long considered strong family discipline the foundation of both political order and economic prosperity. East Asian societies long ago articulated elaborate codes for daily life in a network society, including strategies for dealing not only with rival networks, but also with states and markets. Nevertheless, the academic literature has only begun to document this sophistication for Taiwan. Anthropological field research has described the persistence of traditional culture. Government propaganda, business boosterism, and academic analyses have stressed the positive implications of Chinese culture for modern development.

> *Historical.* East Asia's unique traditional culture pervades and persists among the mass population. Economically this has produced a disciplined labor force, modest consumption and high savings. Politically it has produced a docile citizenry, which usually pursues its modest demands for political participation through individual political connections rather than through collective mass mobilization. (Grichting 1970; Ahern 1973; Cohen 1976; Jacobs 1979; Ahern and Gates 1981; Hofheinz and Calder 1982)

Modern. Though less emphasized by the existing literature, Japanese colonial policy preserved and reinforced these economically adaptive mass characteristics while connecting them to modern economic growth, and exposing them to modern economic and political organization, particularly during the Second World War. The resulting unique mixture of mass traditionalism, modernization, and mobilization also contributed greatly to postwar development. (Barclay 1954; Myers and Peattie 1984)

Contemporary. Though less extensively treated in the existing literature, postwar development not only relied upon but also contributed to the fuller achievement of traditional forms of informal political participation, family economic organization, and even community religious practice. To what extent further development will undermine these foundations, with what effect on political stability and economic security, remain open and important questions. (Feuchtwang 1974; Harrell 1982; Gallin and Gallin 1982; Gallin 1984; Greenhalgh 1984; 1988)

Conclusion

Sorting propositions by levels has made it possible to highlight the disagreement between orientations within each level. Of course, all of the orientations, particularly the radical, expect interactions between levels. These are best viewed through the analysis of particular historical situations, as in the chapters that follow.

PREWAR
BACKGROUND

3

Edwin A. Winckler

MASS POLITICAL INCORPORATION
1500–2000

This chapter explores the relationship between external and internal political incorporation, particularly as manifested in the relationship between mass military mobilization and mass political participation. External political incorporation is a relationship negotiated between the political elites of different countries, defining the terms on which each country will participate in the interstate system. Internal political incorporation is a relationship negotiated between elites and masses within each country, defining the terms on which particular categories of the population will relate to state power. On the one hand, the chapter advances some general propositions about the relationship between these external and internal processes. On the other hand, it explores how this relationship has worked out in one locality under successive, historically different interstate systems.

Since this relationship is tortuous, some elaboration of these concepts should be helpful. "External political incorporation" means membership of a state in the variety of interstate political relationships characteristic of an era. "Disincorporation" means exclusion or withdrawal from them. Such external political relationships have important connections with, but are not identical to, external economic and cultural relationships. The variety, significance, and connections of external political relationships have been particularly conspicuous for postwar Taiwan.[1] Throughout the chapter the definition of "peripheral elites" remains deliberately broad, including both political and economic elites, and including both native and foreign residents of the peripheral country (the latter insofar as they have local interests distinct from those of their own core elites).[2] "Internal political incorporation" means membership of an individual (or category of individuals) in the variety of intrastate political relationships characteristic of an era. As used here it centers on core duties or rights of citizens (military service and taxes, external and internal security) but extends also to related civic functions (e.g., educational attendance, social security).[3] Ultimately we are interested in "mass participation." However, "internal political incorporation" is logically, institutionally, and historically prior to actual formal individual political participation. Consequently, this chapter explores why a state does or does not incorporate particular categories, not why particular individuals do or do not participate. In fact the terms of incorporation are probably an important, and neglected, influence on the extent of participation, particularly in situations like Taiwan where citizens are granted incorporation in principle that they are denied in practice.

The most general propositions are as follows. Common interests between elites enable elites to collude to exclude masses, while conflicting interests between elites require elites to mobilize masses against other elites. In the long run, mobilizing masses militarily entails incorporating them politically, though it may take many decades before the necessary institutional and ideological changes work their way through the political system. Among the factors affecting the rate at which this occurs are the relations between national political elites and the timing of political development. The more a national elite depends on other national elites, the less it depends on its own masses, and the longer it can delay mass incorporation. The later the political development, the more a national elite is affected by two contradictory global influences: ideological pressures favoring mass incorporation in principle and political support for containing mass participation in practice.

The general trade-off between elite-elite and elite-mass coalitions underlies much political-historical and social-scientific writing (e.g., Moore 1966; Huntington and Nelson 1976; Wuthnow 1980; 1983), including that on imperialism (Fieldhouse 1973; Robinson 1977). However, the specific relationship between mass military mobilization and mass political incorporation has been explored much more extensively by political historians than by social scientists (Wakeman 1966; Kuhn 1970; McNeill 1982; though see Finer 1975). The effects of the changing global political economy on national political development have of course received much attention (recently reviewed by Lowy 1981 and Thomas 1984, among others). However, the effects of changing global political-military and political-ideological processes on national political development still require further clarification, despite important work (Hintze 1906/1975; Anderson 1974; Tilly 1975; Skocpol 1979; Meyer and Hannan 1979; Bergesen 1980; Bollen 1979; 1980).

The historical situations examined here are Taiwan under imperial Chinese, colonial Japanese, and Nationalist Chinese rule. These three eras involve quite different types of interstate system—the Chinese world-empire, Western capitalist world system, Japanese capitalist subsystem, and socialist world order—with correspondingly different modes of both external and internal political incorporation (fig. 3.1). Moreover, within each era there has been confrontation between different types of interstate system, subjecting Taiwan to competing modes of external political incorporation, with corresponding ambiguities of internal po-

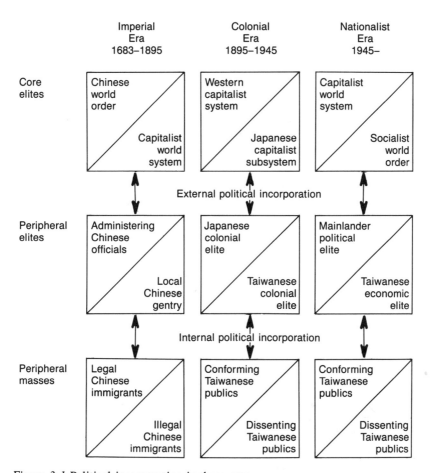

Figure 3.1 Political incorporation in three eras.

litical incorporation, specific to each era. Externally Taiwan has never been fully and unambiguously incorporated in any of these political systems, and internally the majority of the population has never been fully and unambiguously incorporated either.

I use the political history of this corner of the world system to address three main theoretical questions. What has been the impact of core military-political struggles on peripheral elites (Fieldhouse 1966; Bergesen 1980)? What has been the impact of the military response of peripheral elites on the military-political status of peripheral masses (Hintze 1906/1975; Skocpol 1979)? What has been the impact of actual or potential mass response on the military-political institutions deployed against them by core and peripheral elites (Walton 1984; Thomas 1984)? Some social scientists have been properly skeptical about the strength of core-periphery interactions, particularly "merely political" interactions under preindustrial technology (Stinchcombe 1982). On the other hand, other theorizing strengthens the presumption that supranational politics should strongly condition national and subnational politics (e.g., Waltz 1979). In fact, I find the relationship between external and internal political incorporation quite intimate on Taiwan in all three eras.

The chapter's approach to political participation synthesizes elements from existing literatures—liberal-individualist, conservative-statist, and radical-globalist. The first section starts from recent political outcomes on Taiwan and then briefly reviews alternative approaches to explaining them. The body of the chapter follows the relationship between external and internal political incorporation through the imperial, colonial, and nationalist eras on Taiwan. The conclusion briefly reiterates the requisite level of complexity necessary for treating "late-late" political development.

Approaches to Explaining Mass Political Participation

The ultimate dependent variable in this discussion is the current level of mass political participation on Taiwan. Mass participation on postwar Taiwan is rather high if measured by the number of voters in elections. Except for a modest residence requirement, virtually all adults are eligible to vote, and voter turnout has averaged about 70 percent for most of the elections in the postwar era (Lin 1981, 14–15; Copper 1984). Mass participation is rather low, however, if measured in terms of the extent to which voters have a choice between alternative party slates, or in terms of the importance of the offices for which elections are allowed. Only the Nationalist party has the formal organization and media access to present a full slate of candidates. Elections apply only to local, not to provincial or national executives. Elections do apply to national and provincial as well as local representatives, but none of these has much influence on government policy. Moreover the conduct of campaigns is highly restricted (Mancall 1963a; Mendel 1970; Lin 1981). This mixed picture corresponds well to Linz's expectation for an authoritarian situation, in which electoral participation typically is permitted but circumscribed (Linz 1978; Winckler 1984).

Broadly speaking, liberal, conservative, and radical approaches to explaining such mixed state systems are complementary, each defining a broader context for the one before. For a "late-late" politically developing case such as Taiwan, the first directs attention to peripheral masses, the second to peripheral elites and the third to core elites.

Liberal approaches to political participation focus on differences between ordinary individuals. Designed to analyze earlier developing polities, they assume that individuals are modern citizens with equal access to electoral institutions, and they inquire into the economic, social, and cultural characteristics that determine how particular types of individuals participate (Campbell et al. 1960; Nie et al. 1979; Verba et al. 1978). People on Taiwan have enough access to elections that these are fruitful questions to ask. However, because it is only since about 1980 that the Nationalist government began publicly releasing detailed and comprehensive electoral returns, such analysis has only recently gotten seriously underway.

Preliminary indications are that many of the findings of comparative electoral analysis will apply to Taiwan. For example, there certainly is some relationship between ethnic background and voting behavior, with mainlanders more loyal to Nationalist party candidates and Taiwanese more selective (Key 1949; Jacobs 1976). There probably is some relationship to geographic mobility, with participation declining as individuals move from rural environments in which they can be mobilized by community leaders to urban environments in which they more autonomously balance competing demands on their time (Huntington and Nelson 1976; Huang 1971). There may be a positive relationship between higher educational attainment or higher occupational status and more critical, anti-establishment voting, as liberal modernization theory implies and Taiwanese opposition politicians claim (Verba et al. 1978). Influences conflict, however. Modern urban institutions can also mobilize even middle class voters behind the establishment (Wilson 1970; Huang 1971). Traditional personal loyalties reduce the salience of substantive issues of any kind (Fried 1966; Jacobs 1976). In any case, on Taiwan the voting behavior of ordinary citizens cannot explain the extent of internal political incorporation itself since Taiwan's constitutional arrangements have not been subject to popular vote.

Conservative approaches to explaining political participation focus on the terms of internal political incorporation offered to mass publics by national elites. This approach was first elaborated to analyze the expansion of participation in Europe, but it has since been applied elsewhere. Thus Bendix (1964/1977), following Marshall (1964), analyzed the institutionalization of modern citizenship in Europe, emphasizing the constraints placed on mass incorporation by state elites and class stratification. More recently Huntington and Nelson have analyzed the choices about mass participation that face the elites of contemporary developing countries, emphasizing the inhibiting as well as facilitating effects of socioeconomic modernization on the propensity of the masses themselves to participate (Huntington and Nelson 1976).

A particularly useful strand in the conservative literature argues that ultimately the most decisive determinant of political incorporation is military mobilization. Weber (1925/1968) argued that in traditional societies it was the level at which revenues were converted into military capacity—by local lords, regional barons, or central bureaucracy—that attained the greatest political autonomy. Building on Weber, Andreski (1954/1968) argued that, across an even broader range of types of societies, the level of mass political democracy was proportional to the level of mass military mobilization. Most recently McNeill (1982) has argued that in Europe the nineteenth-century transition from limited professional military forces to mass national military mobilization required defining soldiers as citizens and extending them rights of both political participation and economic welfare. All three of these authors are following a transition from a traditional state that directly incorporated only local elites, who in turn indirectly incorporated local masses, to a modern state that eliminates intermediate elites and directly incorporates the entire population.

This "conservative-statist" approach applies well to Taiwan and the East Asian countries with which it has been involved. As will be seen below, both between and within historical eras, the level of modern citizenship rights promised the masses is roughly proportional to the level of modern military duties required of them. Some problems remain, however. The conservative-statist approach still takes national histories one at a time and so does not offer a systematic global-historical model of which countries face what kinds of external challenges. Moreover, elites promise the masses political rights more often than they deliver them. In the "garrison state" model (a liberal critique of statist tendencies for which developments in East Asia provided much of the inspiration), modern mass military mobilization appeared to lead to mass regimentation, not mass participation (Lasswell 1937; 1941). To explain such differences in mass outcomes requires turning to the "radical-globalist" literature.

Radical-globalist approaches to political participation focus on the different terms of external political incorporation imposed on national elites by their different positions within the global political system at different stages of world history. For example, Perry Anderson (1974) has compared early state modernization in Western and Eastern Europe. Eastern Europe had a different internal historical heritage (less classical city-state and Roman-imperial influence and therefore less of a Renaissance) and developed in a different external geopolitical environment (military pressure from the European states to the west that had modernized earlier), with correspondingly different consequences for democratic development (state cooption of both traditional rural and modern urban elites).

Generalizing this account, one can differentiate political development along core-periphery and earlier-later dimensions (Black 1966, 95–126). Political development in the main European core powers was largely independent in the sense that it was driven primarily by elite competition within and between the main core powers themselves. As long as core elites maintained cooperation, within or across countries, they could forestall mass mobilization. However, once core elites fell into mortal struggle (after about 1850), they mobilized core masses (Quester 1977; McNeill 1982).

In contrast, political development in the periphery has been dependent in the sense that it has been driven as much by interaction between core and periphery as by interaction (foreign or domestic) within the periphery (Meyer and Hannan 1979, 187–249; Bergesen 1980, 77–158, 189–277). Core influences themselves both promote and constrain mass incorporation, and juxtapose advanced stages of core development with backward stages of peripheral development. In particular, contradictions arise between globally accepted ideologies of mass incorporation, on the one hand, and both external support for constraining actual mass participation and internal lack of political, economic, or cultural supports for expanding it, on the other. Interdependence within the world system (political, economic, and cultural) has increased at an accelerating rate, and many of the later-incorporated territories have weaker states, poorer economies, and thinner cultures that are more vulnerable to external influences. Consequently, in general, the more peripheral the state and the later the development, the stronger the core impact, the greater the dependence, and the more acute both external and internal contradictions.

Different segments of the elites of a peripheral country may react to dependence and its contradictions with varying combinations of external collaboration or resistance and internal authoritarianism or democracy. To the extent that core elites and peripheral elites cooperate, they can minimize the mobilization of peripheral masses. To the extent that core elites and peripheral elites fall into conflict, however, peripheral elites may mobilize peripheral masses against core elites (Skocpol 1979; Walton 1984). In either case, the incentives are strong for peripheral elites within each country to contain their own internal conflicts, in order to present a united front to both core elites and peripheral masses. A frequent result is that peripheral elites endorse mass political incorporation in principle but restrict it in practice.

In sum, the coalitional-incorporationist approach taken by this chapter attempts to include the world-historical scope of radical-globalist inquiries, the focus on national elites of conservative-statist contributions, and the attention to mass populations of liberal-individualist research. The brief formulation introduced here does not claim to answer the question of what, in particular cases, the terms of external and internal incorporation will be. It does, however, claim to direct attention to the key processes involved. In any case, it establishes the analytical program I shall now briefly pursue for Taiwan in its imperial, colonial, and nationalist eras.

Imperial Chinese Rule

Until 1895 Taiwan stood at the interface between the traditional Chinese world order and the modern capitalist world system. Developments in the core of each had significant effects on Taiwan. For the two centuries after 1683 Taiwan was partially incorporated into the traditional Chinese empire; consequently its institutions for internal political incorporation emanated from the Chinese core. Because China had been the most successful of the traditional world-empires—long fending off Westerners through traditional means—it experimented only tardily and reluctantly with Western military technology, much less Western military organization. Consequently, both the level of modern mass military mobilization and the development of modern citizenship roles remained low, both in the core of late imperial mainland China and on imperially peripheral Taiwan (Teng and Fairbank 1954; Wright 1957; Wakeman 1966; Kuhn 1970; Wakeman and Grant 1975; Kierman and Fairbank 1974).

As a state of subcontinental scale under premodern technology, China faced at least two sets of dilemmas debated by its core elites on the mainland. Externally the principal tension was between continental and maritime orientations, with the continental military threat usually maintaining priority (Fairbank 1968a). Internally the principal tension was the often unfavorable trade-off between the additional revenues from new settlement and the additional costs of new administration. Already stretched to the limit, the traditional Chinese state had to minimize the number of subnational administrative units, adding only territories that were particularly crucial militarily or particularly productive economically. Moreover, the state had to reconcile itself to the minimum level of control over peripheral elites necessary to maintain order and collect revenues (Skinner 1977a; Zelin 1985).

Peripheral Taiwan repeatedly presented acute forms of both external and internal dilemmas. Externally, mainland Ch'ing elites had to balance the security costs of incorporating Taiwan against the security needs of other areas, against the security risks on Taiwan itself, and against the increasing economic benefits of Taiwan, particularly to the southeast coast (Liu and Smith 1980). Internally, Ch'ing elites on the mainland long wavered between the advantages of regarding Chinese on Taiwan as only temporary sojourners still incorporated via their old mainland communities of origin, or as permanent settlers incorporated via their new island communities of settlement (Shepherd 1981, 157–244).

1500s

In the 1500s the main development in the European core of the emerging modern capitalist world system (at this time a commercial capitalist world system) was the transition away from medieval world-empires, Christian and otherwise (Wallerstein 1974). The main struggle in the emerging European core was between the two Iberian powers, Portugal and Spain (Modelski 1978). The more maritime-oriented Portuguese opened the route eastward through the Indian Ocean to East Asia. They pioneered the "functional" approach to global expansion, a network of entrepots with minimal hinterlands. The more continental-oriented Spaniards coopted Italian maritime skills to open the route westward across the Atlantic to the Americas and then across the Pacific to the Far East. They continued a more "territorial" approach to global expansion, seeking land-based resources and incurring the costs of areal administration. The Portuguese and Spanish met and overlapped halfway around the world in East Asia, the Portuguese choosing Macau as their Far Eastern entrepot and the Spanish choosing the Philippines as their Far Eastern colony.

In the 1500s the main development in the Chinese world order was the gradual decline of the Ming dynasty and an accompanying shift in the terms of incorporation of the entire southeast coast into the Chinese empire. Earlier, the Ming had attempted to restore official control of the rapidly expanding private trade of the southeast coast with southeast Asia. By the 1500s, however, maritime trade fell increasingly under unofficial management, and the southeast coast itself fell prey to pirate attacks. Internally this caused both the commercialization and the militarization of precisely those southeastern coastal communities that would later settle Taiwan (Wills 1979; Leonard 1984).

In the 1500s Taiwan itself remained largely in the "external arena" of both the Chinese world-empire and the emerging Europe-centered capitalist world system. So far there had been remarkably little official contact between the Chinese mainland and Taiwan. Chinese regarded Taiwan as part of the kingdom of Liu-ch'iu, which itself occupied the dual status of nominal tributary to both China and Japan (Sakai 1968; T. Ch'en 1968). As for non-Chinese, Taiwan lay across both the north-south and west-east trade routes of the western Pacific. Consequently its southern harbors were used by Chinese, Japanese, Portuguese, and Spanish pirates and traders as "free ports" for transactions and transshipments, already somewhat analogous to their internationalized role today (So 1975).

Already there was some Chinese agricultural settlement around Tainan, the port with the easiest passage from mainland Fukien (Kuo 1973a, 21–30). Most of Taiwan, however, remained occupied by plains and mountain aborigines. Their diverse characteristics may or may not partly result from Taiwan's diverse external accessibility to northeast, continental, and southeast Asia (C. Ch'en 1968; Ferrell 1969). In any case, they represent a band level of social organization, with world-empires and world systems, one of Wallerstein's three basic types of social system (Wallerstein 1974). The incorporation or displacement of the plains aborigines did not get seriously under way until the 1600s and 1700s, and that of the mountain aborigines until the 1800s and 1900s. In the meantime they constituted a significant deterrent to both commerce and settlement and remained a significant security cost into the twentieth century (Linck-Kesting 1979; Shepherd 1981).

1600s

In the 1600s the main development in the European core of the capitalist world system was the institutionalization and expansion of global commerce (Wallerstein 1974). The main conflict within the core was between the declining Spanish and rising Dutch, with the Dutch establishing their independence of the Spanish and coopting much of the commercial network of the Portuguese to become the first global hegemon (Modelski 1978). The Dutch appeared in East Asia around 1600 and, failing to displace the Portuguese and Spanish from Macau and the Philippines, chose southern Taiwan as their major East Asian entrepot, ejecting the Spanish from northern Taiwan (Beckmann 1973; Wills 1974).

In the 1600s the main political development in the core of the Chinese world order was the overrunning of the Chinese Ming dynasty by the Manchu Ch'ing dynasty invading from the north. The Manchus conquered southern China last and held it least securely, facing major revolts there as late as the 1670s. Consequently, the Ch'ing could not fully turn its attention to the southeast coast until the 1680s, and it could not ignore Taiwan, because a major Ming loyalist, Cheng Ch'eng-kung, had fled there to continue resistance after the Ch'ing had expelled him from the southeast coast. As John Wills (1979) has brilliantly analyzed, each successive phase of the Ch'ing incorporation of the southeast coast in the late 1600s reflects a different mix of bureaucratic, market, and network mechanisms. The Ch'ing tolerated a transition period in which it allowed trade and tried to coopt the secessionist Cheng regime through network ties. However, as the Ch'ing consolidated its power over the mainland it applied military force and bureaucratic rationalization to the southeast coast, now including Taiwan.

Thus, in the 1600s, externally Taiwan wobbled between the influence of Dutch power at its zenith and Chinese power at a nadir during the Ming-to-Ch'ing transition. The Dutch initiated formal settlement, the retreating Cheng forces expelled the Dutch and accelerated settlement, the Ch'ing finally expelled the Chengs. The Ch'ing then had to decide whether the security benefits of controlling the island were worth the security costs of administering it. Since it posed both an external security threat (if occupied by foreigners) and an internal security threat (if occupied by secessionists), after some debate the security benefits were deemed worth some security cost. To assert its sovereignty the Ch'ing declared the island a prefecture of Fukien province. However to minimize security costs it forbade Chinese to settle there (Leonard 1984, 63–78; Wills 1974).

Internally, then, in the 1600s the southern third of the island had experienced first commercial exploitative Dutch colonization, then a traditional-mobilizational regime under the Chengs, and finally preemptive incorporation by the Ch'ing. The Dutch had "pacified" the southern plains aborigines and had encouraged Chinese settlement for crop cultivation. The influx of Cheng armies greatly increased Chinese settlement, in military colonies, and extended "pacification" to the central plains. The Ch'ing attempted to placate the aborigines by minimizing Chinese settlement. In fact there was drastic depopulation in the late 1600s as Ming loyalists and Ch'ing refugees returned to their homes on the newly reopened mainland southeast coast (W. Hsu 1980a; Shepherd 1981, 24–157).

1700s

In the 1700s the main development in the core of the Europe-centered capitalist world system was the first major contraction in the new global economy, accompanied by mercantilism, an early-modern form of defensive commercial nationalism (Wallerstein 1980). The main core political struggle was between the maritime British and continental French over which would succeed to Dutch hegemony (Modelski 1978). This struggle spilled over into North America and South Asia, where both the British and French had penetrated, but not to East Asia, where they had not. The British won, coopting both the Dutch and Portuguese commerical networks (Furber 1976; Chaudhuri 1978).

In the 1700s the main development in the core of the East Asian regional Chinese world order was the achievement of the zenith of Ch'ing power and prosperity. By midcentury, however, the consequent renewed population growth had already begun to overshoot the available land resources in some areas of the mainland. The Ch'ing permitted some resettlement of some frontiers, including Taiwan (Reischauer and Fairbank 1960, 345–93; Wakeman 1970; Zelin 1985).

Externally, then, with Western power at a nadir in East Asia during global hegemonic succession and Chinese power at its apogee, Taiwan remained firmly within the Chinese orbit. Formally, its original terms of external incorporation restricted internal settlement. Informally, however, two sets of processes undermined these restrictions. On the one hand, policy-making elites in the core of the empire disagreed among themselves about the advantages and disadvantages of restricting and liberalizing settlement on Taiwan. Advocates of rival measures alternately gained the upper hand as the disadvantages of each policy recurrently became apparent. On the other hand, the peripheral Chinese elites implementing policy on Taiwan profited greatly by accepting bribes from the peripheral Chinese masses wishing to migrate to Taiwan regardless of state policy. Expanding settlement in the periphery of the empire periodically presented policy makers in its core with new trade-offs to calculate. The upshot was that, informally, settlement continued apace (Shepherd 1981, 157–244).

In classically peripheral fashion, however, both local officials and migrant subjects remained oriented primarily to their positions and places of origin on the mainland. Indeed, the state still formally considered them Fukienese or Kwangtungese, not Taiwanese. Unlike in core areas of the empire, on Taiwan Ch'ing garrison forces, exceptionally numerous, were all outsiders. To minimize further militarization of the already fractious populace, the state mobilized local militia only during emergencies. As problems came to their attention, core elites inaugurated the usual programs of traditional Chinese state building—military pacification of peripheral masses, political incorporation of peripheral elites. But these programs proceeded only slowly, and internal political incorporation remained fragile and incomplete (Kuo 1973a; Shepherd 1981, 157–244).

Small wonder that internally, under these frontier conditions, the principal acts of "political participation" by the peripheral masses on Taiwan in the 1700s were periodic traditional mobilizations. Some of these uprisings were directed at local officials in attempts to limit state exactions or to seize state resources. Others were directed by migrant communities against each other. Many uprisings involved elements of both (W. Hsu 1980b; Lamley 1981). In the earlier stages of settlement when kinsmen were few, the main basis of mass mobilization was common mainland community of origin. In the later stages, as lineages and communities flourished on Taiwan, they too could mobilize (Pasternak 1969; 1972). Some of the most ambitious uprisings, organized by secret societies imported from the southeast coast, swept the entire island and required several dispatches of additional troops from the mainland to quell (Davidson 1903, 63–83).

1800s

In the 1800s the main development in the core of the capitalist world system was the transition from commercial, mercantile capitalism to industrial, free-trade capitalism. This produced renewed expansion for much of the century, but some contraction and defensive territorial imperialism toward the end (Gordon 1980; Bousquet 1980). The decisive victory of maritime Britain over continental France at the beginning of the century was followed by the apogee of the British global free-trade regime in the middle of the century, and by gradual relative British decline and accompanying struggle between core powers toward the end of the century (Modelski 1978; Smith 1981).

In the late 1700s the French political revolution had introduced mass military mobilization to modern warfare and the English industrial revolution had created new potential for military logistics and military weapons. Neither, however, was much applied to wars in the European core until the mid–1800s. By 1860 these core developments spilled over into core-periphery relations, beginning to widen the gap in military power, economic welfare, and cultural dominance between the European core and even the most advanced parts of the periphery, such as East Asia (McNeill 1965/1979; Headrick 1981). In its ascending phase (1840–1860), Britain forcibly opened China to free trade. In its declining phase (after 1860), Britain attempted to stabilize Ch'ing sovereignty over China against other imperialists and coopted Japan as an ally against Russia (Fairbank 1953; Wright 1957, 21–42; Nish 1966; Edwardes 1967; Iriye 1970).

In the 1800s the main regional developments in the erstwhile Chinese world-order were, from midcentury, the decline of China and the rise of Japan. The expansion of the West, including Russia overland and Britain and others by sea, required China not only to modernize its continental capabilities but also to supplement them with an equally modern maritime capability. Moreover, China had to apply these simultaneously on several external fronts at once, while dealing with several major internal rebellions at the same time. It is not surprising that ultimately imperial China failed fully to meet these multiple challenges. Elite military reorganization and military technological modernization succeeded against the internal Taiping rebels in the interior but failed against the external foreign invaders along the coast. Even when China's military technology was adequate for dealing with modern Western forces, its military organization was not, in terms of both elite coordination and mass mobilization (Fairbank, Reischauer, and Craig 1965, 313–487; P. Cohen 1970; Hsu 1980; Hao and Wang 1980; Liu and Smith 1980).

By the mid–1800s, then, externally Taiwan was again "up for grabs" between the expanding modern world system and the now declining Ch'ing dynasty. In 1860 China conceded the opening of five treaty ports, all of them along the southeast coast, two of them on Taiwan itself. British, Americans, French, German, and Japanese began landing on Taiwan to protect shipwrecked sailors, purchase commodities (camphor, tea, coal), and propagate Christianity. Moreover, the advent of steam vessels set off a scramble for coaling stations, among which northern Taiwan initially appeared an attractive candidate. China responded by more fully incorporating Taiwan into the empire, actively promoting settlement (1874–75, following Japanese incursion), and finally promoting Taiwan to provincial status (in 1884, facing French attack). However, despite some precarious modernization in the late 1880s, progress was fitful. Necessarily, the Ch'ing balanced resources against threats to its continental frontier (Kansu-Sinkiang). Unnecessarily, the court later squandered resources on extravagances (construction of a new summer palace to replace that destroyed by Westerners in 1860). Britain, however, backed China's claim to Taiwan until the end of the century (Yen 1965; Gordon 1970; Lien 1973; Liu and Smith 1980; Kim 1980).

Internally, the early 1800s saw both the peak inflow of migrants and the peak of struggles between successive migrants for the most advantageous land, water and other resources. As elsewhere in China, around midcentury the central court mobilized local elites and local masses to combat foreign intrusions. However, as elsewhere, this mobilization was largely traditional in both its preindustrial technology and its network organization (Wakeman 1966; MacKay 1895, 164–71). The modernizing reforms toward the end of the century actually antagonized many local elites by finally bringing them within the Ch'ing tax system. Nevertheless, after about 1860 internal communal conflict began to die down. Existing research does not resolve whether this was related to external involvement (military threat, economic opportunity) or to internal developments (strengthening of administration, completion of settlement) (Lamley 1964; Speidel 1967; Meskill 1979).

Reactions of Chinese on Taiwan to their unceremonious transfer to Japan in 1895 provide some insight into the nature of internal incorporation by the end of the imperial Chinese period. Some of Taiwan's local elite responded to mainland-oriented definitions of political community by returning to their original homes along the southeast coast. Others responded to island-oriented loyalties by briefly defending their home regions on Taiwan. Against the official Ch'ing policy of Li Hung-chang, but with the ultranationalist encouragement of Chang Chih-tung, the Ch'ing governor on Taiwan declared it a temporary republic, in the futile hope of securing Western intervention against Japanese takeover. However, the political formulas underlying both elite commitment and mass mobilization were still based on traditional network mechanisms and traditional military practices (personal fealty, blood oaths, local militia, primitive arms). As in other territories under other powers, it was only Japanese colonization that would forge an islandwide definition of political incorporation as "Taiwanese" (Lamley 1968; 1970; 1973; Meisner 1963).

Colonial Japanese Rule

In 1895 Taiwan became the late-acquired colony of late-developing Japan, placing it at the interfaces between Japan and both the core Western powers that Japan was challenging (particularly the United States) and the peripheral Eastern countries that Japan too was trying to exploit (particularly China). Consequently, during this period Taiwan's institutions for internal incorporation emanated from the Japanese imperial core. Partly because of earlier experience at adapting to the traditional Chinese world order, Japan's response to the modern capitalist world system was rapid and comprehensive internal modernization. In politics Japan drew particularly on German models that combined state autonomy for military modernization with representative institutions for internal control. In independent Japan both modern mass military mobilization and modern citizenship roles increased. In dependent Taiwan both remained low until the Second World War (Fairbank 1965, 179–312, 488–612; Hall 1970, 253–324; Ward 1968; Jansen 1970; Livingston et al. 1973).

The development of modern Japanese political institutions involved an unequal dialogue between authoritarianism and democracy. As regards authoritarianism, centralization and modernization of military institutions had been a key early reform. With remarkable boldness the Meiji elites had replaced traditional samurai with modern citizen-soldiers. They legitimated both state autonomy and citizen loyalty through emperorism. They applied this only apparently traditional ideology to the earliest Japanese citizen-soldiers, then gradually to the core Japanese masses at large. Emperorism was later elaborated to rationalize the rule of Japanese peripheral elites over foreign colonies, and it was eventually applied to the foreign peripheral elites and masses as well (Norman 1940/1975; Halliday 1975, 3–61).

As regards democracy, the Meiji elite accepted the European view that modern mass military mobilization entailed modern mass citizenship rights. They knew that, externally, Japan would not be accepted as a core power until it had modern state forms. The Meiji elite believed that, internally, modern constitutionalism provided an effective way to consolidate the internal control necessary to implement their modernizing policies. The emperor promulgated a constitution in 1889 and granted the first parliamentary elections in 1890. Later this led, unexpectedly, to significant competition between Japanese elites and rapid expansion of Japanese mass participation. As of 1895, however, the Meiji elite continued to dominate the government and the suffrage for electing the parliament remained limited (Akita 1967; Najita 1967; Halliday 1975, 62–81).

On Taiwan, after 1895, the terms of external incorporation largely dictated the terms of internal incorporation. Since Taiwan was a colony, it was partly but not completely politically incorporated into Japan, and the significant peripheral elite was Japanese not Taiwanese. Japan practiced direct rather than indirect rule, and substantial rather than minimal Japanese settlement. Consequently, Japanese elites on Taiwan tended largely to preempt any internal political role for Taiwanese, elite or mass. In addition, Taiwan was incorporated into Japan primarily through military rather than civilian institutions. A few civilian Japanese elite progressives in Japan itself instigated movements by some Taiwanese to demand improvements in the terms of Taiwan's political incorporation, but the conservatives dominant both in Japan and on Taiwan quickly suppressed them (Kublin 1973; Kerr 1974; Tsurumi 1977).

As regards internal incorporation, then, Japanese political formulas were subject to two dimensions of conflict when applied to Taiwan: conflict between conservatives and progressives within Japanese core elites in Japan, and conflict between this diversity of views in Japan and the unanimity of conservatism among Japanese peripheral elites on Taiwan. Politically late-developing Japan's pre-World War II posture toward its late-acquired colony resembled that of post-World War II late-late politically developing states toward their own populations. In principle Japan affirmed an authoritarian constitution that promised some eventual mass political incorporation. In practice on Taiwan Japan implemented mass political incorporation only to the extent that the changing relationship between elites in Japan, elites on Taiwan, and masses on Taiwan required. In the 1920s, when the Japanese elite still sought the approval of Western elites, it implemented some token internal political incorporation of Taiwanese elites. In the 1930s, when the Japanese elite challenged both Western core elites and Japanese and colonial masses, Japan effectively disincorporated both elite and mass Taiwanese, suppressing their previous political participation. In the 1940s, at war with Western elites, the Japanese elite attempted to accelerate the incorporation of all Taiwanese.

1895–1914

From 1895 to 1914 the main political process in the core of the Europe-centered world system was imperialist rivalry. Declining Britain maneuvered to retain its influence against both the continental powers challenging it (Russia and Germany) and the maritime powers it coopted to help meet that challenge (the United States and Japan). It appeared that, with Britain no longer able to contain them, and most other areas of the world already partitioned, core rivalries would finally spill over into the division and occupation of China (Smith 1981; Nish 1966).

From 1895 to 1914 the main East Asian regional development was Japan's own drive for core status in the world system in the face of a rising continental threat from Russia and rising maritime competition from the United States. Japan feared that further decline of China would permit the rise of Russia in continental northeast Asia. Consequently, in 1895 Japan defeated China to preempt Russian advance into Manchuria and Korea, eventually losing some of its continental gains but getting maritime Taiwan as a by-product. In 1905, after a decade of further military preparation, Japan defeated Russia itself, restoring its foothold in Manchuria. Meanwhile the maritime United States, less immediately threatening, extended its directly controlled entrepots across the Pacific to the Philippines, and extended its indirect penetration of East Asia beyond into China. The rotation in office of personal cliques of the early Meiji oligarchs gradually gave way to the alternation in office of elite political parties. These were incorporated, along with the new business class, into the amalgam of emperorship, military, and bureaucracy that formed the relatively consensual core of the Japanese state (Iriye 1972; Halliday 1975, 82–102; Jansen 1984).

From 1895 to 1914 the external question about Taiwan was how it would be incorporated into Japan. Japan's main reason for acquiring Taiwan was political: owning a colony was a prerequisite to Great Power status, and running a colony well should be an additional credential. Since administration was expensive and Japan was poor, economic modernization of Taiwan was largely a way of enabling the island to pay for its own costs (Chang and Myers 1963; Tsurumi 1967; E. Ch'en 1977).

Internally, from 1895 to 1914, the main tasks were gaining and institutionalizing control. Taiwan's existing educational and commercial elites adapted to Japanese rule with varying success. The more conservative Chinese literati withdrew from public life and attempted to continue traditional Chinese elite culture. The less conservative literati joined the merchants in seizing such business opportunities as the Japanese allowed them (Lamley 1964). In 1914 many elite Taiwanese responded favorably to the call of some ostensibly progressive Japanese in Japan to assimilate to Japanese culture in order to attain Japanese political rights. This elite movement was quickly suppressed, however, by the conservative Japanese establishment on Taiwan (Lamley 1970–71). For the Taiwanese masses, political unification and economic modernization arrived through the Japanese local policeman, who combined the roles of civilian garrison soldier and modernization extension worker. This arrangement proved extremely effective for enforcing both political subjugation to colonial rule and economic incorporation into colonial capitalism. However, it allowed no mass military role for Taiwanese and entailed little positive mass political incorporation (E. Ch'en 1968; Ch'en 1973).

1915–1931

The main political development in the global core from 1915 to 1931 was of course the First World War and its political aftermath. During the war distraction of the European powers relieved imperialist pressure on the periphery, while disruption of European industrial production created economic opportunities for the global periphery. At the end of the war, the victory of the democracies and collapse of empires (Austro-Hungarian, Russian, and Ottoman) lowered the prestige of imperialism and raised the prestige of nationalism. In the decade after the war, however, the European Powers attempted to regain some of the political and economic ground they had lost, particularly to Japan (Smith 1981).

Japan was one of the principal beneficiaries of World War I, which left it one of the major powers in East Asia. However, Japan was also one of the principal objects of postwar backlash from the Western Powers, who restricted it to a subordinate military status, at least formally. Nevertheless, within the global framework of liberal capitalist economic internationalism and liberal bourgeois political nationalism, Japan continued to develop both global economic relationships and domestic political democracy (Iriye 1972; Halliday 1975, 116–40; Nakamura 1983; Duus 1968; 1970).

Externally, from 1915 to 1931, as the postwar political prestige of imperialism declined but the economic returns from prewar investment rose, the emphasis in Taiwan's relationship to Japan shifted from political control to economic development. Postwar Taiwanese students in Japan witnessed the flourishing of political parties and the expansion of the electorate there. With some encouragement from progressive Japanese in Japan, elite Taiwanese demanded the extension of participation to Taiwan, either through the Japanese parliament or through home rule. The Japanese establishment tolerated some demands for positive political incorporation but granted no more than the appointment of a few establishment Taiwanese as advisers to the provincial governor and as members of local councils. Underlining the political interdependence of the parts of the Japanese empire, this concession was actually more in response to the Korean revolt of 1919 than to Taiwanese demands themselves (Kublin 1973; E. Ch'en 1972; Kerr 1974).

Internally, from 1915 to 1931, Taiwanese elites remained excluded from any meaningful role in their own governance. Moreover, their periodic petitions for such a role remained within Japanese institutional ideals, and their economic incorporation into the Japanese colonial establishment actually gave the Japanese more economic leverage to keep them in line (Tsurumi 1979). The economic incorporation of the Taiwanese masses into capitalist relations of private agricultural property and industrial wage labor provoked peasant and worker protests. Though encouraged by advisers from Japan's own embattled leftist mass parties, these movements too were quickly contained and later suppressed (E. Ch'en 1972; Hsiao and Sullivan 1983).

1931–1945

The main political development in the global core from 1931 to 1945 was the collapse of collective attempts by the Great Powers to manage global economic and security affairs. The decline of Britain and France, the challenge from Germany and Japan, and the still incomplete rise of the United States and the Soviet Union deprived the core of a hegemon. Core failure again created both economic hardship and economic opportunities for the global periphery and accelerated the partitioning of the world into regional blocs (Kindleberger 1973).

The main East Asian regional development from 1931 to 1941 was Japan's decision to challenge the constraints placed on it by the existing global core, in response to what it perceived as growing security dilemmas. On the continental side, Japan felt it had to intervene to prevent the Chinese nationalists from reunifying China and recovering Japan's ertswhile continental hinterland. On the maritime side Japan's expanding definition of vital security interests came into increasing conflict with U.S. attempts to restrict that expansion. By emphasizing these dilemmas, a minority of junior military extremists succeeded in shifting the balance of power away from the political parties and their originally internationalist economic backers and maneuvering reluctant bureaucratic and military establishments into preemptive showdowns in both continental (1931, 1937) and maritime (1941) directions (Crowley 1966; 1970b; Halliday 1975, 116–40).

Externally, from 1931 to 1945 Taiwan's role in Japan's military preparations gradually increased as maritime military concerns increasingly complemented continental ones. Politically and economically Taiwan's status in the Japan-centered system rose from exploited periphery to both exploited and exploiting semiperiphery, a base from which Japan could incorporate still further Southeast Asian territories. This rise in status culminated at the zenith of Japanese wartime success when Taiwan was itself formally politically incorporated into the Japanese home islands, leaving the newly acquired "outer colonies" to constitute the "East Asian co-prosperity sphere" (Barclay 1954; Lebra 1975; Cumings 1984).

Internally from 1931 to 1945 the narrowing parameters of dissent on Taiwan, as in Japan, left little latitude for Taiwan elite nationalist demands. Moreover, the increasing economic incorporation of Taiwan into Japan meant a decrease in the autonomy of Taiwan's economic elites. Earlier, the agricultural-export component of Taiwanese elite interests suffered as Japan altered the terms of trade in favor of its own exploited rural sector. Later, the industrial component of Taiwanese elite interests suffered as Japan belatedly centralized economic management for military mobilization. As for the Taiwanese masses, earlier the Japanese completely suppressed the peasant and worker movements of the 1930s. Later it finally drafted Taiwanese masses for military service, though still only for supportive rather than combat roles. Nevertheless, even this constituted further internal political incorporation and entailed an intensified effort to persuade Taiwanese that they were Japanese citizens and obliged to die for the emperor. In return, Japan promised universal suffrage and comprehensive elections for 1945 (Kirk 1941–42; Ts'ai et al. 1971/1982; Peattie 1984).

Nationalist Chinese Rule

After 1945 Taiwan became the base-in-exile of a dependent, late-late politically developing state (Nationalist China), affected by the ideological heritage of a politically late developing country (Republican China). From 1917 to 1949 mainland China had stood at the interface between the established capitalist world system and the aspiring socialist world order. From 1949 to 1979 the boundary between blocs retreated to Taiwan itself. Since 1979, when the United States recognized the PRC, the boundary has in some respects returned to the frontier between mainland China and the Soviet Union. Since 1945 Taiwan has been largely but not completely incorporated into the erstwhile Republic of China, which in turn since 1950 has been partly incorporated as a client state into the American-centered world system (Fairbank et al. 1965, 613–717, 804–84; Clough 1978).

Consequently, the external influences on Taiwan's institutions for internal political incorporation have emanated mainly from the interwar Republican experience of the Nationalist elite on the mainland, as modified since World War II by influences from American elites in the core of the world system. On the mainland before 1945 the relatively independent Nationalist state had succeeded in modernizing the military roles of a significant portion of the political elite in some regions but had achieved modern military mobilization and modern citizenship roles for only a small portion of the masses in the country as a whole. On Taiwan since 1945 the relatively dependent Nationalist state has completed both elite and mass military modernization of the island, extending partial but still incomplete political incorporation to the Taiwanese masses (Liu 1956; Kallgren 1963).

The early phase of Chinese constitutional modernization had occurred on the mainland during the last years of the empire and the first years of the Republic (to 1924). China's defeat by Japan in 1895 (conspicuously symbolized by the loss of Taiwan) had made the Chinese elites, now in the global periphery, study Japanese success. The resulting constitutional modernization actually contributed to the fall of the empire, but it did lay the foundation for the quite successful national elections held by the early republic (Wright 1968; Young 1970; Fincher 1981). Unfortunately, both the external and internal circumstances of China's transition from traditional to modern military organization arrested constitutional modernization. Externally, foreign elites expanded their spheres of influence within China and, by foreign loans and political manipulations, affected the balance among Chinese elites. Internally, the early republican period saw military decentralization, not military centralization as in Japan, and lacked the central transitional political symbol provided by the emperor in Japan. Instead of a legitimate peripheral national elite mobilizing patriotic citizens to fight foreign core elites, illegitimate subnational peripheral elites mobilized paid mercenaries to fight each other. Neither modern military mass mobilization nor modern mass citizenship roles advanced much (Yu 1966; Nathan 1976; Pye 1971; Chi 1976).

In the late republican period (after 1924), influenced by the Soviet core of the incipient socialist world order, the Nationalist party had reorganized itself along Leninist rather than electoral lines. It adopted both a more modern, anti-imperialist definition of nationalism and a more modern, professional approach to military leadership. This enabled it to make substantial progress toward unifying China, until this very process alarmed Japan into intervention. However, Nationalist modernization of military roles focused more on officers than men, even in the face of Japanese invasion (Liu 1956; Chi 1982). A series of constitutions (1923, 1930, 1946) reflected the main global political emphases of successive periods (democracy, authoritarianism, democracy). These constitutions, however, had little impact on the actual functioning of the Nationalist state, essentially a military dictatorship extended through a mobilizational party. Few public elections were held, producing little elite electoral competition and little mass electoral expansion (Ch'ien 1961; Tung 1968; Tien 1972; Eastman 1974).

As applied to Taiwan since 1945, the republican Nationalist constitutional experience was subject to multiple tensions. The loss of the mainland to a one-party mass movement persuaded the Nationalist elite of the need for further mass incorporation but also reinforced its conviction that the masses should not be given divisive choices between competing elites. In any case, only gradually did the Nationalist elite shift its definition of the relevant masses from the mainland to Taiwan (Mancall 1964a; Clough 1978). American core elites were also ambivalent: some political incorporation of peripheral masses would be good for stability, but too much could be destabilizing. A predominant emphasis on stability usually helped elites, while occasional emphases on "human rights" sometimes helped masses in the periphery. For their part, the Taiwanese peripheral masses also have been ambivalent. Taiwanese continue to resent mainlander political dominance, but Taiwanese increasingly accept that the mainlanders' "Republic of China" provides the only alternative to political incorporation by the People's Republic of China. However, no authoritative expression of mass opinion on these issues has been possible, because elections have been confined to local arenas and local issues.

Obviously there are many ways to periodize Taiwan's postwar political development, but this chapter will continue to key on major core geopolitical developments—U.S.-Soviet rivalry, the gradual reversal of the PRC's alignment, and the resulting gradual divergence of interests between American core elites and Nationalist peripheral elites. The question is why the consequent gradual convergence of interests between Nationalist elites and Taiwanese masses did not result in more rapid political incorporation of Taiwanese. The answer is that the Nationalist elite is still debating its alternatives.

1945–1960

The main political development in the global core between 1945 and 1960 was the emergence of a global confrontation between the capitalist world system and socialist world order. This involved several stages. Immediately after the war there had been a brief phase in which the United States demobilized at home and promoted decolonization abroad. The late 1940s inaugurated a more conservative course of bolstering allies around the world to contain the Soviet Union, involving much free emergency American military and economic aid. By the late 1950s, however, the costs of such unilateral subsidies were beginning to mount, and the United States began to consider how to put its informal empire on a more self-supporting basis (Packenham 1973).

The main East Asian regional development in the early postwar period was of course the victory of the Chinese Communists and the outbreak of the Korean War. Together these cemented the United States into a hostile relationship with China and continued reluctant American support of Taiwan. Initially the United States attempted to dismantle Japan's domestic and foreign economic organization, but by the late 1940s it began attempting instead to restore Japan as a counterweight to the USSR and PRC in the western Pacific. By the late 1950s Japan's domestic economic development was well under way, and its foreign trading connections had begun to revive (Halliday 1975, 160–203; Nagai and Iriye 1977; Borg and Heinrichs 1980; Nakamura 1981; Tucker 1983).

Externally in this period Taiwan was wrenched away first from its semiperipheral relationship to Japan into an exploitatively peripheral relationship to mainland Nationalist China, and then from subordination to the Nationalist mainland into confrontation with the Communist mainland and dependence on the United States. The arriving mainlanders took over the Japanese role as exogenous elite, governing Taiwan in the name of a wider Republic of China, while planning to recover the mainland. Two skirmishes in the Taiwan Straits (1954 and 1958) confirmed that Taiwan was unlikely to recover the mainland either (Kerr 1966; Clough 1978).

Internally, in the early postwar period Taiwan at first experienced the euphoria of liberation from colonialism and restoration of nationalism characteristic of most of the Southeast Asian territories conquered by Japan. However, as described in chapter 8, the Nationalists soon repressed the more nationalistic small-scale Taiwanese urban elites, while coopting the larger-scale urban elites accustomed to collaborating with the Japanese. The Nationalists weakened small-scale Taiwanese rural elites through land reform, then coopted them by placing them in charge of state rural agencies. The Nationalists inaugurated local elections that, confined to the subnational level, served mostly to divide parochial local elites against each other. Even these carefully manipulated local elections remained backstopped by the same pervasive police network through which the Japanese had controlled the island, plus various overlapping Nationalist secret security agencies for good measure. In the late 1950s suppression of a joint mainlander-Taiwanese attempt to form an opposition political party reaffirmed these rules of the game (Mancall 1963b; Israel 1963; Kallgren 1963; Kerr 1966; Mendel 1970).

1960–1980

The main political development in the global core in the 1960s and 1970s was the decreasing success of U.S. attempts to confine the Soviet Union to merely regional power status, accompanied by increasing attempts to share the costs of security and development more equally with resurgent allies. A militarily activist policy toward containing the spread of the socialist world order in the Third World (particularly of course in Vietnam) proved a costly failure and had to be retrenched. However, an economically activist policy of liberalizing world trade and involving Third World countries in global capitalist development proved spectacularly successful, particularly in East Asia.

The main East Asian regional political development in the 1960s and 1970s was the gradual shift of China from de facto alignment with the Soviet Union, through nonalignment, to de facto alignment with the United States. Japanese economic expansion increasingly overflowed throughout the western Pacific, promoting Japan into the core. Propelled by both American and Japanese involvement, Taiwan and South Korea again moved upward toward semiperipheral roles in the Pacific community (Ozawa 1979; Cumings 1981).

Externally in the 1960s and 1970s Taiwan's political incorporation into the American-centered world system was the inverse of American relations with China. In the 1960s, though still restraining Taiwan from launching offensives against the mainland, the United States allowed Taiwan's offshore security support role to expand, particularly in connection with the Vietnam War. In the 1970s, however, as American relations with China improved, the United States began a protracted process of diplomatic and military disengagement from Taiwan. Nevertheless, meanwhile, Taiwan became ever more deeply enmeshed in both the American and Japanese economies as they used Taiwan's cheap, skilled labor force to compete with each other (Clough 1978; Chiu 1973b; 1979).

Internally in the 1960s and 1970s the political status of Taiwanese publics within the Nationalist state also gradually reversed its emphasis, from exclusion to incorporation, roughly in tandem with the gradual reversal in American-Nationalist party relations. The 1960s were politically quiet, partly because of continued political repression, partly because of unprecedented economic expansion. In the 1970s, however, successive external political and economic shocks provided occasion for challenging the establishment, while generational and leadership transitions provided opportunity for reforming the establishment. Chiang Kai-shek's son Chiang Ching-kuo maneuvered successfully to bring more Taiwanese into the political elite and to establish a populist base among the Taiwanese masses (Israel 1963; Kallgren 1963; Gurtov 1967; Jacobs 1971; Wei 1973; Tien 1975; Copper 1979; Winckler 1984).

1980-

The main core political development by the 1980s was the approach of the Soviet Union to global parity with the United States. The main core economic development was the approach of Japan to economic parity with the United States, in a context of global economic contraction. The rising costs these two developments imposed on the United States impelled further American efforts to displace these costs onto its allies. American business resorted still more extensively to Far Eastern "sourcing" for its increasingly transnationalized network of production and sales. Maritime East Asia became less central militarily, but more central economically, to the core. Geopolitically, on the one hand, after the fall of Vietnam in 1975, the United States again withdrew from direct involvement on the Asian continent to a more purely maritime offshore frontier. On the other hand, with the recognition of the PRC in 1979, the de facto line of indirect confrontation between the United States and the Soviet Union moved west to the continental frontier between China and the Soviet Union. Economically, on the one hand, intensified American-Japanese economic competition meant still more opportunities for skill-intensive industries elsewhere in East Asia. On the other hand, global economic contraction and rising production elsewhere in the Third World intensified competition with East Asia's declining labor-intensive industries.

By the 1980s American involvement with China had reduced the immediate external PRC military threat to Taiwan, but it also had required Taiwan to become more self-sufficient in defending itself. Economically, Taiwan participated in the regional transition from labor-intensive to skill-intensive industries. China in particular provided both a new indirect market for Taiwan's high-technology products and a new indirect competitor for its low-technology products.

Internally on Taiwan, American diplomatic derecognition and the second oil crisis finally convinced progressives within the Nationalist elite of the need to accelerate both political and economic reform. These same challenges, however, convinced conservatives of the need for renewed political repression and revived contradictions between external economic opening and internal political closure. Continuing to lose the support of core elites, neither tendency within the peripheral Nationalist elite can escape the relationship between modern mass military mobilization and modern mass political participation. The conservatives cannot plausibly rely on a largely Taiwanese military to repress a largely Taiwanese population, and the progressives cannot plausibly rely on a largely Taiwanese electorate to support a still largely mainlander political elite. As a result, in the 1980s political liberalization is producing a transition from "hard" to "soft" authoritarianism, but not yet to full democracy. A transition from authoritarianism to democracy—a government responsible to the electorate—is likely to begin only in the 1990s, after generational succession has removed most mainlanders and institutional reform has replaced them with Taiwanese.

Conclusion

This chapter has explored some of the historical reasons for the contemporary combination of mass political participation and mass political constraint on Taiwan. On the one hand, the chapter has encompassed as broadly as possible the interaction among core elites, peripheral elites, and peripheral masses under successive historical situations. On the other hand, it has focused as narrowly as possible on military-political processes—military challenge or security collaboration between core and peripheral elites, military confrontation or common defense between peripheral elites and masses. I have argued that the configuration of elite security dilemmas is the most powerful explanation of the extent of mass political choice. In other words, at least for mass participation on imperial, colonial and nationalist Taiwan, external circumstances strongly condition internal development, and political causes are the most powerful explanation of political effects. In view of this emphasis on politics, I conclude by placing Taiwan's political history back into the context of comparative analysis of both political and nonpolitical influences on political development.

As regards political influences, the few existing quantitative assessments of the relationship between the terms of external political incorporation (particularly of earlier versus later political developers) and the terms of internal political incorporation (particularly democracy versus authoritarianism) have produced contradictory findings. Focusing on the "rise of centralist regimes" in a world system that insists that each sovereign state maintain control of clear national boundaries, Thomas et al. (1979) found a clear prevalence of one-party and military regimes among nation-states that became independent after 1945, when compared with those that had become independent before 1945. In contrast, focusing on the degree of democratic competition as reflected in popular sovereignty and political liberties, Bollen (1979; 1980) found no significant relationship between the timing of political development and the degree of political democracy. Bollen found instead that a larger state economic role inhibited democracy, and that "Protestant culture" promoted it, implying the primacy of internal not external factors.

Bollen's data indicate that the level of postwar democracy in the 1960s was highest for those countries that became independent before 1750 (averaging 71.2 out of a score of 100 representing "perfect democracy"), next highest for those from 1750 to 1850 (65.0), lowest for those from 1850 to 1945 (48.1), and higher again for those that became independent after 1945 (63.6). Both studies indicate that the level of political democracy in the 1960s was lower for countries that became independent in the 1940s and 1950s than for prewar political developers (on Bollen's measures, 58.8 and 39.5), but higher again for those that became independent in the 1960s (73.8). As Thomas et al. note, however, the 1960s' readings on the countries that became independent in the 1960s may be premature, since they reflect more the level of political democracy toward which those countries aspired at independence than the level of political democracy they actually achieved after some years of existence. In any case, Bollen's useful negative findings do not refute the argument of this paper, since he did not distinguish between core and peripheral countries, did not identify the external military-political systems into which countries were actually incorporated, and did not distinguish stages of world system development or phases of world system cycles. In fact, far from proving the priority of internal over external factors, his data indicate a strong relationship between external and internal incorporation. Visual inspection of his country codings suggests that the most important influence promoting democracy in noncore countries is being a "new society" dominated by European settlers or (if an "old society" dominated by non-Europeans) having been strongly affected by long experience as a colony of a particularly democratic core country (usually Britain).

What this points to is the desirability of regarding the internal political condition of a noncore country as, in the first instance, the joint result of its cumulative historical experience with supranational political systems and its contemporary external political incorporation. Some early comparative political analysts emphasized historical background (e.g., Emerson 1960; Hartz 1964; Black 1966). However, cross-national statistical studies in both the modernization theory and world system literatures have largely ignored both historical and contemporary external political contexts. In contrast, this chapter, like earlier historical comparisons, suggests that one should sketch these external political constraints before examining other factors, including internal socioeconomic modernization and indigenous culture. From this point of view, Taiwan has been triply unfortunate in its external political-military experience—authoritarian Chinese imperial heritage and Japanese colonial experience followed by continuing severe postwar external challenge to Nationalist survival. Neither rising mass military mobilization nor rising mass socioeconomic modernization has so far completely overcome this inhibiting legacy.

Doubtless the cumulative experience of external political incorporation is not the only explanation of the contemporary terms of internal political incorporation. Naturally, one would like to explore the effects of leadership struggles, ethnic composition, industrial structure, labor markets, Western ideologies, traditional religion, and other variables. Consequently, this chapter concludes by placing political incorporation back into its economic and cultural context. In doing so, one must not relapse back into either purely endogenous socioeconomic modernization perspectives or an approach to "culture" that treats it as a purely indigenous historical ragbag. Rather, one should focus on the interaction of external and internal processes through mechanisms of incorporation. This should facilitate identifying relevant economic and cultural processes and integrating them with political processes.

Economic incorporation has been, of course, much explored (beginning with "Leninist" theories of imperialism and Polanyi 1944/1967, among others; more recently, for East Asia, see Moulder 1977). Economic incorporation is also likely to be particularly important for domestic politics. Economic incorporation includes both the external economic terms on which a country was incorporated into global product markets, including the extent of the economic role of the state (Seers 1983), and the internal economic terms on which peripheral masses were incorporated into domestic labor markets (Bagchi 1982). Cultural incorporation too, of course, deserves attention.

Political interactions are likely to remain central, however, at least for explaining the terms of internal political incorporation in late-late political developers. Moreover, the terms of external political incorporation probably would strongly condition the degree of influence of other factors. In any case, political interactions must be fully mapped before it can be decided whether or not, as causes of particular outcomes, they have been overwhelmed by economic or cultural influences.

Notes

1. The initial definition of "external political incorporation" as a relationship between "the political elites of different countries" is deliberately general, intended to cover both the situation of earlier political developers in which the national elites are all in the European core (relatively equal and relatively independent) and the situation of later political developers in which the distinction between core elites and peripheral elites becomes increasingly important (accompanied by inequality and dependence).

2. The complex short-run interactions between political factions and economic fractions within the peripheral elite are temporarily bracketed in order to shift attention to long-run interactions among core elites, peripheral elites, and peripheral masses. The short-run intraelite complexities are explored for the formative early postwar period on Taiwan in chapter 8 of this volume.

3. The definition of internal political incorporation also is deliberately broad, though by now more standardized in the literature. Our usage follows that of Marshall and Bendix (as elaborated particularly in Meyer and Hannan 1979).

4

Susan Greenhalgh

SUPRANATIONAL PROCESSES OF INCOME DISTRIBUTION

**Problematique: External Linkages and
Internal Distribution**

All of the East Asian Newly Industrialized Countries (NICs), but especially Taiwan,[1] challenge the conventional views of both liberal and radical scholars about trends in inequality over the course of economic development. Following Kuznets (1955), in the 1960s and 1970s liberal economists generally maintained that over the course of development inequality exhibited a U-shaped pattern, rising in the early stages of growth, then falling in the final phase of transition to industrial status (Adelman and Morris 1973; Paukert 1973). At least since the 1960s, radical political economists have argued that inequality in Third World countries consistently worsened as integration into global economic systems proceeded (Frank 1969c; 1972; Wallerstein 1974). Yet on Taiwan, over a full century that spanned several different phases of development and integration into the global economy, the sometimes fragmentary data available suggest that during most periods economic inequality either remained stable or declined, finally evening off at a level that is remarkably low by the standards of both developing and developed societies.

Taiwan's good distributional performance has provoked reexamination of both the ''things get worse before they get better'' view of liberal economists and the ''things go from bad to worse'' view of radical political economists. Liberal economists have somewhat modified their theories to account for Taiwan's relatively even distribution, arguing that if the basic growth path is right, it is possible for economic growth to be compatible with improved distribution in every phase of the transition to modern industrial growth. Economists have identified several liberal state economic policies that they claim account for Taiwan's good distribution, in particular land reform and export expansion. These scholars regard supranational forces as merely conditioning factors, and they reject the radical-globalist analyses of dependency and world systems theories as irrelevant to Taiwan.

Political economists writing in the mid–1980s have largely accepted the liberal economic view of which specific policies were crucial, but they have added missing national-level political components that help explain why the Nationalist state had both the capability and the willingness to adopt such policies on Taiwan. Political economists have identified geopolitical conditions that account for the adoption of these policies. Yet they too see national-level factors—in particular, the policies of a strong developmentalist state—as the main source of Taiwan's equitable growth. In their view, radical globalism, with its stress on extreme dependency and inequality, appears inappropriate if not obsolete in the context of East Asia.

This dialogue between orientations has improved the explanations of income distribution on Taiwan, forging a ''new statist synthesis'' of important, mostly national-level, components of liberal and radical orientations. This chapter, however, argues that such a statist synthesis remains incomplete. It overemphasizes the role of deliberate state strategy while neglecting other historical processes, most of them supranational. Even with regard to deliberate state strategy, the statist synthesis underestimates the importance of supranational influences and actors in both the adoption and implementation of state policies. Consequently, it needs to be supplemented by a ''new globalist synthesis'' of supranational components from the liberal, radical, and conservative orientations.

This chapter looks again at the role of external linkages in explaining Taiwan's relatively egalitarian income distribution. First it reviews the data available about economic distribution on Taiwan from the mid–1800s to the present. Next the radical-globalist explanations of distribution on Taiwan are discussed, including an examination of a succession of different types of dependency experienced by the island. None of these types of dependency had the disequalizing effects that the dependency and world systems literatures of the 1960s-early 1980s expected. Third, the new statist synthesis, on which recent writers of all orientations appear to be converging, is analyzed. Given the limitations of this perspective, a new globalist synthesis is offered, reasserting the strong influence of supranational processes on subnational distribution. The conclusion summarizes the chapter's main findings and highlights their implications for theories of economic inequality.

Trends in Economic Inequality, 1850s–1985

Except for a brief period during and after World War II, and the 1950s, for which data are not reliable, over the course of the twentieth century the data available indicate that the level of economic inequality on Taiwan remained unchanged or declined slightly, declined further, and then leveled off within a range that is very low relative to other developing countries.[2]

To facilitate exposition of the data, Taiwan's history is periodized here into the conventional political phases: late Chinese imperial era (1858–1895), Japanese colonial period (1895–1945), and Chinese Nationalist phase (1945–1985, the last year for which income data are available).

Late Ch'ing Period, 1858–1895

Although nothing is known for sure about the level of economic inequality on Taiwan during the early and mid-Ch'ing (1644–mid-1800s), historians surmise that in the frontier conditions of a subsistence agrarian economy, low economic integration, high population transience, susceptibility to disease, and frequent ethnic conflict, there were few opportunities for the accumulation of wealth (Myers 1972a; 1972b).

After 1858, when treaty ports were first opened to international trade, opportunities for upward mobility increased rapidly, resulting in marked economic differences within the literati (Lamley 1964, 16–17). There is some evidence that commercialization in the late nineteenth century increased the concentration of landholdings. Using data from a Japanese land survey, Wickberg (1970, 84–85) has shown that in the last years of the Ch'ing the degree of concentration of landholding varied with degree of commercialization and proximity to urban centers. These data, however, are from northern Taiwan, where opening of treaty ports probably had the greatest impact; the more limited penetration of local systems over most of the island (Chang and Myers 1963) suggests that the trend toward concentration may have been less pronounced outside the north.

Japanese Colonial Period, 1895–1945

The first decade of Japanese rule produced a general leveling of economic differences among Chinese on Taiwan. While new employment opportunities and rising wages and farm prices improved the livelihood of peasants and workers, the confiscation of property and elimination of the "large-rent households" (*ta-tsu hu*) undermined the position of the rich.[3] The literati, who had been the most influential members of Ch'ing society, were very badly hurt, for they were deprived of their profession and ill-equipped to take up other forms of work (Lamley 1964).

After the initial leveling, changes in the degree of inequality on Taiwan were limited and, if anything, in the direction of greater equality, at least until the advent of World War II. Although the available quantitative evidence is all from the agricultural sector, this is not an overwhelming drawback, for throughout the period the vast majority of the population (60–70 percent) was in agriculture (Ho 1978a, 82). In the nonagricultural sector one can only speculate that inequalities among the Taiwanese were not great, for discriminatory policies of the Japanese worked in many ways to prevent accumulation of wealth by entrepreneurial families (Barclay 1954, 58–72; Tsurumi 1980). Unfortunately, little is known about the relative income positions of the two sectors.

Turning to the data on agriculture, there was very little change in the distribution of owner-cultivator families by size of landholding between 1920 and 1939 (table 4.1, panel A). There may have been some concentration of land in the 10 hectare and above class (panel B). As Wickberg (1981, 233–34) has pointed out, however, this concentration did not occur at the expense of the smallest size class. Furthermore, it may reflect land purchases by Japanese sugar companies and land reclamation by individual financiers, rather than increases in concentration of ownership by wealthy Taiwanese families.

Table 4.2 shows changes in tenure status of farm families between 1910 and 1945. Again the picture suggests continuity rather than change. The most significant change, increase in the proportion of part-owners, has equivocal distributional implications, for it measures both upward mobility from the tenant group and downward mobility from the owner-cultivator group (Ho 1978a, 43; Wickberg 1981, 234).

Data on income and expenditure of farm families by tenure status were collected in surveys of 1931, 1937, 1941, and 1950. Although these data are subject to reservations, they do provide an opportunity to make very crude estimates of trends in the degree of inequality during this period. A measure that is appropriate for data grouped by a small number of classes such as the tenure groups found on Taiwan is Kuznets's total disparity measure (TDM). Like the more familiar Gini coefficient of inequality, the TDM varies directly with the level of inequality, that is, the higher the TDM, the higher the inequality.

Using the data on income and expenditure by tenure class published by Chang (1969, 39, 41) and data on population share by tenure class provided by Ho (1978a, 355), I have computed TDMs for the three "series" of data available: income for three tenure groups for 1931 and 1950; expenditure for three tenure groups for 1931 and 1950; and expenditure for two tenure groups for 1931, 1937, 1941, and 1951.[5] The results of these calculations must be viewed with considerable caution, but they do provide a basis for informed speculation about trends in rural inequality in the 1930s and 1940s.

The results of the calculations can be found in table 4.3. Data in column 1 suggest that the distribution of income among tenure groups may have become more equal between 1931 and 1950. Expenditure data, which are commonly used as a proxy for income, suggest a similar trend toward equalization, with most of the change occurring between 1931 and 1937 (columns 2 and 3). Column 3 also indicates some rise in inequality in the 1940s. The real rise in inequality was probably much greater than these data imply, however, for the 1950 figure reflects the impact of the 37.5 percent rent reduction of 1949. The rent reduction lowered the expenditures of tenants, thus equalizing expenditures across tenure groups (Chang 1969, 41).

In sum, all three data sets point to significant continuity in the distribution of

Table 4.1

Changes in the Distribution of Landholding, 1920–1939

A

Size of landholding (*chia*)	Percentage of owner-cultivator families			Percentage change
	1920	1932	1939	1920–1939
Under .5	42.68	38.37	43.22	+ .54
.5–1	21.40	20.89	20.87	− .53
1–2	17.46	18.74	17.19	− .27
2–3	7.01	8.12	7.44	+ .43
3–5	5.74	6.65	5.62	− .12
5–7	2.22	2.69	2.27	+ .05
7–10	1.46	1.80	1.44	− .02
10–20	1.35	1.72	1.26	− .09
20–30	.33	.47	.35	+ .02
Above 30	.35	.54	.34	− .01

B

Size of landholding (hectare)	Percentage of cultivated land by size class	
	1920	1939
Under 1	15	14
1–10	50	45
Over 10	35	41

Sources: A: Ho (1978a: 349–50).
B: Wickberg, personal communication.
Note: 1 chia = .9699 hectare.

income and wealth, with perhaps slight trends toward greater equality of income during the 1930s and greater inequality of income during the 1940s. This conclusion is supported by more disaggregated indices of levels of living, which show that the material welfare of the Taiwanese improved up to the late 1930s and then deteriorated in the 1940s (Chang 1969, 43–62; Ho 1978a, 91–102).

Nationalist Period, 1945–1985

Data on levels of income equality in the Nationalist period fall into two subsets, partial survey data collected in the 1950s and early 1960s, and more complete, islandwide survey data covering the years 1964 to 1985 (see table 4.4).[6] During the 1950s inequality may have been quite high, although the empirical basis for this conclusion is wobbly. Measured by the Gini coefficient, an aggregate index of inequality that ranges from a low of 0 to a high of 1.00, in the mid–1960s

Table 4.2

Changes in Tenure Status of Farm Families, 1910–1945

Tenure class	Percentage of population in each tenure class						% change	
	1910	1925	1930	1935	1940	1945	1910– 1930	1910– 1945
Owner-cultivators	33.7	29.0	29.1	31.4	32.0	29.8	−4.6	−3.9
Part-owner/ part-tenants	23.5	30.1	30.7	30.6	31.2	29.5	+7.2	+6.0
Tenants	42.8	40.9	40.2	38.0	36.8	40.7	−2.6	−2.1

Sources: Ho (1978a: 43, 355); Wickberg, personal communication.

Table 4.3

Changes in Level of Inequality in Income and Expenditure of Farm Families, 1931-1950

Year	Total disparity measure (TDM)		
	Income (3 tenure groups) (1)	Expenditure (3 tenure groups) (2)	Expenditure (2 tenure groups) (3)
1931	16.3	24.2	31.0
1937	n.a.	n.a.	9.0
1941	n.a.	n.a.	9.8
1950	5.7	9.2	11.4

Sources: Data on income and expenditures by tenure group from Chang (1969: 39, 41).
Data on share of tenure groups in total population from Ho (1978a: 355).
Notes: The three tenure groups in columns 1 and 2 are: owner, part-owner, tenant.
The two tenure groups in column 3 are: owner, tenant.
The TDM measures the sum of the differences, signs ignored, between the percentage shares of given groups within the population in total number and in total income.
N.a. = not available.

inequality remained at a stable and relatively low .36 for several years, then dropped to a very low level of about .31 in the early 1970s, where it has remained, fluctuating only slightly from year to year, through the mid–1980s. The ratio of the income of the top fifth of households to that of the bottom fifth of households moved in a similar fashion. This ratio declined from about 5.3 in the mid- and late 1960s to 4.4–4.6 in the early 1970s before falling to a low of about 4.2 in the years 1976–1981. In the early to mid–1980s the ratio increased slightly to 4.3–4.5. Although these official data most certainly understate the true level of income inequality because, inter alia, the underlying surveys undersample wealthy

Table 4.4

Trends in Income Inequality among All Households, 1964-1985

Year	GINI Coefficient Official figures (1)	Adjusted figures (2)	Ratio of income of top fifth of households to bottom fifth (3)
1964	.360	.321	5.33
1965	—	—	—
1966	.358	.323	5.25
1967	—	—	—
1968	.362	.326	5.28
1969	—	—	5.28
1970	.321	.293	4.58
1971	—	.295	—
1972	.318	.290	4.49
1973	.313	—	—
1974	.319	—	4.37
1975	.312	—	—
1976	.307	—	4.18
1977	.311	—	4.21
1978	.306	—	4.18
1979	.312	—	4.34
1980	.303	—	4.17
1981	.306	—	4.21
1982	.308	—	4.29
1983	.313	—	4.36
1984	.312	—	4.40
1985	.317	—	4.50

Sources: Column 1: DGBAS, various years; 2: Fei, Ranis, and Kuo (1979: 92-93, 55); 3: *Taiwan Statistical Data Book* (1985).

households, such problems also plague surveys conducted in other countries. From a comparative perspective, what is most noteworthy about Taiwan is that throughout the two decades for which sound data are available, the level of inequality was exceptionally low by the standards of developing and developed countries. Of forty-five countries for which recent income distribution data are available, only two had ratios of the top to bottom fifth of households that were lower than Taiwan's ratio of 4.5 in 1985. And in these countries, Japan and the Netherlands, that ratio was 4.4 or 4.3, only a fraction lower than Taiwan's (computed from World 1986, 226-27).

Radical-Globalist Analyses and Inequality on Taiwan

What is the role of global factors in this pattern of distribution? To answer this question, I begin by exploring the radical-globalist hypotheses advanced in the 1960s-early 1980s relating external ties to internal distribution.

Dependency and World System Views of Inequality

The principle bodies of radical-globalist literature predicting changes in economic inequality are the world system and the dependency approaches. Although these two theories are similar in some respects, they differ in important ways.

The world system paradigm posits a global stratification system and distinguishes different categories, or zones, of countries within that system, specifying a distinctive external role and internal structure for each zone (for elaboration see chapter 1). The perspective predicts a direct relationship between centrality in the world system and equality in the distribution of income. Although this approach has achieved considerable empirical success,[7] it has certain limitations. Of relevance here is its failure to operationalize the categories in the stratification system in a way that allows unambiguous location of countries within the system.

The dependency perspective focuses on the trade and other relations between particular core and dependent countries, and the structural distortions these cause in the latter.[8] For dependent countries the perspective predicts high and rising levels of regional, sectoral, and class income inequality. A principle defect of the dependency literature is its failure to distinguish among different types of dependency. Most writers assume that various forms of dependency have similar effects. A more plausible assumption is that different types of dependency involve different political-economic structures, different processes of penetration and incorporation, and thus different effects on dependent countries. Measuring dependency is also problematic. Although scholars have reached some agreement on measures of different types of dependency, they have not used them to determine the dominant type of dependency, nor have they established empirical cutoff points to indicate degrees of dependency of each type. Finally, as noted throughout this volume, the dependency model is based on the Latin American experience; the question of how it should be modified to fit the experiences of East Asian countries has only recently begun to receive sustained attention (Deyo 1987b; Gold 1986b).

Ideally, then, the world system paradigm should allow one to set the grand stage—identifying the historical era and the position in the world system—while the dependency model should enable one to fill in the details of the political, economic, and other transactions in which a country engages. Transitions between world system levels should have predictable implications for income distribution; different kinds of dependency should affect income distribution through different causal paths.

Unfortunately, in practice distinctions among dependency types are seldom drawn, and distinctions among systemic levels are seldom agreed upon. For example, mid-1970s Taiwan has been variously characterized as peripheral (Evans 1979); transitional between peripheral and semiperipheral (Chirot 1977; Mahler 1980; Snyder and Kick 1979); dependent to an above average degree (Barrett and Whyte 1982); heavily dependent (Gates 1979); and too special to be fitted within the dependency perspective (Amsden 1979). Clearly, these are summary judgments that lump together two major dimensions, dependency and global position, and several subdimensions.

Type of Dependency and Global Position: Historical Overview for Taiwan

Structural position in the world system is based on role played in the division of labor in the capitalist world economy. Using the shorthand introduced by Wallerstein (1979), these can be called core, semiperiphery, and periphery, based on levels of profit, technology, wages, and industrial diversification (see chapter 1 of this volume).[9]

Type of dependency refers to the general political-economic form that dependency takes. In the modern world system the major types of dependency are colonial, aid, trade, investment, and technology dependency. As working definitions, one can say that colonial dependency exists when one country is formally colonized by another. Aid and investment dependency exist when levels of foreign development assistance and private foreign investment, respectively, are high relative to the domestic sources devoted to the same ends. Trade dependency exists when asymmetric trade relations exist such that one partner benefits more than the other, or when the proportion of trade in total economic activity is so high that a country becomes vulnerable to shifts in external markets. Technology dependency exists when external actors control important technology, especially industrial technologies that are central to a country's development strategy. Since elements of two or more types of dependency usually coexist within a country, it is important to ascertain the whole mix of dependent relations in a given historical period, for each type of dependency involves different political and economic structures, and thus different effects on the developing country. In some periods it is possible to identify a major form of dependency, one that is overwhelmingly important, or one that acts as a critical impediment to further growth.

For Taiwan, a qualitative evaluation yields the following simple picture (see table 4.5). Empirical support for this picture will be presented below. Taiwan was first incorporated into the periphery of the world system in the years around 1858, when opening of its first treaty port led to a surge of foreign trade in primary commodities. From 1895 until 1945 Taiwan was a colony of Japan, a country attempting to move upward in the world system by establishing its own East Asian sphere of economic influence.

Table 4.5

Taiwan's Position in the World System and Main Types of Dependency, c. 1858–Present

Years	Type of dependency	Structural position in world system
c. 1858–1895	Trade dependency	Periphery
1895–1945	Colonial dependency	Colony of semi- peripheral power
1945–1949	(Transition period)	Periphery
1949–early 1960s	Aid dependency Trade and tech. secondary Investment minor	Periphery and client of major core power
Early 1960s– early 1970s	Trade dependency Technology secondary Investment minor	Periphery
Early 1970s– present	Technology dependency Trade secondary Investment minor	Semiperiphery

Following decolonization and a brief transition period from 1945 to 1949, the removal of the Nationalist government from mainland China to Taiwan made Taiwan for the first time a de facto independent actor in the world system. During the 1950s the island was in the periphery of the world system, exporting limited amounts of processed raw materials, while concentrating most of its resources on internal development via import substitution. From 1951 to 1965 Taiwan received massive amounts of U.S. foreign aid. Aid played a central role in Taiwan's development and stabilization. By relieving critical economic bottlenecks, it allowed the government to concentrate its resources on political stabilization. For most of this period, then, the dominant type of dependency was aid dependency, with trade and technology dependency holding secondary positions.

A period of trade dependency, during which technology and investment dependency were minor themes, began in the early 1960s with the promulgation of statutes to increase foreign trade and investment. A decade later, in the early 1970s, Taiwan began to shift from peripheral to semiperipheral status in the world economy. This shift was accomplished by moving from the export of low-wage, labor-intensive, light manufactures to the export of higher-wage, more technology-, skill-, and capital-intensive intermediate goods. It was also accomplished by Taiwan's building up its own periphery, mostly in Southeast Asia, which was dependent on Taiwan for investment, foreign aid, and trade in capital-intensive intermediate goods (Lin 1973, 130–33).[10] During this latest phase, which extends to the present, difficulty in obtaining the most advanced technology has probably been a greater constraint on economic growth and structural development than has reliance on external markets. For this reason the 1970s and 1980s might better be considered periods of technology dependence in which trade dependence played a secondary role.

Colonial Dependency

From 1895 to 1945, when Taiwan was subject to direct rule by Japan, the degree of political, economic, and social subordination of the Taiwanese was extremely high (see chapter 5). Politically, the Taiwanese were deprived of any say in their government, and they were subject to ruthless police control (Tsurumi 1980). Economically, Taiwan's agriculture and industry were revamped to produce goods needed for Japanese consumption and military expansion. Trade was reoriented to Japan, so that by 1935, 90 percent of Taiwan's exports went to the home islands (Ho 1978a, 392). Socially, the Taiwanese were subordinate to the Japanese, facing more limited job opportunities, lower pay, and discrimination in housing, education, and other social services (Barclay 1954).

According to world system and dependency theorists colonialism exacerbates economic inequality within the colonial population. Some of the principle mechanisms by which inequality is said to increase are set forth in the following hypotheses:

1. Colonial economic policies impoverish peasants by forcing them to plant export crops, thus exposing them to the uncertainties and fluctuations of the world market (Chirot 1977; Frank 1969c).

2. Under colonialism the forced transformation of a natural subsistence economy to export-oriented peripheral capitalism results in the stagnation of agriculture, manifested in a regression to more labor-intensive production techniques, a concentration of landholdings, and a rise in land rents. These processes produce greater inequality within the agricultural sector, and thus greater inequality in the economy as a whole (Amin 1976; Chirot 1977).

3. Under the system of colonial exchange, competition from imported manufactures leads to the destruction of local handicrafts and a decline in the income of the poor (Amin 1976).

4. Colonialism fosters the development of a lumpenbourgeoisie, a class of landlords and merchants who suppress the growth of a national industrial bourgeoisie. The growth of a national bourgeoisie would lead to a more diversified, internally oriented pattern of economic growth and a more equal distribution of income (Chirot 1977; Frank 1972).

5. Transportation and other infrastructure built under colonialism is oriented toward the ports of exit. By linking areas of the colony to the external world rather than to one another, colonialism fosters regional and sectoral income disparities (Chirot 1977; Frank 1969b; 1969c).

These hypotheses have very little support from Taiwan. The only significant change in Taiwan's structure of agricultural production, an increase in the export crop sugar cane, did not expose peasants to world market fluctuations because they had a guaranteed market in Japan (Ho 1978a, 356, 392). Agriculture did not stagnate; on the contrary, it achieved a remarkable and sustained rate of growth (Ho 1978a, 53–56). Imports of Japanese manufactures did lead to a reduction in full-time handicraft jobs, but the concurrent increase in manufacturing employment was twice as large (Ho 1978a, 78–80). Although no national industrial bourgeoisie emerged during the colonial period, this was due to colonial policies, not to suppression by a lumpenbourgeoisie. A significant Taiwanese lumpenbourgeoisie did not emerge for the simple reason that Japanese nationals monopolized all the relevant economic niches (Ho 1978a, 101, 324; Tsurumi 1980). Japanese infrastructural developments linked areas of Taiwan not only to Japan, but also to each other (Chang and Myers 1963, 440–42; Ranis 1979, 115, 216). As a result, regional disparities in income were not large.

Aid Dependency

From 1951 until the early to mid–1960s Taiwan was heavily dependent on U.S. aid for political and economic survival. (Aid was phased out gradually in the early 1960s and ended formally in 1965.) Data on the extent of dependency during this period can be found in table 4.6, which shows Taiwan's position on various indices of dependency relative to other peripheral and semiperipheral countries. Measures of dependency in the 1950s and early to mid–1960s are shown in columns 2–4.[11] To gauge the extent of Taiwan's aid dependency, column 2 shows 1960–1970 foreign grants and loans disbursed as a percentage of 1965 gross national product (GNP).[12] By this measure Taiwan was 1.5 times as aid dependent as the average developing country, and it was 1.8 times as aid dependent as the average semiperipheral country included here (henceforth simply the semiperiphery).

During this period neither trade nor investment dependency was high. Although there are many possible measures of trade dependency, one that goes beyond amount of trade to tap the structure of trade relations is Galtung's (1971) "level of processing" variable (column 3). On this index countries that import raw materials and export manufactured goods—the typical more developed country pattern—rank highest, while countries that import manufactured goods and export raw materials—the less developed country pattern—rank lowest.[13] Clearly, a high level of processing indicates a low degree of trade dependency. Although Taiwan's level of processing (.05) was lower than that of the core (.23), it was much higher than that of the semiperiphery (-.42) and the periphery and semiperiphery together (-.44).

Measuring investment dependency as the accumulated stock of private overseas direct investment (PODI) at the end of 1967 as a percentage of 1965 GNP, one finds that Taiwan was only 50 percent as dependent on foreign investment as the average peripheral or semiperipheral country (column 4). Though these measures are by no means complete, they do support the contention that during this period aid dependency was the dominant form of dependency on Taiwan.[14] Dependency and world systems theorists have posited several mechanisms through which foreign aid and other features of Taiwan's political economy during the 1950s may have worked to increase economic disparities:

6. In the aftermath of colonialism the class structure is dominated by a tiny export elite who ally with foreign actors and attempt to influence state policy to increase their own incomes and prevent the development of an indigenous industrial bourgeoisie (Frank 1972; Rubinson 1976).

7. Industrialization by import substitution exacerbates inequalities by relying on capital-intensive techniques, which keep unemployment high and wages low, and by producing for the privileged, who squander scarce resources in luxury-good consumption (Amin 1976; Frank 1972).

8. Foreign aid inhibits equalization by supporting primarily capital-intensive industrial projects and neglecting the agricultural sector, where the bulk of the low-income population is found (Goulet and Hudson 1971; Hayter 1971).

9. Aid strengthens those in power, enabling them to avoid changes in institutions, such as land tenure, that form the major obstacles to more equal income distribution (Goulet and Hudson 1971; Hayter 1971).

10. Aid facilitates the penetration of multinational corporations, which are the main agents of disequalization (Hayter 1971).

These hypotheses have very little support from Taiwan. In the decade after colonialism the government not only eliminated or squeezed out the tiny Taiwanese "export elite" of landlords and merchants; it also provided protection for native industry and encouraged the emergence of a national bourgeoisie (Ho 1978a, 128–29; Lin 1973, 45–47). Although the household income data for the 1950s are flimsy (see note 6), import substitution industrialization may have been marked by high income inequality, as suggested by hypothesis 7. This could have been due to a bias toward capital-intensivity, as hypothesized. However, it could not have resulted from the production of luxury goods: most of the goods manufactured in the 1950s were light consumer items (Ho 1978a, 194). The effects of aid on Taiwan are contrary to those hypothesized. A sizable percentage of aid funds went either directly or indirectly to agriculture. Furthermore, aid administrators actively supported reform of the land tenure system (Jacoby 1966, 129–49; chapters 6 and 7, this volume). Though aid institutions were instrumental in bringing multinational corporations to Taiwan in the 1960s, the distributional impact of foreign investment was not necessarily negative (this is examined in the next section). Thus, at most one of these hypotheses (number 7) might be supported by the Taiwan case.

Table 4.6

Selected Comparative Indices of Dependency and World System Position, 1950s–1980s

		1950s to mid-1960s		
		Aid dependency	Trade dependency	Investment dependency
	1958 GDP per capita U.S. $ (1)	1960–70 grants and loans as % of 1965 GNP (2)	1960 level of processing (3)	Stock PODI end-1967 as % 1965 GNP (4)
East Asian "success stories"				
S. Korea	128	139.1	−.21	2.6
Taiwan	108	46.8	.05	5.2
Hong Kong	257	11.8	.19	17.8
Singapore	435	18.3	.04	19.6
Other candidates for semiperiphery in 1970s				
India	69	26.1	.03	2.7
Kenya	90	73.7	−.54	20.2
Egypt	110	49.5	−.35	1.2
Philippines	198	28.4	−.63	14.0
Nigeria	48	18.8	−.69	2.3
Ivory Coast	131	66.1	−.76	20.9
Colombia	221	30.6	−.71	14.3
Mexico	292	19.4	−.71	9.2
Brazil	268	18.8	−.48	17.0
Argentina	530	14.4	−.67	10.9
Iran	n.a.	34.9	−.83	12.1
Venezuela	776	14.7	−.82	45.7
Average SP	131	26.3	−.42	10.3
Taiwan: Avg. SP	82.4%	177.9%	.47 above avg.	50.5%
All developing countries	149	31.9	−.44	11.0
Taiwan: All LDCs	72.5%	146.7%	.49 above avg.	47.3%
All developed countries	1,512	n.a.	.23	n.a.

Sources:

Column 1: United Nations (1967); 2: Organization for Economic Cooperation and Development (1972); *World Handbook of Political and Social Indicators*, 1972, Taylor and Hudson; 3: *Taiwan Statistical Data Book* (1980); World Bank (1981); United Nations (1979); 4: OECD (1972); Taylor and Hudson (1972); 5, 6: World Bank (1980; 1985); 7, 8: OECD (1973; 1975; 1977; 1980; 1981; 1982).

Table 4.6 (continued)

		1970s to mid-1980s			
		Aid dependency		Trade dependency	
1978 GNP per capita U.S. $ (5)	1983 GNP per capita U.S. $ (6)	1972–75 grants and loans as % of 1973 GNP (7)	1979–81 grants and loans as % of 1980 GNP (8)	1978 level of processing (9)	Partner concentra-tion % exports to 2 major trade partners 1977 (10)
1160	2010	30.1	1.4	.26	52.4
1400	2724	18.3	.0	.59	54.2
3040	6000	25.5	.1	.19	40.8
3290	6620	19.0	.7	−.11	29.8
180	260	5.4	2.3	.17	23.3
330	340	23.3	16.7	−.54	30.8
390	700	45.7	18.1	−.33	33.7
510	760	18.3	3.1	−.28	58.8
560	770	6.6	.2	−.78	51.3
840	710	43.5	4.8	−.68	40.5
850	1430	11.5	.7	−.60	48.7
1290	2240	22.6	.2	−.40	71.0
1570	1880	23.0	.3	−.16	26.5
1910	2070	3.4	.0	−.47	18.4
2160	n.a.	12.5	.0	n.a.	27.4
2910	3840	4.5	.0	−.80	60.9
1399	n.a.	15.6	1.2	−.16	40.7
100.0%		117.3%	1.7%	.75 above avg.	133.2%
696	n.a.	17.9	2.6	−.35	46.2
201.1%		102.2%	.8%	.94 above avg.	117.3%
8070	11060	n.a.	n.a.	.19	n.a.

Sources (continued):
Column 9: World Bank (1980; 1981); *Taiwan Statistical Data Book* (1980); 10: United Nations (1979); 11, 12: World Bank (1980; 1983); 13: World Bank (1985); 14: OECD (1973; 1975; 1979); Simon (1980); 15: OECD (1979); Simon (1980); 16: World Bank (1985).

Notes:
Includes two groups of countries with which Taiwan is frequently compared, East Asian

Table 4.6 (continued)

Selected Comparative Indices of Dependency and World System Position, 1950s-1980s

1970s to mid-1980s

	Trade dependency			Investment dependency	
	Commod. concen. % 3 major commod in total exports 1977 (11)	Commod. concen. % 3 major commod in total exports 1981 (12)	Imp. and exp. as % 1983 GNP (13)	1974–77 PODI as % 1977 GNP (14)	Stock PODI end-1977 as % 1977 GNP (15)	Net PODI 1983 as % 1983 GNP (16)
S. Korea	1.9	1.8	63.0	2.0	4.1	n.a.
Taiwan	2.0	1.7	89.0	1.0	3.2	.3
Hong Kong	.8	.5	144.5	7.3	14.4	n.a.
Singapore	4.3	3.3	302.1	14.0	23.4	8.4
India	14.0	16.4	12.2	.7	2.5	n.a.
Kenya	56.4	64.4	33.5	5.5	12.2	.8
Egypt	48.1	95.5	46.8	n.a.	n.a.	2.7
Philippines	39.0	26.4	32.6	3.4	7.8	.3
Nigeria	84.3	91.6	48.7	n.a.	8.1	.5
Ivory Coast	71.6	55.5	57.6	2.2	8.8	n.a.
Colombia	73.3	52.0	20.5	2.3	7.1	.7
Mexico	36.1	69.5	17.5	2.8	7.2	.3
Brazil	30.4	23.7	17.2	2.0	6.6	.6
Argentina	24.7	29.4	15.6	.8	5.8	.3
Iran	94.2	91.9	n.a.	n.a.	1.2	n.a.
Venezuela	65.6	67.4	32.7	n.a.	9.0	n.a.
Average SP	37.6	40.7	33.1	2.1	5.5	.6
Taiwan: Avg. SP	5.3%	4.2%	268.9%	47.6%	58.2%	43.1%
All developing countries	58.3	50.3	36.9	1.5	5.6	.7
Taiwan: All LDCs	3.4%	3.4	241.2%	66.7%	57.1%	36.8%
All developed countries	n.a.	8.3	28.7	n.a.	n.a.	n.a.

Notes (continued):
''success stories'' and partial set of countries designated by more than one author as semiperipheral in 1970s (based on Chirot 1977, 179–81; Evans 1979, 290–314; Mahler 1980, 142; Snyder and Kick 1979, 1110; Wallerstein 1976).

Trade and Technology Dependency

From the mid–1960s to the present, the dominant forms of dependency on Taiwan have been trade and technology, with investment dependency holding a distinctly secondary position. Although different types of dependency predominated in different decades, we treat these two decades together because the distributional processes operating during them are similar. During the 1960s Taiwan occupied a peripheral position in the world economy, exporting labor-intensive light manufactures to the core. From the early 1970s on, it has occupied a semiperipheral position, exporting increasingly capital- and skill-intensive goods, not only to the core, but also to areas more peripheral than itself.

Indices of dependency during these phases are shown in table 4.6, columns 7–16. Measuring aid dependency as grants and loans as a percentage of GNP, one finds that Taiwan was about as aid dependent as the average peripheral or semiperipheral country in the early 1970s (column 7). By the early 1980s aid to Taiwan had fallen off drastically, leaving the island only about 1 percent as aid dependent as other noncore countries (column 8).

There are three measures of investment dependency, two short-term measures of capital inflows, and a longer-term measure of accumulated capital stocks.[15] One flow measure is 1974–77 private overseas direct investment (PODI) as a percentage of 1977 GNP (column 14). By this measure Taiwan was about one-half as dependent on foreign investment as the average semiperipheral or noncore country. The stock measure is the accumulated stock of PODI at the end of 1977 as a percentage of 1977 GNP (column 15). By this index Taiwan was only about 55–60 percent as dependent on foreign investment as the average semiperipheral or developing country. Because similar data are not available for the 1980s, I use instead 1983 net direct private investment as a percentage of 1983 GNP (column 16). (This is the net amount invested or reinvested by nonresidents in enterprises in which they or other nonresidents exercise significant managerial control.) By this index, in the early 1980s Taiwan was only about 40 percent as investment dependent as the average semiperipheral or developing country.

Another dimension of a country's position in global investment relationships

---

Table 4.6 notes (continued)

Developing countries include low- and middle-income countries as well as capital surplus oil exporters. Sample sizes range from 61 to 129. Developed countries include high-income or industrialized countries. Sample sizes range from 18 to 28.

In columns 10–12 all averages median figures. In other columns all averages weighted averages. In columns 14 and 15 end-1977 stock PODI for Taiwan based on arrived investment from Simon (1980). OECD figures appear to be approved levels, and differ wildly from figures for earlier years.

Net PODI is net amount invested or reinvested by nonresidents in enterprises in which they or other nonresidents exercise significant managerial control. These net figures take into account value of direct investment abroad by residents of country in question.

SP = semiperiphery; n.a. = not available.

is the investment of local capital in other countries. On this dimension Taiwan occupies an intermediate position. Although investment outward has been later and substantially lower than investment inward, it has been growing rapidly since the mid-1970s. By 1984 Taiwan enterprises had invested over U.S. $300 million abroad, of which perhaps one-third was in Southeast Asia (the first wave), and two-fifths was in the United States (Dong 1985).

Measures of trade dependency are displayed in columns 9–13. Following Galtung's analysis (1971, 85–91), two aspects of trade dependency can be delineated, a gap in the level of processing between trading partners (introduced above), and a gap in the number of partners such that core countries trade with many partners, while dependent countries interact primarily with one core country. To these can be added three other facets of trade dependency: commodity concentration, the reliance on a small number of commodity exports (or imports); marketing dependency, which exists when a large proportion of a country's exports are bought and marketed by foreign purchasing agents and trading firms; and trade as a share of total economic activity. Although extensive use of trade can bring benefits not available otherwise, it also increases vulnerability to fluctuations in, and tariffs and other restrictions on, external markets.

On the level-of-processing index Taiwan shows an extremely low level of dependency in the late 1970s (column 9). The average was -.35 for all developing countries and .19 for all industrialized countries; it was an even higher .59 for Taiwan. Furthermore, relative to other noncore countries, Taiwan's exports were highly diversified (columns 11, 12). Using as a measure of commodity concentration the percentage of the three major commodities in total exports in 1977, one finds a median percentage of 37.6 for semiperipheral countries and 58.3 for developing countries. On Taiwan, however, the three major commodities made up only 2.0 percent of total exports. These figures were little changed in the early 1980s (column 12). But if the content and diversity of Taiwan's imports and exports indicate low levels of dependency, its position in the trading structure and the importance of trade in the economy indicate otherwise. On a measure of partner concentration, the percentage of exports going to the two major trading partners, Taiwan's trading pattern was 1.2 to 1.3 times as concentrated as that of the median semiperipheral and peripheral country (column 10). With respect to dependency on foreign buyers and trading companies for marketing, available information suggests that as much as 50 percent of Taiwan's exports may be marketed by foreign corporations and trading firms. Finally, trade comprises a huge slice of economic life on the island. In 1983, the value of imports and exports equaled 89 percent of GNP (column 13). By this measure Taiwan was two to three times as trade dependent as the average semiperipheral or developing country.

In sum, these indices suggest that, relative to other countries, in the 1970s and 1980s Taiwan exhibited a moderate degree of trade dependency and a low level of investment dependence.[16] On trade dependence Taiwan was low in processing and commodity concentration, moderately high in partner concentration, very high in the amount of trade in economic activity, and possibly very high in marketing dependency.

With respect to technological dependency, in comparative studies Taiwan is often counted among the technological leaders of the Third World (e.g., Hveem 1983). Technological leadership is a relative matter, however, for compared to core countries and to its perceived technological needs for further development and structural change, the island is quite dependent on foreign corporations for much of its advanced technology. Throughout the 1970s and 1980s technological dependency has been considered one of the major constraints on further upgrading of the economic structure (chapter 10).

What are the implications of trade and technology dependency for income distribution? Several hypotheses have been advanced by world system and dependency theorists, all suggesting that high trade and technology dependency, especially that induced by foreign investment, is associated with high inequality. Some of the major hypotheses are as follows:

11. Taking advantage of the elite's desire for luxury goods, foreign firms orient manufacturing technologies to the production of capital-intensive goods, leaving the masses jobless and excluded from consumption (Amin 1976; Evans 1979).

12. Because it encourages capital-intensive production, foreign investment destroys jobs in manufacturing and leads to a hypertrophy of the urban services sector. Because inequality in this sector is very high, an increase in its size increases the overall level of inequality (Evans and Timberlake 1980, but see Fiala 1983; Amin 1976).

13. Multinational-corporation-led development and MNC-controlled technology transfer inhibit economic diversification and the extension of spread and multiplier effects. Thus they provide few opportunities for local entrepreneurship and capital accumulation (Amin 1976; Rubinson 1976; Hveem 1983).

14. MNC penetration weakens the bargaining power of labor and results in wage levels that are very low (Bornschier and Ballmer-Cao 1979; Rubinson 1976).

15. Spatial concentration of foreign firms in a few towns and enclaves aggravates existing inequalities among regions, sectors, and labor markets (Amin 1976).

16. In semiperipheral countries where foreign investment is high, a triple alliance among MNCs, the state and elite local capital will exert pressure to shift returns from labor to capital, thus exacerbating inequalities in the distribution of income (Evans 1979).

Again, the radical-globalist hypotheses have little support from Taiwan. Not only has Taiwan's industrialization been largely labor-intensive, but also most of the island's foreign investment has been in labor-intensive sectors of production (Ho 1978a, 209; Ranis 1979, 232–42). The services sector is not overinflated; on the contrary, it is growing more slowly than the manufacturing sector and is relatively small by Third World standards (Galenson 1979b, 387–89). As hypothesized, MNC investment produced few spread and multiplier effects, at least initially. Since the recession in the mid–1970s, however, subcontracting, local sourcing, and worker training have increased rapidly, especially in certain industries (e.g., automotive, electronics) (Simon 1980, 483–519). At no time does it appear that MNC investment retarded the process of industrial diversification, which has proceeded rapidly since the mid–1960s (Ho 1978a, 130). Although it is true that the labor force is not organized to bargain for higher wages, this appears to be due more to state prohibition against unions and strikes than to any activities of the MNCs (Galenson 1979b; this issue requires more research). Even without unions, however, wages have risen rapidly as a result of market forces. Although foreign firms are to a certain extent concentrated in industrial enclaves, this has not led to spatial concentration of family income, for workers remit their wages to families living outside the enclaves. Finally, although there is a triple alliance of some sort on Taiwan (see Gold chapter 9), the effects of this alliance appear to be the opposite of those hypothesized, for during the years the alliance was forming, the share of labor in family income rose, while that of capital fell (DGBAS, various years).

New Statist and Globalist Analyses of Inequality on Taiwan

Why do the dependency and world systems hypotheses, which have considerable support from Latin America, have so little support from Taiwan? There are two logical possibilities. Either (1) the role of supranational factors is misspecified, that is, the hypotheses omit certain macrolevel variables or ignore some of the ways in which such factors work, or (2) supranational processes are not important forces shaping subnational distribution—in other words, dependency and world system theories misspecify the analytic level. Both groups of new statist theorists—economists and political economists—adhere to the second position. I believe that the first is correct. Before making my case, though, it is important to look carefully at the arguments advanced by these other schools of thought.

Toward a New Statist Synthesis: Economists

In the late 1970s liberal economists examined Taiwan's deviation from liberal expectations that distribution would deterioriate before improving and explained it by two factors: the initially equal distribution of assets, and the labor intensivity of most economic activities, in particular of the export industries whose expansion quickly absorbed Taiwan's surplus labor and bid up wage rates. In these liberal accounts the important thing about the state's policies of land reform and export promotion is that they maximized the role of the market. There seems to be little doubt that these two policies did play a large role in facilitating equitable growth on Taiwan. Nevertheless, the liberal economists' account remains incomplete, in particular because it takes these policies for granted. This account explains neither the capability of the state to adopt such policies nor its desire to do so.

The classic liberal economic analysis of distribution on Taiwan is the 1979 monograph by Fei, Ranis, and Kuo, *Growth with Equity: The Taiwan Case*. Disputing the widely held view that inequality must rise before it falls (Kuznets 1955; Adelman and Morris 1973; Paukert 1973), their major conclusion is that growth and equity are not necessarily competitive. In fact, they showed that, on Taiwan at least, income distribution improved during every phase of the transition from colonialism to the modern economic growth of the early 1970s, when their analysis concluded (p. 310; also Kuo 1983, 93–134; Kuo, Ranis, and Fei 1981).

These authors identify two policies that they believe largely explain Taiwan's equitable postwar distribution: the land reform in the early 1950s, and the switch from import substitution to export-oriented, labor-intensive industrialization in the early 1960s. During both postwar phases of economic growth a number of other conditions also contributed to this outcome. In the import substitution phase of the 1950s, conditions conducive to equity included the government's continued support of agriculture after the land reform, the relatively even initial distribution of industrial assets, the comparatively mild version of import substitution, and the decentralization of industrial operations. In the export promotion phase of the 1960s and early 1970s, conditions fostering improved distribution included the rapid absorption of surplus labor into labor-intensive industries, the resulting increase in real wages beginning in the late 1960s, and the substantial class mobility that existed. In both phases the small difference in wages and incomes between the farm and nonfarm sectors and the unusually high and well-distributed levels of literacy and education also promoted equitable growth.

With regard to the role of external factors, like most liberal economists these authors either ignore them or dismiss them as unimportant. An example of the latter approach is Ranis's (1974) emphatic rejection of the view, popular among dependency theorists in the early 1970s, that U.S. aid funds were responsible for Taiwan's good developmental performance (which underlay its good distributional performance); at most, he asserts, the availability of aid in the late 1950s and early 1960s provided a little buffering for a system about to embark on a new and untested growth path. By reassuring key members of the financial community, aid ''facilitated the policy changes required for the restructuring which could take place once the necessary *local decisions* had been made'' (Ranis 1974, 290, emphasis added). Nowhere is the role of U.S. advisers in promoting the switch to export-oriented industrialization or in pushing land reform a decade earlier visible; rather, in the liberal accounts, these two monumentally important developmental shifts are outcomes of local Nationalist state decisions (on land reform see Fei, Ranis, and Kuo 1979, 37–46; on the role of U.S. advisers see chapters 6 and 7, this volume). Although export-oriented industrialization, a strategy entailing heavy interdependencies with global economic and political systems, is identified by these scholars as a major route to equitable growth (see also Adelman 1985), at most, features of that global system are treated as conditioning factors that shape the choice of policy paths.[17]

With respect to the role of the state, Fei, Ranis, and Kuo distinguish three distributional roles of the government (1979, 5): (1) through setting the policy environment (via land reform, trade, industrialization, and other policies), the government can play a critical role in determining the kind of growth path adopted and thus the primary (i.e., pretax) distribution of income; (2) through participation in the productive activity of public enterprises the government can affect distribution directly; (3) through its taxation and expenditure policies the government affects the secondary (after tax) distribution of income. The book's empirical examination of the government's effects on the secondary distribution of income (the third role) shows that the Nationalist state's taxation policies were distributionally neutral during the period investigated, 1964–1973 (pp. 279–89). Throughout the book, however, the authors make it clear that they believe the Nationalist state had a major impact on the primary distribution of income through its choice of Taiwan's basic growth path (the first role; also Kuo, Ranis, and Fei 1981, esp. 145–46; for a general liberal economic exposition of the view that distribution follows from development strategy see Adelman 1985). Although the state bequeathed much of its direct role in determining income distribution to the market in the 1960s, in the liberal economic view the two early state policies, because they established the island's basic growth path, are largely responsible for its *long-term* distributional path. It is for this reason that the Fei, Ranis, and Kuo view is characterized as statist.

Liberal economists have made important contributions to the understanding of Taiwan's relatively low level of inequality by isolating critical elements of the domestic economy shaping that outcome. Nevertheless, their account is incomplete, misleading, and in some respects even implausible. It is incomplete in that it says what the important policies are, but nothing about the political requirements for adopting them. Put another way, it explores the proximate determinants of favorable distribution while ignoring the ultimate ones. The liberal economists' account is also imbalanced in that it gives too much credit to the Nationalist state for making the decisions that defined the island's basic growth and distributional paths. As I will argue below, there is much circumstantial evidence that U.S. aid administrators had important hands in the decisions to implement land reform and shift from import substitution to export promotion. Finally, an account that regards supranational processes merely as "conditioning factors" is simply implausible in the case of Taiwan. As documented throughout this volume, Taiwan has been penetrated by foreign political or economic influences in every postwar decade.

The New Statist Synthesis: Political Economists

In the 1980s political economists (mostly political scientists and sociologists) examined Taiwan's deviation from radical expectations of deteriorating distribution and explained it largely by the state's adoption of the same two policies. Unlike the economists, however, the political economists address the questions of the state's ability and desire to adopt these policies. In their view the state was able to adopt them because it was largely autonomous from domestic economic interests, and this autonomy in turn derived in large part from military strength brought from the mainland and military support received from the United States. The state wished to adopt such policies largely for political reasons, namely, to destroy the economic base of Taiwanese landlord elites, and to consolidate the political support of rural Taiwanese masses.

Nevertheless, despite these additions to the economic account, the political economic interpretation also remains incomplete. It probably understates direct supranational political influences on the willingness of the Nationalist state to adopt the policies of land reform and export-oriented development. The external political threat of the 1940s and the external economic opportunities of the 1960s, which appear as "favorable environmental conditions" in the liberal economic accounts, were more exceptional and compelling influences than recognized. Moreover, they were supplemented by direct political intervention by supranational actors to encourage, not to say force, the adoption of these policies.

So far, the most extensive statements by political economists critiquing radical theories as applied in East Asia appear in a volume edited by Deyo (1987b) entitled *The Political Economy of the New Asian Industrialism*. Most of the authors in that volume have turned to the strong developmentalist state to explain the failure of dependency theories to account for developmental outcomes in East Asia. Although the volume does not contain a chapter-length treatment of income distribution, two chapters touch on distribution briefly (Johnson and Koo), and two treat it at some length (Deyo and Evans).

These expositions confront two fundamental problems of earlier radical theories of inequality when applied to Taiwan. Radical globalists had claimed that high economic dependency should lead to high inequality, but on Taiwan it apparently has not. Radical statists had claimed that an authoritarian political regime promoting export expansion would exclude labor from political influence and suppress demands for higher wages, leading to high inequality, but on Taiwan apparently it has not.

With regard to the dependency-equality paradox, Evans argues that Taiwan does not contradict the dependency proposition that high levels and long periods of foreign penetration produce high inequality because foreign penetration of the island was neither uninterrupted nor high. First, he points out, after the departure of Japan there was a break in foreign penetration in the 1950s that may have provided a critical breathing space before foreign investment began to come in in earnest in the 1960s. Second, he argues, on Taiwan economic dependency (which he equates with dependency on foreign investment) has been only moderate relative to that in Latin America, thus one would expect inequality to be lower. Thus, foreign economic penetration might be harmful elsewhere, but on Taiwan its moderate level leaves the peripheral state room for maneuver and the peripheral society ownership of its economy.

Unfortunately, Evans's formulation does not completely remove the dependency-equality paradox. It does not do justice to the pervasive and prolonged distributional impact of prewar Japanese colonialism, clearly a crucial phase of Taiwan's dependency. For the postwar period, it stresses foreign investment while ignoring aid and trade, whose high levels on Taiwan radical theories had claimed should also have led to high inequality (see hypotheses in previous section).

For Johnson and Koo, the coexistence of high economic dependence with low inequality on Taiwan can be explained by the presence of a strong developmentalist state. Both authors argue that deliberate state actions—either policies to ensure equitable distribution (Johnson 1987, 145, 151), or a welfare orientation and attention to equity problems (Koo 1987, 178)—are in large part responsible for the low level of inequality on Taiwan. The problem here is that even though many state actions had favorable distributional consequences, many others did not. For example, in the 1950s the Nationalists discriminated against agriculture to provision the military, feed the cities, and fund industry, leaving rural families lagging far behind their urban counterparts in income and consumption (Ho 1978a). Far from supranational influences uniformly harming distribution and national policies uniformly helping it, the U.S. aid mission to Taiwan lobbied unsuccessfully for the abolition of these urban-biased policies until the end of aid in 1965.

In response to the second dilemma, the coexistence of low inequality with an exclusionary state that represses labor, Evans (1987, 217–20) replies that one must analyze distributional outcomes in the context of specific class configurations and developmental strategies. On Taiwan, he argues, the destruction of the landlord class during land reform and the strategy of export-oriented industrialization worked to improve distribution despite the existence of a state interested in keeping labor costs competitive.

Evans's emphasis on state strategy is further developed by Deyo (1987a, 242–43), who argues that "economic strategy and structure" help to eliminate the apparent incompatibility between a repressive state and an egalitarian income distribution. Among the distributionally beneficial strategies and structures he cites are export-oriented industrialization, which fostered the employment of multiple wage workers by low-income families and did not lead to segmented labor markets; progressive declines in unemployment and consequent rises in wages; and the recent (1980s) restructuring, which has led to increased investment in education, housing, and health and, in turn, a decline in absolute poverty. (Deyo's discussion here refers to the four East Asian NICs, not just Taiwan.)

An examination of state strategies is certainly a critical part of a discussion of Taiwan's income distribution. Yet what is noteworthy here is that these authors identify as crucial precisely the same features of Taiwan's growth path that earlier writers in the liberal economic tradition isolated: land reform and export-oriented industrialization. The sole exception is Deyo's point about the restructuring in the 1980s, which happened after the Fei, Ranis, and Kuo volume was published.

Taken together, these accounts represent a new statist synthesis in which both liberal economists and a group perhaps best described as neoliberal political economists (several of the authors discussed here—Deyo, Evans, Koo—doubtless intend to advance radical views, but seem to have backed into more liberal positions) maintain that the state and its developmental strategies are the key factors in Taiwan's economic distribution. Although the political economists do not go as far as the liberal economists in attributing the key policy decisions solely to the Nationalist state, by neglecting to mention the role of the U.S. aid mission in promoting these policies, they imply that the policies were only state-engendered. In this new statist synthesis, global and subglobal regional factors are generally seen as contextual, conditioning influences that have little independent effect on determining distributional outcomes.[18]

Among the political economists, the new statist interpretation of Taiwan's equitable distribution represents, in my view, an overreaction to the failure of the dependency and world systems hypotheses to explain that outcome. Although these hypotheses fared poorly in explaining the Taiwan case, it does not follow that one must reject the fundamental insight of the radical-globalist paradigms. Instead of downplaying the role of supranational political and economic forces, it is possible to expand the range and operational modes of such factors to produce an explanation that is more complete and more consistent with the political and economic facts of Taiwan's recent history.

Toward a New Globalist Synthesis: Initial Equalization of Assets

To see the centrality of supranational influences in Taiwan's subnational distribution it is useful to look again at the two strategies both sets of authors agree were crucial: land reform and export-oriented industrialization. In both cases, I argue, existing analyses oversimplify the redistributive processes involved and underestimate the influence of external political and economic forces. Although many of the distributionally critical supranational factors are standard features of Taiwan's political economic history, remarkably, they have not appeared in explanations of trends in inequality on the island. Although not wishing to retell an oft-told story, I believe it important to point out the impact these processes had on Taiwan's income distribution. In this and the following section I draw from the liberal, radical, and conservative orientations to sketch the outlines of a "new globalist synthesis" helping to explain Taiwan's pattern of relatively equitable growth.

⸺ Land reform was probably the most important determinant of the distribution of assets among the Taiwanese masses. Exclusive attention to that reform, however, diverts attention from other forms of asset change that affected the distribution of wealth between elites and masses, and between mainlanders and Taiwanese. Of particular importance are the redistribution of financial, industrial, and other physical assets, and of access to political power that occurred in the 1940s (see chapter 8). Significantly, all of these forms of redistribution were the results of external processes beyond state control. The Japanese had centralized control of most industrial assets on Taiwan to mobilize them for war, a process that removed them from Taiwanese economic elites and turned them over to the Nationalist political elite after retrocession of the island to China. Many physical assets were destroyed by the war, and many financial assets were wiped out by the postwar inflation in which the consumer price index rose tenfold a year during 1946–1949, and 500 percent in 1949–1950 (Lundberg 1979). Not only was the economic power of the Taiwanese elite stripped away; their political power was also removed by the events of the late 1940s. In fact, the land reform of 1949–1953 looms so large to contemporary observers because, after the wartime and postwar disruptions of the 1940s, there were few assets besides land left to redistribute. The contingent that arrived from the mainland in the late 1940s and early 1950s brought substantial holdings of human capital in the form of advanced education and technical skills but, with the exception of a few large industrialists who were able to ship plants to Taiwan (see chapter 5), their arrival probably did not substantially alter the distribution of physical assets. All of these factors are "conservative" in that they are unique and political, and unlikely to be duplicated elsewhere.

Even if one follows current thinking and focuses only on the land reform, it is hard to sustain the argument that it was the result primarily of Nationalist state policy. Supranational actors were influential in every phase of the reform, from decision to implementation to distributional results.

The decision to carry out the land reform was made by a mainland-based (i.e., external) state and heavily influenced by a foreign government whose motive was achievement of a global geopolitical strategy. To begin with, when the reform was launched, the Nationalist state itself was more an external than internal actor, operating from its main political base in East China and in the interests of preserving its position within China as a whole. The decisions to carry out the rent reduction, sale of public lands, and land-to-the-tiller programs were strongly influenced by the United States through the work of the Sino-American Joint Commission on Rural Reconstruction (JCRR), a semi-autonomous organ of U.S. aid administration within the Nationalist government. The JCRR involvement in

Nationalist land reform went back to mainland days (JCRR 1950; also Tang 1954; chapter 7 this volume). On Taiwan JCRR was actively involved in all three phases of the 1949–1953 reform, its liberal values coloring many facets of the reform process (see chapter 6). It helped to work out the schedule for the 37.5 percent rent reduction with the Taiwan provincial government. The land ownership classification of 1951 was carried out largely on its initiative, and the commission made important recommendations for the sale of public lands in the same year. JCRR contributed fully to the drafting, discussion, and final adoption of the Land-to-the-Tiller Act and the Regulations Governing the Issuance of Land Bonds in Kind. American efforts to promote land reform, in turn, were part of the larger American strategy of containing communism, a point familiar to radical theorists. This strategy involved preempting revolutionary communist redistribution by sponsoring reformist capitalist redistribution.

The implementation of the reform was marked by significant foreign participation and facilitated by a decade of externally imposed disruptions of social and economic life. American aid officials played key roles in working out the details of how these reforms would be structured and provided crucial financial and technical support for their implementation (see, for example, Ho 1978a; Hsiao 1981; chapters 6 and 7 this volume). Perhaps more fundamentally, the relative ease with which the rent reduction and land-to-the-tiller measures were carried out was significantly conditioned by the social and economic disturbances caused by a decade of wartime operations and military conscriptions, and postwar political and economic chaos, all with external origins. The disruption of institutions, social relationships, and agricultural routines facilitated reformist efforts to effect fundamental changes in rural life by creating a social climate within which drastic reform of the land ownership system became politically thinkable. These kinds of factors, which appear in economists' accounts as "favorable initial conditions," are in fact crucial parts of the explanation for why Taiwan's land reform was implemented with relative success.

The immediate distributional consequences of the land reform were due not only to the provisions of the reform, but also to a set of complementary policies, which were also influenced by external actors and institutions. Aid officials were instrumental in devising the agricultural policies of the 1950s; Japanese-installed institutions (in particular, the farmers' associations) were built on in implementing them; and Nationalist officials were keen on successfully implementing them, for increasing rice production was deemed necessary for building up the military in preparation for war against an external enemy.

Thus, the egalitarian consequences of the land reform can be traced not only to the policies of the Nationalist state, but also to specific supranational circumstances surrounding the reform, in particular, World War II and the social upheavals it caused, the strategies and goals of the United States, and the continued struggle between Nationalist and Communist Chinese regimes for control of the country.

Toward a New Globalist Synthesis: Labor-Intensive Export Expansion

The existing view of the equalizing effects of export expansion also oversimplifies the processes involved—particularly by neglecting changes in export strategy after the 1960s—and exaggerates the influence of the Nationalist state on the decision and implementation phases of the reform, and on its distributional consequences.

Current scholarship identifies Taiwan's strategy of export expansion as critical to its falling, then low, inequality in the 1960s–1980s. However, although these writers have explained the mechanisms by which export expansion lowered inequality in the 1960s—rapid absorption of surplus labor followed by rising wages—they have not explained what maintained low levels of inequality in the 1970s and 1980s, after the labor surplus was absorbed. (This criticism is less applicable to the Fei, Ranis, and Kuo volume, whose coverage ends in the early 1970s.)

Though little research has been done on this question, a few factors, especially supranational ones, can be identified that worked to keep inequality down by further raising the incomes of the lower and middle classes. Supranational factors were far from the only forces making for low overall inequality in the 1970s and 1980s. However, more than merely conditioning factors, they were critical causes of that outcome.[19] For example, beginning in the late 1960s and early 1970s, competition from lower-wage countries, combined with growing use of import restrictions by industrialized countries, forced Taiwan to begin shifting from labor-intensive to skill-intensive industries that bring higher wages to the work force. Also, the increasing number of foreign firms and buyers on the island, along with the growing sophistication of larger Taiwanese firms, generated an abundance of opportunities for small- and micro-scale entrepreneurship through subcontracting. The result was an explosion of rural, family-run factories that, although vulnerable to market fluctuations, gave rural families opportunities to share in the economic benefits of Taiwan's access to foreign markets. Thus, the explanation for low inequality in the 1970s and 1980s lies not simply in the promotion of labor-intensive exports. Equally important was how that initial strategy was built on and adapted to changing conditions in the domestic and global economies.

Even if only the late 1950s-early 1960s policy shift emphasized in the current literature is examined, one sees that the Nationalist state was but one of several, mostly external, influences on the decision to adopt this policy. Key supranational influences were foreign aid officials and their government's strategy to protect its capitalist clients. The evidence suggests that U.S. AID exerted strong and continuous influence on the formulation of Nationalist export-promotion policies through written analyses, oral persuasion, and threats to withhold aid. In the late

1950s and early 1960s, AID sponsored or strongly supported many of the measures to improve the investment climate, including the centerpiece of the reform package, the nineteen-point program or economic and financial reform (Jacoby 1966, 129–49; also chapter 7, this volume). The American interest in promoting this reform, in turn, was part of a larger effort to shift from the more expensive direct military involvement to self-financing, indirect economic involvement as a strategy for protecting capitalism from communism.

Supranational factors—in particular, conditions in the global economy—also shaped the way the reform package was implemented in the 1960s. As liberal economists have noted, it was only the opening to the world market that enabled Taiwan to identify its comparative advantage, and it was the world market that identified that advantage as in labor-intensive exports. Thus, the labor intensivity of Taiwan's exports was the product of the disproportion between the largeness of world (especially American) markets and the smallness and cheapness of Taiwan's labor force, and the adjustment that conjuncture brought forth, namely, rapid labor absorption into labor-intensive production, followed by rising wages. This is a "conservative" point because it requires a very specific combination of circumstances—domestically, a baseline of labor-intensive, labor-surplus agriculture, and supranationally, a large demand in core markets combined with a small number of rival peripheral suppliers—that is unlikely to be repeated in other developing countries. As radical theorists would add, however, the development of labor-intensive industries was not simply a matter of Taiwan's adjusting to external markets. It also involved the active search for cheap labor by Japanese and American firms fleeing expensive labor at home and seeking competitive edges over each other.

The egalitarian effects of the switch to export-oriented industrialization were facilitated by advantageous global timing. It was the boom in the world economy in the 1960s that supported the development of labor-intensive exports, which both economists and political economists consider the primary cause of income equalization in the 1960s. Furthermore, by fueling massive export-oriented industrialization in the 1960s, the global economic boom enabled Taiwan to achieve newly industrialized status by the early 1970s. By raising its position in the world-economy before the crises of the 1970s, Taiwan had more resources to withstand the disequalizing forces of recession and core protectionism that marked that decade and the one that has followed.

Thus, the distributional success of the export-promotion strategy was due not simply to the policies of a strong developmentalist state. In large part this outcome stemmed from the specific supranational context in which the strategy was carried out. Behind Taiwan's falling and then low inequality in the 1960s–1980s lay, inter alia, changes in American geopolitical strategies in the 1950s, the boom in the world economy in the 1960s, and growing competition from lower-wage countries in the 1970s and 1980s.

Conclusion

To recapitulate, essentially the radical-globalist argument of the 1960s-early 1980s was that the economic logic of global capitalism would force the national elites of developing countries to adopt policies detrimental to the masses. In parts of East Asia, however, national elites adopted policies that ultimately proved beneficial to their populations, at least in terms of income increase and distribution.

Consequently, liberal and later radical theorists (as well as conservative theorists; see chapter 2) concluded that peripheral states have more autonomy, both external and internal, than earlier radicals had thought. The emphasis then shifted to deliberate strategies that developmentalist Third World states have adopted to combat disequalizing external influences. The trouble with this account of the developmental strategies of East Asian states is that the United States lobbied strongly for the adoption of the land reform and export promotion policies to which the new statists attribute their relatively equal income distribution. Radical globalists may have been wrong that external influences always worsen internal distribution, but they were not wrong that external influences exert a pervasive influence on internal outcomes, at least on Taiwan.

In rejecting the radical-globalist theories of the dangers of dependency, political economists have begun to abandon examination of supranational determinants of subnational distribution. In fact, we have seen that there is little difference between the explanations of Taiwan's good distributional performance offered by the economists and the political economists. Both are "neoliberal" in emphasizing the importance of the state in adopting market-maximizing policies. Indeed, they emphasize the same two policies, land reform and export expansion.

Although these two policies doubtless had the egalitarian effects claimed, the new statist account is inadequate in that it oversimplifies the nature of these processes and ignores the role of external forces in shaping the decisions to adopt these policies and the ways the policies were carried out. With respect to the redistribution of assets, not only land but also financial and industrial properties and even access to political power changed hands in the 1940s and early 1950s. External forces played a critical role in redistributing these assets. Wartime Japanese mobilization, war-end Nationalist takeover, and postwar inflation and American influence all had a hand in leveling the ownership of property in those formative decades.

With regard to the labor intensity of exports, Taiwan's success at export promotion required not only the adoption of market-oriented policies and early entry into booming global markets. Equally crucial was the active search for low-wage labor by foreign buyers and foreign investors eager to escape rising labor costs at home and undercut low-wage competitors abroad.

Foreign influences were not merely conditioning factors, but rather fundamental ingredients of Taiwan's distributional success. These supranational conditions require restatement because, although many of them were noted in passing in early accounts by economists, they neither received the emphasis they deserved nor were incorporated into theories of Taiwan's economic distribution. More recently, interest in such factors appears to have waned, as economists and political economists alike turn their attention to states and state policies.

While the present analysis supports the most basic assumption of the radical-globalist accounts, it also suggests several ways in which the dependency and world systems perspectives require modification. First, despite the greater visibility of foreign investment as a mechanism for foreign influence, the East Asian cases indicate that investment may not be the most important conduit for foreign influence on distribution in the more advanced Third World countries. More important in some places may be foreign aid, whose distributional effects become visible only over the long term. Second, in addition to the detrimental distributional effects of aid emphasized by these theories, Taiwan shows that when geopolitical and temporal conditions are right, foreign aid can have beneficial distributional consequences. Through its role in advancing and shaping the two early and critical reforms discussed here, U.S. AID was a major force behind the decline in inequality in the 1950s and 1960s.

The supranational conditions underlying Taiwan's path of "growth with equity" are historically specific and unlikely to obtain for other later developers. This bring one to the policy implications of Taiwan's experience. Emphasizing national-level factors, as both sets of theorists do, is sensible if one is looking for measures that other countries could adopt to improve their distributional records. But the question this chapter raises is: What if much of the explanation for Taiwan's relatively equal income distribution lies in conditions outside of deliberately adopted national policies? If that is the case, as we have argued it is, then Taiwan's distributional experience may have little direct policy relevance for other countries.

Notes

1. Although all four East Asian NICs—Hong Kong, Singapore, South Korea, and Taiwan—can boast levels of income inequality that are lower than those in most developing countries, only Taiwan has achieved and maintained a very low level of inequality. In the city-states Hong Kong and Singapore the Gini coefficient of inequality (which ranges from a low of .00 to a high of 1.00) has remained above .40. In Hong Kong it fell from .49 in 1966 to .41 in 1971, then rose again, reaching .45 in 1981. In Singapore it declined from .50 in 1966 to .46 in 1980 (Fields 1984). In South Korea the Gini fell from .45 in 1960 to .34 in 1965 and .33 in 1970, but then rose to .39 in 1975 and 1980 (Koo 1984).

I wish to thank Christopher Chase-Dunn, Richard Rubinson, Robert Wade, Edgar Wickberg, and Edwin Winckler for their comments on earlier drafts of this chapter.

2. Although a fully elaborated theory would deal with the distribution of different types of economic goods, due to problems of data quality and availability, most authors restrict their scope to the distribution of income. Given the robustness and historical depth of the income data for Taiwan, I have chosen to follow the same approach, and to supplement income with data on wealth for periods where income data are inadequate.

Though the official income data are of fairly high quality, it should be noted that they are based on a unit of analysis, the coresidential household, that is different from what for most of the postwar decades has been the operative unit of income acquisition in the society, the family (*chia*). Use of a household unit probably had little impact on the level of inequality when most family members lived together in a single household. Since the 1960s, however, when dispersal of family members into separate households became common, use of the household unit has probably produced a level of inequality that is lower than the level of inequality among family income units (Greenhalgh 1982).

3. Lamley (1964, 292–93) reports that during the 1895 takeover some of the rich suffered losses from property damage, confiscation and theft. During the land reform of 1905, the rights of the *ta-tsu hu* were bought by the government with bonds. While some families managed to invest their bonds in income-generating enterprises, most divided the bonds among branches of the family, thereby destroying their earlier economic power.

4. The TDM is a very simple measure that represents the sum of the differences, signs ignored, between the percentage shares of given groups within the population in total number and in total income (technical properties of the measure are discussed in Kuznets 1976, 11–13). Though the TDM is usually applied to a larger number of size classes than the data here include, nevertheless it should permit rough estimation of cross-temporal trends within the data set.

5. The assumption underlying these calculations is that the sample data are representative of the island as a whole. Although it is not possible to confirm this assumption on the basis of information provided by Chang, the exercise yields interesting results nonetheless.

6. The data for the earlier period are based on small, unrepresentative samples and should not be relied on. In these samples the Gini coefficient was .56 in 1953 and .44 in 1959. Data for the latter period are based on large, representative samples and sophisticated data processing techniques and hence yield distributional data that are fairly reliable. More thorough reviews of the data quality can be found in Fei, Ranis, and Kuo 1979, 10–13, 65; Ho 1978a, 140–43; Kuo 1975, 81–92; Kuznets 1979, 98–113.

7. Cross-national studies include Bornschier (1983); Bornschier and Ballmer-Cao (1979); Bornschier, Chase-Dunn, and Rubinson (1978); Mahler (1980); Nolan (1983); Ward (1978). A classic single-country study is Leys (1974).

8. Caporaso (1978) argues that the dependency literature contains two distinct (though latent) paradigms: "dependence," a concept in the liberal tradition that refers to external reliance of whole nation-states on other actors; and "dependency," a structural (radical, in the terms of this volume) concept that refers to the incorporation of developing regions, classes, etc. into the global capitalist system and the resulting structural distortions. (The usefulness of Caporaso's distinctions for understanding Taiwan is debated by Barrett and Whyte [1984] and Hammer [1984].) Here I treat both concepts, though somewhat differently. The dependence concept refers only to external reliance, and so fits readily into hypotheses about the origins of inequality. The dependency concept is more difficult to treat in hypothetical fashion because it logically entails both cause (reliance) and consequence (distortion). My approach removes this circularity by separating the three facets of dependency isolated by Caparaso into two independent variables (reliance, lack of choice) and one dependent variable (internal distortions) and asking whether the causes are necessarily associated with the consequences.

9. Tylecote and Lonsdale-Brown (1982, 258–62) have pointed out conceptual and measurement problems with Wallerstein's criteria for delineating position in the world economy. As an alternative they suggest degree of possession of high technology. This suggestion is promising, but the data necessary to implement it are not available.

10. Southeast Asian dependence on Taiwan for trade is reflected in growing trade

imbalances in Taiwan's favor that grew rapidly after 1970 (Hong Kong), 1973–74 (Singapore, Philippines), and 1978 (Thailand). Technical aid missions sent to Southeast Asia mushroomed during the Vietnam War (1964–69), remained relatively numerous in the early 1970s, dropped off during 1975–78, then increased steadily in the late 1970s and early 1980s (CEPD 1983, 240–43, 191–95). Investment patterns of Taiwan's business groups suggest that up through the late 1970s the majority of investments abroad were in Southeast Asia (based on analysis of China Credit Information Service, *Business Groups in Taiwan, 1978*).

11. For theoretical explanations of these measures see Chase-Dunn (1979); Galtung (1971); Mahler (1980); Rubinson (1976).

12. Although it would have been desirable to include a measure of aid in the 1950s, the relevant data could not be located. For foreign investment, too, the earliest data available are for the 1960s.

13. The formula for the level of processing variable is:

$$\frac{(a + d) - (b + c)}{(a + d) + (b + c)}$$

where a is the value of raw materials imported; b is the value of raw materials exported; c is the value of processed goods imported; and d is the value of processed goods exported. This is a relatively crude index, for it uses a dichotomous measure of level of processing (raw materials/processed goods), whereas a continuous measure would be more appropriate. A more elaborate version of the measure has been developed (Delacroix 1977), but I do not have the data necessary to employ it.

14. To determine the dominant form of dependency in a country, it is necessary to have not only international comparisons of each type of dependency, but also intranational comparisons of different types of dependency. Unfortunately, the existing measures of different types of dependency are not comparable. (Thus, for example, a comparison between a .05 level of trade dependency and a 3.4 percent level of investment dependency is meaningless.) Until comparable measures are available, one must rely on cross-country comparisons of each type of dependency to suggest the dominant type of dependency.

15. Bornschier, Chase-Dunn, and Rubinson (1978) have suggested that stocks and flows of foreign investment have different effects on economic growth. While current inflows of capital stimulate short-term increases in growth due to contribution to capital formation and demand, the long-run effects of foreign investment are structural distortions of the economy and lowered economic growth. This view is critically discussed by Szymanski (1983).

16. The conclusion about investment differs from that of Barrett and Whyte (1982, 1070), who have argued that investment dependency was above the average in the 1970s. Their conclusion was based on the growth rate of foreign investment between the early and late 1960s. However, such a measure says little about the absolute level of investment dependency, for a high growth rate may simply indicate a very low initial level of investment.

17. This approach to the world economy is also manifest in the work of Adelman, whose views on inequality are informed by close study of the Korean and, to a lesser extent, Taiwan experiences. For example, in a recent article on poverty-reduction strategies for the 1980s she writes that the policies that are most effective in producing equitable growth paths change over time in response to, inter alia, changes in the economic and political "environment" in which a country operates (1985, 65).

18. Although the Deyo volume's treatment of inequality on Taiwan is limited, this statist interpretation of these authors' views is supported by a more lengthy discussion of

distributional trends in South Korea published by Koo elsewhere (1984). In that article Koo maintains that the developmentalist state must be placed at the center of analyses of Third World economic distribution. Sounding not unlike Adelman, who writes in the liberal economic vein, Koo argues that the world economy should be viewed as a contextual variable that may constrain but not determine the policies adopted by Third World states.

19. Koo (1984) argues for a strong role for state policies in producing a rise in Korean inequality in the 1970s. The different distributional outcomes experienced by Korea and Taiwan in the 1970s may be due to differences in policies or differences in subnational social and economic structures. A careful comparison of the changing patterns and determinants of inequality in Taiwan and South Korea would shed a great deal of light on the theoretical issues addressed in this chapter.

5

Thomas B. Gold

COLONIAL ORIGINS OF TAIWANESE CAPITALISM

Colonization marked the incorporation of particular societies into the world system, or the intensification of previous linkages. Marx and Lenin viewed the global expansion of advanced capitalism as progressive in the sense that it would batter down precapitalist modes of production wherever they existed and bring about capitalism on a world scale, a prerequisite to socialist revolution.

Subsequent radical writers have adopted a different view, not surprising, considering that the prediction of Marx and Lenin did not materialize. These contemporary observers argue that imperialism articulated with precapitalist modes in such a way as to preserve those modes and block the development of full-scale capitalism.[1] Although incorporated into capitalist cycles of exchange and reproduction, their own economies and relations of production did not undergo transformation in the direction of capitalism. The exploitation of these economies and the reinforcement of the power of reactionary elites created a legacy obstructing capitalist development well after the termination of a formal colonial relationship.

As with so many other aspects of its development experience, Taiwan's colonial interlude poses an anomaly to theories of imperialist occupation. In this chapter I will examine key aspects of Taiwan's experience of colonialism and decolonization that differed from that in Latin America, Africa, and elsewhere in Asia to evaluate its consequences for later development. I also hope in the process to introduce the case of Japanese colonialism to the larger discourse on the subject.

Japanese Colonial Occupation of Taiwan

The distinctive nature of Taiwan's colonial experience can be traced to the unique nature of Japanese capitalism and imperialism. The origins of Japanese imperialism lie in Western imperialism, of which Japan itself was a victim.[2] In the mid-nineteenth century, the European and American Powers had forced China and Japan to sign unequal treaties granting them extraterritoriality and tariff control. But the Japanese response differed from that of China, formerly its mentor. The Japanese, who overthrew the 250-year-old Tokugawa shogunate, restored the Meiji Emperor, and ended Japan's 200-year isolationist policy in 1868, had as their overriding goal national wealth and military strength in order to regain independence and achieve security. Internal development and international independence were inextricably intertwined objectives.

Analyzing sources of Western power, Japan's new leaders undertook a thorough restructuring of the nation's feudal political and social system. Central to the project was economic development, in particular, industrialization. In the absence of an indigenous capitalist class, the Meiji state itself both set goals for the nation's economy and performed the necessary entrepreneurial functions of capital accumulation, investment, and production. After establishing several new enterprises, it sold some of them off to private investors, most of whom were large bankers.[3] The resulting conglomerates (zaibatsu) continued to remain dependent on the state, which generally acted in their interests.

It would be a great error to explain Japanese imperialism by a simplistic application of Lenin's (1939) analysis of Western imperialism, namely, that it represented, in the first instance, a stage of advanced capitalism. Japan's capitalism was still quite fragile when the nation embarked on imperialist adventures. The need for raw materials to fuel the growing industry and population was one impetus to Japan's turn to the outside at the end of the nineteenth century, but a search for investments and markets to solve problems of capital surplus and a falling rate of profit did not exist. Other, primarily political and military, reasons offer better explanations (Duus 1984).

Japan wanted to establish a cordon sanitaire against Western imperialists. It also determined to demonstrate to the Westerners that it had arrived: it had successfully industrialized and militarized and deserved to be treated as an equal; it should regain sovereignty and tariff autonomy. Taking overseas colonies, as the Powers had, would be convincing proof of this achievement. There was also an element of missionary zeal: Japan would teach other Asians the benefits of modernization (Takekoshi 1907).

Few areas of the world remained to be colonized, and Japan was not in a position to wrest a colony from a Western empire. It could, however, secure territories nominally controlled by its weak neighbor, China. It turned to Taiwan, Korea, and Manchuria as its major colonial possessions.

Taiwan had been a prefecture of the mainland province of Fukien since an army of the newly established Ch'ing dynasty had defeated loyalists of the previous Ming dynasty in 1683. But the Peking-based government expended little effort to administer this disease- and rebellion-ridden frontier island.

This changed as Western imperialists and, to a lesser degree, Japan began to make demands on Peking that included opening Taiwan along with the mainland to trade, settlement, and Christianity. In 1884, forced to take resolute action, Peking sent General Liu Ming-ch'uan to implement some of the defense-related self-strengthening policies on Taiwan that other administrators were attempting to carry out on the mainland. To emphasize its importance, Peking upgraded Taiwan to provincial status in 1887. Governor Liu made gains in military and defense modernization and infrastructure. But his successors after 1891 did not follow through.

Social and Political Control

Unlike the Western colonial powers, which had long-standing mercantile relations with the areas they colonized, Japan had few prior economic interests on Taiwan to defend, and it did not have relations with local classes who could be counted on to support Japanese rule. Rather, Japan was ceded Taiwan and the Pescadores as booty after defeating China in the Sino-Japanese War (1894–95), and it had to establish its presence there more or less from scratch.

Japan's colonial policy on Taiwan was influenced by Japan's evolving relations with the Western metropoles, on one hand, and China, on the other. Although Japan enjoyed enhanced status after its decisive military victory over China, it found itself in the frustrating position of still granting imperialist privileges to foreigners at home, and being treated generally as inferior. In fact, Russia, France, and Germany forced it to relinquish additional territories that China had initally ceded it. To end this humiliation, Japan had to demonstrate its effectiveness. It did this by moving rapidly and forcefully to eradicate resistance, to prevent other imperialists from meddling, and to establish unquestioned administrative control over Taiwan. This partially explains the harshness of the early policy.

After five months of fierce fighting,[4] including the subjugation of a hastily proclaimed Republic of Taiwan, the Japanese declared the island secure, then began to establish a structure of control to suppress further outbreaks and ensure their unchallenged hegemony.[5] The supreme authority, the Government-General (Sōtokufu), had extensive political, bureaucratic, military, and legislative powers over the colony. The first nine governors-general, up to 1919, were active military officers.

Japanese held the top posts in all three levels of local administration; the only exceptions were a handful of Japan-educated Taiwanese who were appointed village headmen later in the occupation. At a lower level, that of the hokō (units of 100 households),[6] Taiwanese were the elected leaders, but they were closely supervised by police. Only one-sixth of Taiwan's police force was made up of local people, and no Taiwanese was appointed above the rank of captain. In sum, direct and ruthless Japanese political control penetrated deep into every village on the island, rapidly enforcing and then maintaining the submission of the populace (Ch'en 1970, 148).

Japan's position vis à vis the Western Powers improved rapidly. In quick succession, extraterritoriality was abolished (1899) and Japan regained tariff autonomy (1910); it joined the Allied Expeditionary Force against the Boxers in China (1900); formed an alliance with Britain (1902); defeated Russia in war (1905); and annexed Korea (1910). Japanese self-confidence increased, pushed along by economic expansion brought on by European involvement and destruction in World War I. With this security, and prodded by a liberal period in its domestic politics after 1919 and the Wilsonian call for self-determination, Japan relaxed its repressive rule in Taiwan, appointing civilian governors with reduced legislative power and changing to a policy of integration.

One element in the integration policy for Taiwan was "local autonomy," or home rule, through the establishment of deliberative councils at local levels in 1920. Although Taiwanese could sit on the councils, the groups were dominated by Japanese residents and had only advisory power until reforms of 1935. At that time they were granted severely limited and ineffective decision-making power. At the top level of administration, the governor-general established a Consultative Council (Hyōgikai), which had no Taiwanese on it until 1921. Its functions were more honorific than substantive, however. In this period there were organizations and movements within Taiwan society calling for a range of reforms, mostly aimed at granting the people a better position within the empire, not seeking independence or reunification with China.[7]

In the 1930s, as Japan began to plan for a southward military thrust into China and Southeast Asia, launched from Taiwan, the authorities stepped up efforts to coerce the assimilation of the Taiwanese to Japanese culture. They appointed a retired military man as the seventeenth governor-general in 1936. A new crackdown ensued throughout the empire. In the waning days of the Pacific War, Tokyo announced the end of Taiwan's colonial status and its inclusion into Japan, but this had little effect on the populace.

Compared to the Western imperialists, Japan's administration of its colony was more direct and penetrated deeper into society, while its absorption of natives into government was much more restricted, resembling the French more than the British pattern (Gann 1984).

Economic Control

Japan's original economic objective for Taiwan was to develop the island's agriculture to supply the home islands with food and raw materials. These resources would enable Japan to attain its goals of increasing its industry-based wealth and power, maintaining independence, and achieving parity with the Europeans. Taiwan's function changed only with Japan's stepped-up preparations for war from the mid–1930s, as it introduced defense-related industries into the island and turned it into a base from which to launch the southward advance. The Korean and Manchurian colonies hosted industries from their inception.

Japanese administrators applied developmentalist lessons from the home is-lands to their colonies. In particular, the state took the lead in capital accumula-tion, preparing the productive infrastructure until private (Japanese) capital was capable of taking over the job. While suppressing resistance to its control, the Sōtokufu instituted financial reforms that incorporated Taiwan into the yen econ-omy and tariffs that reoriented trade from China to Japan. Japanese trading firms replaced British and other foreign houses, which were expelled.

Beginning in the term of the fourth governor-general, Kodama Gentarō, and his civil administrator Gotō Shimpei (1898–1906),[8] the Sōtokufu invested in building up the physical and social infrastructure. The former included transpor-tation and communication networks as well as harbor improvement, irrigation systems, and energy, while the latter included social order, public health, and education, especially in the Japanese language. A two-track education system kept most Taiwanese in an inferior position (Tsurumi 1977). The Sōtokufu established monopolies on opium, salt, camphor, tobacco, and liquor to control these vital commodities and generate revenues. It established the Bank of Taiwan in 1899 as a development bank.

Sugar and rice were the major primary commodities that Taiwan was to supply in exchange for Japanese manufactured goods. The first step to increasing agri-cultural production and tax revenues was a land survey in 1901, followed by a land reform in 1905. The *ta-tsu hu* (original landholders) were forced to accept government bonds in payment for their land, while the *hsiao-tsu hu* (original cultivators, who often took on tenants) were given title to the land and held responsible for paying a tax based on estimates of land productivity.

Next, the Sōtokufu moved to increase production by introducing new tech-niques and seeds to the peasants through farmers' associations, which all peasants were compelled to join (Ho 1978a, 63). Rural credit cooperatives made working capital available to them. Most important, and in contrast to Western imperialist policy, rural social organization and methods of production were not fundamen-tally altered: the basic unit of production continued to be the family farm; peasants or landlords retained ownership of the land and tools; and they sold their surplus, in this case to the Japanese. Sugar, the most important crop, was not grown on plantations, except in a few cases, but rather by peasant households. The government divided the island into a maximum of fifty sugar districts, compelling cane growers to sell their output to the mill assigned to their region at set prices. This severely limited the freedom of action of the farmers (Williams 1980, 232–34). The Japanese police enforced this serf-like relationship of peas-ant and mill (Kerr 1974, 101). What one sees, then, is the removal of an unpro-ductive rentier stratum, followed by state-led policies to increase production on family farms and state-enforced means of extracting and utilizing the surplus.

Having created a stable investment climate, the Sōtokufu went further and offered financial inducements to solicit Japanese companies to take over. After the turn of the century, and especially after the stimulus provided by the defeat of

Table 5.1

Types of Companies Owned by Taiwanese and Japanese, 1929

Company Type	Total Capital (1,000 yen)	Japanese	Taiwanese	Other
Limited by shares	287,939	78.40%	19.81%	1.79%
Mixed partnership*	16,567	67.97	32.03	—
Unlimited liability	7,941	23.59	76.42	—
Total	312,447	76.46	21.89	1.65

Source: Chang (1955, 96).
*Some shareholders have limited liability, some do not.

Russia, private corporations began to invest, with sugar refining the major target (Chang and Myers 1963, 443–44).

The Sōtokufu used its legal power to protect the interests and dominance of Japanese investors and circumscribe Taiwanese participation in the developing modern sector. By more or less tying peasants to the land and coercing them to provide sugar cane at fixed prices to specified mills, it guaranteed a steady supply of raw materials to Japanese refiners. By limiting the number of mills that could be set up in a geographical area, it protected the investor already there, in most cases a Japanese. In the industrial sector, Executive Law No. 16 prohibited companies that had only Chinese investors from using the word *kaisha* (company) in their name. This meant that purely Taiwanese firms had to maintain antiquated forms of ownership and management, whereas modern companies had to have a significant Japanese presence (Shih 1980, 316). This law was abolished in 1924. Table 5.1 illustrates the results of this law: the overwhelming dominance of Japanese in the companies limited by shares, the bulk of the modern sector. Once Japanese corporations began to invest in Taiwan, their state-backed economic power was so great as to make effective Taiwanese competition highly unlikely. In this way, the traditional Chinese-owned sugar mills were quickly wiped out (Chang and Myers 1963, 445). And any "Taiwanese" firm of consequence was really controlled by Japanese.

Table 5.2 shows sugar firms listed in an economic report from 1924. The miniscule size of the firms headed by Taiwanese, relative to those owned by Japanese, is evident. What is more, in many cases, apparently independent Japanese enterprises were actually subsidiaries of huge financial-industrial-trade conglomerates, zaibatsu, that were much more highly integrated than Western monopoly capital firms.

Table 5.3 shows the division of labor among the various sectors. Clearly, Japanese capital dominated industry whereas Taiwanese were relegated to tradi-

Table 5.2

Comparison of the Registered Capital of Selected Sugar Refineries, 1924
Unit: 1,000 yen

Company Name	Registered Capital
Japanese companies	
Meiji Sugar	37,500
Toyo Sugar	36,250
Taiwan Sugar	63,000
Ta-feng Development	5,000
Taiwanese companies	
Lin Pen-yüan Sugar	3,000
A-hou Sugar	3,000
Hsin-hsing Sugar	1,200

Source: *Taiwan Ginkō* (Bank of Taiwan), *Taiwan Kaisha Tekiyo* (1924, 40–42).

tional sectors such as agriculture and commerce. Finally, table 5.4 illustrates the imbalance in ownership of large corporations. It also shows that as the Second World War progressed, the Japanese swallowed up Taiwanese capital, further decreasing its share.

In addition to these forms of domination of the capitalist sector, Japanese migrants filled the important roles in the economy as well as in the administration, precluding Taiwanese participation. Throughout the Japanese period nearly 70 percent of Taiwanese were employed in agriculture.

Japan's main objective in Taiwan was to produce an agricultural surplus, but this surplus was not simply removed from the island. On the contrary, one of the two main crops, sugar, was processed on Taiwan in modern mills dispersed throughout the countryside. Furthermore, as Japan prepared for war, it diversified and deepened industrial production on Taiwan, moving from food processing into heavy, defense-related industries (Chang 1980). This differs from Western imperialism, where the relation between colonies and center was primarily in the sphere of trade, without a concomitant development of the productive forces.

Given all of this, what opportunities for upward mobility were there for ambitious Taiwanese in this system? Quite obviously, the previous Chinese mobility channels had been eliminated: the former political elite fled back to the mainland and was replaced by Japanese. The social elite (gentry and literati) was treated with respect, and many individuals were given low-level posts under strict Japanese supervision (Kerr 1974, 71–73). However, the substitution of modern Japanese education for the Confucian system removed a pillar of the gentry's power and offered a different set of education-based rewards. The discriminatory

Table 5.3

Taiwanese and Japanese Capital by Sectors, 1929

Sector	Total Share capital (1,000 yen)	Japanese	Taiwanese	Other
Industry	198,941	90.73%	8.44%	0.83%
Mining	17,107	71.57	20.12	8.31
Agriculture	9,399	47.17	52.79	0.04
Commerce	53,242	43.44	52.74	3.82
Transportation	5,781	55.11	44.47	0.42
Marine	3,417	65.13	34.32	0.55
Total	287,887	78.40	19.81	1.79

Source: Chang (1955, 97).

Table 5.4

Trends in Capital of Joint-Stock Companies Belonging to Japanese and Taiwanese

Companies with paid-in capital from 200,000 to 5 million yen

Year	Total Capital (1,000 yen)	Japanese			Taiwanese	Other
		In Japan	In Taiwan	Total		
1938	72,076	25.5%	34.1%	59.6%	38.5%	1.9%
1939	80,588	27.4	34.6	62.0	36.3	1.7
1940	93,433	31.9	35.8	67.7	30.9	1.4
1941	117,619	36.4	36.3	72.7	25.5	1.8

Companies with paid-in capital above 5 million yen

1938	302,184	77.7	18.5	96.2	3.6	0.2
1939	325,811	76.9	19.7	96.6	3.1	0.3
1940	361,810	75.6	21.1	96.7	3.0	0.3
1941	414,210	76.5	20.4	96.9	2.8	0.3

Source: Chang (1955, 97).

education system's primary objective was to train a corps of literate and skilled workers. A few Taiwanese were able to receive advanced education in Taiwan or Japan, but the areas open for study were restricted primarily to medicine and primary school teaching (Tsurumi 1977, 23–24).

Although commerce and handicraft production presented routes to wealth and prestige, few Taiwanese could be much more than petty-bourgeois shopkeepers or owners of handicraft workshops because of the restrictions noted above. But a few of them became extremely wealthy entrepreneurs. Within the Japanese colonial structure, the only way to achieve this was through collaboration.

The Collaborator-Entrepreneur Elite

Although Japan's predominance in Taiwan's economy and polity was secure, local collaborators performed several useful functions for the Japanese rulers. They facilitated penetration of Taiwanese society and could be used to ensure control. They presented exemplary models to their compatriots of how one could prosper through collaboration. And their business enterprises stimulated overall economic activity and generated more surplus for the empire.

The collaborative elite derived from two groups: One was a handful of wealthy and powerful landowning gentry that the Japanese coopted to prevent them from forming an opposition and to utilize their economic surplus. The other was a group of men from merchant backgrounds with no prestige in the precolonial Chinese society who took a chance on the Japanese and, through active collaboration, received bountiful rewards.

In this section I describe the experience of five collaborators. These five were unanimously deemed to be the most important, influential, and wealthy of the colonial-era collaborators by Who's Whos, biographies, scholarly studies, and interviews with older Taiwanese familiar with the era. The sketches that follow are designed to show the backgrounds and careers of the collaborator-entrepreneurs, how they were a product of the structures created by the Japanese, and how they were ultimately manipulated by the Japanese. The order in which they are introduced illustrates the continuum from eager collaboration to active resistance cum reluctant collaboration.[9]

Ku Hsien-jung (1864–1938)

Clearly the most controversial collaborator was Ku Hsien-jung. He came from Lukang, a port in west-central Taiwan. He was a trader and adventurer of unclear origins. Of his own volition, Ku facilitated the peaceful entry of the Japanese forces into Taipei and then helped them pacify the rest of the island. For his efforts, he was awarded the Sixth Order of the Rising Sun and a post in the security apparatus. Ku was given monopoly privileges for camphor, opium, and tobacco and then put in charge of the extremely profitable and powerful salt monopoly for the island. He used the income from these privileges as capital for his own enterprises. He received extensive landholdings in central Taiwan from the Sōtokufu and also purchased land in Japan.

Trade remained at the center of Ku's business activity. His other investments extended to sugar, land development, manufacturing and retailing. Most major Taiwanese firms listed him as a director.

Ku was also a major political figure. He served on the Governor-General's Advisory Council and was the first Taiwanese to sit in the Japanese House of Peers. Although regarded by some as the paradigmatic running dog, Ku was actually a complex figure. He helped set up the Public Interest Society in 1923 to counter the home rule petitions of the Taiwan Culture Society and later became its president. Yet at the same time he also contributed to the establishment of *Taiwan Magazine* and the progressive Taiwan Youth Association in Tokyo. He was active in trying to improve Sino-Japanese relations in the early 1930s. By the end of the Japanese period, most of his companies, now run by his sons, were forcibly merged into larger Japanese companies, leaving the family only land and financial investments.

Lin Hsiung-cheng (1888–1948) and the House of Lin Pen-yüan

The other Taiwanese most noted for active collaboration were the descendants of an apocryphal ancestor, Lin Pen-yüan. Based in the Pan-ch'iao area outside Taipei, the Lins were one of the island's wealthiest families under the Ch'ing and were targeted by the Japanese for cooptation. Subsequently, they became inextricably tied to the colonial regime.

The Pan-ch'iao Lins emerged on the strength of the ancestor Lin P'ing-hou, who had become rich via trade and then used his wealth to purchase an office in the late Ch'ing government. While buying land on Taiwan, he established a base for the family on the mainland in Amoy. He contributed to the suppression of rebels on Taiwan.

His son, Kuo-hua, continued land development efforts and relocated the family in Pan-ch'iao, where they became Taiwan's largest landholders as well as active in tea trade and finance. Lin Kuo-hua's son Wei-jang was successful in the civil service examinations and also helped pacify the turbulent Taiwan frontier society. Another son, Wei-yüan, was active in civil affairs and concerned with China's self-strengthening efforts. He contributed money to Ting Jih-ch'ang to help build a navy and supported other defense efforts. Wei-yüan also supported Liu Ming-ch'uan's modernization program. He turned down an offer to serve as speaker of the Parliament in the abortive Taiwan Republic and fled to Amoy ahead of the Japanese.

The Lins were thus an exceptionally wealthy and prominent family well before the Japanese arrived. They were a prime target for cooptation. In 1900 a deal was struck whereby the Lins helped the Bank of Taiwan set up a branch in Amoy, in exchange for which the Japanese afforded protection to them and helped them establish the major Taiwanese-owned sugar refining company, Lin Pen-yüan Sugar, in 1909.

The Lin's capital was also absorbed into the Huanan Bank. Established in 1919, it combined Taiwanese, Overseas Chinese, mainland Chinese, and Japanese capital and functioned in the designs of imperial Japan for economic penetration into China and Southeast Asia.

Although the Lins' directly owned companies were mostly in real estate and credit, the family was involved in a large number of joint ventures with Japanese companies in such diverse sectors as steel, gum, and chemicals. The Pan-ch'iao Lins were dependent on the Japanese and joined Ku Hsien-jung to form the short-lived Public Interest Society on Japanese orders.

Lin Hsiung-cheng headed the first *fang* (nuclear unit) in the family, and it received the most attention from the rank-conscious Japanese. Lin was a prominent figure in business and civil affairs and sat on the Governor-General's Advisory Council. His wife was the daughter of the noted early Chinese entrepreneur, Sheng Hsüan-huai, and he invested in Sheng's enterprises. Another prominent family member was Lin Po-shou (1894-) of the second *fang*, who was educated in Japan and Europe.

The family declined considerably in the 1930s. Its core company, Lin Pen-yüan Sugar, had been merged into Japanese concerns in the late 1920s, and the Lins turned over many of their business affairs to their clerks. According to contemporary materials, the clerks milked the companies for their own profit.

Yen Yun-nien (1874–1923)

Another man who was rewarded for assisting the Japanese in their takeover was Yen Yun-nien of Keelung, the northern port city. The Yens came to Taiwan during the Chia-ch'ing period (1796–1820) as fishermen. To avoid the violent warfare between settlers originating from Chang-chou and Ch'üan-chou in Fukien, they moved closer to Keelung and bought land from which they prospered. Yen Yun-nien opened up retail stores with two brothers.

Yen, who was appointed family representative when the Japanese arrived to quash bandits, swore allegiance to the emperor, which protected the family. Yen developed good relations with the Japanese by acting as interpreter for their garrison. This was the foundation for his subsequent accumulation and investment strategy.

The Keelung-Juifang area was famous for its coal mines, but mining rights were reserved for Japanese investors. In 1896 the Fujita Gumi Company received mining rights in the region. An official of the firm went to the local police to find a Taiwanese who spoke Japanese to serve as a labor subcontractor. Yen was recommended and, in 1900, started supplying goods and laborers to Fujita. He studied Japanese management and mining and wanted to increase the area he was already mining. He collected capital from friends and relatives and, with his savings from his days as an interpreter, expanded his claim. He also improved his relations with Fujita and other Japanese concerns. In 1914, Fujita's operation floundered and Yen took it over and revived it.

Fujita had been cooperating with Mitsui, and in 1918 the latter invested with

Yen to establish the Keelung Coal Mining Company and, later, the T'ai-yang Mining Company. Yen mined both his own land and Japanese land, selling all his output to Mitsui. He proceeded to buy up shares in other companies in the area until he had over sixty concessions in Taiwan's major coal-producing region.

Yen Yun-nien was on the Governor-General's Advisory Council. When he died he left diverse holdings that included coal mining, light railroads, forestry, marine products, retail stores, and credit institutions, some of them joint ventures with both Japanese and Taiwanese firms. Because of their ventures in limestone and coal, the Yen companies prospered with Japan's emerging war industry in the 1930s, but they were forced into mergers in the 1940s.

Ch'en Chung-ho (1854–1931)

A similar pattern was followed by Ch'en Chung-ho of Kaohsiung, the southern port city first called Takao. Prior to Taiwan's cession to Japan, Ch'en was the major sugar trader between the island and Japan. His Ho-hsing Company had a store in Yokohama as early as 1873. He assisted the Japanese in the Sino-Japanese War and fled to Amoy afterward, fearful of attacks by his fellow Taiwanese. He was persuaded to return in 1897 by the Sōtokufu. He continued to speak on behalf of the Japanese and acted as the head of a *hokō* unit. The authorities gave Ch'en the Sixth Order of the Rising Sun. He also helped the Japanese in their war against Russia (1904–1905) and continued to receive honors for his loyalty. The Sōtokufu helped him invest in the Japanese owned Taiwan Sugar Company, and in 1903 it aided him in establishing the Hsin-hsing Sugar Company, the flagship of his enterprises. With the exception of the requisite Japanese, nearly all of the central people in the company were his Japan-educated sons.

Ch'en's business was centered on sugar, and he rose or fell with world markets. He lost money after the Russo-Japanese War and did not recover until the sugar boom following World War I. Where other families used capital from land to invest in industry, he used the capital accumulated from sugar to invest in land. His other major investments were in salt manufacture and trade. Ch'en himself was not on the Governor-General's Council, but his eldest son, Ch'i-chen, was.

Lin Hsien-t'ang (1881–1956)

At the other end of the spectrum is Lin Hsien-t'ang of the famous Lin family of Wu-feng in central Taiwan near Taichung. They were not related to the Pan-ch'iao family of the same surname.

In the mid-nineteenth century the family head, Lin Wen-ch'a, raised a private army among local boys and assisted in quelling one of the numerous rebellions that peppered the island's history. He followed this with successful military exploits in the anti-Taiping crusade on the mainland, earning several titles and honors. The family's new official gentry status brought it many opportunities to build up wealth and power, and it adopted the life-style and civil behavior of Chinese gentry families.

The Lins were closely associated with Taiwan's reformist modernizing governor, Liu Ming-ch'uan. They diversified their economic activities beyond the traditional control of land and water into camphor, aided by monopoly rights granted by Liu; trade with the mainland; retail stores; and real estate on the mainland.

At first, Lin Ch'ao-tung, family leader in 1895, agreed to join the anti-Japanese resistance. But its poor leadership and destructive in-fighting convinced him it was hopeless, and he withdrew to China. The remaining family members did not participate in the armed defense of the island.

The family's leading figure in the Japanese period was Lin Hsien-t'ang. Although he invested in companies via bonds given him in compensation for *ta-tsu* rights taken in the land reform, Lin directly set up only three enterprises, and these were established only after Executive Law No. 16 was abolished in 1924. Taiwanese held all of the important positions in his *kaisha*. In 1926 he established the Taito Trust Company with the express purpose of using its funds to support Taiwanese-owned enterprises. His *ta-tsu* compensation formed the initial capital for the Changhua Bank, but due to Law No. 16 it had to have Japanese leadership. In spite of this, Lin held various positions in it, eventually becoming chairman of the board.

Lin contributed funds to set up schools to promote higher education among Taiwanese. He also participated directly in politics, becoming the most distinguished spokesman for Taiwanese home rule. While he was establishing companies like Taito Trust and supporting organizations such as the New People's Society aimed at strengthening the economic and political position of Taiwanese, Lin was constantly being courted by the Japanese. In 1921 he was appointed to the Governor-General's Advisory Council, but he was removed two years later for continued activism on behalf of Taiwanese rights.

Three of these men, Ku, Yen, and Ch'en, were parvenus with no stake in the precolonial system. They gambled that the future lay with the Japanese and sought out the occupiers and collaborated with them. They combined their entrepreneurial talents with official protection and sponsorship to grow wealthy. The two Lin families came from Chinese landlord gentry background but were not opposed to business: both had supported Liu Ming-ch'uan's modernization program and themselves had invested in commercial undertakings. The Japanese eagerly courted them. Lin Hsiung-cheng and his family collaborated economically and politically, while Lin Hsien-t'ang used his influence to promote Taiwanese interests, seeking reform of the colonial system. Others in his family, however, were less able to resist Japanese enticements.

These men had different geographic bailiwicks but invested in similar economic sectors. All of them had extensive holdings in land, the traditional Chinese source of wealth, and a sector less subject to Japanese interference. Also, all of them had some investments in sugar mills. This was Taiwan's premier industry, and through their own initiative and, more importantly, Japanese assistance to reward collaboration, they shared in its profits. Sugar mills were the core enterprises of Ch'en Chung-ho and Lin Pen-yüan, and the others had them in their portfolios.

Furthermore, all had major investments in financial enterprises. Traditionally, Chinese have combined landholding with moneylending, but the Japanese encouraged this as a way of channeling Taiwanese capital into production. Because Japanese sat on bank and corporation boards, they had great power to see this through. Each collaborator in question had his own trust companies and banks, but they were all pressed by the Japanese to invest jointly in the Taisei Fire, Casualty, and Marine Insurance Company. Along with Taiwan-based Japanese capitalists, they each put in five million yen (T'u 1975, 416–20). The Huanan Bank, in which all but Ku invested, was an example of a financial undertaking used by the Japanese to further their expansionist schemes in Southeast Asia.

Although the collaborators had mutual investments and social relationships, each family controlled a large number of its own companies. This lack of unity facilitated Japanese control.

In addition to financial rewards and honorary political office, the Japanese gave a great deal of publicity to these men as examples to their fellow islanders. The families adopted many Japanese customs in return. Their economic, political, and cultural interests became externally oriented, to a certain extent disarticulating them from mainstream Taiwanese society.

The collaborator-entrepreneurs flourished during good times in Japan, such as the post-World War I boom and the subsequent liberal era. But when the Pacific War came closer to home, the Japanese restricted their freedom of action. To consolidate resources and mobilize for war, the Japanese bought out most of their industrial holdings. Land and financial investments, however, remained in the entrepreneurs' hands into the Nationalist period (T'u 1975, 446).

The Collaborators in the Postcolonial Period

Tracing the fate of the collaborator-entrepreneur elite after the departure of their colonial supporters requires a look first at the circumstances of Taiwan's decolonization. Decolonization from Japan was not followed by independence. Rather, based on the Cairo Declaration of 1943, the Allies handed Taiwan over to the Republic of China at the end of World War II. Unlike the former European colonies, on Taiwan there had been no armed liberation struggle; there was no united political elite with an army and ideology poised to run its own affairs. The pervasive Japanese police had effectively blocked the emergence of such an elite.

To assert Chinese control and to fill the political vacuum created by the Japanese departure, Chinese leader Chiang Kai-shek sent in an administration of mainland officials, who took over Japanese positions at all levels of government.

The politically fragmented Taiwanese had no organized means to express their own wishes. The ex-collaborators remained quiet, as their ties to the ROC's mortal enemy of fourteen years of brutal war rendered them too suspect in Chinese eyes to represent their people effectively. An exception was Lin Hsien-t'ang, who was invited to Nanking to witness the Japanese surrender in 1945.

Violent spontaneous demonstrations against the regime in 1947 resulted in the government massacre of up to twenty thousand Taiwanese (Kerr 1965). Community leaders and the educated elite were the main targets. The ex-collaborators' families suffered losses as well.

After the Nationalists retreated to Taiwan late in 1949 and the island became a de facto independent entity, the economic and political structures that emerged were remarkably similar to the colonial ones. Politically, a minority group monopolized the administration, controlled the means of violence, used thorough political repression to consolidate its rule, and extended its control down to the community level. In the economic sphere, the state owned majority shares in heavy industry and banking (based primarily on confiscated Japanese companies) and became increasingly involved in directing economic development. A crucial difference from the colonial period, however, is that the Nationalists did not restrict entrepreneurial activities of the Taiwanese.

The Nationalists moved to coopt and neutralize the remaining Japanese-period collaborators. Politically, the collaborators made peace with the Nationalists and sided with them in their determined opposition to communism. Not unexpectedly, perhaps, the most visible has been C. F. Koo (Ku Chen-fu), son of Ku Hsien-jung. He sits on the Central Executive Committee of the Nationalist party and helps to manage some of its business ventures. He is also chairman of the quasi-official Industrial and Commercial Association (his father had chaired a comparable body). He frequently represents Taiwan business interests abroad as a quasi-governmental ambassador. Members of the Ch'en and Yen families sit on the board of the Industrial and Commercial Association. Ch'en Ch'i-ch'uan was Nationalist mayor of Kaohsiung twice in the 1950s, and his brother Ch'i-ch'ing has been a delegate to the national assembly and has served in the Taiwan provincial government. Lin Po-shou of Pan-ch'iao is also an eminent public figure, as are other members of his family.

Economically, the Japanese-period collaborator-entrepreneurs were restricted in their activities in the early days after the retreat of the KMT to Taiwan. Soon after Retrocession in 1945, the Chinese confiscated all Japanese-owned industrial assets and turned them into state enterprises. These included many former Taiwanese properties that had been swallowed up during the war mobilization. The Nationalists also took over Japanese banking interests, in effect becoming majority shareholders in nominally private institutions such as the Changhua and Huanan Banks. The old shareholders did remain on the boards, however. The land reform of 1949–1953 removed the remaining foundation of the elite's traditional power. They were compensated, however, with shares in four state-owned enterprises, later sold to private investors, and thus had an opportunity for continued business activity.

Among those four corporations,[10] the sons of the collaborators concentrated the family resources in the Taiwan Cement Corporation. Lin Po-shou became the first chairman of the board, succeeded by C. F. Koo. Koo built it up and diversified its interests to create one of Taiwan's leading business groups. Yen Ch'in-hsien and Ch'en Ch'i-ch'ing have sat on the board. Lin Ming-ch'eng, also of Pan-ch'iao, is a permanent supervisor. Possibly quite by design, Lin Hsien-t'ang has no descendant representing him.

The descendants of the collaborators have their own business interests as well. For instance, the Yen family continues to own T'ai-yang Mining and a host of small enterprises. Lin Hsien-t'ang's son, P'an-lung, is an entrepreneur in his own right.

The Colonial Legacy: Postcolonial Capitalism

No accurate analysis of Taiwan's political economy can start with the Nationalist Chinese period. And the Japanese legacy cannot be reduced and written off, as some have tried,[11] to infrastructure and a few factories, most of which suffered American bombing. As I have tried to illustrate in the above brief review, the legacy is more profound and long lasting. In addition to unifying weights, measures, and currency, building a modern infrastructure, and introducing industry, which it dispersed around the island, avoiding the primate-city phenomenon common to other colonies, Japan's legacy can be seen in the following:

First, the Japanese removed the traditional elite, its material base, and the educational-bureaucratic system that gave it political and ideological hegemony. They replaced it with a new elite comprising Japanese and collaborating Taiwanese businessmen, a revolutionary move in a formally anticommercial society.

Second, Japan demonstrated the benefits of a meritocratically staffed administrative apparatus. The people saw clearly the improvements in health, sanitation, education, and material living standards that the state had brought about directly and through stimulating and guiding private investment. The Japanese introduced institutions central to successful state-led capitalist development.[12]

Third, the Japanese showed the potential for business success despite the existence of exclusionary politics. Great wealth involved collaboration with the powerful state, but one could also make money, albeit on a smaller scale, in spite of politics.

Fourth, Japan left a structure for pervasive political control and penetration down to the grass roots.

Fifth, while maintaining a precapitalist mode of production in agriculture, Japan systematically introduced new technology to raise production, dramatically breaking down peasant resistance to trying new things.

Sixth, the Japanese invested in human capital cultivation and the introduction of new values, anticipating, not fearing, change.

The Chinese Nationalists inherited and occupied the structure that the Japanese erected. They also inherited a population with certain expectations for their government. Although bungling tragically in the first few years, the Chinese nonetheless later successfully built on the legacy left by the Japanese. They legitimized a career in business, giving it prestige and patriotic significance. They took an activist role in the economy, building developmentalist institutions while also creating an investment climate conducive to private enterprise. While maintaining a hard authoritarian political system, at least until very recently, they allowed great scope for business activity, with collaboration with the state a major track to success. They removed impediments to the rapid development of agriculture, maintaining the family farm, introducing new technology and products, and facilitating a transition to industry and commerce.

Although the Japanese-era elite maintained social prestige and a business presence, its political activities were vastly circumscribed and it was surpassed in status by a new group of people. The Japanese had developed Taiwan's productive forces but restricted access to the major benefits. The Nationalist Chinese removed the remaining barriers, paving the way for explosive release of those forces.

Notes

1. For a lucid and witty review of the literature, see Foster-Carter (1978).
2. See Myers and Peattie (1984) for an excellent collection of articles on the subject. See also Cumings (1984).
3. Hirschmeier (1964) provides the best description of the process.
4. For discussions of Taiwanese resistance, see Hsu (1972), Shih (1980), and Lamley (1970).
5. This discussion follows E. Ch'en (1970) and C. Ch'en (1973). Both authors have essays in Myers and Peattie (1984) on related subjects.
6. For a more detailed discussion see Ch'en (1970, 144–48).
7. See Hsu (1972) and Shih (1980) for details.
8. For a more detailed discussion of these men and their policies, see C. Ch'en (1973), Chang and Myers (1963), and various articles in Myers and Peattie (1984).
9. The general discussion of the five collaborators derives from the following sources supplemented by interviews: Kawata (1917); Miyagawa (1926); Iwasaki (1903); Ozono (1916, 1931a, 1913b); Shih (1980); *Taiwan jinshikan* (1934); *Taiwan minkan shokuinroku* (1920); T'u (1975); and various issues of the journal *Taiwan jitsugyōkai* (Taiwan Entrepreneur's World). Specific works on each man are: for Ku Hsien-jung, *Ko Kenei-o den* (Biography of Ku Hsien-jung) (1940) and Ozono (1921); for the Pan-ch'iao Lins, Ozono (1931c) and Lin (1975); for Yen Yun-nien, Kubota (1924), *T'ai-yang K'uang-yeh Kung-ssu ssu-shih-nien chih* (1958), and Wang (1976–77); for Ch'en Chung-ho, Miyazaki (1932); for Lin Hsien-t'ang, Meskill (1979), Hsu (1972), Kerr (1974), and Shih (1980). Shih has tables listing specific companies in which they were active.
10. These were Taiwan Cement, Taiwan Pulp and Paper, Taiwan Industrial and Mining, and Taiwan Agricultural and Forestry. The last two were amalgams of small enterprises which were auctioned off separately.
11. Most works done on Taiwan or with the government's blessing do not even begin their study until 1952, when the economy had recovered from Nationalist-induced destruction. See, inter alia, Kuo, Ranis, and Fei (1981).
12. For a lucid analysis of these institutions, see Johnson (1985).

POSTWAR FORMATION

6

Richard E. Barrett

AUTONOMY AND DIVERSITY IN THE AMERICAN STATE ON TAIWAN

Introduction: Core Penetration of the Periphery

A major cause of global social change in the world system model is the ubiquitous impact of Western capitalism on the Third World. Like invading army ants, foreign capitalists appear everywhere during the nineteenth and twentieth centuries in a feverish search for resources and markets. Sometimes the doors to trade and investment are open and Western capitalists can enter on their own, involving their home states only later. Although this pattern was common in many areas of Africa and Latin America, in many Asian nations these doors were shut and civilian capitalists required military aid from their home states to pry them open. Thus the interrelationships between state and bourgeoisie in both core and peripheral nations become a necessary focus of research.

This problem of the separate interests and capabilities of capitalists and states in core and periphery is particularly crucial in East Asia, where neither of the major nations (China and Japan) became a colony of a great power. Moreover, a look at the historical record within any of these core powers indicates that there were conflicts over the extent to which imperialist domination was either necessary or desirable, and that these conflicts occurred within the government and the bourgeoisie, as well as between them.

Core and Periphery

Not all of these interrelationships have received the attention one might expect from scholars using the "radical globalist" world system perspective. Certain theorists who have dealt with Asia, such as Moulder (1977), Trimberger (1978), and Skocpol (1979), assign the exogenous variable of foreign penetration—either by capitalists or by their states—a major role in explaining why certain Asian nations did or did not industrialize. In contrast to previous analyses stressing sociocultural differences between China and Japan, Moulder emphasizes the similarity of their premodern states. She explains their later economic divergence in terms of differences in Western impact and differences in their mode of incorporation into the capitalist world system. In Trimberger's account of Meiji Japan, the major motivation for "revolution from above" is a xenophobic reaction to foreign intrusion by the upper classes. Skocpol's analysis of the French, Russian, and Chinese revolutions makes defeat by a foreign power or intense pressure from foreign states a major contributor to loss of legitimacy by the ruling class.

Given the importance of foreign capitalist intrusion and pressure by foreign states in these theories, one might expect their authors to deal with these major exogenous variables at some length. In general, they do not. Although Moulder catalogues Western outrages against Chinese nationalism, she does not demonstrate how extraterritoriality, indemnities, foreign missionaries, and trade caused underdevelopment. Trimberger makes no attempt to show that variations in foreign pressure (or variations in Japanese perceptions of foreign intrusion) produced variations in government development policies in the course of the Meiji Restoration. Skocpol is able to give only a "high-medium-low" scaling to the foreign pressures on these states (Perry 1980).

States and Classes

Although core states have received little attention from world system theorists, "radical statist" neo-Marxian theorists have discovered both the autonomy of these states and differences between them. Much of this literature attempts to explain the rise of the modern bourgeois welfare state, a development not foreseen by Marx (Gough 1975). Although originally about internal developments in core societies, arguments over neo-Marxist theories of the state suggest alternative interpretations of core-periphery relations as well.

The principal authors in this debate, Poulantzas (1978) and Miliband (1969; 1973), agree that the state is not simply a reflection of bourgeois interests (this is crass economism) but rather achieves some "relative autonomy." They part company, however, on what this means or how it happens. Poulantzas sees the autonomy as coming from domination by a strong state over bourgeois interests (Bonapartism). Pluralist institutions of bourgeois democracy (political parties, elections, separation of power, etc.) camouflage this state monopoly.

Miliband, on the other hand, points out that Marx's concept of Bonapartism referred to a specific case where the bourgeoisie was in temporary disarray, enabling the state to increase its influence. Miliband contends that, normally, one must understand political competition within bourgeois parliamentary democracies in terms of the different fractions within the dominant capitalist class. One difficulty in evaluating the usefulness of the concept of relative autonomy is that most of its proponents treat it as a categorical fact rather than as a measurable variable. Miliband considers it as a temporary state but does not specify the conditions that lead to its emergence, its magnitude, or its disappearance.

More explicit attention to the assessment of state autonomy would improve some world system analyses. For example, Moulder (1977, 102–105) discusses why core states (principally Britain) bothered to penetrate China, whereas some core states (such as Britain and the United States) actually encouraged Japan to resist unequal treaties and territorial encroachment soon after Commodore Perry forced Japan to establish links with the world system.[1] She claims that the British state acted because British industrialists saw China as a market for the "overproduction" of the capitalist system. However, she fails to document either that the industrialists held such views or that the British government acquiesced to them. In fact, using much better evidence than Moulder's, Hamilton (1977) has shown that British manufacturers had concluded before 1900 that the China market was a chimera.[2] Evidently the British state was acting at least partially on its own behalf in China, but Moulder does not explore this.

Moulder argues that the supposed lack of markets in Japan resulted in a lack of penetration by core states. However, she does not document the political process or the interactions between capitalists and state officials in core states that brought about the decision not to attempt penetration of Japanese markets. Moreover, she does not explore the geopolitical considerations that may have outweighed commercial possibilities and that also had major influences on policy formulation in core states.[3]

Trimberger (1978, 7–8), on the other hand, explicitly uses the concept of relative autonomy to explain why the state sponsored economic modernization in Japan. Like most world system theorists, however, she seldom attempts to show how the relative autonomy of core governments affected their policies toward the periphery.

The major argument of this chapter is that any world system analysis of development in Third World nations is incomplete without an analysis of the action of core states and interest groups. Since the United States government dominated the financial, monetary, military, and trade parameters of the capitalist world system between 1945 and the early 1970s, it should receive the major share of theorists' attention.

Second, the emergence of the U.S. government from World War II as a large, complex bureaucracy means that any analysis must also take account of both the attempts of external bourgeois groups to influence it and the relatively autonomous bureaucracies that were both the cause and effect of its growth. In foreign affairs, these bourgeois interests tended to bifurcate into two groups: Europe firsters and Asia firsters. Within the government, shifting coalitions of bureaucratic actors pursued three contradictory foreign policy goals: containment, rollback, and reform.

As will be shown below, these three goals tended to be identified with various segments of the government bureaucracy, and elements of the bureaucracy without direct ties to outside interests tended to develop their own ideology. U.S. policy toward Taiwan was guided by these intragovernmental coalitions. The island's eventual mode of integration into the capitalist world system can be explained more convincingly by examining how Taiwan functioned in internal U.S. government debates over the direction of the world system than by attempting to show that American bourgeois groups had a direct stake in opening Taiwan up for exploitation in the immediate postwar decade.

Autonomy in American China Policy

If the accounts of these comparative sociologists and social theorists seem inadequate, to what theoretical model can we turn? Franz Schurmann is one of a very few authors who have tried to come to grips with both the theoretical and historical issues involved in analysis of the interactions of state and bourgeoisie in international affairs. *The Logic of World Power* (1973) analyzes the triangular interaction among the United States, China, and the Soviet Union and takes into consideration both the autonomy and dependence of each state's foreign policy vis à vis domestic social forces. Moreover, his analysis attempts to account for both consensus and diversity of views within the foreign policy establishment of each state. Accordingly, a summary and critique of his argument should provide a robust theoretical framework for further historical analysis of the Taiwan case.

Ideology and Interests

Schurmann differs from many radical American historians in that he does not view the emergence of the postwar American "empire" as the natural culmination of economically based Manifest Destiny policies and turn-of-the-century American imperialist yearnings.[4] Instead, he attributes the distinctive nature of the postwar American empire—and the conflicts within the United States over its direction—to two things: the rapid expansion of the domestic power of the American state under Franklin Roosevelt and the application of that state's ideology on a global scale. Schurmann puts particular emphasis on the precedents set by the ideological war that Roosevelt self-consciously waged on the Axis powers. As will be seen, this reformist ideology may explain more of postwar outcomes on Taiwan than even his theory allows.

Schurmann also maintains that to understand the transmutation of the 1940 vision of "one world" into the late 1940s' bipolar view (one free world and an unfree one) requires the examination of interests as well as ideology. Classifying American business interests according to their geographic orientation, Schurmann and others have divided them into internationalist Europe firsters and nationalist Asia firsters. In general, the Europe firsters—Easterners interested in free trade, large-scale banking, and heavy industry—favored a rapid recovery of Europe's devastated economy and an early resumption of prewar trading patterns. They favored devoting American attention and resources to mutual security pacts such as the North Atlantic Treaty Organization (NATO), to the Marshall Plan for European economic recovery, and to other policies calculated to contain world communism.

The Asia firsters—Southerners, Midwesterners, and Westerners interested in realizing America's potential for political and economic leadership in the Pacific—favored developing links with Asian nations. In general, the Asia firsters were the low-technology, Main Street (as opposed to Wall Street) bourgeoisie. They saw revived European industries as competitors in export markets. For them, destruction of European industries presented an ideal condition for American economic and political penetration of Asian countries.

Thus, for Schurmann postwar American "imperialism" is the outcome of a triangular struggle among the expanding power and ideology of the American state (as ultimately expressed in the doctrine of containment), on the one hand, and the two principal interest-based policies of the American bourgeoisie, internationalism and nationalism, on the other. The state registers both its own autonomous political interests and the conflict of economic interests in society. All three of these currents can be found even within particular bureaus of the state. The White House usually adopts containment, the State Department generally advocates internationalism, and the Pentagon tends to reflect whatever variant of nationalism is in vogue at any given time. The containment of communism remains the state's strategy and rationale for foreign policy decisions made by the executive branch. In Schurmann's account of the influences on the chief executive's decisions, however, internationalism and nationalism struggle with considerable success to force reinterpretations of the rationales behind policies and to influence the concrete content of that strategy over time.

Reform and Defense

How well does Schurmann's scheme work in accounting for postwar outcomes, particularly those on Taiwan? The materials explored in the remainder of this chapter suggest that Schurmann, too, may have understated the degree of autonomy of the American state.

Schurmann sees Roosevelt's ideological legacy as a belief that American domestic problems could be ameliorated through state-directed programs of reform, and that the international order could be reshaped to conform with American ideals. He feels that this statist ideology yielded rapidly to the economic interests of the nationalists and internationalists. Instead, the record suggests that Roosevelt's depression reformism and wartime idealism merged and became successfully institutionalized in America's foreign policy bureaucracies. The post-Rooseveltian American state's distinctly meliorist ideology remained strong long after 1945 and formed the ideological (as opposed to interest-based) justification for the Marshall Plan and other early foreign aid ventures. This ameliorative ideology was strongest within the government bureaus directly concerned with the provision of aid.

Thus my hypothesis is that the "relative autonomy" of this group of meliorist bureaucrats and the ideological nature of the Second World War led them to support foreign policies that encouraged the emergence and survival of bourgeois democracies in the periphery. They were, as Schurmann stipulates, constrained by core bourgeois interests, but these included the geopolitical interests of the American state as well as the (usually economic) interests of American citizens in foreign countries.

The international ameliorative agencies achieved their partial autonomy from domestic social and economic interests as part of the overall expansion of the American state as it fought depression and wartime enemies. These agencies survived the beginning of the cold war because they were able to justify long-term economic and social "nation-building" in terms acceptable to advocates of geopolitical containment, economic internationalism and rollback nationalism.

For advocates of containment, foreign aid bolstered the political stability of the Free World and encouraged defections from the communist bloc. For economic internationalists it revived economic activity in old trading partners and attracted the participation of new states in the capitalist world system. For advocates of rollback, foreign aid helped to strengthen friendly governments, subvert neutral ones, and demonstrate the objective superiority of the capitalist system in the Third World. While these groups were skeptical of the value of ameliorative aid for its own sake, the initial success of the aid program in rehabilitating certain European nations led them to concede the usefulness of the program and to grant these agencies considerable latitude in the actual operation of these programs.

Clearly, this reformist ideology and the interests of the American state or of specific American bourgeois groups could come into conflict in concrete situations. For example, in situations where national security or vital national interests were at stake, the U.S. government showed a tendency to support unsavory allies, or to patch together temporary (and unsatisfying) solutions that would promise to stabilize the situation for a period of time (typically until the end of a presidential term). American allies and client states recognized this tendency, and those in key areas were often able to get American aid with a minimum of reformist interference by exploiting it.

When national security stakes were less clear-cut, the influence of American bourgeois groups with investments or trade interests in particular countries could deflect the foreign policy bureaucrats from using foreign aid for reformist purposes. However, because the influence of bourgeois groups on U.S. policy toward aid for Taiwan was very limited, it will be excluded from this analysis.[5]

Taiwan was a key area for U.S. postwar aid administrators because it represented the first attempt at the social and economic development of a largely rural nation rather than the rebuilding of a previously industrialized one. Unlike in the European nations, there was no set of political and economic institutions that could be rebuilt by simply adding capital and technology. Instead, the aid administrators had to evolve a new ideology of "nation-building" and "development" and concoct programs to give this set of ideas concrete expression. In many senses, the Taiwan aid program was the avatar of U.S. AID programs in many Third World nations (especially in Southeast Asia) during the 1950s and 1960s.

Parameters of American China Policy

Despite the diverse influences affecting American China policy, at any given point during this period it displayed considerable coherence. This coherence was evidently the result of both external and internal parameters. On the one hand, the American state was constrained by its foreign partners and their domestic allies. On the other hand, the American state evolved effective procedures for achieving internal consensus.

Interstate Relations

Since the late 1930s, official and unofficial American representatives had been urging the Nationalist party (Kuomintang) to "reform itself" and to build a stronger base for its anti-Japanese and anti-Communist efforts through land reform, elimination of corruption, and other programs. Most of the historical evidence indicates that before 1949 on both Taiwan and the mainland such advice was routinely ignored, various restrictions to prevent the misuse of U.S. aid were subverted, and the Kuomintang factions continued with their normal patrimonial procedures in apportioning resources.[6]

Why was the Chinese government able to resist American pressures for a better accounting of how this aid was used? Briefly, during most of World War II, the Nationalist Chinese government was able to threaten to "drop out of the war" (i.e., sign a separate peace with the Japanese) unless they received aid with few strings attached. As Tang Tsou (1963), Barbara Tuchman (1972), and others have chronicled, this strategy worked for most of the 1941–45 period, but after 1945 the Nationalists lost their ability to threaten to pursue a policy that would directly affect U.S. security interests. From 1945 on, there was increasing conflict between the two wartime allies over the size and allotment of aid requests.

In the postwar councils of American power, decisions about the allocation of government resources were weighed against how much they would contribute to the overall goal of U.S. security in the face of a perceived Soviet threat. Much of the congressional debate about the relative merits of giving economic and military aid to Chiang Kai-shek in the 1946–49 period revolved around whether or not such aid would help to accomplish this overall goal. The Europe firsters (usually Democratic supporters of Secretary of State Marshall, and later Acheson) claimed that such aid was needed in Europe, and that aid to Chiang would be a marginal or wasted investment. The Asia firsters (often Republican legislators) attempted to justify China aid on a number of grounds, including an early version of the "domino theory." They claimed that the fall of Chiang's government would not only mean the loss of China to communism, but would also open the door to communist subversion in much of Southeast Asia. Since Japan and the European nations had been major prewar trading partners of these regions, they would become more vulnerable to Communist pressure as well.

The public record of the congressional debates of this period has been available for scrutiny for many years. In addition, the publication of the well-known "China White Paper" (U.S. Department of State 1949) has provided valuable documentary evidence of how the Truman administration thought the American public should interpret the U.S.-Kuomintang conflict.[7] However, most scholars who wrote on the topic during the 1950s and 1960s (such as Tsou 1963) did not, apparently, have access to the high-level documents that showed the attitudes and plans of powerful government officials.

The publication of the "Pentagon Papers" in 1971 made available a number of National Security Council memoranda from the late 1940s (U.S. Department of Defense 1971). Although the bulk of the material pertains to Vietnam, some of it deals with American policy in Asia as a whole, or with American policy toward China and Taiwan in particular. These materials do not reveal the details of bureaucratic infighting, but they do indicate the parameters of U.S. policy established as a result.

Intrastate Consensus

The National Security Council (NSC) staff worked in conjunction with the other major departments involved in the administration of national security policy (such as State, Defense, and Treasury, the Central Intelligence Agency, and other groups) to try to pull together agendas of the vital national interests of the United States. These agendas have been given concrete form in various NSC staff memoranda, and such memoranda form the basis for NSC deliberations and are often forwarded to the White House for approval as administration policy.[8]

Although such NSC memoranda do not always indicate what actions the United States will take if threatened in an unexpected manner, they do indicate the general views of elite groups and identify real or potential foreign political developments considered threatening to American interests. They define a rough hierarchy of goals that guide operational decisions about what should be risked when and where. Although these NSC memoranda have not achieved perfect coordination of American policies, they do establish the general limits within which bureaucratic struggles should be contained.[9]

By 1949, the Truman administration had written off the Nationalist Chinese cause on both the mainland and Taiwan. National Security Report No. 48/1 (presented to the NSC on 23 December 1949), ''The Position of the United States with Regard to Asia (draft),'' explicitly endorses the Central Intelligence Agency's estimate of 19 October 1949 (''ORE 76–49, concurred in by the intelligence organizations of the Departments of State, Army, Navy, and Air Force'') and quotes directly from it:

> Without major armed intervention, U.S. political, economic and logistic support of the present Nationalist island regime cannot insure [*sic*] its indefinite survival as a non-communist base. . . . Failing U.S. military occupation and control, a non-communist regime on Taiwan will probably succumb to the Chinese Communists by the end of 1950. (U.S. Department of Defense 1971, 2:245)

This report both holds the Joint Chiefs of Staff to their earlier assessment that ''the strategic importance of Taiwan does not justify overt military action'' and states the State Department's concern that U.S. intervention would provide the Chinese Communists with an ''irredentist issue'' that would ''rally almost unanimous public sentiment behind them in China'' (ibid., 244–45).

As a consequence of these arguments, the basic national security objectives endorsed by the NSC staff (and later by the administration) included:

> The United States should continue the policies of avoiding military and political support of any non-communist elements in China unless such elements are willing actively to resist communism with or without United States aid. . . .
> The United States should continue the policy set forth in NSC 37/2 and 37/5 of attempting to deny Formosa and the Pescadores to the Chinese Communists through diplomatic and economic means within the limitations imposed by the fact that successful achievement of this objective will primarily depend on prompt initiation and faithful implementation of essential measures of self-help by the non-communist administration of the islands. (Ibid., 270–71)

Thus, as a general policy, the Truman administration was only willing to bet a very short stack of chips on the survival of Taiwan as an independent polity, and it was also determined to make this limited commitment contingent on internal reform and ''self-help'' and to leave open the option to ''pull the plug'' or perhaps to intervene if the international situation dictated it.[10] This document suggests the exploration of more U.S. options in China policy in the future, but its very latitude was a reflection of (and perhaps caused by) the differences in views about the role of U.S. aid to Taiwan among various segments of the American foreign policy bureaucracy.

Diversity in American China Policy

Acting upon a request submitted under the provisions of the Freedom of Information Act, the National Archives recently declassified the records of the U.S.

consulate at Taipei, Taiwan, for the 1947–49 period. My preliminary survey of these and other documentary data on U.S.-Nationalist Chinese relations leads me to believe that there were three fairly distinct points of view on the correct role for the United States government in Taiwan after the fall of the Kuomintang regime on the mainland.[11] These three points of view appear to have been generally associated with certain bureaucratic organizations within the U.S. government; however, insufficient research has been done to identify precisely the amount of overlap between policy and organization, or whether there were significant deviations from these patterns by certain units or individuals within these bureaucracies.

Agency Views

The three principal organizational attitudes toward American policy regarding Taiwan in the late 1940s are as follows. First, the U.S. military favored a politically stable, pro-American regime on Taiwan. It was unwilling, however, to commit many resources to this goal until the outbreak of the Korean War, and particularly after the entry of the armed forces of the People's Republic of China into that conflict (December 1950). As the NSC memo (48/1) quoted above shows, the Joint Chiefs were willing to place Taiwan outside the Pacific "defense umbrella" in 1949. They showed no great desire to commit U.S. forces to a continuation of the Chinese civil war by establishing an extensive military advisory presence on the island, or by introducing U.S. combat or occupation forces to the island. Although U.S. military supplies were diverted to Taiwan (instead of going to China) throughout 1949, and a few U.S. military officers arrived there to survey training opportunities, these activities were not of a scale to indicate any serious intention to help Taiwan defend itself successfully from attack by the People's Republic or to emerge as an independent polity. In the U.S. military view, political stability and military strength were the key goals; social reform, particularly if it took resources away from the military or resulted in political instability, was of low priority.

The second distinct view was Secretary of State Acheson's conception that while limited support for Taiwan might provide short-run benefits, continued diplomatic recognition and support of the Nationalist regime would put a serious obstacle in relations between the United States and the People's Republic (see Cohen 1980, 26). Some elements of this view have already been noted above in the discussion of NSC Report 48/1; elsewhere in that report mention is made of the problems inherent in a policy that sought to "isolate" or "contain" China. The State Department realized early on that reestablishing relations with the People's Republic after a period of denying recognition would be a long and difficult political and procedural problem. As a result, in 1949 at least, the State Department stressed a low-profile American diplomatic presence on Taiwan. It backed away both from firmly supporting Chiang and from attempting to aid groups that might take power from Chiang and put Taiwan more firmly in the American orbit.[12]

Third, in contrast to the military and State Department views, which tended to stress limited U.S. involvement in Taiwan and support (at least temporarily) for the Nationalist regime, the bureaucrats within the foreign aid establishment appear to have been primarily interested in the improvement of living standards of Taiwanese peasants and relatively unconcerned with the survival of the regime. In fact, some of these bureaucrats appear to have had a hidden agenda of using the foreign aid program to help engineer the eventual downfall of the Kuomintang and to replace it by United Nations trusteeship status for the island.[13] In their view, the aid program should aim only at the improvement of living standards and economic stability and should not become one more cog in the Kuomintang patronage machine.

Policy Evolution

During the period between December 1949 and June 1950, the proposal for UN trusteeship for Taiwan received serious attention from high State Department officials. As Warren Cohen (1980, 25–32) has shown, Undersecretary of State Dean Rusk, George Kennan (head of the department's Policy Planning Staff), and others felt that the best way of seizing the psychological initiative in the struggles against communism in East and Southeast Asia would be for the United States to disassociate itself from Chiang Kai-shek and the Kuomintang and to force Chiang to turn the island over to the United Nations. This temporary congruence of interests between tough-minded anticommunists like Kennan (who had no high expectations of good relations with Communist China in the near future, but who also had no sympathy for Chiang) and universalist reformers like Rusk (who were unwilling to consign the Taiwanese to a corrupt dictatorship of the right or a totalitarian state of the left) was a fundamentally unstable one, but it provided sufficient high-level support for a reformist foreign aid program to take hold in Taiwan over the next several years.

The outbreak of the Korean War dashed Acheson's hopes for an early rapprochement with China, and entry of Chinese "volunteer" troops into Korea in November 1950 demolished any domestic American support for diplomatic or other ties with China. Yet, as Cohen (1980, 42–48) has shown, State Department policy toward Taiwan remained ambivalent even after the initiation of armed conflict between China and the United States. Acheson and many of his top advisers (particularly Rusk) were disenchanted with Chiang and the Kuomintang, and tried to fashion an aid program that would allow the island to survive without making a clear political commitment to the current regime. This policy would allow the United States to continue to pursue opportunities to detach China from the Soviet orbit or, failing that, to develop a group of "liberal reformers" who could take power in Taiwan.

Success of U.S. Aid Bureaucrats

The ideological predilections of the American foreign aid bureaucrats (as well as their assessment of local conditions) led them to support programs that stressed "small capitalist" values and individual participation in the economy (and to a lesser extent in the polity). In the early 1950s, this support took the form of programs designed to encourage the emergence of an economically viable class of small family farmers through land reform and the reconstitution of democratic farmers' associations with significant power over the distribution of rural resources (see Shen 1970; Ladejinsky 1977, 95–108, 142–47). By the late 1950s, the American aid group was supporting the development of small-scale and domestically controlled private industry and encouraging the transfer of public enterprises to the indigenous bourgeoisie as the best means of rapid industrial development (Jacoby 1966, 138–49).

Bureaucratic Influences

There are at least five bureaucratic reasons why aid administrators were able to push this idealistic "interventionist" view fairly successfully within the American foreign policy establishment and in the field on Taiwan during the early 1950s.

First, the American aid-disbursement process was becoming increasingly bureaucratic during the late 1940s and early 1950s. Much less American aid was flowing to countries like China through such quasi-international agencies as the United Nations Relief and Rehabilitation Administration (UNRRA), and more aid was beginning to flow directly through the Economic Cooperation Administration (ECA), an agency of the U.S. government (see Jacoby 1966, on the Taiwan ECA program). As a result, the U.S. government was able to demand greater accountability over how aid funds were spent.

Second, this bureaucratization of the program meant that, increasingly, aid was apportioned on a programmatic rather than simply a country basis. Agencies that evaluated the aid programs were now apt to compare performance of similar aid projects or programs across countries in order to establish their cost-effectiveness and the efficiency of the staff who administered them. The inclusion of China under the ECA meant that its aid program would have to meet standards similar to those applied to the Marshall Plan countries and other nations receiving U.S. funds. American aid administrators on Taiwan were under pressure to justify the cost-effectiveness of their programs. Although the U.S. aid program on Taiwan probably never reached the standards of efficiency of the aid program in the Marshall Plan nations of Western Europe, this outside standard gave the American administrators a convenient stick which which to nudge recalcitrant Chinese officials who were straying from the path of efficient administration.

Third, these bureaucratic changes in the administration of aid would not have had much impact on Taiwan if most of the rest of the Truman administration had not written off the island as a bad investment. The aid administrators were the only group (at least before the outbreak of the Korean War) who were willing to put resources into Taiwan, and the Kuomintang was forced to ally itself with them. Although the aid agency demanded a high price in terms of reform, the Kuomintang had little choice if it wished to survive.

Fourth, the view that the United States could and should give aid to the Chinese people—but not necessarily tie itself to support for the Kuomintang—was a view that had historical antecedents on the mainland among General Stillwell's staff and on Taiwan among American personnel during the 1945–49 period. Although these American consular officials were later effectively isolated or silenced, the record of Kuomintang mismanagement in China before 1949 and on Taiwan during the 1945–48 period remained part of the written record and oral lore available to members of the American community there. As a result, ECA officials had a clearer idea of what abuses would have to be corrected if their programs were not to be discredited by corruption and failure.

Finally, American aid officials had access to the extensive Japanese colonial statistics on agricultural and industrial production on Taiwan.[14] As a result, they had a much better idea of the possibilities for improvement of the Taiwanese economy than they had ever had in administering rehabilitation or developmental programs on the mainland. On Taiwan, they could deduce guidelines for judging the cost-effectiveness of various projects. The combination of historical knowledge of patterns of Kuomintang mismanagement, possession of a yardstick against which present performance could be measured, and commitment to broad-based economic improvement rather than to the survival of a regime made the ECA and the Joint Commission on Rural Reconstruction (JCRR) much more effective agents of social change and economic improvement than most foreign aid programs.

External Influences

Schurmann's view of the evolution of American policy in the Pacific put considerable emphasis on the role of the Asia firsters, particularly on the amalgam of interest groups generally known as the "China Lobby." It may be useful to review why U.S. aid bureaucrats were able to carry out a reformist program in Taiwan despite strong American interest groups, which had, in the recent past, successfully opposed putting strings on aid to Nationalist China.

Schurmann (1973) argued that major support for Chiang Kai-shek came from American missionaries (who saw China as ripe for conversion after the 1911 revolution), businessmen (who saw Carl Crow's proverbial "four hundred million customers"), and the U.S. Navy (which saw its interests tied to a Pacific-first strategy). These groups were at least partially successful in mobilizing domestic support for Chiang's regime and later in leading a search-and-destroy mission to find those who had "lost China." However, they were primarily concerned with Taiwan as a symbol of American foreign policy (i.e., rollback rather than containment) rather than with direct implementation of their interests on the island itself.

In the late 1940s and 1950s most Protestant and Catholic missionaries left or were driven out of China, and some went to Taiwan. Although they found a safe haven there, they never made massive efforts to convert the population. The Catholic missionaries tended to minister to the needs of the mainlander flock, while the Protestants achieved their greatest success on Taiwan among marginal groups (such as the mountain aborigines and college students caught between Chinese and Western culture). The close alliance between the Kuomintang and conservative fundamentalist American Protestant denominations is primarily a phenomenon external to Taiwan. Church groups on Taiwan have never played as important a role in mobilizing antigovernment opposition as in Korea, but relations between the state and certain Taiwanese denominations (such as the Presbyterians, who have deep historical roots on the island) are often cool.

Most of the Asia firsters among the American business community in the late 1940s were not interested in immediate investment in postwar Asia because the possibilities for profit in the domestic market loomed so large (Schurmann 1973, 115). Rather, they wanted unrestricted Asian markets as a guarantee of future expansion in that direction. In the late 1940s or 1950s even businessmen did not see Taiwan as a significant market or source of cheap labor, but rather as a symbol of an overall commitment to Pacific expansionism.[15]

Schurmann has stressed the support of the American military, particularly the navy under Admiral Radford, for Taiwan's survival. The navy wanted a chain of bases stretching from Japan to Australia that would help to implement its strategy of forward defense in the western Pacific. Taiwan was part of this chain, but oddly enough its inclusion did not require the construction of major naval bases there.[16] It was important to the navy that Taiwan be denied to any adversary of the United States (which in the late 1940s meant the Soviet Union and very possibly the emergent People's Republic of China), and that it complete the image of a littoral strategy demanding a strong naval presence. Consequently, internal conditions on Taiwan did not matter much, so long as the island did not go communist. Had the U.S. Navy established military bases on the island, it might well have opposed land reform and other aid initiatives as destabilizing influences.

Because reform on Taiwan would help to rehabilitate Chiang's public relations image in the United States, and because they actually had little interest in events on Taiwan (as opposed to Taiwan's external and symbolic importance), these three interest groups did not give Chiang's government much help in forestalling demands for reform by American aid officials. It is a curious twist of fate that among the three states in East Asia that enjoyed strong support by the American Right (Chiang's Taiwan, Rhee's Korea, and Diem's South Vietnam), it was their favorite leader, Chiang, who suffered the deepest penetration by American aid agencies and who had to implement the most far-reaching economic and social reforms. Rhee and Diem were more successful in using the presence of American armed forces or a precarious political and military situation as means of playing off American bureaucratic actors and interests against those attempting to push for reforms.

Conclusion

During the 1950s, the U.S. government engaged in a delicate balancing act aimed at satisfying its various domestic constituencies while maintaining a maximum of flexibility on the Taiwan issue. While attacking the legitimacy of the People's Republic (rollback), it kept Chiang's army firmly leashed on Taiwan, allowing the Nationalist Chinese air force only symbolic victories to demonstrate the superiority of American arms technology to other client states without striking serious blows at China's internal stability. Beginning with the appointment of Karl Rankin as ambassador to Taipei in August 1950, the State Department held to a policy of sending envoys who were favorable to the Kuomintang and who avoided giving the impression that the United States encouraged reform in the Kuomintang, more political rights for Taiwanese, or support for bourgeois-democratic movements within Taiwan (see Rankin 1964, 142–45). However, the Taiwan foreign aid program and U.S. trade policies toward the island resulted in massive structural changes in the economy. One of the world's few successful nonrevolutionary land reform programs was carried out, income distribution became more equitable, and a large industrial labor force and a growing middle class became enmeshed in the capitalist world trading system.

This chapter has stressed the importance of "conservative" factors in these outcomes, particularly the ideological nature of the U.S. aid program. The major alternative explanation for Taiwan's postwar success in agriculture and later in industry is that the Kuomintang turned over a new leaf, whether from fear of the Taiwanese peasantry (see Hsiao 1981) or because the Nationalist government "arrived in Taiwan in 1949 purged and chastened" (Clough 1978, 33). While individuals may have conversion experiences, organizations seldom do; I remain unconvinced that the Nationalist Chinese would have undertaken a series of reforms that penetrated to the core of class relations through fear or remorse alone.

It is unlikely that the Joint Commission on Rural Reconstruction, the Council on U.S. Aid, and a variety of other mechanisms for solidifying joint control over aid at just above the operational level (as well as the liberal use of U.S. technical experts and evaluators) were particularly welcomed by the Kuomintang. Whereas domestic considerations (the China Lobby), the military balance of power, and the State Department's long-term goal of detaching China from the Soviet orbit all forced the aid reformers into a relatively nonpolitical track in Taiwan, their effective control of resources enabled them to extract concessions and reforms that brought about economic development and the emergence of Taiwan as a major trading partner of the United States. In this sense, the foreign aid program at least achieved Tyler Dennett's 1921 description of the goal of American diplomacy in Asia: the development of trading partners through the "open door" policy.

The Taiwan case points up the importance of the United States government as a vigorous actor in the world system and the complexity of motives of the bureaucratic groups within it. As Schurmann has suggested, the postwar period saw the emergence of an "ideology of empire" within the U.S. government. Yet while there was a general acceptance within the government of the goals of maintaining a stable international capitalist system and "international security," there was great diversity in opinion over the long- and short-run strategies best suited to accomplishing that goal.

In general, the evidence suggests that, in the Taiwan case, the bureaucratic actors were not heavily influenced by outside bourgeois interest groups. Instead, the data suggest that at least some nations now firmly within the capitalist world system owe their postwar integration to the logic of bureaucratic rather than capitalist expansion.

Notes

1. In his seminal 1921 work, Tyler Dennett suggested that the goal of U.S. policy toward both China and Japan in the nineteenth and early twentieth centuries was a "demand for most favored nation treatment." He says that while the United States took initial advantage of British gunboat diplomacy to obtain concessions from China, its later policy there and its consistent policy toward Japan was to strengthen the indigenous states so that they would not be forced to grant special trading privileges to other Western powers (see May and Thompson 1972, x-xi).

2. Murphey (1974, 47-49) has estimated that Chinese imports of foreign goods grew only three to four times between 1870 and 1930 (a low rate of increase), and that Chinese per capita consumption of foreign goods remained among the lowest in the world.

3. Furthermore, the tabular data presented by Moulder (1977, tables 3, 4) on the more rapid growth of U.S.-Japanese (compared to U.S.-Chinese) trade contradict the argument she makes in the text. Historians have been aware of the slow growth of the China trade since the work of Griswold (1938), and May's more recent work confirms that by the 1900-1909 decade the value of U.S. trade with China was surpassed by the value of trade with either Japan or Southeast Asia. By the 1910-1919 decade the U.S.-China trade was surpassed by U.S. trade with "other Asia" as well (May and Thompson 1972, xiii-xiv).

4. This group of radical American historians (which included William Appleman Williams, Walter LeFeber, and Thomas McCormick) emerged in the early 1960s. In general, they stressed that American foreign policy since the Spanish-American War has been directed toward "a coherent bid for 'informal empire' by the realistic representatives of hard-pressed but ultimately confident corporate capitalists" (Young 1972, 131).

5. Daniel Ellsberg (1972) has given an excellent summary of how this "national

security crisis'' process worked in the Vietnamese case in the 1960s. As Stueck (1981, 126–37) has shown, American support for Nationalist China appears to have been based more on ideology than on the direct interests of domestic bourgeois groups. See also note 15 below.

6. Because this overall relationship has been treated by many scholars, such as Tsou (1963), Young (1963), Tuchman (1972). and Schaller (1979), it will not be reviewed here.

7. As pro-Nationalist party scholars—and others—have pointed out, the "China White Paper" was a sanitized version of U.S. government files on the subject.

8. For a discussion of the relative importance of the NSC as a policy-making group under different presidents, see Ransom (1963, 28–55).

Allen Whiting has suggested that the "1949 NSC decisions assigning strategic importance to Taiwan in the event of war should be looked at as a bureaucratic compromise." However, because of the Sino-Soviet alliance and the unexpected outbreak of the Korean War, the policy of nonintervention in Taiwan became untenable and "the compromise turned into a trap" (see Heinrichs 1980, 119–28). Yet in NSC 37/7 (22 August 1949), and reaffirmed in NSC 48/1 (23 December 1949), the Joint Chiefs of Staff said that "the strategic importance of Taiwan does not justify overt action." Later in NSC 48/1, Taiwan is not included in the "military minimum position in Asia (a chain of strategic islands including Japan, the Ryukyus, and the Philippines)" (U.S. Department of Defense 1971, 2:, 245, 257).

9. See Tsou (1963, 441–551) or Stueck (1981, 113–52) for a discussion of the congressional politics surrounding the passage of foreign aid bills at that time.

10. Gaddis (1980, 93) has claimed that "at no point during 1949 and 1950 was Washington prepared to acquiesce in control of the island by forces hostile to the United States and capable of taking military action against other links in the offshore chain." However, his account ignores Acheson's readiness to abandon Taiwan as the price for detaching the Communist Chinese from the Soviet bloc (see Cohen 1980, 28–30). His analysis also overemphasizes the influence on the Pentagon of the hawkish views of General MacArthur and retired Admiral Forrest P. Sherman, while ignoring the dissent of Army Chief of Staff J. Lawton Collins from such a forward policy (see Stueck 1981, 139–40).

11. The consular records from 1950 on are still classified but may become available for similar declassification requests in the near future.

12. Livingston Merchant's February 1949 evaluation of political trends within Taiwan recommended against State Department support for an independent Taiwan freed from both the Kuomintang and the Communists (Cohen 1980, 27).

13. For a bald statement of the "UN Trusteeship view," see the letter of 15 February 1949 from Roger Lapham, chief of mission, Taiwan Economic Cooperation Administration, to Paul G. Hoffman, administrator, ECA, Washington, D.C.

14. See Kerr (1965) for a listing of some of these sources; see also Paine (1946) and Taipei consular files, 1947–49.

15. The specific reasons why American investment was not attracted to Taiwan until the late 1960s have been explored in Barrett and Whyte (1982, 1074–77) and Schreiber (1970).

16. Taiwan's natural harbors are few and small, a fact well known to the U.S. Navy since it leapfrogged Taiwan for Okinawa from the Philippines in 1944–45.

7

Denis Fred Simon

EXTERNAL INCORPORATION AND INTERNAL REFORM

Introduction: Americans versus Chinese

In general, the modal outcome predicted for most developing countries by dependency theorists is retarded, or at best distorted, development. This outcome is produced largely through politically enforced "unequal exchange" in the global marketplace. Nevertheless, even world system theory allows for the possibility that some—albeit only a few—countries will succeed in upgrading their status within the global division of labor either through "development by invitation" or through exceptionally vigorous and fortuitous transformation (Ruggie 1983; Wallerstein 1976). The exact circumstances under which this occurs, however, and the nature of the process that determines such exceptional outcomes remain to be explored in detail, particularly for the twentieth century. In this regard, the role of "conservative" interstate political-military relations, as opposed to "liberal" intramarket commercial relations, requires more emphasis.

As reiterated throughout this volume, Taiwan is a classic case of "development by invitation," and a rare case of development combining growth with equity (Kuo, Ranis, and Fei 1981; ODC 1979). Relations between the Nationalist state and the American government played a crucial role in this process, particularly in the early 1950s when the "invitation" to develop was first issued and the "terms" of that invitation were initially defined. This chapter deals with a very critical stage in that formative process, the negotiations between the U.S. AID agency and the government on Taiwan over the "third phase" of "land reform" in the early 1950s. Even though the land reform program ostensibly was geared only to the agrarian sector, the third phase reforms also had an important impact on the ownership of capital in the industrial sector. The issues were: How large would be the role of the private versus the public sector? How concentrated would the ownership of capital be in the private sector? And which Taiwanese, if any, would be allowed to participate in the private industrial sector? Since AID administrators had opinions about each of these issues, in all three substantive areas the more general question arose of how much influence the United States would have over economic decision making on Taiwan.

In the early 1950s, the extent of U.S. involvement the Chinese government would allow in critical areas of decision making was a highly charged issue. The Nationalist regime clearly was dependent on the United States for economic and military assistance as well as political support. The Chinese government was disturbed by apparent American efforts to influence events within Taiwan. Much of the U.S. influence was articulated through the U.S. Mutual Security Agency (MSA) office in Taipei. The MSA mission on Taiwan was primarily oriented toward assisting the Nationalist troops to develop a viable defense capability. This effort had both a military and an economic dimension. The former was focused on the construction of military facilities and the training of personnel, while the latter was aimed at building Taiwan's infrastructure so that the economy could support the military effort. The MSA mission would eventually be broken into two parts, one becoming the MAAG—Military Assistance Advisory Group—and the other becoming the AID mission.

Although not every U.S. Mutual Security Agency memo was converted instantly into official Chinese policy on Taiwan, the Nationalist regime's dependence on the United States made acting independently very difficult. Nationalist leaders frequently had to consult the United States—either the U.S. assistance mission, the Department of Defense or the Central Intelligence Agency—when making a major decision. One reason for this state of affairs was the continued U.S. distrust of the Nationalists; another reason was that Taiwan was caught up, for better or worse, in the larger anti-Communist strategic posture of the United States.

Most Kuomintang officials resented their degree of dependence on the United States. Interviews conducted on Taiwan with Chinese economic and political leaders, along with information contained in now unclassified U.S. State and Defense Department reports from Taiwan during this period reflect this resentment. For example, many members of the government did not like the strong ties that existed between the Joint Commission on Rural Reconstruction (JCRR) and the United States. They viewed the JCRR as an "extragovernmental" body that did not always act in accordance with the wishes of the Nationalist government. They also did not approve of the ways that the aid mission could intervene in domestic politics. Most important, Kuomintang leaders resented the limits that the United States placed upon military spending and defense preparations.

Nationalist sensitivities about American interference applied particularly to land reform. The major impetus to implement a comprehensive land reform program had come from the United States. In addition, even though Nationalist interests clearly would be served by following U.S. suggestions in this area, Chinese attitudes toward resolution of important social and political questions differed fundamentally from the attitudes being articulated by various U.S. agencies on the island.

This sensitivity to U.S. interference became particularly acute with regard to the critical third phase of land reform. Wolf Ladejinsky, the American land reform expert who had worked very closely with the Japanese, was invited by the MSA mission to review the Nationalist land reform policy "in an effort to bring to the attention of the Chinese government some of the problems involved in the Third Phase of the Land-to-the-Tiller Program, particularly those related to the transfer of Government enterprises" (MSA 27 July 1953). The KMT was quite perturbed about this outside pressure from the United States and stated that all final decisions regarding the matter would be made without outside involvement.

Yet the United States attempted to force a reevaluation of the pace and method of the program through such persons as K. Y. Yin and through the Industrial Development Commission, a branch of the government-run Economic Stabilization Board (ESB). The United States tried to encourage the participation of the JCRR in the matter, but the commission was reluctant to become directly involved and clearly had its own problems with respect to criticisms of the high degree of "independence" that it had from the Nationalist government (MSA 28 October 1953).

In many respects, the fundamental terms of Taiwan's incorporation into the postwar global political economy were decided in the course of determining how landlords would be compensated for their lands that were to be distributed to the "tiller." More specifically, the key elements of Taiwan's emerging pattern of industrial development were decided during the latter stages of the land reform process. To understand how this happened, some of the details of the process of land reform on Taiwan must first be reviewed. In the following sections each of the main issues in the third phase of land reform—public versus private ownership, concentration versus dispersion of shares, and mainlander versus Taiwanese interests—will be discussed, including both the positions of the actors and how the issues were resolved. The chapter's conclusion returns to the question of American influence over Chinese economic decision making, discussing the other form of U.S. intervention in the 1950s—AID—and its consequences for Taiwan's later development.[1]

Taiwan's land reform was composed of three steps: (1) a rent reduction program that reduced all land rents to 37.5 percent of the main crop yield; (2) a sale of public lands; and (3) the land-to-the-tiller program, which consisted of an attempt to equalize the distribution of land holdings by turning tenants into owner-cultivators and shifting the socioeconomic base of the landlords out of the rural sector—and, it was hoped, into the immature but growing industrial sector (Apthorpe 1979). It is the third phase that forms the heart of the chapter.

Under the provisions of the program, the government provided compensation to landlords for land surrendered under the dictates of the program guidelines. A landlord could retain three *chia* of land (2.9 hectares) for himself as long as he proved that he would cultivate the plot himself. He was compensated for the remaining portion of his land by (a) 70 percent in land bonds—rice bonds for paddy land and sweet potato bonds for dry land, and (b) 30 percent in stock shares in four government enterprises—Taiwan Cement Corporation, Taiwan Pulp and Paper Corporation, Taiwan Agriculture and Forestry Corporation, and Taiwan Industrial and Mining Corporation. The "stock-to-the-landlord" aspect of compensation is the primary concern here (Koo 1968; Tai 1974).

A key issue about compensation was the present worth and future viability of these corporations. Taiwan's economy was still unstable. Many observers at the time shared the landlords' view that they were being given watered stock in worthless assets. Most expected the primary focal point of economic activity to be in the public sector, then comprising 80 percent of the industrial economy. Hardly anyone anticipated that within ten years the private sector would prove to be the more dynamic portion of the economy, and that within twenty years it would account for the same 80 percent of the industrial economy. Consequently, only a few groups of financier-bureaucrats—mostly mainlanders—competed for ownership of the four companies, using a few prominent Taiwanese landlord-bankers as intermediaries to buy up the stocks from small- and middle-scale Taiwanese landlords.

Public versus Private Control

Foremost among the issues underlying the debate over the corporations was the question of state control within the Taiwan economy. According to the observations of an MSA team in 1952, the Nationalist government had made no serious effort to sell its enterprises to private firms. Citing "discrimination against private enterprise, particularly with respect to raw materials and obtaining credit from the Bank of Taiwan," the report went on to note that "these enterprises are not competitively free and cannot be under existing conditions."

The Chinese government, on the other hand, was very concerned with maintaining economic control. These concerns resulted from the student experiences of many economic leaders (e.g., S. Y. Dao) in Germany, where government control was viewed as the most efficient and effective means to manage the economy. Although MSA officials had begun early to encourage an emphasis on private enterprise, competing external pressures and Chinese domestic considerations made any appreciable movement in this direction quite difficult. The land reform might have earned the political support of the KMT from the rural sector, but, without extensive control of the economy, Nationalist leaders felt quite insecure. Moreover, the regime was obligated in many instances to provide jobs for key Chinese mainlanders in return for their continued support or prior support.

The minister of economic affairs, T. K. Chang, was one of those who preferred state firms to private enterprises. He was skeptical of modern methods of corporate management, doubting the ability of the market mechanism to select top-level personnel or to make critical decisions. Chang's position was clear— because private enterprise on Taiwan depended on state assistance, if private entrepreneurs did not follow government policy, the government could make life very difficult for them. Interviews conducted by the author with former members of the government's Economic Stabilization Board and with former AID officials stationed on Taiwan indicate that many government officials supported Chang's position.

Not surprisingly, Taiwanese private entrepreneurs felt disadvantaged. On the basis of numerous interviews with Taiwanese businessmen, a private MSA consultant reported that "they felt that there was no free competitive enterprise on Taiwan at that time and that there was not equal treatment for all, or freedom of action in business . . . they wanted a free competitive enterprise economy, since it would give them freedom to conduct business in their own rightful way and would relieve them of government discrimination" (MSA 28 January 1952).

American aid officials were concerned about the fate of the private sector in general and the four government enterprises to be transferred to the private sector as compensation for landlords in particular. Documents secured by the author from AID show that members of the U.S. Mutual Security Mission on Taiwan were apprehensive about the ability of these enterprises to survive under private control. As one report suggested, "the factors to assure the success of the program (Land-to-the Tiller) have not been provided" (MSA 12 June 1953). Most of the corporations had serious financial problems, and only through various forms of continued government support and assistance could they survive. A report prepared by one mission adviser dealing with the Taiwan Cement Corporation, which was in the best financial situation of the selected corporations, revealed that "the time for the successful transfer of ownership of this corporation to private stockholders is not in sight" (MSA 6 August 1953).

One MSA report intimated that the political and economic consequences of the failure of any one or all of these enterprises would not only discredit this phase of the land reform but also damage the long-term possibilities for private enterprise on the island. A major debate arose between the U.S. security mission and T. K. Chang about the timing and method of implementation of the compensation portion of the program (MSA 20 July 1953). U.S. personnel encouraged the Nationalist government to delay the transfer of the enterprises until the various management and financial problems could be resolved. One document secured from U.S. AID revealed that, even with the high chances of failure of the four enterprises under private control without government assistance, Chang was "quite persistent in his determination to turn all the four corporations over to the landlords to see how they make out and to prove a point" (MSA 20 July 1953).

Even though the United States attempted to delay the transfer of the government corporations until a more economically and politically opportune time, the program went forward as planned. The Nationalist government, as part of its "emotional psyche" for dealing with the United States, refused to allow American officials to dictate Chinese policy on this issue. Accordingly, the role of the private sector continued to be an issue throughout the rest of the period of U.S. AID presence on the island (until 1965). Further complicated by the question of external involvement in Taiwan's internal affairs, the issue generated substantial debate within the Nationalist government. Spurred on by the issue of state control, the controversy over the role of the private sector became particularly heated during the latter part of the 1950s when attention focused on whether to "open" Taiwan to extensive foreign trade and investment.

During this debate, the Nationalist government was for the most part reluctant to open the Taiwan economy to outside forces and was adamant in its belief that the local economy would be destabilized by allowing greater economic openness. Some local businessmen, and a sizable number of government officials and academics, took the opposite position, arguing that the only way to promote economic development in general was to allow market forces to play a greater role. This latter group believed that competitive dynamics would stimulate improvements in product quality and variety and would prove conducive to the island's long-term viability. Although the government eventually did partly succumb to both U.S. and internal pressures, its commitment to the maintenance of a free and competitive private sector remained somewhat suspect.

The departure of AID in 1965 alleviated some of the pressure on the Nationalist government regarding further development of a private sector. By that time, however, as a result of previous AID policies, the steady growth in foreign investment, the attractiveness of export opportunities, and, most important, the success experienced by many Taiwanese entrepreneurs, the government was left with no choice but to acknowledge the existence of an already dynamic and growing private sector. Since that time, the continuation of a U.S. commitment to Taiwan has been based, in part, on the economic success achieved by the regime while employing a capitalist style of development. Even though the United States no longer involves itself in the workings of the economic system on Taiwan, the continued presence of U.S. foreign investment and private technical assistance serves to strengthen not only the private sector, but also the need for the Nationalist government to maintain its support for that sector.

The informal support of the United States and the government's public commitment to private sector development, however, have not alleviated the anxiety and apprehension of the largely Taiwanese private sector regarding government intentions and policies. The majority of Taiwanese entrepreneurs continue to remain wary of the central government. Among most businessmen, young and old, the general preference is for remaining aloof from the government, and to obtain assistance only when government interference is minimal. Otherwise, as several local businessmen remarked during interviews, the government may find out too much about various corporate activities and exert unwanted influence on the behavior of privately owned firms.

Concentrated versus Dispersed Assets

The settlement concluded during the third phase of land reform also explains a second feature of Taiwan's postwar political economy, the so-called alliance that exists today between certain segments of big business and the government. Paradoxically, however, it is not the distribution of industrial stock to landlords that explains the particular individuals participating in that alliance. Most of the landlords who received stock quickly resold it to larger landlords who had already entered into commercial banking and industrial investment long before land reform began. Even so, of the four corporations whose stock was distributed, only the Taiwan Cement Corporation fell into the hands of what could be considered "former landlords," even commercially and industrially entrepreneurial ones. The other three corporations were captured by mainlander financier-bureaucrats. Thus, even though the third phase of land reform determined that there would be a private industrial sector, it also determined that, at least initially, ownership of that sector would be concentrated in relatively few hands. This section explores what made ownership of stock in these four industrial corporations so unattractive to so many landlords, and how reconcentration of ownership in them occurred.

Landlords obviously were concerned about the real value of the assets they were receiving as compensation for their land. Initially, the assets of the government corporations were undervalued, so at the time of Taiwan's currency reevaluation, revision of the estimated value of the firms would be made. Even though the currency exchange rate moved from a ratio of NT$5.00 (US$1.00) to NT$15.65 (US$1.00), a threefold increase, the assets of the firms were revalued to reflect a sevenfold increase from the initial assessments. This inflated increase was unjustified considering that very little change had taken place in the value of the land or physical plant. The increase most likely reflected the common belief that the stock in these firms was relatively worthless.

Questions also existed concerning the most effective way to run these firms (*Industry of Free China* 1954). The role of the government in management was a potentially important issue because the government continued to possess holdings in several of the firms. Nevertheless, government assistance was not readily forthcoming for the reasons cited, and not until several years later did the government agree to render substantial assistance to the firms in financial difficulty. Finally, the shares to be distributed to approximately 40,000 landlords were divided up so that any one landlord could not have a controlling interest in any one corporation. Thus, these former landowners had no good prospect of accumulating new economic power.

As a result, most of the industrial stock distributed to landlords was quickly resold. Analysis of the disposition of the shares reveals that most of the landlords were aware of the problems just cited. For example, each share of stock in the Taiwan Agriculture and Forestry Corporation (TAFC) was given a value of

NT$10.00. Yet, many of the small-scale landlords sold their shares for prices ranging from NT$2.50 to NT$4.50 (U.S. AID 18 March 1955). These shares, according to one report made by MSA in March 1955, were ''bought by bureaucrats, businessmen, and capitalists'' a few days after the first shareholders' meeting. Out of twenty-three members of the upper-level management (all Taiwanese), ten were import-export merchants; six were public servants; two were businessmen; one was a medical doctor; and four had been landlords. Furthermore, out of about 3.3 million shares owned by these twenty-three persons, the four former landlords controlled only about 10 percent.

The situation was similar for the Taiwan Industrial and Mining Corporation (TIMC). Of the twenty-five members of upper-level management (twenty-four Taiwanese and one mainlander), six were businessmen; six, coal mine owners; three were import-export merchants; two were textile manufacturers; two were stockbrokers; two were public servants; one was a medical doctor; and three were former landlords (one large-scale landlord and two small-scale landlords). Out of the 3.7 million shares controlled by these twenty-five persons, the three former landlords held less than 10 percent (U.S. AID 31 March 1955).

The major shareholders of TAFC and TIMC decided to sell most of each company's units to separate shareholders. For example, the shareholders of the TIMC decided to make available fifty-five units to both stockholders and outside individuals. The TAFC decided to sell thirty-six unit factories on the open market. Even though the government did retain shares in both of these firms, the shareholders' decisions were part of any effort to raise sufficient capital to remain independent of government controls. Perhaps the most successful case of a breakaway firm is the Taiwan Pineapple Company. The government still has an interest in the firm, but by the late 1970s the company had become the core of one of the major business groups on Taiwan.

One of the two other firms, the Taiwan Cement Corporation (TCC), remains one of the largest corporate entities on the island. During the early period of Taiwan's development, the TCC prospered because various government-sponsored projects required large quantities of cement and related products. Moreover, because it was able to build on the contacts made by several of the directors during the period of Japanese rule, the company served as a link in arranging various cooperative projects with Japan.

The fourth corporation, the Taiwan Pulp and Paper Corporation (TPPC), became a refuge of sorts for many retired servicemen and former government officials of the Nationalist regime. Although it remains a major producer of paper on Taiwan, it has not had the success of the Taiwan Cement Corporation.

It appears that a large percentage of the island's future entrepreneurs had worked in Japanese companies during the 1930s and 1940s. Many of these people, such as the director of one of the locally owned beverage companies, assumed control of various enterprises when the Japanese left in 1945. Many of these new owners were trusted employees of the Japanese. Interviews conducted with several of them reveal that Japan preferred to surrender these enterprises to former employees rather than to the Nationalist government. Few of these firms, however, developed into major corporations.

The question therefore arises as to the origins of most of the current industrial "bourgeoisie" in Taiwan, since it is clear that they did not originate primarily from the class of small to middle landlords or the group of former employees of Japanese firms. The initial answer to this question is mixed. As with the rise of a business class in the West, Taiwan's business leaders came from a variety of sources (see also chapter 9). Many of those with previous ties to the mainland, especially those with ties to the Nationalist government, used those connections to reestablish similar types of enterprises on Taiwan. As for those of Taiwanese origin, there does not appear to be a definitive pattern. Yet they do share one characteristic: they pursued economic opportunities when it became clear that the avenues for obtaining political power were closed. The factors creating this situation are discussed in the next section.

Mainlander versus Taiwanese Interests

A third issue brought to the forefront by the transfer of government enterprises was the nature of the Taiwanese-mainlander relationship. This relationship was political before it was economic. Moreover, the terms upon which they related to one another had been established prior to the redistribution of industrial assets during land reform (Kerr 1965). Governor K. C. Wu, mayor of Shanghai during the 1940s and governor of Taiwan in the early 1950s, had been a strong advocate of better Taiwanese-mainlander relations. He provided opportunities for Taiwanese to hold political positions within his cabinet. According to several sources, however, his retirement in 1954, though officially attributed to poor health, most probably represented the defeat of his efforts to provide a forum within the central government for the articulation of local Taiwanese interests.

U.S. officials were well aware of both the political and economic consequences of Nationalist policies for the Taiwanese. State control of the economy and Taiwanese-mainlander relations were inextricably linked. American officials saw free enterprise as a way to enhance the political leverage of the Taiwanese, in spite of government policy. U.S. actions in this regard were designed to use the economy as the main ground on which to fight this political battle.

Even the strictly economic problems of mainlander-Taiwanese relations predated and went beyond those of land reform. Local private capital (mostly Taiwanese) was hampered by action or inaction (whether deliberate or not) of the Nationalist government. As early as 1950, the Economic Cooperation Administration, the precursor to AID, noted this problem and requested permission from the U.S. government to set up a small industries program to extend assistance "to help private industry which is largely Formosan" (ECA 18 September 1950). After making an extensive field survey of business attitudes and practices among local businessmen in 1952, a consultant to the MSA mission noted the acute difficulties between Taiwanese and mainlanders. Based on discussions with several Taiwanese manufacturers, the consultant reported that "they stated emphatically that they employed no mainlanders in their plants and had no intention of doing so, and added that no Taiwanese hold responsible positions in government factories."

Nationalist economic discrimination against Taiwanese during this period led one observer to comment that "the Chinese government has not cultivated the loyalty and cooperation of the Taiwanese people" (MSA 11 December 1953). For example, a series of field interviews conducted by mission personnel showed a dearth of Taiwanese in executive positions in government or government-owned industries, but visits to several Taiwanese-owned businesses showed the mission that "trained Taiwanese personnel was available."

The land reform was an effective way for the Nationalist regime to remove the only potentially strong alternative locus of authority on the island. In contrast to the situation on the China mainland, the KMT did not have a vested interest in the land tenure system on Taiwan; here politically it could only gain by facilitating social transformation. The key source of rural power, land, was not yet under effective Nationalist government control. Dispossessing landlords from their power bases and moving them into the still immature industrial sector would make them very much dependent on the Nationalist government for all types of assistance.

The land-to-the-tiller program initially met strong opposition from several local groups. Even a JCRR study noted that the Taiwan Provincial Assembly (a landlord stronghold) tried to block the program at its inception. Only President Chiang Kai-shek's formal intervention in the debate curtailed effective opposition (JCRR 1965). Nevertheless, the opposition had its effect on the formation of policy, as can be seen in the change in the proportions of industrial stocks and land bonds paid out as compensation for land. The original provision was for 50 percent each in land bonds and industrial stocks. Instead, the proportion for industrial stocks was reduced to 30 percent and the proportion for land bonds increased to 70 percent.

The process of land reform in the 1950s provides insights into the isolation of most local small- and medium-scale businesses from the Nationalist government even today. Small- and medium-scale landlords did not fare well under the land reform program. Martin Yang (1970) reports that of five hundred landlords, about 91 percent of the large-scale landlords and more than 98 percent of the small-scale landlords sold their shares in either one or several lots. Many of the bonds held by owners of small and medium-size farms were sold to the owners of bigger farms and to nonrural persons, often at a considerable loss. Many landlords sold because they were neither willing nor able to change occupations. Yang's survey also indicated that less than 10 percent of the small-scale landlords and only about 17 percent of the large-scale landlords used their money to establish businesses after selling their stock. Few of those that followed that path started industrial concerns. Some small-scale landlords did establish commercial firms and trading companies, but only after a long period of difficult adjustment.

The ambivalence of the local businessmen and former landlords toward the government still exists today. In many respects, it owes its origins to the experiences of these individuals and their families during the land-to-the-tiller program. Stripped of their main source of wealth, many of these persons eventually left the island. Some became the base of the Taiwan independence movement in Japan and the United States. Moreover, according to various reports on Taiwan during the late 1970s and early 1980s, others who remained on the island have been a source of financial support for many "independent party" candidates and, more recently, the Democratic Progressive party in local elections.

Conclusion: Aid versus Investment

The body of this chapter has focused on a key episode in the formative phase of Taiwan's postwar political economy, that is, direct U.S. intervention to secure a private sector and to guarantee Taiwanese participation in it. It has argued that American intervention was successful on both counts, but that, at least for the short run, Taiwanese participation in industrial investment was less than American officials may have hoped. In the long run, however, Taiwanese participation became extensive. Though there have been many reasons for this, both U.S. intervention in the third phase of land reform and other U.S. actions deserve much credit.

By way of conclusion, the principal form of U.S. intervention in the Taiwan economy in the 1950s, U.S. aid, will be examined. The AID mission was instrumental in promoting private investment in industry, both Chinese and foreign. The nature of American assistance also progressed through three stages: first, paying for imports of key commodities; second, financing key infrastructure projects to facilitate domestic development; and third, promotion of export trade and foreign investment. Eventually, foreign investment replaced aid as the catalytic element in Taiwan's development (Simon 1987). Of course, there was an appreciable degree of local initiative involved, but the fact remains that AID helped shape the parameters in which domestic entrepreneurs began to operate.

During the period of U.S. assistance to Taiwan (1951–1965), total U.S. aid amounted to approximately U.S. $1.5 billion. Almost two-thirds of all aid, not including military assistance, went toward the development of infrastructure projects and human resources, 37 percent and 26 percent respectively. Moreover, about 67 percent of U.S. assistance went to public enterprises; 27 percent to mixed enterprises; and only 6 percent to solely private enterprises (Ho 1978a). These figures apparently suggest that U.S. aid did very little to promote the development of private enterprise on the island.

Yet, as noted, just the opposite is true. As Ho has suggested, aid allocation was designed to support investments with substantial external economies. These external economies included investments in power, transportation, and communications. In addition, in 1958, an Office for Private Investment was established within the AID mission. The formation of the Industrial Development and Investment Center, along with the formation of the China Productivity Center, helped to provide encouragement and assistance to the private sector. In such key industries as glass, synthetic fibers, PVC, soda ash, and hardboard, American funds acted as a stimulus by helping to promote and support private-sector involvement.

Jacoby (1966) argues that AID's policy of concentrating investment on infrastructure and human resources turned out to be the cornerstone of Taiwan's rapid development because it created a favorable environment for private investment. Even though the land reform failed to stimulate substantial private-sector participation by smaller businessmen, U.S. AID provided the framework for potentially more profitable private business investments. In this way, AID played a critical role in helping to reverse the former Nationalist government policy of extensive state control.

The AID mission also helped to pry open the Taiwan economy to private foreign participation. The nature of the Taiwan economy at the time, combined with the political-military situation in the Taiwan Straits, had inhibited the arrival of foreign investment in Taiwan in the 1950s and early 1960s. Most of the foreign capital coming into Taiwan during that period was from overseas Chinese. Only after the aid mission had helped stabilize the economy did these flows begin to increase appreciably. The third phase of aid, which began to achieve momentum in the late 1950s, moved away from specific project support and was designed to complement, and in some cases direct, the shift in the Taiwan economy away from import substitution toward export promotion. This shift in orientation achieved its expression in the government's 1960 Nineteen Point Economic Program (Jacoby 1966). Above all, this third phase attempted to encourage the Nationalist leadership to develop economic policies that were more developmental and less control-oriented (Ho 1978a). The controls of the previous period, which included multiple exchange rates, foreign exchange controls, and various state subsidies, had outlived their usefulness.

Interestingly enough, however, this program (which had the effect of liberalizing the Taiwan economy) was introduced only after the U.S. AID mission had used various incentives and threats to force the Nationalist government to adopt such a program. In particular, the U.S. mission threatened in various ways to diminish its level of funding for Taiwan and to cut various projects from the future aid plan. These threats evidently proved successful, but only after causing much controversy both between AID and the Nationalist government and within the Chinese government itself.

Total dependence on foreign capital—aid and foreign investment—averaged about 12 percent of Taiwan's gross domestic capital formation during the 1952–1974 period. Taiwan was particularly dependent on U.S. assistance during the period 1951–1965. In fact, the United States financed an average of about 40 percent of capital formation per year during the period of U.S. assistance to the island (CEPD 1979). As aid decreased, however, foreign investment increased. Foreign investment financed the following percentages of GDCF: (1) 1.7 percent during 1952–1960; (2) 5.7 percent, 1961–1968; and (3) 6.9 percent, 1969–1974. These figures might appear to suggest that aid merely laid the groundwork for a new form of dependence (CEPD 1979; Griffin 1973).

Here again, however, the opposite is true. Actually, the United States spent considerable time promoting general policies and industries that would allow Taiwan to compete effectively in the international market (Simon 1987). Indeed, the success of the U.S. assistance program is perhaps the main reason why Taiwan has not moved toward total dependency upon foreign corporations. AID fostered Taiwan's ability to take care of its domestic food needs and to stimulate its industrial development internally. It also strengthened the state and fostered its ability to formulate and implement effective economic policies (Winckler 1987). These policies were designed to minimize Taiwan's dependence on external sources of capital. As long as Taiwan could generate sufficient resources to assure a favorable balance-of-payments situation, to maintain a stable foreign exchange position, and to offer a series of competitive exports, the United States would not need to be concerned about the viability of the economy.

Eventually, Taiwan became the first "graduate" of U.S. AID. By 1965, when U.S. assistance to Taiwan was terminated, export-promotion policies were well under way, foreign investment had begun to achieve momentum, and the government exhibited an ability to manage its own economic development in the future. The combination of internal reform and external incorporation, however exceptional, made Taiwan's development one of the major success stories of the post-World War II period.

Note

1. This paper is based on field research conducted by the author in Taiwan between 1977 and 1978 on information obtained through a Freedom of Information Act request to the Department of State. Much of the information was obtained from interview with former AID officials who served in Taiwan and from former and current government officials on Taiwan. These persons have all requested that their identities remain anonymous.

8

Edwin A. Winckler

ELITE POLITICAL STRUGGLE
1945–1985

Introduction

What have been the principal power showdowns within the Nationalist state on
Taiwan since 1949? What have been the principal confrontations between economic elites within the Chinese society on Taiwan since 1945? These historical
questions are fundamental to any discussion of the mechanics of Taiwan's relationship to the world system, the nature of its authoritarian regime, or the
consequences of either of these for domestic social outcomes. The generalized
influence of the "world system," "the state," or "the bourgeoisie" must pass
through particular social networks, and particular contests within those networks, before resulting in particular outcomes. Yet, largely because of the extreme discretion of Nationalist institutions, there is still no circumstantial account of the elite politics of Taiwan's development, in Chinese or any other
language. Accordingly, what follows is a "heuristic history" intended to provoke
argument about these general questions and to orient discussion of specific
episodes on Taiwan.[1]

Analytical Themes

Analytically, the chapter stresses three themes. The first is the role of networks in
structuring transactions within the state and bourgeoisie. The second is the role of
networks in achieving the initial cooperation between the Nationalist state and
Taiwanese bourgeoisie. The third is the role of networks in consolidating a lasting
political-economic establishment on Taiwan. Thus the chapter examines Chinese
elite actors dealing with each other through personal relationships within the
surprisingly small social field connecting the tops of the relevant domestic state
and business institutions. Some might dismiss these transactions as petty personal
history of just the sort that more scientific analysis should supersede. On the

contrary, these patterns of "conservative" social organization are crucial to the larger political-economic outcomes. Moreover, the argument is not that socio-logical analyses must allow for historical accident, but that network mechanisms are crucial to how both states and markets actually work.[2]

First, then, as regards the role of networks within state and bourgeoisie, the distinction is made between bureaucratically based *factions* struggling for power within the state and economic *fractions* of classes competing for wealth within society.[3] The chapter argues that the principal factions within the Nationalist state have been based on rival security agencies, manipulated by top political leaders in the course of a protracted succession process. Economic fractions within the Taiwanese elite reflect the differential success of different Taiwanese landlord-banker-businessmen at translating landed capital into commercial capital, and commercial capital into industrial capital, in the context of transition from Japanese colonialism to Nationalist rule under American influence.

Second, in 1945–1954 mainlander factions and Taiwanese fractions remained remarkably isolated from each other, largely because of their differing external origins (Republican China and imperial Japan). The occupying Nationalist state largely suspended both economic markets and political elections, two social mechanisms through which these two elites might otherwise have come to terms with each other. Consequently, linkage between state and society relied heavily on personal relationships. Competing state factions sought out competing economic fractions, and vice versa. The few brokers in a position to sell access between these two groups faced high political and economic risks but stood to make high political and economic profits. Throughout, the state remained dominant and the economic future of elite Taiwanese depended principally on the political fortunes of the Nationalist officials with whom they tentatively allied.[4]

Third, the chapter focuses on how individuals achieved membership in the political-economic establishment, not on how they influenced particular economic policy outcomes. It describes the political incorporation of some domestic elite class fractions in a particular political-economic regime, and the political exclusion of other elite class fractions. A companion chapter in this volume (chapter 3) explores the relationship between external political incorporation and the internal political incorporation or exclusion of "mass" classes.[5]

Historical Background

Historically, since the chapter basically concerns control of the central government level of the Nationalist state, as far as Taiwan is concerned the topic begins in earnest only after the arrival of the main Nationalist forces and principal central leaders by 1950. However, the discussion begins with a brief look at what had happened in the 1940s, both on the mainland and on Taiwan, since this establishes crucial parameters within which the later process evolves. Basically, it explains why the range of elite actors involved was so limited.

On the mainland side, several points should be made. First, before 1945 the Nationalist regime already displayed some "statist" autonomy of its military, party, and mass movements from classwide economic interests. To be sure, it was highly constrained by its regional military allies and local landlord constituents, and it was economically exploited by a small circle of businessmen with privileged access to the state. Still, the party ideologues of the Nationalist movement had the ideological objective, if not the political capacity, of implementing rural land reform. As for large-scale businessmen, they remained more dependent on the state than it was on them (Coble 1980).

Second, divergences of interest between the Nationalist state apparatus and the landlord and business classes were exacerbated by the defeats and inflation accompanying the Chinese civil war. State leaders partly blamed misuse of the state by private interests for the loss of the mainland. For its part, business placed little trust in the frequently demanding Nationalist state (Pepper 1978).

Third, most of the class interests adhering to the Nationalist state were sheared off by the move to Taiwan, which principally included government officials, parliamentary representatives, and military personnel. Of course some businessmen came too, but only those most closely associated with and dependent upon the Nationalist state. They became even more dependent in the unfamiliar environment of Taiwan.

Several points should also be made about pre–1950 Taiwan. First, in the course of Japanese rule, elite politicking and mass movements among the Taiwanese had been first widely distributed and then thoroughly repressed. Thus even before the Nationalist occupation in 1945 most organized or radical Taiwanese politicians—particularly leaders of the peasant and labor movements, and particularly any of them who were Communists—had been driven underground or off the island, their organizations smashed (E. Ch'en 1972; Hsiao and Sullivan 1983).

Second, in 1945 agents of the principal factions in the central Nationalist state and dominant class descended on Taiwan to contend for the political positions and economic assets that this rich new prize afforded. "Returnee" Taiwanese who had spent the war on the mainland and arrived with the Nationalists served as bridges between particular mainlander factions and particular "islander" Taiwanese. The island passed from brutal repression under "political study clique" General Ch'en Yi (1946–47), to cosmetic civilianization under Wei Taoming (1947–48), former ambassador to the United States and affiliated with Madame Chiang, to consolidation as a Nationalist retreat under the sophisticated and progressive Whampoa General Ch'en Ch'eng (1948–49) (Kerr 1965).

Third, contrary to Taiwanese expectations of greater political participation under a Chinese regime, by 1949 the Nationalists had put virtually all Taiwanese except those whom the Nationalists had brought with them from the mainland out of public political action. Taiwanese who had conspicuously collaborated with the Japanese stood accused of treason; those who had conspicuously agitated against the Japanese were suspected of being dangerous radicals. Repression of antigovernment demonstrations in late February 1947 had provided the Nationalist state with the opportunity to massacre numerous less prominent potential leaders—most radical urban intelligentsia and some outspoken rural local notables. Though Chiang Kai-shek (CKS) sacrificed military Governor Ch'en Yi—having him publicly shot in the head at the former Japanese race-course in Taipei—Ch'en had accomplished the historic function of politically excluding the already mobilized indigenous Taiwanese (Kerr 1965).

State Struggle

Figure 8.1 provides a speculative overview of power struggles within the Nationalist state on Taiwan since 1945. Looking backward, this is the story of what happened to various components of the Nationalist state—particularly the internal security agencies—after their pell mell retreat from the mainland in 1949. Looking forward, this is the story of the gradual succession of Chiang Ching-kuo (CCK) to the control, first of this security apparatus, and, incrementally, of the state as a whole. There is both an historical and a theoretical relationship between these two perspectives. If Chiang Kai-shek had not become disillusioned with his security lieutenants for losing the mainland, Chiang Ching-kuo might never have succeeded him as his father's right-hand man in this key administrative area. If Chiang Ching-kuo's diagnosis of the essentially security-based nature of the Nationalist state had not been correct, he probably would not have succeeded his father as the key power holder.[6]

Let us briefly review this process diagonally down the figure, involving the manipulation by The Leader of successive state factions at successive points in time. Although there are many complications, these showdowns can be grouped into three overlapping phases related to the institutional sector of the state over which Chiang Ching-kuo was consolidating his control—police, military, and technocracy. Actually all of these struggles began in the early 1950s but were concluded seriatim. Also, each of them involved a parallel struggle in the Nationalist party—itself, for all practical purposes, an arm of the state (Durdin 1975a; 1975b).

Since the power struggles within the Nationalist state had had a long history by 1949, it seems advisable to note some of the institutional and, particularly, personal legacies of the past. Although it is not possible to indulge in too much historical detail, it is important to underline the highly personal nature of Nationalist state factions. The key power holders were remnants of the "thirteen buddhas" left over from the Republican era—fascist lieutenants bound to Chiang Kai-shek by a combination of ideological oath and personal fealty and forming the innermost circles of what was essentially a secret society back-stopping the military and party institutions. Chiang personally groomed upcoming military officers. Tokens of personal connection—ranging from autographed pictures of

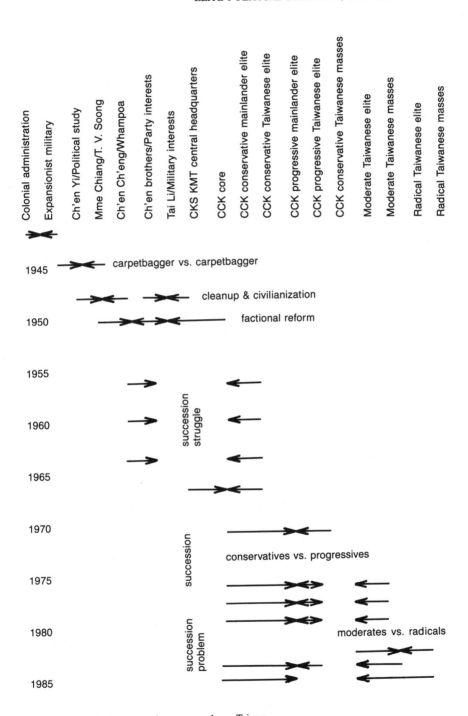

Figure 8.1. State factions and state struggle on Taiwan.

"the Gimo" on their coffee tables to intermarriage with the "royal" family—
socially symbolized their loyalty to him. Similar long-standing personal relationships connected Chiang to his principal lieutenants in other policy areas—General
Ch'en Ch'eng of the Whampoa military school clique as premier, Chang Ch'un of
the political study clique as head of the Presidential Office, and Ku Cheng-kang
as head of the CC clique in the party and national legislature (Eastman 1974; Tien
1972; Chi 1982).

Already in the 1950s Chiang Ching-kuo also had his own personal entourage,
also divided into factions according to the length and origin of association. The
first, inner circle contained three groupings. The southern Kiangsi faction had
joined Chiang Ching-kuo in the 1930s when he was assigned to administer the
former Communist base areas there. Its best-known member has been security
specialist Wang Sheng. The cadre school faction had joined Chiang in Ch'ung-
ch'ing during the Second World War. Its best-known member has been party
organization specialist Li Huan. The third grouping in the inner circle had joined
Chiang Ching-kuo after his return to Nanking in the mid–1940s. A second,
middle circle consisted mostly of cadres whom Chiang trained on Taiwan for
service in the General Political Warfare Department and National Security Bureau. However, it also included some career party officials who committed
themselves to Chiang Ching-kuo early, and a few associated from the period of his
stay in the Soviet Union in the late 1930s. The third, outer circle, included
ordinary cadres and did not display any noteworthy factions (Sun 1961a, 56–59;
Liu 1984, 11–173). Obviously, people were added to these circles—in the 1960s
former party adherents of Ch'en Ch'eng, and in the 1970s the technocrats needed
to run the country—but for basic decisions on political strategy the earlier security and political advisers remained central. Moreover, they remained in conflict,
with Wang Sheng favoring a hard line and Li Huan advocating controlled liberalization.

Security and Party

The principal focus of the first phase of factional struggle within the Nationalist
state on Taiwan revolved essentially around internal security, and the principal
rival factions were based in the security systems of the party and military,
respectively. When Chiang Kai-shek arrived on the island he and his son Chiang
Ching-kuo took more direct control of the internal security apparatus that they
had brought with them. This included two principal rival internal security factions, the military intelligence (*chün t'ung*) group, headed until his 1947 death by
Tai Li, and the party intelligence (*chung t'ung*) group, headed by the Ch'en
brothers. By 1949 Chiang Kai-shek was disappointed in the party intelligence
faction (the Ch'en brothers were widely blamed for Nationalist loss of the mainland) and also suspicious of them (Ch'en Li-fu had once gotten more votes in an
intraparty election than Chiang himself). Essentially Chiang took the opportunity

of retreat, reform, and reorganization to dissolve both intelligence factions. He placed their useful members—disproportionately from military intelligence—in a new party reform and internal security apparatus controlled by his son (Liu 1984, 174–225).

In 1949, Chiang Kai-shek gave Chiang Ching-kuo four tasks: control the military (via the General Political Warfare Department), control security (via the political action committee), control the party (via the party reform commission), and control the young people (via the youth corps) (Sun 1961a, 1–8). This Chiang Ching-kuo proceeded to do, mostly through a political action committee composed mostly of military intelligence types. However, because of Chiang Ching-kuo's youth, senior Chiang security aide T'ang Jung often served as figurehead, and older military intelligence leaders often served as intermediaries to other senior persons. Although Chiang Ching-kuo was not formally in control of this committee, in fact he ran it and gradually purged most members not affiliated with him. The secretariat of the committee eventually became institutionalized as a confidential branch of the Presidential Office, while its training school—the so-called underground university in Shih P'ai—became institutionalized as the National Security Bureau (Sun 1961a, 19–28). The NSB represented an attempt to coordinate the numerous overlapping and competing security agencies under Chiang Ching-kuo as security czar. Evidently it was established with American advice, partly to effect a separation between internal and external security functions, parallel to the distinction between the American Central Intelligence Agency and Federal Bureau of Investigation. The competitive overlapping of functions persisted to some extent—probably because Chiang Kai-shek and Chiang Ching-kuo wanted it that way. Nevertheless, the NSB became the core of Chiang Ching-kuo's power and an inner sanctum to which reportedly he continued to retreat for key decisions even after becoming premier and president.

In the 1950s, Chiang Ching-kuo had already achieved surprising penetration of the party. Of the six sections of the party Central Committee, he personally directed Political Warfare, controlled Propaganda through a subordinate, and had allies running Mainland Operations. In the crucial Organization Department and in Overseas Chinese party affairs, CCK had to rest content with a subordinate as deputy director. The section running Mass Movements evidently did not interest him, perhaps because he had his own mass organization, the Youth Corps (Sun 1961a, 24–38).

In all these areas, according to a contemporary observer, Chiang Ching-kuo relied on five strategies. The first was to rely on his inner circle—the cadres recruited in Kiangsi and Ch'ung-ch'ing. The second was to compromise with his father's veteran cadres by using them wherever possible. The third was to promote new people of his own. The fourth was to coopt people seeking affiliation with him on their own initiative. The fifth was not to rely on, but rather carefully to exclude, other prominent leaders with their own independent power bases. One might add that the overall strategy was informally to penetrate and then formally to preempt successively more "public" policy areas, leaving subordinates in control of those already occupied (Sun 1961a, 60–73).

Military and Party

The principal focus of the second phase of factional struggle within the Nationalist state was the military, and the principal conflict was between commanders and commissars. In fact Chiang Kai-shek had used his son as an agent for control of the military ever since 1950 when—at a time when failure of ideological indoctrination was being advanced as one of the principal causes of the Nationalist loss to the Communists—he made Chiang Ching-kuo director of the General Political Warfare Department. This meant constructing an organization to monitor the reliability of all military officers, bringing Chiang Ching-kuo into conflict with career commanders, but not giving him operational authority over them. In the 1950s line command was still held by Chiang Kai-shek and generals who had served under him since attending the Whampoa Military Academy in Canton in the early 1920s. Allegedly it was Chiang Ching-kuo who purged the American-trained army commander-in-chief, General Sun Li-jen, who had opposed the strengthening of political officers. This was a significant episode because it showed Nationalist determination to maintain control of their own military establishment despite extensive dependence on U.S. military aid. Similarly, the career of powerful Air Force Commander-in-Chief Wang Hsu-ming was derailed when Chiang Ching-kuo had Wang's favorite Chinese opera singer arrested as a Communist agent. After Chiang Ching-kuo's representatives in the navy collected information on corruption by Navy Commander-in-Chief Kuei Yung-ch'ing and his principal subordinates, they were all either transferred or dismissed; Kuei eventually committed suicide (Sun 1961a, 9–18; Liu 1984, 226–55).

The decisive phase of Chiang Ching-kuo's struggle to control the military came, however, in the late 1950s and early 1960s. In 1957 he became the head of the commission to handle the difficult problem of retiring the ROC's excess military personnel. Around this time, again on American advice, a system of periodic rotation of assignments was begun, routinely transferring officers away from potential power bases. Chiang Kai-shek continued personally to supervise all significant military appointments, but Chiang Ching-kuo played a gradually increasing role. Moreover, from 1959 a long-term Chiang Ching-kuo associate (General Yi Ching-ch'iu) ran the military personnel bureau. The few generals unfortunate enough to disagree openly with Chiang Ching-kuo—or to pose a potential threat to him—had a way of ending up as defendants in corruption cases, commandants of military schools, or ambassadors to foreign countries, rather than commanding troops at home. Meanwhile Chiang Ching-kuo attracted the allegiance of some junior members of the Whampoa clique, most of whose senior members basically had snubbed him. Beginning in the early 1960s, key assignments for such lieutenants were appointment as islandwide garrison commander, followed by appointment as provincial governor.[7]

At this time Chiang Ching-kuo was locked in a protracted struggle with Ch'en Ch'eng, not only to eliminate Ch'en's former subordinates within the military, but also to recruit a majority within the party Central Committee. "Three great battles" occurred within the central party in the late 1950s and early 1960s, with Chiang Ching-kuo gradually gaining the upper hand. The provincial party apparatus was also an area of fierce struggle, with Ch'en Ch'eng-affiliated mainlander party managers and Taiwanese local politicians falling victim to electoral defeats and corruption charges. As it turned out, Ch'en Ch'eng succumbed to cancer in the mid-1960s, but before he died he advised his followers to dissolve themselves as a faction and to join Chiang Ching-kuo as individuals whenever possible. Meanwhile, as Chiang Kai-shek gave up operational control of even central party affairs, Chiang Ching-kuo finally succeeded in placing his own men as head of the party Organization Department (Li Huan in 1963), Cadre Control Board (General Yi in 1966), party secretary-general (Chang Pao-shu in 1968), and other positions of formal party authority.[8]

Another potential military rival Chiang Ching-kuo may have outmaneuvered at this time was his own German-trained younger half-brother, General Chiang Wei-kuo, the country's principal tank commander. In late 1963 Wei-kuo was transferred from line command to military education, and the prospect of his replacement by a Chiang Ching-kuo protégé precipitated an abortive coup attempt by the senior vice-commander being passed over (Mendel 1970, 127–28). Reportedly this in turn further undermined Wei-kuo's political standing.

With the decline in the health of Ch'en Ch'eng and the retirement from very old age of long-term defense minister Yu Ta-wei (whose daughter married one of Chiang Ching-kuo's sons), Chiang Ching-kuo first became vice-minister of defense (1964–65) and then became full minister (1966–69). Now having line control of military commanders as well as the Political Warfare Department, he implemented a general reorganization. Among other things he somewhat demoted the political officers relative to the line commanders, thus reducing his dependence on the political warfare system and winning some gratitude from line officers. The General Political Warfare Department nevertheless remained significant; one of Chiang Ching-kuo's first acts upon the death of his father in 1975 was to appoint his own security czar, Wang Sheng, as its head (Liu 1984, 299–317).

A final potential rival eliminated in the mid-1960s was long-term Chiang Kai-shek protégé and Chiang Ching-kuo colleague P'eng Meng-chi. A younger Whampoa product, P'eng had won his spurs by his ferocity toward Taiwanese as Kaohsiung city garrison commander during the February 1947 massacre. In the late 1940s and early 1950s he commanded the "pacification forces" for the entire island. He remained a favorite of Chiang Kai-shek into the 1960s and went out of his way to reassure Chiang Ching-kuo that he had no intention of competing with him for ultimate power. Nevertheless, in 1966 he was shipped abroad as ambassador to Thailand and later Japan.

Technocracy and Party

The third and final phase of Chiang Ching-kuo's succession focused principally on the area of financial and economic policy, again with significant developments in the party. On the one hand, Chiang Ching-kuo had never been strong in economic institutions and business connections. Partly this was because they were dominated by T. V. Soong lieutenants associated with Madame Chiang or political study faction members sponsored by Ch'en Ch'eng. Partly it was because they were not in fact crucial to obtaining control of the state. On the other hand, Chiang Ching-kuo had nevertheless developed his own shadow cabinet of competent technocrats in the Retired Servicemen's Commission, the Youth Corps, the provincial government, and the Defense Ministry.[9]

In 1969, having thoroughly consolidated his position within the military, Chiang Ching-kuo became deputy premier, with financially expert and politically compliant Yen Chia-kan as premier. Chiang Ching-kuo began personally to chair the Financial and Economic Committee, a weekly meeting coordinating economic policy among the relevant agencies. Suddenly Hsu Po-yuan, the party's long-time financial specialist associated with Madame Chiang, fell victim to the "banana scandal." Li Kuo-ting, successor to Yin Chung-jung as czar of economic policy, surrendered the chairmanship of the powerful extraconstitutional Economic Planning Agency to a long-time rival and (now) Chiang Ching-kuo associate Fei Hua. Chiang Ching-kuo temporarily continued to use the planning agency to oversee economic policy. However, when he became premier in 1973 he transferred much of the planning commission's power back to the constitutional ministries, deflating the commission and winning support at the ministries of economics and finance. Yen Chia-kan became vice-president, positioned to succeed Chiang K'ai-shek as president. Meanwhile, Chiang Ching-kuo gathered the instruments of policy making around the premier's office. When Chiang Kai-shek died in 1975, Yen became president and Chiang Ching-kuo continued to run the country from the premiership. When Chiang Ching-kuo finally became president himself in 1978 he appointed a compliant technocrat as premier and took the main policy-making power with him to the Presidential Office. The long and carefully prepared succession was over (Liu 1984, 318–59).

Nevertheless, many ultraconservative Chiang Kai-shek followers remained among line party cadres and national legislators, constituting a potential source of criticism if Chiang Ching-kuo moved too blatantly to abandon his father's ideological legacy (recovery of the mainland) or to threaten their institutional prerogatives (opening their posts to Taiwanese). The architect of Chiang Ching-kuo's strategy in party and electoral affairs was Li Huan. He combined limited Taiwanization among party officials with a shift in electoral strategy, from playing the leaders of parochial local political machines off against each other to nominating well-educated, nonfactional "good government" candidates instead. The party swept the local elections of 1973 and Li was up; it lost four of twenty local executiveships in 1977 and he was out. Moreover, the apparent liberality of Li Huan's policy opened the door to escalating opposition challenges in the second half of the 1970s. Chiang Ching-kuo himself reverted to a more heavy-handed approach, evidently shifting his reliance from Li Huan back to Wang Sheng. Nevertheless the overall strategy of casting Chiang Ching-kuo as a "populist" leader in touch with the masses did largely succeed (Tien 1975; Winckler 1984).[10]

Class Conflict

Having sketched the most important struggles surrounding the institutionaliza-tion and succession of power within the state, the discussion now turns to the basic conflicts surrounding the production and appropriation of surplus value within the economy. Figure 8.2 provides a speculative overview. Looking back-ward, this is the story of what happened to diverse class fractions that had originated in previous socioeconomic regimes on both Taiwan and the mainland. Elite Taiwanese who had remained on Taiwan ended the Japanese period with various degrees of landlordization, commercialization, and collaboration. Taiwanese who had joined the Nationalists on the mainland ended the Republican period with various standings in the Nationalist political and economic establish-ment. Mainlanders who had come to Taiwan arrived at different times with different ranks in different organizations run by different factions. Looking forward, this is the story of the emergence of a large-scale sector selectively incorporating old and new, Taiwanese and mainlander, business and politics.[11]

The relationship between these backward and forward perspectives is again both historical and theoretical. Despite the political convulsions involved, there is significant continuity between the old and new establishments. This continuity is more one of structural position (as intermediary between state and society) than it is one of ideological orientation (pro-Japanese or pro-Nationalist). In the long run, the Nationalist state found it easier to collaborate with large-scale Taiwanese businessmen who had collaborated with the Japanese than to cope with the middle- and small-scale Taiwanese businessmen who had opposed the Japanese, sometimes in the name of Chinese nationalism.

Once again, going down the diagonal of the figure, I will sketch the successive confrontation between coalitions of class fractions and the emergence of succes-sive dominant coalitions within the new establishment. The first confrontation was *ins versus ins*, the showdown and selective merger in the late 1940s of Japanese-affiliated and Nationalist-affiliated elites, in the context of a command-ist state and of sharply restricted economic and political competition. The second was *ins versus outs*, skirmishing in the course of the 1950s between those

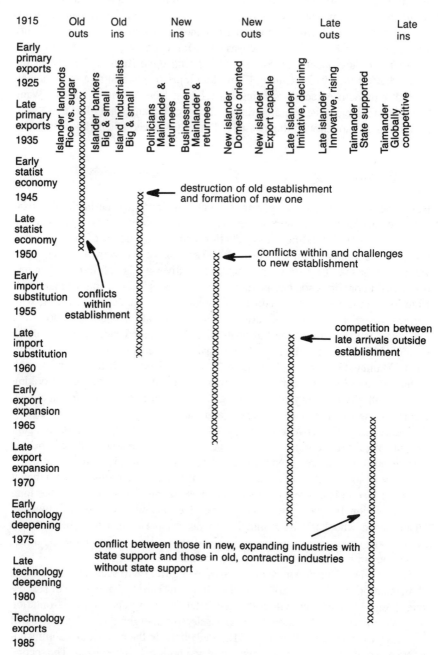

Figure 8.2. Class fractions and class conflict on Taiwan.
Notes: XXX indicates principal contradiction. "Taimander" indicates convergence of Taiwanese and mainlanders.

satisfied with the resulting establishment and malcontents attempting to gatecrash or reshape it. This significant economic and political competition was initiated as deliberate policy by at least some factions within the state. The third was *outs versus outs*, a generalized process of economic and political competition between successive new cohorts of entrepreneurs to which accelerated, more externally oriented economic development gave rise. These challenges did not, however, significantly reduce the hegemony of the original establishment.

Since class formation on Taiwan had had a long history by 1945, it seems advisable again to note some of the institutional and personal legacy of the past. Here it is important to underline that for investigating the role of circulation of capital in elite politics, the concept of "landlord" in the existing literature about Taiwan is grossly inadequate. By 1945 capital, not land, was already the key elite political asset, and consequently Nationalist bank reform was a more fundamental attack on the existing Taiwanese upper elite than land reform. Consequently, I emphasize financial role rather than land ownership in characterizing the class fractions that constituted the pre–1945 Taiwanese political-economic elite.

Economically, most large-scale Taiwanese were landlords who had come to political terms with the Japanese and who had become involved in the export of primary agricultural products to Japan (for capsule descriptions of the major Japanese-period collaborator-entrepreneurs see chapter 5). Some, however, made their money from coal mines, domestic commerce, or professional services. Banks owned by Japanese had served mostly large-scale Japanese firms rather than Taiwanese. Therefore some prominent Taiwanese had used their profits and connections to establish banks through which to diversify their enterprises and expand their political influence. However, even these few large-scale banks ostensibly owned by Taiwanese basically functioned to collect money on Taiwan and siphon it off for investment in Japan.

Politically, some large-scale Taiwanese businessmen demanded equal citizenship, home rule or other political rights within the Japanese empire. Some used business entrepreneurship as a means to challenge Japanese political monopoly. These are included as having politically "come to terms" with the Japanese, however, because they remained within the legal framework prescribed by Japan. This class was in crisis after 1945 because its Japanese political support and export market had been cut off, and because the Nationalists actively moved to curb its political influence and expropriate its economic assets.

Equally interesting politically are middle- and small-scale Taiwanese businessmen. Like the large-scale landlord-banker-businessmen, by 1945 they were already commercial capitalists rather than merely landlords. The Japanese had outlawed the traditional Chinese "rotating credit association," presumably to force savings out of the unorganized money market into the large-scale sector. However, the Japanese did provide the legal basis for small-scale local banks and credit cooperatives, legal forms that the Taiwanese therefore used extensively. Although these middle- and small-scale cooperative banks controlled a miniscule portion of the total capital on Taiwan, they did provide platforms for economic and political entrepreneurship. Local bankers accounted for a large proportion of the local representatives appointed or elected in the 1930s and for many of the politicians who emerged in 1945. Many of these were also landlords. Some—a higher proportion than among the large-scale Taiwanese bankers—were also local businessmen or professionals. Many of the local businessmen depended on Japanese political patronage, particularly monopoly rights to distribution of particular commodities (e.g., liquor) or provision of particular services (e.g., transportation) within particular localities. In contrast, some of the profession-als—local doctors, lawyers, journalists—were economically relatively indepen-dent of the Japanese government. Some among these were very pro-Japanese, but many favored more political rights for Taiwanese, and a few even advocated imitation of the Nationalist movement on mainland China.

In summary, as of 1945, Taiwanese distinguished the following categories among themselves. Islanders (*a-hae*) were those who had remained on Taiwan during the Japanese period and had had no relationship with the Chinese Nation-alists before 1945. Most large-scale Taiwanese during the Japanese period were islanders. Pro-mainlander Taiwanese (*k'ao-shan*) had mostly remained on Taiwan but had expressed support for Chinese nationalism or formed relation-ships with Chinese nationalists. Such pro-mainlanders probably constituted an extreme minority even of small-scale businessmen, but probably most of them were small-scale operators, particularly independent professionals. Returnee Taiwanese (*pan-shan*) had gone to the mainland during the Japanese period, served under the Nationalist government, and returned with it in 1945 as part of the new establishment. Probably most of these returnees were Taiwanese of modest means who had gone to the mainland because of lack of educational opportunities or economic stakes on Taiwan.

Ins versus Ins

The principal focus of conflict in the first phase, 1945–1954, was between the old and new establishments—between the Taiwanese elites who had prospered under Japanese rule and the returnee Taiwanese and mainland Chinese taking over the economy under Nationalist auspices. In the old establishment, islander Taiwan-ese "in" and "out" with the colonial administration who had quarreled during the Japanese period now found themselves jointly defending themselves against the newcomers from the mainland. In the new establishment there were tensions between returnee Taiwanese and mainland Chinese, but they cooperated effec-tively in appropriating as much of the wealth and power of the old establishment as possible.

The key distinction within the old establishment was between those who sooner or later formed a working relationship with the Nationalist state and those who did not. Not surprisingly in this turbulent period, the factors affecting this outcome were complex. They probably included the changing needs of the Nationalist state, the nature of the economic assets of the Taiwanese, and the political connections and commitments of the Taiwanese, in that order.

The attitudes of successive early Nationalist administrations toward Taiwanese changed drastically over time, as did also, of course, the attitude of Taiwanese toward Nationalist administration. The Ch'en Yi regime accused some of the elite Taiwanese most conspicuously associated with the Japanese of collaboration, but incorporated some of those elite Taiwanese regarded as Taiwanese or Nationalist patriots into an appointive provincial representative assembly. Many of the latter, however, resigned in disgust after Nationalist repression of the 1947 Taiwanese mass protests. The ensuing Wei Tao-ming and Ch'en Ch'eng administrations attempted to incorporate a few pro-Nationalist islander Taiwanese into the provincial government administration, but this was resisted by the returnee Taiwanese who claimed the few Taiwanese slots for themselves. One objective of Wu Kuo-chen in accepting the provincial governorship from 1950–1953 was to increase the representation of Taiwanese, particularly islanders.

The highly visible economic assets of the large-scale islander Taiwanese landlord-banker-businessmen made them threatening to the Nationalist state, but also vulnerable to it. The highly provincial and extractive Nationalist administrations of the late 1940s kept them on the defensive with political charges and economic reforms. The more international and developmental Nationalist administrations of the early 1950s allowed some to buy their way back into the development process. Some large-scale "old ins" sooner or later rejected Nationalist rule and withdrew from politics, and even from business, on Taiwan. Some tried to succeed within the new Nationalist order but failed. Others eventually succeeded in joining the "new ins." Those who succeeded had to transform themselves from bankers, spreading their investments among a diversified portfolio of speculative investments, into industrialists, concentrating their investments on a limited number of factories. This made their economic assets still more vulnerable to political regulation. Although preserving substantial insider political influence, they could not engage in opposition politics except at the cost of their economic interests, which as time went on became unexpectedly enormous.

In general the fate of middle- and small-scale Taiwanese cooperative bankers was gradual integration into an islandwide and government-managed system of cooperative banks. This gave these banks more efficient management and some protection against corruption; it also robbed them of their financial and political autonomy. Rural credit functions were transferred to government-managed farmers' associations. Local businessmen wedded to traditional primary exports or Japanese monopoly privileges were particularly prone to decline. Eventually the need for political and economic services of middle- and small-scale Taiwanese businessmen secured for many of them a regular if limited expansion of income and influence, and for some of them promotion into the new establishment.

In the 1945–1954 period the underlying distinction within the new establishment was that between politicians and businessmen—between those operating basically from the state and those operating basically from the market. In this period, however, the state intervened heavily in the market and the market turned the state into an auction. Some individuals moved back and forth between political and economic roles. Most political leaders were mainlanders, but some business leaders were Taiwanese. Further ethnic segmentation remained significant in both politics and business, between Hokkien and Hakka within the Taiwanese, and between mainlanders from northern, central, and southern China.

The next section will delve somewhat more deeply into the new establishment. In general, among mainland Chinese, the many politicians ran the government (see the discussion of state struggle in the first half of this chapter) and the few big businessmen (mostly from Shanghai) gained a disproportionate share of the first wave of import substitution industries (mostly textiles). The political, economic, and social alliances and conflicts within the mainlander elite can really be deciphered only by someone familiar with their relations on the mainland from 1920 to 1950. In general, however, their eventual fate was determined by the ties they were able to form with Chiang Ching-kuo as he emerged as the island's future leader between 1950 and 1970.

The returnee Taiwanese were mostly politicians with state positions that, while not high in comparison with those of the mainlander political elite, certainly gave them considerable stature vis à vis their Taiwanese compatriots. However, returnee Taiwanese who had achieved high military or security positions during the Sino-Japanese and civil wars on the mainland were soon forced out of those positions into local politics or local business on Taiwan. Other prominent returnee Taiwanese politicians performing less sensitive political roles retained both political and economic positions so long as the mainlander state faction with which they were associated remained on top. If their mainlander allies lost power within the state, or if their relationship with powerful mainlanders declined, they might well be forced to choose between politics and business, forced to abandon politics for business, or, conceivably, forced to relinquish both. There were few businessmen among the returnee Taiwanese.

Ins versus Outs

The principal focus of conflict during the second phase, roughly 1954–1962/1965, was between the largely Nationalist-affiliated Taiwanese "ins" who (in competition and collaboration with mainlander businessmen) dominated the large-scale private sector economy, and the formerly anti-Japanese local politicians and still political-economic "outs." These "outs" were confined to smaller-scale enterprises and attempted—unsuccessfully—to mobilize smaller businessmen, local nonparty politicians, and mass support to increase their political leverage on the state. Certainly there were plenty of ambitious Chinese, both mainlander and Taiwanese, trying to improve their political access for both political and economic purposes. Even returnee Taiwanese businessmen sought mainlander politicians to use for access to the Nationalist state. Islander Taiwanese politicians sought both mainlander Chinese and returnee Taiwanese for the same purpose. Mainlanders even sought Taiwanese to use as fronts when there was something to be gained from it, as in the purchase of some Japanese industries being sold by the Nationalist state. "Outs" were those who had no such "in," or had had such connections but were now slipping.

One should not overstate the degree of challenge to the establishment that the "outs" were able or willing to display. In fact the dominance of the new establishment was so pronounced that often it was only the instigation and support of some members of the establishment trying to improve their position within it that activated the middle- and small-scale "outs." The suppression of any subversive collaboration between "ins" and "outs" suggests that the Nationalist state required that members of the economic establishment remain politically dependent. They should not build a multivalent independent organizational base even within the establishment itself, let alone a "mass" base in the middle- and small-scale sectors beyond.

The "ins" attempting to mobilize "outs" included two sorts, both of which soon lost the double game they were attempting to play. From the "old ins" were a few prominent Taiwanese who wanted to circumvent restrictions on their investment activities by using "outs" as proxies, or who wanted to probe the susceptibility of the Nationalist system to a resurgence of autonomous Taiwanese political activity. A good example is Lin Po-hsiu, whose family were the biggest landlords in northern Taiwan under the Ch'ing, one of the largest and most cooperative landlord-banker-businessmen under the Japanese, and one of the largest shareholders in the new economic establishment under the Nationalists. He helped finance Taiwanese Kao Yu-shu's successful independent campaign for mayor of Taipei in 1954, represented Taiwanese bankers in attempting to replace Lin Ting-li as deputy speaker of the provincial assembly in the mid–1950s, and obliquely supported the movement to form a second political party in the late 1950s.

Also attempting to mobilize "outs," from the "new ins" were some of the returnee politicians and returnee financiers who had run into trouble. The ideal type started with political instinct, organizing ability, and business acumen rather than established power, wealth, or prestige. He attempted to convert his political access into economic position, only to find that he was affiliated with a losing faction within the state and lacked the economic resources to stay in the game on his own. Meanwhile he had probably alarmed stronger economic and political competitors by such success as he had achieved.

A close approximation to the ideal type is Lin Ting-li. Lin had evidently been a spy for Japan in Amoy during the 1930s, where he was recruited by the political intelligence faction as a double agent for the Nationalists. He returned to Taiwan with the Nationalists and played an important—again evidently double—role as a bridge between the Nationalists and Taiwanese during the 28 February 1947 massacre. He pursued an ambitious, three-pronged, power-amassing career as politician (deputy speaker of the provincial assembly), publisher (creator of the influential *United Daily News*), and businessman (as a front for islander Taiwanese, most prominently in the Taiwan Agricultural and Forestry Corporation). Although some business ownership was permissible, the Nationalist state did not want an independent Taiwanese businessman involved in politics or publishing, particularly one with a security background. Lin was forced to sell his newspaper and was transferred from politics to jail on a charge of communicating with Taiwanese in Japan who advocated "Taiwan independence."

The exceptional "in" who proves the rule by successfully mobilizing "outs" to enhance his position was—who else—Chiang Ching-kuo. Indeed, he was probably responsible for the "rule," since it was probably he who was knocking off all the other competitors. Beginning in the late 1950s, Chiang Ching-kuo started to reach out to potential allies among the Taiwanese elite, using as his bridge precisely the person with whom he had replaced Lin Ting-li as deputy speaker of the provincial assembly, Hsieh Tung-min. Originally from central Taiwan, Hsieh had spent the war on the mainland as a member of the team preparing to take over Taiwan for the Nationalists. At retrocession he was assigned to southern Taiwan, where he formed additional relationships with prominent families. He was among the first Taiwanese to hold posts in the central party and provincial government. Through his collaboration with Chiang Ching-kuo he later became speaker of the provincial assembly, governor of Taiwan province, and vice-president of the central government.

Outs versus Outs

The principal focus of the third phase, since the opening of the island to the world economy and acceleration of economic development in the mid–1960s, has been competition for access to the establishment between successive cohorts of industrialists or politicians spawned by economic growth and social modernization. As export-oriented economic development gained momentum, the new wealth generated by economic development, and the new political sophistication generated among Taiwanese businessmen by contact with other countries, began to flood the political marketplace. The issues and price of politics rose beyond the means of a few Taiwanese families or the Nationalist party easily to control. Clearly there has been some conflict of interest between the public and private sector of the economy, between internally and externally oriented businessmen, and between the successive industries that have risen, prospered, and begun to decline. Certainly there has been much jockeying over economic policy through such—largely informal—channels as exist for input from the establishment to the state. Nevertheless, in the 1960s and 1970s there was remarkably little conflict between fractions within the new establishment, presumably because most of the time the economy was expanding so rapidly that everyone had more remunerative things to do. The real question has been when and on what terms "new wealth" would be admitted not just to prosperity but also to long-term political power.[12]

The principal breakthroughs came with the 1973 and 1977 elections, in connection with both Chiang Ching-kuo's political succession and the evolving requirements of economic development. Before 1973 the Nationalist party had pursued a divide-and-rule strategy, choosing its candidates for local office largely from among the parochial rural factions the manipulation of which had been the party's strategy for twenty-five years. In 1973 Chiang Ching-kuo's political adviser Li Huan chose candidates instead from among the bright young businessmen whose emergence has just been noted, or from among bright young politicians who would run both the economic development and social welfare of their localities in the managerial style that accelerating socioeconomic development required. As further explored in chapter 3, this was the turning point from vertical, rural-based, "zero-sum" patron-client politics toward horizontal, class-based, growth-oriented politics.

The 1977 elections carried the incorporation of the new bourgeoisie a step further. The state put out the word that, for the first time in thirty years, the involvement of businessmen in non-Nationalist local politics was permissible. Of course it was still best if they supported Nationalist candidates or waited their own turn for nomination by the Nationalist party. However, if they short-circuited the process by supporting independent candidates of their own or jumped the gun by running as independent candidates themselves, it would not be interpreted as incipient treason, and no retaliation would occur. Criticism of the efficiency and probity of local government—so long as it did not challenge the basic legitimacy of the Nationalist regime—was allowable, even encouraged. Subsequent elections (1980, 1983) extended this formula to elections for national representatives.

Conclusion

This brings the story of the postwar convergence of Nationalist political and Taiwanese economic elites to a temporary close. The heuristic history has illustrated the main theme stated at the outset, namely, the centrality of "conservative" personal networks to the workings of both state and market, and to connecting the two. Within the state, power derived from personal relations to The Leader. Within the market, wealth derived from family firms with personal access to the state. Contrary to what radical statists might expect (see chapter 1), state and market remained at arm's length, largely because of the distinction between mainlanders dominating one and Taiwanese dominating the other. The gap was bridged by co-opting selected Taiwanese into the Nationalist establishment, few at first but more later.

On balance this sequential incorporation of Taiwanese economic elites has enhanced the stability of the Nationalist regime, keeping it at least somewhat representative of Taiwan's rapidly developing society. The early arrived, upper-elite members of the late Japanese and early Nationalist periods achieved high positions as national or provincial corporate directors or economic advisers. The later arriving, lower-elite members achieved lower positions as appointive administrators or elected representatives, first at the local and provincial and later at the national levels.

Taiwanese elites gained incorporation but lost autonomy. Earlier the newly arrived Nationalist party had itself depended on the limited number of historically distinguished, rural-based regional-elite families, who had definite territorial political bases and social positions of their own. That is why these families were accommodated, and why they remained influential for so long. In the 1980s, however, most potential Taiwanese political candidates are dependent on the increasingly sophisticated Nationalist party organization. There are many aspirants, they lack their own political bases, and they can be rotated out of office before they have time to build such bases.

Whether the incorporation of Taiwanese economic elites has made the Nationalist establishment more representative of the political aspirations of the mass of Taiwanese remains a moot question. On the one hand, Taiwanese voters continue to give large majorities to Nationalist candidates. On the other hand, non-Nationalist challengers remain hamstrung by denial of the right to form an opposition political party (until 1987), and by restrictions on access to the media, among other constraints. Tensions between "ins," and between "ins" and "outs," have produced repeated cycles of expansion and contraction in both the volume and the vehemence of mass political participation. Mass political incorporation, however, is the topic of chapter 3.

Notes

1. Aside from the documentary sources cited in the text and footnotes, this chapter is based on extensive conversations with many types of informants, and extensive reading in Chinese newspaper clipping files from 1969 to 1984 on Taiwan. Given the random pattern in which bits of information arise from such sources, and particularly given the fact that what is reported here are interpretations synthesized from many such sources, it has not been feasible to cite particular informants or clippings. I note any important points about which I remain particularly uncertain. The purpose of this piece however, is not to provide a definitive descriptive history of elite struggle on postwar Taiwan, but rather simply to suggest some categories for interpreting that history.

2. For theoretical references on networks, see the section on cultural conservatism in chapter 2 of this volume.

3. "Faction" points to coalitions—conscious and interpersonal—based on access to state power and aimed at improving that access. "Fraction" points to similarities of interest—conscious or unconscious, interpersonal or interorganizational—arising from

similarity in types of economic activity (commercial agriculture, light industry, real restate, commercial banking, etc.).

4. The implicit argument, not elaborated here, is that there are only a limited number of mechanisms through which political and economic elites could have related—bureaucracy, markets, elections, and networks. Most systems rely primarily on one basic mechanisms, supplemented, to overcome its defects, by one or more of the others. In the early postwar period on Taiwan, the system was basically bureaucratic, supplemented (since markets and elections were largely suspended for elite transactions) mostly by networks. On mechanisms see Dahl and Lindblom (1953) and Lindblom (1977); on entrepreneurship, risk, and return see Knight 1921).

5. Thus the chapter is limited to a preliminary "positional" sketch and does not include systematic "reputational" or "decisional" analysis. It does, however, include "nondecisional" elements, that is, assessment of the extent to which elites could prevent issues from being raised at all. For good short summaries of a long and difficult argument about methodologies for elite studies, see Walton (1966) and Bachrach and Baratz (1962).

6. Data on political positions and career lines for this section come from three serials: the annual *China Yearbook* published by the Government Information Office; directories of ROC officials issued periodically by the U.S. embassy (and successor American Institute in Taiwan); and numerous issues of official lists of Chinese government personnel printed for in-house use by the national, provincial, and local governments on Taiwan.

7. See, for example, the careers of Huang Chieh and Ch'en Ta-ch'ing, as given in contemporaneous issues of the *China Yearbook*.

8. Evidently the "three great battles" between Ch'en Ch'eng and Chiang Ching-kuo included the elections for the Eighth National Congress of the Nationalist party in October 1957 and for the Ninth National Congress in November 1963, but what the third was, I am not sure. The Seventh National Congress had been in 1952 and the Tenth was in 1969. Ch'en Ch'eng died on 5 March 1965.

9. Persons in these organizational examples include Chao Chu-yu of VACRS (Vocational Assistance Commission for Retired Servicemen), Chou Hung-tao of the provincial Department of Finance, and Wang Shao-yu of the provincial Monopoly Bureau.

10. Interestingly, in connection with the emphasis on personal networks in this chapter, Li's real problem was not that he lost some electoral races in 1977 but that his network of Taiwanese protégés had proved unreliable. Wang later overreached himself and was exiled as ambassador to Paraguay in 1983. A cautious approach to electoral liberalization persisted until 1986.

11. Data on business positions and career lines for this section come from three types of sources, many of them in several successive editions over time: biographic directories of businessmen, organizational profiles of individual companies and business groups, and sectoral histories of industrial development. Among biographic directories of businessmen, see particularly Republic of China Chamber of Industry and Commerce (1955; 1963; 1970) and China Credit Information Service (1973; 1978). On individual companies see China Credit Information Service (1978) and *Commonwealth Magazine*; on business groups see China Credit Information Service (1970; 1972; 1974; 1976; 1978; 1983/1984) (the last available in English for the first time). Among sectoral histories of industrial development, on the public sector see particularly China Institute of Engineers (1958) and on the private sector H. Ch'en (1957).

12. On the changing economic background of local political leaders, see Y. Ch'en (1981). Based on comprehensive information from the provincial party headquarters, this is one of the few major published systematic studies of elite political incorporation on Taiwan. However, it should be noted that the occupations self-reported by local candidates often do not reflect the real thrust of their economic activities.

LATER
DEVELOPMENT

9

Thomas B. Gold

ENTREPRENEURS, MULTINATIONALS, AND THE STATE

This chapter follows the structure of Evans's (1979) study of Brazil, examining the interaction through time among the key members of Taiwan's economic elite—private capital, multinational corporations, and the state. I argue that on Taiwan the state played a much greater role than in the commonly analyzed Latin American cases. For this and other reasons, Taiwan avoided much of the social, economic, and political disarticulation and exclusion prevalent in Latin America and has begun a transition away from hard authoritarianism toward a more pluralist democratic system. By presenting data on Taiwan, in this chapter I hope to facilitate comparison with other, non-Asian cases of dependent development and in this way contribute to the construction of a badly needed new paradigm for development studies.

The Analysis of Dependent Development

Students of the dynamic capitalist societies of East Asia have lagged far behind Latin Americanists when it comes to adding to stocks of development theories. Latin Americans were the first to challenge the liberal modernization paradigm that dominated development theory after World War II.[1] Modernization is an optimistic approach to the study of development which asserts that, through the removal of cultural and social structural obstacles to the acceptance and implementation of new ways of behavior, all societies can follow a universal road to becoming modern. "Modern" features of society include forms of management and production, orientations to the world and society, and types of political activity that closely resemble an idealized picture of the United States.

Scholars of all disciplines set out to pinpoint the inhibitors of modernization through fieldwork, social history, and macrosociological comparisons. They devised tables to chart the progress toward modernity of backward nations along particular variables. Advocates believed that a range of external forces could play an important part in diffusing modern values and behaviors to nonmodern societies. These included foreign aid programs, direct foreign investment, loans, education, and training. A number of scholars participated in modernization research, but the project was also tied rather closely to cold war American foreign policy (Peck 1976). This policy sought to bring the supposed benefits of the American style of life to the rest of the world and prevent the Soviet alternative from taking root. Communism was not modern; it was an aberration.

Latin American economists affiliated with the United Nations' Economic Commission for Latin America began to challenge the analysis and prescriptions of modernizationists in the late 1940s. They argued that economic links with the developed countries, based on supposed comparative advantage in certain primary goods exports, were based on unequal terms of trade that, far from stimulating modernization, added structural barriers to it.

In the 1960s other Latin Americans extended this radical line of analysis. In their view it was not just an unequal economic relationship (primarily one of trade), but also the political and social aspects of that relationship, that reinforced and deepened what they called ''dependency'' (dos Santos 1970). Dependency denotes a structural relationship wherein foreign actors, in particular multinational corporations (MNCs), allied with conservative elements in Latin American societies who facilitated external (MNC) control over economic activity as well as social and political life.

Dependency is a profoundly pessimistic view, which is odd considering its Marxist roots. Marx had predicted that expanding capitalism would burst beyond national borders, batter down all obstacles throughout the noncapitalist world, and bring about global capitalism, a prerequisite to worldwide socialist revolution. Early dependentistas, building on Lenin, argued that, in fact, capitalism in its imperialist stage plundered noncapitalist economies. By allying with reactionary elements within those societies, imperialism prevented the emergence of full-scale capitalism.

Some writers, such as André Gunder Frank (1969a), whose polemics first introduced dependency theory to the English-speaking world, argued that only the severing of ties to the capitalist core and socialist transformation could bring about genuine development. But there are other scholars in the field who are less dogmatic. In Wallerstein's (1979) world systems model, a semiperiphery between the developed core and underdeveloped periphery contains a handful of countries that were able to achieve some measure of economic advancement, basically industrialization. They did this through aggressive state action in a period of world system contraction, invitation by MCS in a period of global expansion, or self-reliance.

Later another group of radical scholars put forward a concept of dependent development to explain the process of development within a context of dependency. Cardoso (1972; 1973; Cardoso and Faletto 1979) and Evans (1979) are prime examples. But they, too, are pessimistic in that in spite of industrialization, the countries in this category suffer a number of consequences, authoritarian politics and great social inequality among the worst.

Works by dependency writers shifted the ground of inquiry away from national and subnational forces to external causes. The most sophisticated analysts, such as Cardoso and Faletto and Evans, did not employ a simplistic zero-sum approach claiming that everything can be blamed on foreign forces and that the core benefits only by underdeveloping the periphery. Instead, they traced the interactions between external actors, primarily MNCs, and internal ones, such as traditional oligarchies, local capital, and the state. They illuminated the complex nature of a "situation of dependency" (Palma 1978) and where it might lead.

Evans's important study of Brazil predicts a number of consequences inherent in dependent development. These include disarticulation between technology and social structure, as MNCs bring in capital-intensive production techniques that exacerbate rather than solve problems of unemployment; disarticulation between MNCs and local capital, as the MNCs import needed parts rather than source them locally; disarticulation between a domestic-oriented and an internationalized bourgeoisie; disarticulation between locally produced goods and consumer tastes for foreign products; exclusion of most of the masses—workers and peasants in particular—from the fruits of industrial growth; and exclusion of the popular sector from political activity in which it had previously been active.

The works of Cardoso, Evans, and others had a galvanizing effect on the development field throughout the 1970s, a time when the United States and its ideas about modernization and how to bring it about were on the defensive (Cardoso 1977).

As for East Asia, it seemed impervious to these goings on. Many of the major modernizationists were scholars of East Asia.[2] They had analyzed cultural and structural factors in China that inhibited its modernization and the differences in Japan that led it down a different road. But the victorious Chinese and Vietnamese revolutions provided seemingly incontrovertible proof that America did not have the answer to the question of how to bring Japan's nonmodern neighbors along.

Meanwhile, almost unnoticed, Taiwan, South Korea, Hong Kong, and Singapore began to register phenomenally rapid rates of economic growth and industrialization. Virtually the only scholars to write about it (native or foreign) were liberal economists (see also chapter 2).[3] They analyzed the reams of data provided by local governments, worked up equations and models, and began to publish their results. Although noting the role of government in development, they did not go deeper to analyze the state's structure or relation with society, or the interplay of economic with political variables. They did not engage in any discourse with the Latin America-oriented dependentistas. Other social scientists in Asia or elsewhere did not attempt the sort of comprehensive sociological (radical political economic) analysis of any East Asian capitalist nations.

In the mid–1970s, as I became familiar with the dependentistas' generaliza-

tions about development and underdevelopment derived from their studies of
Latin America and, to a much lesser extent, Africa, I grew uneasy at their lack of
fit with what I knew of Taiwan, where I had lived in the early 1970s. I resolved to
test these theories in a part of the world hitherto untouched by them.

My methodology was to start from Peter Evans's "triple alliance" model.[4] In
Dependent Development, he argued that Brazil's dependent development came
about because of the emergence of a tripartite elite comprising local capital (the
elite faction), MNCs, and the state. They conflicted but also collaborated and
shared an interest in having Brazil develop. Continued stagnation or underdevelopment would not provide markets for local or foreign capital, and popular
disaffection could weaken the state. Because the same three actors had led
Taiwan's development, I concluded that in terms of central variables and outcome
(development), Taiwan would provide a suitable test case.

Dependent Development on Taiwan

On all commonly accepted indicators of development[5]—economic and social—
Taiwan ranks with Brazil and Mexico as one of the handful of newly industrializing countries (NICs) (see table 9.1). In fact, on many indicators, it surpasses the
others.

On some additional variables of extreme importance in the 1980s, Taiwan
looks even better. It maintained a positive current account balance, in mid–1987
had accumulated over U.S. $50 billion in foreign reserves, and had a debt service
ratio under 5 percent of exports of goods and services. On the last figure,
comparable ratios for Brazil, Mexico, and Korea in 1984 were 35.8 percent, 48.6
percent, and 15.8 percent, respectively (World Bank 1986, 213).[6]

Taiwan is not only a case of GNP growth and industrialization, but also one of
development. Table 9.2 demonstrates the process of deepening and diversifying
of the industrial structure. By the 1980s, automobiles, electronics, and computers
were beginning to dominate industry, with former leaders such as textiles declining.

As to dependency, several indicators can be cited to show the degree to which
Taiwan's economy has been conditioned by external factors. Most important are
trade figures, and table 9.3 shows how Taiwan has become increasingly dependent on trade. In 1984, the value of foreign trade was more than 90 percent of the
book value of GNP at current prices (CEPD 1986), a decline from highs above 96
percent. The trade has also consistently concentrated on two partners. Taiwan has
relied on Japan for over one-fourth of imports since the 1950s, in many years
much more. U.S. imports were over 20 percent of Taiwan's total and accounted
for half of Taiwan's exports (CEPD 1986, 214, 216). Japan took only 11 percent
of Taiwan's exports in 1985. While direct foreign investment (DFI) has only once
accounted for more than 10 percent of gross domestic capital formation (11.3
percent in 1972), it has been concentrated in certain sectors that have led

Taiwan's economic growth, thus playing a significant role in shaping the structure of the economy. The most visible example of this is the electronics industry, which in 1977 accounted for 16 percent of export value and was 85 percent foreign owned (Gold 1981, 126; for other measures of dependency, see table 4.6).

DFI has played an important role in the economy, but local and state capital have accounted for most of the value of industrial production. The state owns and operates more than ten enterprises, mainly in upstream industries and infrastructure, while private investors own everything else.

All three members of the "triple alliance" are active in Taiwan. They compete in some sectors, complement and collaborate in others, and actually invest jointly in a few. In the following sections I review Taiwan's dependent development and the emergence of the triple alliance.

Colonial Taiwan, 1895-1945

The developmentalist Japanese colonial administration invested in the island to develop its capacity to produce sugar and rice for export to the rest of the empire in exchange for manufactured goods. Peasants grew sugar on their own land and were bound to sell it to Japanese-owned mills. Japanese firms dominated trade. Japanese conglomerates (zaibatsu), capitalists, and the government itself owned the modern industrial plant, which was centered on sugar refining. Laws restricted Taiwanese participation in the modern sector. Massive immigration of Japanese laborers obviated the need to create a Taiwanese proletariat. The educational system was not aimed at improving Taiwanese mobility chances, but rather at producing better-educated subjects. Power was monopolized by Japanese.

Industrial development in Taiwan came as a response to the needs of the Japanese empire, not from aggressive demands or action by Taiwanese. As the Pacific War intensified and shipping was interrupted, the authorities were forced to build some factories to increase local self-sufficiency.

Although capitalist forms of production were introduced into Taiwan, the absolute majority of owners and workers were Japanese expatriates in an enclave sector. As a result, the effect on Taiwanese social structure was circumscribed, although it did demonstrate to the populace the potential of capitalist industrialization and state guidance of development. The Japanese allied with some members of the traditional landowning bureaucratic elite, but most of their efforts went into creating a new class of collaborators, which they promoted as a native aristocracy (see chapter 5).

Horizontal Import Substitution, 1946-1959

After Japan's surrender, Taiwan was turned over to the Republic of China (ROC), headed by Chiang Kai-shek and the Kuomintang (KMT) or Nationalist

Table 9.1 **Indicators of Development**

	(1) Population (millions) mid-1984	(2) GNP per capita: $ 1984	(3) GNP per capita avg. annual growth rate 1965-1984	(4) GDP growth rate	
				1965-1973	1973-1984
Taiwan	19.0	3,063	7.0	11.0	8.1
South Korea	40.1	2,110	6.6	10.0	7.2
Singapore	2.5	7,260	7.8	13.0	8.2
Hong Kong	5.4	6,330	6.2	7.9	9.1
Brazil	132.6	1,720	4.6	9.8	4.4
Mexico	76.8	2,040	2.9	7.9	5.1
Chile	11.8	1,700	-0.1	3.4	2.7
Argentina	30.1	2,230	0.3	4.3	0.4
Nigeria	96.5	730	2.8	9.7	0.7
Côte d'Ivoire	9.9	610	0.2	7.1	3.7

	(5) Distribution of GDP (%)						(6) Labor force (%)			
	Agriculture		Industry Total		Manufacturing		Agriculture		Industry	
	1965	1984	1965	1984	1965	1984	1965	1980	1965	1980
Taiwan	27	8	29	45	20	36	47	20	22	42
South Korea	38	14	25	40	18	28	56	36	14	27
Singapore	3	1	24	39	15	25	5	2	27	38
Hong Kong	2	1	40	22	24	—	6	2	53	51
Brazil	19	13[a]	33	35[a]	26	27[a]	48	31	20	27
Mexico	14	9	31	40	21	24	50	37	22	29
Chile	9	6[a]	40	39[a]	24	21[a]	27	16	29	25
Argentina	17	12	42	39	33	30[a]	18	13	34	34
Nigeria	53	27	19	30	7	4[a]	72	68	10	12
Côte d'Ivoire	36	28	17	26[a]	10	17	81	65	5	8

	(7) Avg. annual rate of inflation		(8) Life expectancy at birth (years) 1984	(9) Adult literacy rate 1975
	1965-1973	1973-1984		
Taiwan	1.8b	7.6c	71	82d
South Korea	15.5	17.6b	68	93
Singapore	3.1	4.4	76	75d
Hong Kong	6.4	9.8	72	90
Brazil	23.2	71.4	64	76d
Mexico	4.8	31.5	66	72
Chile	50.3	75.4	70	88
Argentina	24.1	180.8	70	94
Nigeria	10.3	13.0	50	—
Côte d'Ivoire	4.1	11.7	52	20

a. 1983.
b. 1963–1972.
c. 1973–1985.
d. years other than 1975.
Sources: For all but Taiwan (except col. 9), World Bank 1986 (pages as indicated): Cols. 1, 2, 3, 7, pp. 180; col. 4, pp. 182-83; col. 5, pp. 184-85; col. 6, pp. 238-39. Column 9: World Bank 1980.
For Taiwan, CEPD 1986 (pages as indicated): col. 1, p. 4; cols. 2, 3, p. 24; col. 4, p. 21; col. 5, p. 39; col. 6, p. 15; col. 7, p. 175; col. 8, p. 312.

Table 9.2

Contribution to Real GDP by Early, Middle, and Late Industries

	% of Real GDP at Factor Cost		
	1952-1954	1959-1961	1967-1969
1. Early industries	6.5	7.7	7.0
Food, beverages, and tobacco	3.8	5.5	3.2
Leather	0.1	—	—
Textiles	2.6	2.2	3.8
2. Middle industries	3.2	4.2	7.3
Nonmetallic mineral products	0.5	1.1	1.5
Rubber products	0.1	0.2	0.3
Wood and wood products	0.8	0.9	0.9
Chemicals and products of petroleum and coal	1.8	2.0	4.6
3. Late industries	2.0	4.7	9.3
Apparel	0.4	0.6	1.0
Paper and paper products	0.8	1.7	2.0
Basic metals	0.1	0.6	0.4
Metal products, machinery (including electrical machinery), and transport equipment	0.7	1.8	5.9
4. 1 + 2 + 3	11.7	16.6	23.6

Source: Ho (1978a, 204).

party. Taiwan was a province of the ROC. Unlike in other former colonies, there had been no independence movement. Influential community and intellectual leaders from the Japanese period were the target of mainland Chinese government massacres in 1947. Those who did not flee were either liquidated or suppressed, leaving a vacuum at the top. As the Nationalist state retreated from the mainland it monopolized political and economic power, imposing a new, external elite on top of Taiwan society. The constraints on economic development were staggering: a bankrupt government; murderous inflation; an industrial plant decimated by U.S. bombs and mainland carpetbaggers; a hostile population; well over a million civilian and military refugees on the state payroll; no foreign allies or capital; and the Chinese Communist People's Liberation Army poised to liberate the island.

The populace had to be fed, clothed, sheltered, and provided with a means of livelihood. The Nationalist state needed revenue immediately in order to effect this as well as to feed its war machine to preserve itself against the Communist and potential internal threats. Owning virtually all of the assets in the industrial sector, by virtue of confiscating Japanese assets and transferring some from the mainland, the state necessarily took the lead in reviving produc-

Table 9.3

Trade as a Percent of Gross Domestic Product at Current Prices

	(1) Exports as % of GDP	(2) Rate of growth of exports	(3) Imports as % of GDP	(4) Rate of growth of imports	(5) Trade as % of GDP
1952	8.6	—	14.8	—	23.4
1953	8.7	35.1	12.0	8.7	20.7
1954	5.8	−26.9	13.2	20.0	19.0
1955	6.4	32.2	10.5	−4.8	16.9
1956	8.6	52.9	14.0	52.6	22.6
1957	9.2	25.4	13.2	9.6	22.4
1958	8.6	5.1	12.5	6.6	21.1
1959	11.1	47.8	16.3	50.2	27.4
1960	9.6	4.5	17.4	28.2	27.0
1961	11.2	30.9	18.5	19.4	29.7
1962	11.4	11.8	15.9	−5.6	27.3
1963	15.3	52.1	16.9	19.0	32.2
1964	17.1	30.7	16.9	18.5	34.0
1965	16.0	3.6	19.9	29.9	35.9
1966	17.1	19.3	19.9	11.9	37.0
1967	17.7	19.5	22.3	29.5	40.0
1968	18.7	23.2	21.4	12.1	40.1
1969	21.4	33.0	24.8	34.3	46.2
1970	26.3	41.2	27.1	25.7	53.4
1971	31.4	39.1	28.2	21.0	59.6
1972	38.0	45.0	32.1	36.3	70.1
1973	41.9	42.8	35.6	43.9	77.5
1974	39.2	25.2	48.7	82.9	87.9
1975	34.5	−5.7	38.7	−14.7	73.2
1976	44.2	53.8	41.2	27.7	85.4
1977	43.3	14.6	39.5	12.0	82.8
1978	47.8	31.9	41.7	26.1	89.5
1979	49.1	23.6	45.1	30.5	94.2
1980	48.4	22.9	48.4	33.5	96.8
1981	47.4	16.5	44.5	9.4	91.9
1982	46.5	4.2	39.6	−5.5	86.1
1983	49.3	16.3	39.9	10.6	89.2
1984	53.4	19.8	38.6	7.0	92.0
1985	51.9	1.5	34.0	−7.9	85.9

Source: CEPD (1986). Columns 1, 3, 4 calculated from pp. 21 and 202; columns 2, 5 from p. 204.

tion and controlling inflation and its causes.

The arrival of generous American military and civilian aid after the outbreak of the Korean War in mid–1950 alleviated the sense of urgency. The state turned to corporatist means of ensuring its hegemonic position vis à vis society. The land reform, completed in 1953, distributed land to a peasant majority that had not agitated for it, then incorporated these peasants into a network of state-controlled farmers' associations. With American help, investments were made in the rural sector and agricultural production grew rapidly.

In the cold war environment, the United States needed a model of successful capitalist development as an alternative to Russian-backed Communist China, and through the predecessor to its Agency for International Development (AID, formally established in 1961), guided and helped the Nationalists in this effort (see chapters 6 and 7). One condition for aid was the promotion of a private sector. Beginning in the 1950s, the state was pressured to create a climate conducive to private capital investment and to divest itself of some of its enterprises in the light industrial sector. It retained those in the heavy and defense industries.

Nevertheless, by its continued control of upstream industry, fiscal instruments, and the disbursal of imported raw materials, the state ensured that the emerging bourgeoisie would be dependent on it and would be active in only certain sectors, such as textiles and food processing. The businessmen were mobilized to join the quasi-official Federation for the Promotion of Industry and Commerce, established in 1951, a further organizational means of incorporating them.

In the decade of the 1950s, growth occurred mainly in the highly protected import substitution industries of the consumer goods sector. Import substitution industrialization (ISI) was "horizontal" in that factories producing domestically needed goods developed across a broad front, but few industries had any depth. Except for small inputs from Overseas Chinese, all of the capital was invested by local businessmen. There was dependence on American financial help, raw materials, capital equipment, and advisers, but nearly all of the demand for the output was domestic. There was no dependent exchange relationship with a core country. The import of consumer goods was negligible. A bourgeoisie was emerging composed of a few favored mainlander emigres and a fast-growing Taiwanese component. But, as a class, it could not use political means to influence social relations: the state bureaucracy, not tied to the bourgeoisie but increasingly committed to capitalist development (helped by U.S. pressure in that direction), retained its hegemonic position and acted in the bourgeoisie's interests without allowing itself to become its instrument. One important way it served capitalist interests was repression of the emerging industrial proletariat, through the use of martial law and puppet unions.

In this increasingly stable environment, stimulated by American assistance and blocked from participation in politics, Chinese entrepreneurs—both Taiwanese and mainlander—scrambled to invest, and the economy grew.

Export-Oriented Industrialization, 1960–1973

Toward the end of the decade, the economy began to stagnate as the small domestic market was saturated. In addition, there were disincentives to export. To break this impasse, with much American insistence, the state decided to liberalize the economy by giving more scope to market forces, promoting the export of the original import substitution goods, and soliciting foreign investment in selected industries to help in diversification and deepening. While liberal in pushing exports, it maintained protectionist barriers around the domestic economy.

As AID retrenched in anticipation of Taiwan's "graduation" from official assistance, it solicited private lenders and investors to take its place. The dynamic for the economy thus shifted radically from internal demand and investment to external demand and direct foreign investment in new growth sectors. Not only did export demand account for a rapidly expanding percentage of Taiwan's industrial production, but, in addition, this trade was dominated by Japanese trading houses and American mass buyers instead of local merchants. This compounded the effects of export dependence, undermining the ability of local producers to respond effectively.

The first large foreign investors created an enclave exemplified by the Export Processing Zone (EPZ) at Kaohsiung. They employed cheap female labor to assemble imported parts for reexport. Taiwan's electronics export industry began this way. Smaller foreign investors entered joint ventures with local businessmen to leap tariff barriers and to spread risk. The export-fueled GNP shot upward, helped immeasurably by the fortuitous expansion in world trade. Local investors were not idle at this time; they also entered growth fields such as electronics, aggressively seeking Japanese partners, or, with state assistance, entered subcontracting relationships with large MNCs. It is important to emphasize that export-oriented industrialization (EOI) did not mean the end of ISI, but the evolution of a close relationship whereby local capital now produced largely for export the parts, components, and finished goods that were previously produced for domestic consumption. The state took the lead in opening new foreign markets, soliciting DFI, linking domestic and foreign capital, and fine-tuning the investment climate.

The result was a complex linkage between foreign and local investors, with nearly all of the domestic bourgeoisie "internationalized" to a greater or lesser degree. It was still not a triple alliance, but the foundation for one was in place: all three capitals were active and carving out spheres of influence. Local capital  was strongest in textiles, food processing, plastics, and other light industrial, low capital, labor-intensive sectors, including production of parts, components, and packaging for MNC assembly plants. MNCs dominated the electronics industry and were also strong in chemicals and machinery. The state continued to control upstream industries such as petroleum refining, and defense and infrastructure.

Capitalist relations of production dominated society. Even peasant families supplied part-time factory workers or themselves invested in industry. But the political sphere was still the preserve of the Nationalist regime, continuing to act in the interests of capital but not being controlled by it. Attempts by intellectuals to press the regime for reforms were handily squashed.

Export-Oriented Vertical Import Substitution, 1974-

The emergence of the triple alliance coincided with the beginning of a new phase of development in the early 1970s. Again, the economy had reached its limits as labor became scarce, infrastructure became outdated, export markets were restricted by quotas on cheap goods, and Taiwan faced increasing competition from other developing countries trying to copy its strategy. Compounding the economic impasse, the Republic of China on Taiwan became increasingly isolated diplomatically as the People's Republic of China on the mainland emerged from its self-imposed isolation.

Only at this stage did the state begin pushing for vertical ISI (something the Latin Americans had done without an intervening EOI stage) and accumulating foreign reserves and knowhow to support deepening. ISI was "vertical" in that it involved the addition of earlier and later stages of processing to industries established earlier. This push was symbolized by the Ten Major Construction Projects in both infrastructure (highway and airport construction, railroad expansion and electrification, nuclear power plants, port modernization) and industry (petrochemicals, steel, and shipbuilding). The state retained control over the former but sought investment by private local and foreign investors in the latter. The major objective was to integrate vertically all of Taiwan's leading export industries, and then upgrade them, increase value added, and expand into new sectors from this base. The petrochemical sector was targeted for major investment on the eve of the 1974 oil crisis. Some large local capitalists, producers of synthetic fibers and plastics in particular, wanted to integrate operations but needed foreign technical and capital participation. MNCs were eager to sell their knowhow and capture a share of Taiwan's huge indirect export market to third countries in synthetic fibers and plastics. Despite the oil crisis, the projects went ahead, with the state playing a larger role than originally intended. Another sector in which a triple alliance was attempted but fell apart due to conflict among the partners was automobiles.

Thus it was a case of both deepening and diversifying domestically by continuing to rely on external markets as the major stimulus for development, that is, simultaneous implementation of ISI and EOI. The state, following the Japanese example, also planned to slough off industries becoming uncompetitive internationally, such as low-end textiles, electronics, and footwear, and to direct investment from all three capitals into new sectors such as microelectronics and capital equipment. The first projects took shape in a new high-technology industrial park, located in Hsinchu, which was targeted as a locus for triple ventures in electronics, biotechnology, and other cutting edge sectors.

In the late 1970s, for the first time in three decades, Taiwanese social forces outside the KMT began to mobilize autonomously for political action, challenging the ethnic division of labor in which mainlanders dominated politics, Taiwanese the economy. The state employed repressive measures against these forces but at the same time, under Chiang Ching-kuo's leadership, recognized the necessity of bringing more Taiwanese into government at the higher levels and moving toward a more democratic form of participation. In late 1986, the KMT made several bold moves, including the announced termination of martial law after almost forty years, and permission to organize new political parties. Elections for ''national'' and local office became increasingly open and fair, but not to the point of actually threatening KMT hegemony.

Local Capital

Table 9.4 shows the structure of Taiwan's industrial sector: a small number of large firms in a sea of smaller ones. Does this mean the same thing as Evans's distinction between elite capital and the rest? I would contend that there are important differences. First, Taiwan's capitalists cannot be distinguished by whether or not they are ''internationalized.'' In an economy as trade dependent as Taiwan's, virtually all enterprises are involved in the international economy. As exporters, most of the small firms and many large conglomerates rely on foreign buyers and trading houses to handle their marketing; thus we cannot distinguish elite capitalists on the basis of controlling their own trade. Second, joint ventures with foreign capital are not the preserve of large corporations, as will be shown below. Triple ventures among local, foreign, and state capital are the preserve of large corporations, however, and we might cite this handful of firms as elite. Most of them have some political connection as well, setting them off from the rest of the class.

Finally, one cannot claim that Taiwan has a bourgeois fraction based on foreign consumption patterns. Strict control of imported consumer goods prevented such a fraction from developing in the 1950s, and the general rise in living standards and access to foreign items has been remarkably evenly distributed since then.

The following discussion refers mainly to the largest business groups, only some of which participate in triple alliances. However, the pattern and characteristics can be more widely generalized to other business groups and capitalists.

Taiwan's capitalists emerged under different conditions determined by the way in which the island's economy was being incorporated into the world system.[7] The inflation and chaos of the early 1950s permitted fortunes to be made by

Table 9.4

Manufacturing Enterprises by Number of Workers, Census Years

Number of workers per enterprise	1961 Enterprises	Workers	1966 Enterprises	Workers	1971 Enterprises	Workers
1-9	46,145	141,121	19,982	75,621	29,274	113,507
10-29	3,872	63,985	3,726	50,275	10,785	126,429
30-49	737	27,430	2,476	74,805	2,028	77,267
50-99	426	29,052	754	51,176	1,600	110,785
100-499	318	63,723	640	132,764	1,628	339,389
500 and over	69	128,961	131	205,019	321	434,162
All size classes	51,567	454,272	27,709	589,660	42,636	1,201,539

Source: Ho (1978a, 378).

speculation. But the biggest beneficiaries were a small cohort of textilers who brought some of their equipment to Taiwan from Shanghai, and a smaller group from Shantung, many of whom also entered flour milling once on Taiwan. The government rewarded the textilers for their loyalty through a policy of providing them with raw cotton (imported by the American aid agency and passed through the government) to spin and weave on consignment. The state supplied necessary funds and paid for the goods. By controlling raw materials, financing, and marketing, the state more or less eliminated competition and created a virtual no-risk environment for its friends. Although this policy lasted only a short time, it gave these entrepreneurs, such as Hsu Yu-hsiang (Far Eastern), Yen Ch'ing-ling (Tai-yuen), and Pao Ch'ao-yun (Chung-hsing), a head start in capital accumulation. The textile sector's strength is demonstrated by the fact that in 1976, 33 of the top 106 business groups had a textile firm at their core (CCIS 1976: 26). Many successfully diversified and upgraded production in the 1980s to deal with protectionism and loss of competitiveness, but others, the Shantungese in particular, failed to do so.

The second group of capitalists emerged via the land reform in 1953, when landlords were given shares of stock in four state enterprises (Taiwan Cement, Taiwan Pulp and Paper, Taiwan Industry and Mining, and Taiwan Agricultural and Forestry), in compensation for confiscation of their land. Only a few landlords became industrialists, however; most sold off the shares, believing them worthless. The latter two companies were really hodgepodges of small Japanese-era firms and were split up and sold separately to the highest bidder. The buyers were in only a few instances landlords; most were merchants, political figures, and mainlanders (see chapter 7). While many of the new owners sold off the assets for speculative gain, others, such as C. F. Koo (Taiwan Cement), T. T. Chao (petrochemicals, plastics), and Hsieh Ch'eng-yuan (Taiwan Pineapple), built on them in the favorable import substitution environment and became industrial magnates.

The U.S. aid mission's policy of seeking out potential entrepreneurs and setting them up in newly created pilot firms also started some capitalists on their way. The most famous example is Wang Yung-ch'ing, a former lumberyard owner who saw the potential of plastics while in Japan. With his mainlander partner, T. T. Chao, he took up an AID offer and began a polyvinyl chloride plant. Wang diversified into rayon, polyester, and petrochemicals and made extensive foreign investments near raw materials in the United States and elsewhere. He is now believed to be the richest man on Taiwan.

With the switch to export orientation and foreign investment, many older entrepreneurs, such as the textilers, joined with foreign buyers and Overseas Chinese merchants. Far Eastern Textile has been particularly aggressive in this. A new group of entrepreneurs came on the scene, made up of Taiwanese traders who, via technical cooperation agreements and joint ventures with Japanese firms they had represented, began to manufacture electronic goods for the local market, then for export. Hung Chien-ch'uan imported electrical products from Japan, becoming general agent for Matsushita. Through technical agreements and joint ventures, he built Matsushita Electric (Taiwan) into one of the island's largest conglomerates. Hung was considered little more than a front man for Japanese capital. On the other hand, Ch'en Mao-pang built up Taiwan Sharp in the same way, but broke with the Japanese and successfully promoted his own Sampo brand.

In the 1970s and 1980s, the government led a push for second-stage, export-oriented import substitution, especially in petrochemicals and microelectronics. Some new faces emerged, mostly the foreign-trained sons of successful businessmen. C. C. Hung's son, Richard, armed with a Ph.D. degree from Michigan State, entered semiconductors and upscale electronics, promoting his own Proton brand name abroad while also producing for foreign labels. Berkeley-trained Matthew Miao, son of a leading Shantung textile-petrochemical magnate, built a hugely successful computer firm, Mitac. This new group of entrepreneurs is eager to develop a local research and development (R&D) capability and to reduce dependence on imported technology. Many were recruited back to Taiwan from American corporations like Xerox and IBM to put their expertise to patriotic use.

Relations with MNCs have changed over time and vary by industry. In sectors where the local bourgeoisie easily dominates production, such as textiles or food processing, local firms rely on foreign trading companies and buyers for export. In the petrochemical and microelectronic sectors, relations are collaborative, often with the state as partner. MNCs supply capital and technology while the local partner supplies capital and downstream plants to purchase the output. Despite progress in local R&D, due in part to state help, there is still dependence on transferred technology, from Japan in particular.

The relationship between local firms and MNCs is most complex in the electronics sector. At first it was complementary, with Taiwanese producing parts for foreign assemblers, or collaborative, using joint ventures for the same ends. A few competed directly. But many local capitalists, especially those allied with small Japanese manufacturers backed by Japanese trading firms, found themselves tied into a web of contractual agreements that prevented their competing in the market or even handling their own procurement and marketing. The barriers to entry in domestic and international markets are so high that only a handful of Taiwan companies, such as Tatung and Proton, have been able to merchandise their goods under their own brand name. In contrast, large Korean companies, whose size and capital strength greatly exceed those of Taiwan's firms, have been better able to promote their own brand names. As a result, Korean brands such as Hyundai, Gold Star, and Samsung are now common household names in the United States.

One bargaining chip that local capitalists hold is their willingness to share the riskiness of long-term investments in Taiwan. More importantly, they own downstream plants making end products, so they are the major purchasers of the output of ventures in intermediate goods. Also, especially in the early days of import substitution, their very existence gave them some leverage with foreign (mostly Japanese) firms eager to penetrate the protected local market. Japanese also valued them as an entree with a government that had fought Japanese imperialism for fourteen years. As costs to MNCs of importing parts from abroad increased, the existence of local suppliers also gave leverage to domestic firms, though most relationships between local and foreign firms are not formal joint ventures.

As regards the state, the local bourgeoisie remains in a decidedly subordinate position. Although it has its own professional associations and consciousness of itself as a class, it has little direct influence on policy formation, and most contact with the government is in the form of receiving instructions. The technocrats in the state apparatus claim to be solicitous of the needs and interests of the capitalist class, but the capitalists do not see it that way. There is virtually none of the interchange of personnel between them such as is seen in Japan. During the economic downturn of 1985, with business confidence further shaken by a scandal involving the high-flying Cathay conglomerate and several high officials, Premier Yu Kuo-hua appointed an Economic Revitalization Committee of business leaders, academics, and technocrats to suggest ways out of the impasse. Its pious proposals were ignored, in part due to the global recovery late in the year that rendered concerted action unnecessary, at least for the short run. In the mid–1980s the state wants to upgrade the industrial structure and close down noncompetitive sectors. This represents a threat to a sizable segment of the bourgeoisie, large and small. Fearing economic disaster and potential political upheaval, the state has gone slow in acting on this plan.

Although its trade associations can approach the government on economic matters, the bourgeoisie has no political organizations at its disposal, and most businessmen do not dare become involved in politics directly. The KMT nominated a scion of the Taiwanese-owned Cathay conglomerate for the Legislative Yuan in 1983. Subsequent revelations of corruption involving Cathay and certain officials confirmed to many people that business and politics should remain separate. The state's firm control of economic and legal levers effectively deters local entrepreneurs from nonconformist behavior, as do still vivid memories of the 1947 massacre. Fear of being too visible inhibits their growing beyond a certain size, thus compromising their international competitiveness.

The capitalists' main bargaining leverage with the state comes from their role as big employers and earners of foreign exchange. Their links with the MNCs help tie Taiwan into the world system and ensure a continued international identity. Capitalists have a certain amount of bargaining power due to heavy borrowing from state banks. Good examples are Tatung and Hualong, two companies whose near collapse threatened the health of the economy as well as state banks. The intimate political relations between their chairmen and the Nationalist party played a role in their receiving bailouts. If Taiwan is to be an anti-Communist alternative, it must have a private sector. But the Nationalist state's inherent distrust of capitalists (and Taiwanese) is a fundamental contradiction that means that the state must support them even as it controls them.

The bourgeoisie's role in local accumulation centers on its ability to earn foreign exchange both through direct exports and through supplying MNCs and thereby increasing local value added. Though it is subordinate to the other two actors, it is an essential element in Taiwan's economic and social development. The entrepreneurial spirit of the entire society provides a limitless supply of people willing to risk capital in business ventures. The large size of the petty bourgeoisie and state restrictions on capital concentration have helped distribute wealth throughout the society.

Foreign Capital

After the Japanese withdrew there was a hiatus when there was no foreign investment to speak of. Not until the mid-1960s was there activity on this front; it then rapidly gained momentum. Tables 9.5 and 9.6 demonstrate that there have been three main sources of foreign investment, most of which has gone into manufacturing. There are major differences in the behavior of the three investors. These differences have played a critical role in shaping Taiwan's dependent development.

Americans

The American investors in Taiwan include some of the nation's largest corporations, such as RCA, General Instruments, Texas Instruments, Ford, National

Table 9.5

Private Foreign and Overseas Chinese Investment Approvals
Unit: U.S. $1,000

	(1) Total		(2) Overseas Chinese	(3)	(4) Foreign subtotal	(5)	(6) U.S.A.	(7)	(8) Japan	(9)	(10)
	Cases	Amount	Cases	Amount	Cases	Amount	Cases	Amount	Cases	Amount	% of GDCF
1952	5	1,067	5	1,067	—	—	—	—	—	—	0.5
1953	14	3,695	12	1,654	2	2,041	1	1,881	1	160	1.6
1954	8	2,220	3	128	5	2,092	3	2,028	1	14	0.9
1955	5	4,599	3	176	2	4,423	2	4,423	—	—	1.8
1956	15	3,493	13	2,484	2	1,009	2	1,009	—	—	1.6
1957	14	1,622	10	1,574	4	48	1	11	3	37	0.6
1958	9	2,518	6	1,402	3	1,116	—	—	3	1,116	0.8
1959	2	965	—	820	2	145	1	100	1	45	0.4
1960	14	15,473	6	1,135	8	14,338	5	14,029	3	309	4.5
1961	29	14,304	24	8,340	5	5,964	1	4,288	3	1,301	4.1
1962	36	5,203	10	1,660	26	3,543	8	738	16	2,664	4.9
1963	38	18,050	22	7,703	16	10,347	9	8,734	6	1,397	4.7
1964	41	19,897	28	8,007	13	11,890	7	10,196	2	728	4.0
1965	66	41,610	30	6,470	36	35,140	17	31,104	14	2,081	6.4
1966	103	29,281	51	8,377	52	20,904	15	17,711	35	2,447	4.0

Year											
1967	212	57,006	105	18,340	107	38,666	18	15,714	76	15,947	6.2
1968	325	89,894	203	36,449	122	53,445	20	34,555	96	14,855	7.9
1969	201	109,437	90	27,499	111	81,938	30	27,862	75	17,379	8.9
1970	151	138,896	80	29,731	71	109,165	16	67,816	51	28,530	9.4
1971	130	162,956	86	37,808	44	125,148	18	43,736	18	12,400	11.3
1972	166	126,656	114	26,466	52	100,190	17	37,307	26	7,728	7.0
1973	351	248,854	201	55,166	150	193,688	29	66,876	92	44,599	8.9
1974	168	189,376	85	80,640	83	108,736	21	38,760	50	38,901	3.6
1975	85	118,175	44	47,235	41	70,940	12	41,165	22	23,234	2.5
1976	98	141,519	53	39,487	45	102,032	8	21,767	26	30,760	2.5
1977	102	163,909	52	68,723	50	95,186	17	24,242	20	24,145	2.7
1978	116	212,929	50	76,210	66	136,719	18	69,765	43	50,336	2.7
1979	113	328,835	50	147,352	63	181,483	19	80,375	39	50,462	3.0
1980	110	465,964	39	222,584	71	243,380	15	110,093	35	86,081	3.3
1981	105	395,757	32	39,463	73	356,294	25	203,213	27	64,623	2.8
1982	132	380,006	50	59,720	82	320,286	33	79,606	24	152,164	3.2
1983	149	404,468	49	29,086	100	375,382	35	93,294	33	196,770	3.5
1984	174	558,741	74	39,770	100	518,971	41	231,175	28	113,978	4.5
1985	174	702,460	67	41,757	107	660,703	42	332,760	32	145,236	6.5
Total	3,471	5,159,835	1,747	1,174,483	1,724	3,985,352	505	1,716,333	900	1,130,427	—

Note: "Europeans" and "Others" not included.
Sources: Cols. 1-9, CEPD (1986, 262, 264); col. 10, Ranis (1979, 250) through 1974, then calculated from CEPD (1986, 44, 262).

Table 9.6

Statistics on Overseas Chinese and Foreign Investment by Industry and Area, 1952-1985

Unit: U.S. $1,000

Industry	Total		Overseas Chinese		Foreign total	
	Cases	Amount	Cases	Amount	Cases	Amount
Agriculture and forestry	17	3,265	15	3,163	2	102
Fishery and animal husbandry	58	23,685	50	16,829	8	6,856
Food and beverage processing	167	136,077	103	50,715	64	83,362
Textile	292	164,019	193	100,953	99	63,066
Pulp paper and products	48	28,375	32	12,730	16	15,645
Chemicals	608	922,180	249	88,045	359	834,135
Nonmetallic mineral products	168	359,695	98	288,903	70	70,792
Basic metals and metal products	323	349,862	88	19,914	235	329,948
Machinery equipment and instrument	209	502,635	51	31,209	158	471,426
Electronic and electric products	544	1,520,812	121	39,474	423	1,481,338
Construction of buildings	161	105,486	153	94,498	8	10,988
Foreign trade	173	24,067	169	11,667	4	12,400
Banking and insurance	60	232,894	21	82,283	39	150,611
Transportation	75	59,432	68	51,367	7	8,065
Services	232	595,727	133	227,284	99	368,443
Other	336	131,624	203	55,449	133	76,175

Source: TSDB (1986, 265).

Distillers, and Gulf Oil. Although in the 1950s there were some joint ventures with state enterprises, American DFI began mainly in the mid–1960s. It was encouraged by the U.S. government, which sought to use MNCs to replace AID, thereby ensuring the survival and viability of a non-Communist Chinese model of development. The most common motive for MNCs was to recapture U.S. market share in certain goods, such as consumer electronics, which was being lost to cheap Japanese imports. In addition to labor that was only a fraction of the cost of U.S. labor, Taiwan offered incentives for DFI with few restrictions, at the very time that Latin American nations were beginning to enforce regulations and controls on American MNCs.

The American MNCs' move to Taiwan represented an oligopolistic reaction, as major producers jumped on the bandwagon to cut costs in order to remain competitive. This is very clear in the television industry, where, within three years, Sylvania-Philco (1966), Admiral (1967), RCA (1967), Motorola (1969), and Zenith (1970) opened assembly plants. In due course many of their suppliers also set up manufacturing facilities to retain their customers.

From tables 9.5 and 9.6 one can see the relatively large size of individual U.S. investments. Through 1985, U.S. cases represented 14.5 percent of the total but 33 percent of the capital. This represented 29 percent of approved cases and 43 percent of capital of non-Overseas Chinese foreign investment. The average American investment was U.S $3.39 million. Most of the investments are wholly owned subsidiaries with initial capital supplied by the parent firm.

American MNCs came to Taiwan to take advantage of the low-cost labor, thus it is natural that production technology is labor intensive. The actual products were developed at R&D facilities at headquarters, but engineers on Taiwan, local and expatriate, carry on research to improve production efficiency.

With the exception of suppliers who make intermediate components for assemblage in other American subsidiaries on the island, most American MNCs export their finished products back to the U.S. market for which they were initially designed. Until the 1980s, those who sold in the restricted domestic market were generally producers of chemical products used in agriculture or the plastics industry, that is, not makers of consumer goods. There are several cases of indigenous enterprises marketing locally goods made on Taiwan under license from an American corporation, most notably in the garment industry. For example, Far Eastern Textile manufactures Manhattan shirts and BVD underwear. Starting in the 1980s, American fast-food companies began operating in Taiwan. Some, such as MacDonalds, were extremely successful. They stimulated other American firms to try their luck and spawned local competitors as well. Other service-sector industries, such as insurance and transport, entered the market in the mid–1980s. American banks and volume buyers (such as K-Mart) have long played a very important role, even though the size of their investment may be small.

Japanese

The Japanese corporations with investments in Taiwan are much more diverse than their American counterparts. At one extreme are large corporations such as SONY, Sharp, Matsushita, Hitachi, and Teijin. But the majority are small and medium-size enterprises that are subcontractors and suppliers to the giants at home.

The smaller, specialized firms set up manufacturing plants abroad to continue to serve their customers at home. However, unlike the haphazard bandwagon sequence followed by American firms, their migration has been part of a national strategy. Led by the Ministry of International Trade and Industry (MITI), Japan's postwar economic growth has proceeded through several stages, characterized by cooperation and consensus between government and business. By the early 1970s, Japan faced several obstacles to continued rapid growth: labor shortages, high wages and other costs, lack of available land, concern for pollution, appreciation of the yen and sizable foreign exchange reserves, quotas in export markets, a challenge from revived American manufacturers, and competition in certain goods from Taiwan and South Korea, which had successfully copied Japan's experience. To solve these problems, MITI developed a strategy that was a commitment to the product life cycle: labor-intensive, technologically simple parts of light industries would move to areas with abundant low-cost labor; polluters and raw material guzzlers would go to countries with lax environmental protection codes and abundant natural resources. The home islands would concentrate on capital- and knowledge-intensive clean industries, as well as R&D.

Taiwan's function in this global strategy was to give small and medium manufacturers in declining industries a new lease on life. Taiwan was selected over other possible sites for such reasons as its proximity; a nostalgia on Taiwan for Japanese culture (which is much less evident in another former colony, Korea; see chapter 12); and the bilingualism and familiarity with Japanese customs and business practices among older Taiwanese, a great help to the small-time Japanese entrepreneurs who were suddenly going global.

Being small at home, Japanese companies also maintained small investments in Taiwan. Although Japanese investments accounted for 52 percent of the non-Overseas Chinese foreign cases, they represented only 28 percent of foreign capital, 26 percent of total foreign cases, and 22 percent of total capital. The average investment was U.S. $1.25 million. This represents a rapid increase in size over time, as the upward evaluation of the yen, combined with Japan's industrial restructuring, pushed a number of larger firms to Taiwan.

Most Japanese investments in Taiwan, especially those for Taiwan's domestic market, are joint ventures with local entrepreneurs. Japanese capital commitment may be low, but in the agreement the Japanese partners commonly reserve powers of control for themselves and require the new venture to import equipment and materials from the parent company in Japan. Because of the often tense state of Taiwan-Japan relations, having a local partner is wise politically for the Japanese investor. The large firms are quite capable of bringing in their own capital, but the smaller enterprises must rely on Japan's mammoth general trading companies (*sogo shosha*) for assistance of all sorts.

At home, too, these trading companies, many of which are the descendants of the prewar zaibatsu, assist small and large firms at every stage of the production process: raw material procurement, provision of working capital, distribution, and marketing. When MITI encouraged the small firms to invest abroad, they naturally turned to the trading companies for advice and assistance. Many of the investments are joint ventures between the Japanese firm and a trading company that maintains the same basic relationship, only now on a global scale: wherever practicable, the trading company will import Japanese components to Taiwan for further processing, and then export them back to Japan if further work is needed and the facilities still exist there. The objective is to retain as much value added for Japan as possible, going abroad to cut corners only at certain necessary stages. One reason a high-visibility joint venture between Toyota, local capital, and the state-owned China Steel collapsed in 1984 was the question of the proportion of locally produced parts the Chinese state demanded.

The production technology used by Japanese-invested firms tends to be labor intensive. Product development is almost always kept at home. Even in joint ventures with local entrepreneurs that involve technology licensing, the Japanese tend to keep the key elements secret. Electronics and pharmaceuticals are frequently cited examples of this practice.

The Japanese firms are diverse in their target markets. Whereas U.S. MNCs mainly export finished goods to the home market for which they were designed, Japanese consumer goods are inherently more suitable to Taiwan (or other Asian) consumers' tastes, or are adapted to become so. Examples are electronics, motorcycles, and foodstuffs. Many other consumer products are exported to markets all over the world. Components and intermediates are destined for assemblage in other factories in Taiwan, Japan, or one of several other offshore locations. The trading companies also play a major role in third-country trade from Taiwan, even if no other Japanese firms are involved.

Overseas Chinese

The Nationalist government designates as "Overseas Chinese" those persons of Chinese descent residing outside Taiwan. In the several countries of Southeast Asia they have played a role analogous to the Jews of Europe: denied full participation in the political and social life of the nations where they reside, they channeled their energies into economic activities.

Those who invest in Taiwan represent a range from large corporations to small merchants. The motives behind their investments in Taiwan go beyond purely economic ones. Hounded at home by governments committed to putting economic power in the hands of the ethnic majority, they wish to invest in a more supportive environment. Many Southeast Asian nations are politically and socially unstable, and the threat of anti-Chinese pogroms is constant, especially in Indonesia and Malaysia. Taiwan offers greater stability and a higher caliber, if more costly, work force. Many investors come from Hong Kong, seeing Taiwan as preferable to the colony's own investment environment. A final reason is purely political: the Overseas Chinese are an object of aggressive propaganda by both the Taipei and Peking regimes, which desire their loyalty and financial support as well as influence with their home states. Since the early 1980s Peking, like Taipei, has been creating a battery of incentives to solicit their DFI, in direct competition with Taiwan. It has adopted Special Economic Zones, tax holidays, and other benefits. Most capital has come from Hong Kong Chinese who seek political insurance against Hong Kong's 1997 return to Chinese sovereignty.

The size of Overseas Chinese investments in Taiwan is generally small. Through 1985, they had invested in 50 percent of the cases but only 23 percent of the capital, an average of U.S. $672,285 each. Nearly three-quarters of their investments are joint ventures. Since the 1950s when they were the main foreign investors, many Overseas Chinese "investors" have been little more than front men for local businessmen. By having an Overseas Chinese attached to it, a project receives certain financial incentives and clout with local officials. Its backers also can repatriate profits, a convenient way for nervous indigenous entrepreneurs to get capital out of Taiwan to a safer, longer-term haven. Overseas Chinese bring in some funds but also rely on local sources, both institutional and private.

Overseas Chinese investments are concentrated in the light industrial and service or speculative sectors (such as construction and real estate), where Taiwan's own capitalists are active. They are thus direct competitors. Coming in many cases from countries less developed than Taiwan, they contribute little in the way of advanced technology, either in the goods they make or in manufacturing techniques.

The environment for foreign investment activities on Taiwan has changed markedly over time. In the unsettled and restrictive conditions up to the late 1950s, AID-sponsored projects and speculative Overseas Chinese investments were the bulk of DFI. During the fifteen years of AID activity, the U.S. aid mission, in close concert with the top echelons of the state, established a pattern of dependence on the United States for capital, technology, markets, and business ideology among a segment of the bourgeoisie and state. Japanese firms began to appear when domestic Japanese constraints on capital outflow were relaxed, and as the Nationalist government urged local producers to enter into technical cooperation agreements. Cultural and business ties of long duration influenced the Taiwanese segment of the bourgeoisie to seek Japanese partners who were also more accustomed to a subcontract-based business strategy.

Currency, legal, and bureaucratic reforms of 1958–60, urged and partly designed by American advisers, stimulated increased investments from abroad. The decisions to create an electronics sector and an EPZ, both on American counsel, sparked the greatest inflow of capital.

One sees a variety of MNC-local capital relations, but in general they are characterized by asymmetry. One example is trade, where American buyers or the large Japanese trading houses dominate Taiwan's global marketing. Another example is supply relations, such as electronics, where local firms provide parts for foreign assemblers. In actual joint ventures, locals investing with Japanese generally find themselves in a dependent relationship, even if they are the majority partner. American joint ventures usually are with very large firms and characterized by a less lopsided relationship.

The state has continuously revised statutes for encouraging foreign investment and tried to channel it into certain sectors (see chapter 10). In 1984, favored sectors included certain types of heavy machinery, automobile parts, and computer-related hardware and software. The state and MNCs received a shock in 1985 when citizens of Lukang spontaneously organized to protest Dupont's plans to put a $160 million titanium dioxide plant in their backyard. The authorities had to table the application, reflecting new popular concern over the heavily polluted environment.

The state's strategy of upgrading Taiwan's industrial structure away from the no longer viable labor-intensive, low-technology industries conflicts with the objectives of MNCs that went to Taiwan for just those things in the first place. This is especially true with the Japanese, who are implementing a similar strategy at home. The state is trying to increase local value added, which also conflicts with Japanese strategy. It is having more success, however, in getting Americans to buy locally and to invest in high-technology upstream operations.

Through direct investments, procurement of parts, or marketing of locally manufactured goods, MNCs have assisted Taiwan in finding and occupying a niche in the international economic system. In the process, they have cooperated in gearing production on Taiwan to the demands of that system. Their contribution to accumulation in Taiwan has come more from trade and subcontracting than actual DFI.

Taiwan's international balance of payments position is excellent, so MNCs do not derive leverage from their ability to bring in capital. Their bargaining position is based more on their control of technology that Taiwan needs to upgrade its industry, and of markets to absorb Taiwan's output. But the greatest element in their package is that they contribute another tie between Taiwan as an entity and other entities with legitimacy in international affairs. The MNC offices have taken the place of embassies on the island. As the PRC began to solicit DFI and other relations with MNCs, many of them closed or scaled down their Taiwan operations or utilized dummy corporations to participate in what they hoped would be an economic bonanza on the mainland. As these hopes have dwindled and the PRC has adopted a conciliatory posture toward Taiwan, seeing MNCs as a form of bridge, many MNCs have become very active on both sides of the Taiwan Straits. In the 1980s, Taiwan has faced crises of a post-Chiang transition and Communist pressure to reunify. Many local businessmen have been loath to make the investments necessary for the state-planned upgrading. MNC percentage of gross domestic capital formation increased as a result, as foreigners demonstrated more confidence in Taiwan's future than did its own people.

The State and State Capital

The state[8] has been the key actor in shaping Taiwan's dependent development: it has created a stable investment climate, devised indicative plans and through them selected priority industries for special treatment, and invested itself through its own enterprises and joint ventures. It thus combines features of the Brazilian state in its direct participation in accumulation, with features of the Japanese state in its aggressive application of "administrative guidance" to shape development.[9]

This is a potent combination, but it is not unique to Taiwan. It derives its particular efficacy there from the nature of state-society relations (Gold 1986b). The Nationalist state cannot be reduced to a structure of class domination based on a capitalist economic system. It did not emerge from within Taiwanese society, nor is it a response to economic or political struggles there. The Nationalist state came to the island full blown with its army, bureaucracy, and technocrats but no base in Taiwanese society. By a textbook application of revolution from above[10] it eliminated real or potential enemies (community leaders, intelligentsia, landlords) and incorporated other social forces (peasants, workers, and capitalists). There was a radical separation of economy and policy enforced by martial law, one-party dominance, secret police, and rule of the island by two levels of bureaucracy: the mainlander-monopolized national government of the Republic of China, where real power lies, and the Taiwan provincial government and below, where Taiwanese do have increasing say over a circumscribed range of issues. The cohesiveness of the political elite, at least externally, has been a unique feature of the regime. Chiang Kai-shek was able to eliminate the various factions and cliques that helped ruin him on the mainland and build a solid core of loyalists who, in a hostile domestic and international environment, banded together to support economic construction for the ultimate purpose of mainland recovery. The political impetus underlying industrial policy in this threatened garrison state should not be underestimated. Even more remarkable has been effective civilizan control of the military, at least by the Chiangs, something Korea has yet to achieve. Chiang Ching-kuo's rise involved removing many of his father's supporters, but it was generally done behind the scenes without attracting great public attention (see chapter 8).

Taiwanese have wide scope for economic activity as long as it is not perceived as threatening to the state or social stability, and entrepreneurs do not engage in political activity. Rumors of examples of businessmen who have become too visible and independent and then were whittled down by the state serve as a disincentive. Further, the 1947 events (see chapter 3) are still deep in the Taiwanese collective unconscious.

Aware of its competition across the Taiwan Straits and the reasons why it lost power there, the Nationalist regime adopted a policy of growth with stability to prevent a recurrence of the rampant and uncontrollable inflation of the 1940s.

Taiwan has a free-enterprise economy within a larger state-dominated economy. The state controls most of the economic levers, the financial system in particular (Wade 1985), and has several means of extracting surplus for its own use. It plays such a large role in the economy for several reasons: its bureaucrat-capitalist heritage from the mainland; its confiscation of Japanese enterprises in 1946; and its control of large amounts of capital for projects that private investors cannot undertake. The National Father Sun Yat-sen laid the legitimate groundwork for a major economic role for the state and restriction of private capital in his theoretical writings, the Three Principles of the People.

The state can use a variety of levers to guide the economy. Its fiscal powers of taxation, rebates, foreign exchange, and special loans are one set of means. Through its control of banking it also influences investment decisions. It owns several key upstream and infrastructural enterprises, such as China Petroleum, Taiwan Power, and BES Engineering. Finally, by formulating plans, it selects sectors for special assistance.

Through the 1950s and 1960s, the state divested itself of many enterprises and directed its efforts at improving the investment climate for local and foreign private business, writing plans, and promoting trade and foreign investment. The recession of the mid–1970s and commitment of its prestige to the successful completion of the Ten Major Construction Projects brought it back into direct economic activity. In the 1980s it promoted a new set of similar projects. As local private investment tapered off and capital fled abroad, the state (and MNCs) filled the gap.

The state's basic strategy for local accumulation has been to broker Taiwan into a niche in the world capitalist system that would ensure a constant flow of capital, stimulate industrial development, and increase foreign exchange earnings. This was not easy. Unlike the less developed countries of Latin America, Africa, and Southeast Asia, Taiwan had almost no exploitable natural resources that would lure foreign investors and give the state a handle on them. Its tea, rice, and sugar were not vital to the survival of the West. Taiwan's only resource was its abundant, low-cost, literate, trainable, and disciplined labor force. As rising production costs in the West and Japan reduced their competitiveness, and as companies developed global production strategies and capabilities, Taiwan's comparative advantage in cheap labor, plus a battery of other incentives, became lures for MNCs. The state's bargaining chip was its ability to provide labor, political and social stability, a responsive bureaucracy, and financial incentives.

As Taiwan faces protectionist markets and competition from lower-cost developing countries following its example, the state's technocrats must keep seeking
new products and processes to ensure survival. The state has discouraged foreign
investment in traditional export sectors and developed incentives to promote new
ones, microelectronics and machinery in particular.

It must convince investors in high-technology and capital-intensive industries
that Taiwan has something to offer them that they cannot get at home. Labor is
still relatively cheap for the quality, but the main effort is going into building
local R&D capacity, improving the quality of suppliers, and trying to develop the
island as a place to transship goods and services from the core to less developed
countries. Instead of cheap laborers, Taiwan now advertises cheap engineers.
Efforts are under way in the mid–1980s to develop offshore banking as a way of
luring financial houses from Hong Kong, which is destined for Communist
control.

To advance these goals, Taiwan is using the usual tax incentives plus the new
Hsinchu Science and Industry Park, which combines the economic benefits of an
EPZ and ultramodern R&D facilities (see chapter 10). It is also willing to invest
as a partner where needed. The state is constrained in this upgrading, however, by
the reality that it cannot push MNCs too far. It cannot be too "nationalistic"
because it is not a nation in the eyes of most of the world. As the Nationalist state
retrenches from its unchallenged dominance over society, replacing martial law
and a one-party system with more pluralistic electoral politics and feisty institutions, its ability to mobilize society and ensure a stable investment climate will be
compromised. The opposition Democratic Progressive party, established in late
1986, favors business and foreign investment, which may smooth the transition to
a new generation of political and business leaders.

Conclusion

This analysis has shown that dependent development on Taiwan resulted from the
dynamic interaction of state, multinational, and local capital pursuing their own
interests. In Evans's model (1979, 38), when MNCs begin production in a
developing economy, their interest in low wages, income concentration to provide a market for their products, technology transfer and reliance on external
suppliers results in several forms of "disarticulation." In particular, their capital-intensive technology excludes a large portion of the working class from the
modern sector, and only a tiny elite segment of the bourgeoisie can ally with them.
Their dependence on imported materials prevents the development of linkages
with domestic suppliers and fabricators. They market goods designed for core
country consumers, and thus promote a class fraction divorced from local production and tastes.

Taiwan has not experienced these adverse effects from MNC penetration.
There are several explanations for this, but the key variable is likely to be the

structure of the triple alliance itself, wherein the Nationalist state is much stronger than Brazil's and the other two partners are much weaker.

It was shown that, unlike the Brazilian state, the Nationalist state was implanted from outside and did not represent the political expression of domestic economic relations. The autonomous, militarized, ideological Nationalist state preceded, shaped, and dominated social forces, removing politics from society's agenda, but providing numerous other channels for mobility and status. It created a political environment for economic development and for three decades did not allow emerging economic interests to influence social relations through the political process. Its ideological commitment to social equality, substantial investment in compulsory free education, support of medium and small enterprises and family farms, prevention of the reemergence of large landowners, and disincentives to capital concentration resulted in an admirable record of income distribution (see chapter 4).

For society's part, a fifty-year tradition of repression by outsiders in Taiwan plus the ethnic (mainlander/Taiwanese) division of labor, backed by state power, facilitated acceptance of this situation. Upward mobility through educational and economic achievement stimulated Taiwanese participation in business. Their entrepreneurial skills—especially in mobilizing family capital and talent—and responsiveness to perceived opportunities for gain cannot be ignored (see chapter 11). The state's role was crucial but should not be overemphasized. Visible economic success helped dampen potential political disaffection, as did the common acceptance of the need to unite against a Communist threat. This also helped retard the development of proletarian class consciousness and gave repressed workers a sense of a stake in the system.

Beyond this, the party and state elite was notable for its internal cohesion. Chastened by the humiliating loss of the mainland and determined to build a counterexample to the Soviet-backed People's Republic of China, and as it became clear that the stay on Taiwan would be open-ended, Chiang Kai-shek promoted an extraordinarily able cohort of economic technocrats and accepted their advice. These men, while closely tied to American advisers and free-enterprise ideology, quietly applied the Japanese state-led developmentalist model. Their decisions to invest in agriculture and delay going directly from horizontal to vertical ISI helped Taiwan avoid the bankruptcy in the countryside and crippling debt burden characteristic of most Third World economies.

Over the ensuing decades, the developmental state, through direct economic instruments as well as suitable policies whose successful implementation was backed by its hegemonic position vis à vis society, mediated the domestic effects of external dependency. It provided stability and hence predictability, aided the bourgeoisie, restricted MNCs and linked them to the local industrial structure, and invested its own capital to promote development. Development has increasingly mitigated many of the more repressive aspects of state domination. With development, the state has shifted its base of legitimacy to economic performance, an improved standard of living and distribution societywide, and, in the 1980s, meaningful political participation by all citizens, including Taiwanese.

Much of the state's success at mediating the domestic effects of MNC activity derives from the place of Taiwan in MNC strategy. First, their presence was discontinuous, allowing the state and local capital to establish an industrial foundation in the interim years 1946–1965. Because MNCs came to Taiwan primarily to take advantage of cheap labor and inputs, their labor-intensive technology was easily absorbed. Though starting as an enclave, they gradually developed backward and forward linkages with local capital to cut costs further. American MNCs exported their goods while Japanese and Overseas Chinese companies sold standardized mass-consumption items appealing to Asian consumers on Taiwan. The state rigidly controlled the import of consumer goods. These controls helped Taiwan avoid the emergence of a stratum based on foreign or luxury consumption patterns.

Taiwan's experience is based on the combination of too many fortuitous events to be taken as a model for Third World development. But it does illustrate alternatives to dependency besides autonomy and state socialism, neither of which is a proven panacea or viable for Taiwan. The PRC's abandonment of self-reliance and total planning, and redefinition of socialism to include many crucial aspects of the Taiwan experience, provide additional testimony. The main practical lessons Taiwan offers are the possibilities deriving from building on what one has, correct analysis of domestic and international forces, and manipulation of these to one's own benefit.

In terms of theory, Taiwan not only provides another counterexample to early dependency theory, but also raises questions about key assumptions in Evans's model. The major one is the weights assigned to the three members of the alliance. While going beyond theorists of underdevelopment and granting some freedom of maneuver to the state and bourgeoisie, Evans grants too much power to MNCs. The experience of Taiwan raises doubts about MNCs as a generic type, a "logic" of MNC strategies, and the unimportance of cultural variables. It is true that the state on Taiwan is off the scale as far as relative autonomy from class forces is concerned. Taiwan illustrates, however, the potential of a well-integrated and committed developmental state, staffed by competent personnel, to seek out opportunities within the world system and successfully mediate between domestic and global forces to attain maximum benefit.

As a consequence of analyzing Taiwan within the framework of Evans's radical theory, I have largely neglected culture and other factors that are central to the "conservative" orientation (see chapter 2). As some of the other chapters in this volume indicate (chapters 8, 11, and 13), Taiwan and the other East Asian NICs raise once again the question of the role of culture and individual variables—the meat and potatoes of modernization theory—in development. It is necessary to reconsider such normative and structural variables as family, the self as a member of a network of personal relations, education, and authoritarian political culture and tie them with a society's material conditions. This should be done dialectically, linking these conservative factors with the real insights of radical dependency scholarship, to analyze the multiple ways in which external and internal factors interact. Culture provides a set of orientations and strategies for action (Swidler 1986) in response to opportunites and constraints presented by external actors (MNCs, armies, missionaries) and internal ones (authoritarian regimes, access to education, freedom to establish an enterprise). By linking culture to opportunities and constraints, it is possible to avoid national stereotypes, reductionism, and ideological preconceptions.

Notes

1. For overviews of the field, see Gereffi (1983), Taylor (1979), and Valenzuela and Valenzuela (1978).

2. Marion Levy (1953) is a seminal example. More recently, Levy and a team of scholars produced a major work explicitly in the modernization tradition. See Rozman (1981).

3. See, for example, Chang (1968), Galenson (1979), Ho (1978a), Kuo (1983), Li (1976), and Lin (1973).

4. See Gold (1981) for details. Hsiao (1981) was among the first to apply a world systems perspective to Taiwan, focusing on the rural sector. Also, see Crane (1982). Barrett and Whyte (1982) offer a test of the claims of dependency theory against Taiwan. Amsden (1979) and Liu (1975) are early examples of the use of political economy to analyze Taiwan.

5. Gold (1986a) discusses these indicators in more detail. He adopts Cardoso and Faletto's (1979) "historical-structural method" to analyze Taiwan's development.

6. See Gold (1986a) for a discussion.

7. Scholars have only recently begun a study of Taiwan's capitalist class. For a recent promising start, see Numazaki (1986).

8. Amsden (1979; 1985) and Wade (1984; 1985) discuss the role of the state in Taiwan's development, somewhat to the neglect of the other actors discussed here.

9. See the definitive discussion in Johnson (1982).

10. Discussed in Trimberger (1973).

10

Denis Fred Simon

TECHNOLOGY TRANSFER AND NATIONAL AUTONOMY

The mechanisms for technology transfer are as varied as the agents. This variation depends upon the type of technology. . . . It depends in part upon the agent undertaking technology transfer. Is it a firm, a government agency, non-profit, or university? The firm has the ability of using technology at a new site for productive purposes, whereas the government agency or foundation may not be producers. Hence, the firm has options for technology transfer that are not open to other agents. Finally, it depends on the capability of the recipient of the technology to be transferred (a capability which also influences the choice of technology to be transferred). A capable recipient has all options; a recipent that lacks the capability is restricted. (Stewart and Nihei 1987, 10)

Technology Transfer: External Constraints versus Internal Initiative

Harnessing science and technology to serve the needs of national development has been a high-priority goal on the agenda of both the industrialized and developing nations. One of the more pervasive features of the current global system of science and technology, however, has been the persistence and seemingly self-reinforcing nature of a "technology gap" between the developed nations of the North and the developing nations of the South. Yet, while most developing countries are critical of the existing system, they continue to profess their faith in the efficacy of science and technology (S&T) for achieving both economic and political objectives. Among these objectives are greater export competitiveness, increasing vertical mobility in the international division of labor, generating employment, and enhancing the relative status of developing countries vis à vis the industrialized nations. Thus, technology-related issues are of great political significance for the Third World (Marton 1987). Accordingly, it is not surprising to find much of the debate over the creation of a "new international economic order'' in the late 1970s and 1980s focused on how to reconstruct the global science and technology system to better serve the needs of the Third World.

While technology has been a major issue for Third World political leaders, for scholars too it has been the center of much recent debate, especially in the 1970s. The current debate has been sparked, in large part, by the arguments of the radical dependency school. Referring to Latin America, advocates of the dependency view contended that the underdevelopment and technological dependence of the Third World are inextricably related to the growth of the industrialized core (Wilber 1979). Inasmuch as modern technology is needed for development, and modern technology is generated and monopolized by the core, the periphery is in a position of structural weakness vis à vis the core. Not only does the periphery lack the information necessary to make appropriate technological choices (Vaitsos 1973), but the major sellers of technology—transnational corporations— often have monopolistic power and can sell technologies—some of which are obsolete—on terms that impose severe restrictions on the Third World buyer. Thus, technological dependence is a self-reinforcing process over which the Third World has little, if any, control (Fransman 1986; Stewart 1977).

In recent years, scholars and policy makers alike have begun to focus on the role that indigenous factors and local initiative can play in the development of technology in the Third World (Rushing and Brown 1986; Street and James 1979). Reacting to the excessive pessimism of the radical dependency position, several scholars have stressed the ''conservative'' point that a strong state can play a positive role in facilitating indigenous technological development (Grieco 1984; Smith 1979; see also Stepan 1978 on the role of the state in Peru). In particular, these scholars have suggested that the dependency perspective has blinded us to significant improvements that are taking place in the technological capabilities of the more advanced developing nations (Fransman and King 1984; Lall 1979). Thus, in contrast to earlier analyses, which stressed the overall deleterious effects of external factors, recent analyses have begun to focus on the beneficial effects of internal factors on technological development in the periphery.

Although the issue of external constraints versus internal initiative in the development of the Third World technological capabilities has major political and theoretical significance, it is far from being resolved (Freeman and Duvall 1984). Furthermore, much of the literature on which both positions are based draws mainly on Latin American cases. Given the distinctive position of East Asia in the world system documented throughout this volume, it is likely that the process of technology transfer, and the results of these transfers, have differed there from those experienced by most Latin American nations (see Patrick 1987 for an overview of the Japanese case).

The purpose of this chapter is to explore the role of internal and external factors in facilitating or impeding technological progress on Taiwan. Three main questions are addressed. The first section asks how successful Taiwan has been in securing and absorbing advanced technology. Turning from dependent to independent variables, the next section examines the external factors that have affected Taiwan's technological development and asks whether they have stimulated or hindered technological progress on the island. The third section explores the critical internal factors and the extent to which these factors have facilitated technology absorption on Taiwan. The final section assesses the overall effect and relative importance of indigenous and exogenous factors in Taiwan's technological development, and points out the theoretical implications of the Taiwan case and its relevance for other developing nations such as the PRC.

The chapter also addresses the issue of upward mobility in the international division of labor. Taiwan often is cited as a model of successful economic growth and technological absorption (e.g., Ho 1978a). Accordingly, the Taiwan case allows one to see what concrete policy steps a state can take to improve its technological position in the world economy. Yet, while Taiwan has moved into the group of so-called newly industrializing countries, it has not yet moved into the industrialized core. Whether or not this will happen remains to be seen; it is highly dependent upon Taiwan's continued ability to acquire and absorb newer and more advanced foreign technology. Taiwan's technological future is also briefly explored in the final section.

In the discussion of technology transfer four types of actors can be identified. External public actors are foreign governments and their agencies involved in development assistance programs. External private actors include foreign corporations and their subsidiaries in Taiwan. Internal public actors include the state and state corporations. Finally, internal private actors are local firms and their entrepreneurs.

Technology Absorption on Taiwan

How much technological progress has there been on Taiwan? Technological learning may be seen as a continuum made up of three stages. These stages are:

1. Acquisition: the acquisition and application of part or all of an advanced technology.

2. Adaptation: the modification of existing technologies to fit local conditions, such as skill levels and factor proportions.

3. Innovation: the creation of new technology processes or products using local research and development (R&D) skills.

Different levels of technological capabilities reflect different positions on this continuum. For example, reliance on technology cooperation agreements with tie-in clauses requiring the local partner to obtain much of the necessary equipment and process information from the supplier reflects an early phase of acquisition. Use of cooperation agreements that allow the local firm to provide a substantial proportion of the equipment and process know-how or components suggests a more advanced state of acquisition capabilities. A high skill level of the local labor force, especially in advanced technical areas, points to a capacity for adaptation. Possession of research and development facilities as well as other pieces of an indigenous S&T infrastructure indicates a potential for innovation. Because industries vary in their degree of technological complexity, at any given time a country is likely to be at different locations on this continuum according to the nature of the industry and the requisites for entry into global or regional markets.

Where does Taiwan fit on this continuum? At the most general level it can be said that as of the mid–1980s, Taiwan's private sector continued to exhibit a high level of dependence on foreign technology to support its economic activities. Most of the technology used in the island's key production sectors was originally acquired from abroad through licensing agreements, imitation, copying, or technology cooperation arrangements. Most local firms have considered reliance on foreign-made equipment and process technologies as the primary way to meet export demands and production goals in quality and quantity terms. With most local firms falling in the small- to medium-size category, and lacking capital and experience to undertake R&D programs, the absence of "a formally recognized engineering function" on Taiwan has been conspicuous (Little 1973). To overcome the consequences of a weak S&T base, the Taiwan state has been taking an active role in encouraging the importation of advanced technology, developing well-equipped R&D facilities, and improving the technical skills of the labor force.

Recognizing the advantages, and at times the necessity, of using foreign technology, many Taiwan companies have given high priority to engaging in technology cooperation agreements. According to a 1975 report on Taiwan's precision industries, the most successful local firms have been those with strong technology linkages with foreign companies (T. Ch'en 1975). A sizable number of firms in Taiwan's hundred largest business groups have either a capital or a technology transfer relationship with an overseas firms. For example, many of the major items produced by Tatung, one the largest local firms on Taiwan, are manufactured under licensing agreements with foreign firms. In another study, conducted by Taiwan's Investment Commission, eighty-three of the surveyed firms (40.3 percent of the total) depended upon licensing and technology cooperation agreements for 50 percent or more of their production, while sixty-three firms (30.6 percent) depended on licensed technology for 100 percent of their production (Investment Commission 1979). Within the metallurgy and petrochemicals industries, most of the primary technology employed is imported.

Up to 1980, about one-half of the agreements included tie-in clauses that required the local firm to purchase raw materials and parts from the technology supplier. Another quarter included tie-in arrangements for the purchase of machinery and equipment. As with the technology cooperation agreements, tie-in clauses were more prevalent in industries such as petrochemicals, where the technology is relatively sophisticated. These data suggest that for a significant number of local firms in Taiwan, technological learning has progressed only to the stage of acquisition. Additionally, in those sectors where the technology is complex, learning has not progressed beyond an early phase of acquisition.

It also must be recognized, however, that some firms on Taiwan have moved well beyond the acquisition stage. In some cases Taiwan firms have become engaged overseas as foreign investors and/or exporters of technology (Amsden 1981; Lall 1979; chapter 4, this volume). This is particularly true in the electronics and textiles industries. Many of these investments have been in Southeast Asia, where the local technological level tends to be well below that of the Taiwan-based firm. More recently, Taiwan firms such as Tatung and Formosa Plastics have expanded their activities into the United States. In addition, the Taiwan government has long been involved in sharing its agricultural technology with other developing nations as part of an effort to use development assistance as a means to win political support.

The transfer of technology to Taiwan has not been limited to economic projects. Since the late 1960s, Taiwan has shifted from direct reliance on imports of weapons and military equipment to licensed or domestic production in some cases (SIPRI 1975). A large quantity of Bell helicopters are produced domestically as part of an agreement signed with Bell Laboratories in 1969. Taiwan also signed an agreement with the Northrop Corporation for production for the F–5F fighter plane (SIPRI 1978). Concluded in 1973, the license agreement initially involved assembly of knocked-down parts from the United States. Over the course of the 1970s, the percentage of local content increased significantly. By the mid–1980s, Taiwan had begun to design its own fighter aircraft, missiles, and related defense equipment (Pollack 1986). Thus, in military production, Taiwan has been moving from early to late phases of acquisition and even into the stage of adaptation. This shift has been accomplished through the development of an indigenous defense R&D capability (Simon 1986). It also reflects the economy's growing ability to absorb advanced technology and "innovate" in areas vital to the island's economic and military security.

Although Taiwan has had little trouble acquiring foreign technology through cooperation and licensing agreements, it has had more difficulty moving beyond the initial stage of technological acquisition to adaptation and innovation. These advanced stages require a more technically skilled labor force and higher quality R&D facilities. With some important exceptions, both still are in their early stages of development on Taiwan.

Although the overall education and skill level of Taiwan's labor force is comparatively high and there is some underemployment of qualified engineers and technicians, labor shortages are critical in areas where highly specialized technical knowledge is required. These gaps in skills, however, have not blinded foreign and local investors to the overall quality and reliability of the existing labor force. Indeed, many foreign firms have capitalized on this high skill level by inviting Taiwan firms to participate in new types of business ventures. For example, in 1976 the Taiwan Machine Manufacturing Company, a government-sponsored firm, reached an agreement with General Electric to produce high-power steam turbines for power-related used (*Journal of Commerce* 1976). Joint ventures also have been arranged for the design and construction of nuclear power plants (*Economic News* 14 April 1978) and the production of buses (*Asia Research Bulletin* 28 February 1977). Finally, several major companies in high-technology industries have agreed to establish operations in the new Hsinchu Science and Industry Park, hoping to plug into Taiwan R&D capabilities (see below). All of these cases indicate an increasing ability and potential for Taiwan to move into more advanced stages of technological development.

Along with the fact that certain advanced technical skills are still lacking, R&D capabilities are also undeveloped in many cases. Some of the problems of Taiwan's economy stem from the absence of adequate knowledge of market-forecasting techniques and R&D processes. In 1977 the government spent 0.75 percent of its budget on research and development, while the United States and Japan spent considerably higher percentages of their budgets—2.29 and 1.78 percent—on research-related activities (*Economic News* 2 February 1978). This amount has climbed to about 1.2 percent as of 1985. Officials on Taiwan hope to see it increase to 2.0 percent by 1990. Except for a few large companies, most local firms on Taiwan spend less than 0.5 percent of their operating budgets on research and development. One major exception has been in the electronics industry, where technology changes have been frequent and rapid, and local firms have had to develop better R&D facilities in order to keep pace with both local and foreign competitors. Local innovation in the computer industry, for example, has been appreciable.

Generally, however, local firms lack adequate information about new developments in technology taking place abroad. And, while this has begun to change in some respects as a result of the emergence of more dynamic industrial associations and government efforts to disseminate information to industry, the fact remains that keeping abreast of foreign technology is still a difficult problem. Moreover, the initiative for new product development usually comes from sources external to Taiwan, thus local producers have very little control over their technology futures. In the past few years the government has taken steps to improve R&D facilities on Taiwan (see below), but these developments are only beginning to have a significant impact. In many respects, Taiwan's ability to innovate new technologies in the future remains contingent on the ability of the government to implement these improvements in areas of vital importance.

External Factors in Technological Development

What factors have affected the nature of technological change on Taiwan? In this section the role of external factors is considered, including both public and private actors.

External Public Actors

It was not until the Japanese period (1895–1945) that modern science and technology were transferred to Taiwan on a large scale. Most of Japan's efforts on Taiwan were directed toward the agrarian sector, where the use of scientific inputs eventually became a primary source of growth, especially in the area of rice cultivation. The Japanese also helped provide the foundation for the gradual development of both heavy and light industry. In addition, Japan also made significant contributions to developing Taiwan's infrastructure and education system and carried out a development program that promoted the integration of the island both geographically and economically.

The key to Taiwan's ability to absorb modern technology in the post-World War II period lies with the U.S. foreign assistance mission (1951–1965). The U.S. mission served as a vehicle through which modern equipment and technologies, as well as American engineers and technicians, were brought to Taiwan. Access to advanced technologies was ensured because U.S. officials saw benefits in building up the Taiwan economy and ensuring its long-term viability (see chapters 6 and 7). U.S. aid supplied funds for the modernization of production facilities in government and private firms. With aid funds, many Chinese in positions of authority received participant training in the United States (Jacoby 1966). More important, aid monies also supported the expansion of modern energy, communications, and transportation networks throughout the island.

Documents secured from AID reveal that there was a constant flow of U.S. businessmen to the island. Working through AID-sponsored organizations such as the China Productivity Center, business and other technical personnel visited Chinese factories and production sites and provided suggestions about how to improve management, organization, and manufacturing processes. These exchanges helped the economy recover from the destruction left over from World War II and the Chinese civil war.

Aid's impact on industrial technology and organization in the private sector was quite modest, however, when compared to its impact on the public sector. Not only did aid monies provide advanced training and modern equipment to state sector firms; they also helped to expand the infrastructure that was necessary for further industrial development and technology absorption.

Overall, these efforts in both private and public sectors were strengthened as a result of the aid program to encourage U.S. firms to invest in the Taiwan economy. Aid administrators were able to persuade Taiwan government officials to develop an investment law that could be attractive to potential investors. These foreign investors eventually provided a further stimulus for economic development though the training of Taiwan workers and the use of modern machinery and equipment in their production operations. Even though initially many of the foreign firms were involved in low-skill, labor-intensive operations, their demands for managerial efficiency and consistent quality control helped to highlight the importance of these factors to local private entrepreneurs, especially as the economy moved from import substitution to export-oriented development.

External Private Actors

The role of American aid as supplier of technology and equipment in the 1950s was gradually taken over by foreign firms in the 1960s. Foreign firms are attracted to Taiwan because the investment climate has continued to be conducive to the exploitation of their particular production technologies. Taiwan possesses an attractive set of investment incentives (see section on internal public actors), a stable political environment, and a highly educated and trainable labor force.

Between 1952 and 1985, the government approved almost 2,200 technology cooperation agreements with foreign firms. Even though some of these were between foreign and state-owned firms, the majority involved private and foreign corporations. Most technology cooperation agreements have been between Japanese and locally owned firms. As of 1985, technology-related agreements with Japan accounted for approximately 64.5 percent of the total (Investment Commission 1985). Agreements with U.S. firms have accounted for 22 percent of the total.

The importance of technology cooperation varies by industry (Simon 1987). As of 1985, the largest number of agreements has been in the electronics sector, with 582 cases or 26.0 percent of the total. Next to electronics is the chemicals industry (19.6 percent of total), whose development owes much to the technology acquired from foreign firms. In the last few years, as a result of government efforts, technology cooperation agreements have increased most extensively in what might be termed "precision and high-technology" industries.

Accounting for approximately two-thirds of all technology cooperation agreements, Japan has had a disproportionate impact on the process of technological development on Taiwan. One reason for the large number of agreements involving Japanese firms is the geographic proximity of Japan to Taiwan. Another is the relative ease with which Taiwanese and Japanese work with each other, which serves as inducement to Japanese investors (Ozawa 1979).

Another reason can be found in the nature of the agreements themselves. Japanese firms often use a foreign investment-technology agreement linkage as a structure to facilitate the sale of parts and raw materials to local firms or to become involved in marketing a locally manufactured item. The cooperation arrangement also may provide a means for the Japanese firm to gain influence over the production process in the local company. Moreover, the goal of technology transfer among Japanese firms has been not to stimulate greater technological independence of the local partner, but to promote trade and to ensure that these firms help accommodate the needs of other Japanese firms producing on Taiwan (Ozawa 1979; Investment Commission 1979). It is not surprising, then, that local firms often complain about the restrictive clauses and tie-in provisions that accompany technology cooperation arrangements with Japan. In mid-1978, an editorial in Taipei's *Economic Daily News* suggested that 70 percent of the cooperation agreements with Japan had resulted in little actual technology transfer. This same theme was echoed by Taiwan officials during visits by the author to the island in both 1984 and 1986. Even though Japanese firms may transfer more sophisticated production equipment or techniques than are generally employed by most local firms, the ability of the local partner to move out on his own in the future has sometimes been severely constrained due to the external controls imposed by the Japanese supplier.

As suggested, the problem most often encountered on Taiwan has been the tie-in clause that requires the local firm to purchase not only technology, but also raw materials and parts from the supplier (Investment Commission 1979). Yet, while tie-in agreements still continue to be a problem in some industries, since the late 1970s Taiwan has been able to limit the use of many of these clauses, especially those restricting exports. Such restrictions usually are imposed by the technology supplier to reduce the possibility of future competition. In the electronics industry, for example, less than 20 percent of the agreements signed since the late 1970s have export restrictions. The government has made a strong effort to prohibit the use of these and similar clauses since limits on exports, particularly in high technology areas, are inconsistent with its ongoing policies of export promotion and technological upgrading.

Overall, in spite of such problems as tie-in clauses, the acquisition of foreign technology has helped to upgrade the technological capabilities of both public and private firms. Such acquisitions have led to improvements in product quality and variation, reductions in production costs, and increases in local sourcing among both domestic and foreign-invested firms (Simon 1987). Due to these technological improvements, foreign firms have been able to expand their subcontracting relationships with local companies and to include more technologically sophisticated items in their subcontracting agreements.

Of course, along with the benefits, there have been some costs associated with reliance on foreign technology. One of the major problems Taiwan has faced in its efforts to secure advanced technology derives from technology obsolescence. In many cases, Japanese suppliers have been accused of transferring already mature technologies to local recipients. These problems, however, are by no means country-specific or industry-specific. One striking case was discovered during interviews dealing with the U.S.-based Amoco Corporation and the China Petrochemical Development Corporation (T. Ch'en 1975; Simon 1987). The case involves Taiwan's difficulties in trying to predict the shift from DMT to the more sophisticated PTA—both important petrochemical intermediaries in the production of man-made materials—during the course of deciding which type of technology to import.

In particular, this case highlights some of the reasons why Taiwan officials and personnel in state corporations frequently are not able to make better technology choices. First, sometimes decisions about technology imports have been made for political or foreign policy reasons, and therefore certain technological considerations are subordinated to political ones. Second, lacking sufficient knowledge of the specific advantages of alternative technical options as well as adequate technology forecasting skills, local actors must often choose primarily on the basis of price. Third, foreign firms may be anxious to license obsolete or soon-to-be obsolete technology and offer it on inexpensive terms. And, once the initial investment has been made, the local firm is locked into its decision—regardless of what it may later learn about the wisdom of the original decision. This illustrates how the control over technology and information about technology by foreign firms can frustrate the efforts of the host nation to improve its technological capabilities. It also highlights how and why access to information, and possession of a domestic R&D capability, can improve the bargaining position of the periphery nation in commercial negotiations.

Internal Factors in Technological Development

How have internal factors affected the island's technological development? This section explores that question first for private actors, and then for public actors involved in technology acquisition and absorption.

Internal Private Actors

On Taiwan, firm size has an important effect on local capacity to undertake research and development activities. Firm size affects research capacity not only because of financial factors, but also because of the general orientation of Taiwan entrepreneurs who own small firms. In 1971, almost 68 percent of the firms on Taiwan fell into the "small" category, that is, they employ ten or fewer workers (Ho 1980). By 1984, this breakdown had begun to change, though not much. Changes in physical plant and factory organization involve large capital commitments. Most small-scale businessmen either do not have ready access to bank loans or are reluctant to seek government bank loans for political reasons. They tend to obtain their capital from the informal money market—friends, relatives, credit societies, and so forth. Such informal channels are rarely sufficient to cover the costs of major changes in production or process technology (Stites 1982a; on the strengths and weaknesses of family firms see chapter 11).

Managerial personnel in these firms also tend to have short-term outlooks and usually approach production problems from the perspective of symptoms rather than causes. Even if a decision is made to acquire new technology, many local producers do not realize that the application of new equipment or manufacturing techniques frequently requires concomitant changes in other areas of plant operation (Spencer and Worniak 1967; Simon 1987). Efforts by the government to consolidate some of these smaller plants into large operating units have been beset by questions of ownership, management responsibility, and financial control.

One problem often encountered on Taiwan has been commercial spying and theft. Small firms often feel they are left with no option but to acquire product and manufacturing information through such means. In addition, Taiwan is not a member of the World Intellectual Property Organization, nor is it a signee of the International Patent Convention. Moreover, foreign invested firms often complain that after providing overseas training to local workers in technical or managerial areas, many of these persons leave the plant to embark on their own ventures or join other firms. On many occasions, these persons carry production designs with them. This has hurt chances for the widespread introduction of technological improvements, for its has discouraged foreign firms from providing extensive training for fear that their investment will be wasted. It also has convinced some firms to limit their contacts with local companies as well as the level of technology they are willing to bring to the island.

In spite of the problems that such "defections" generate for relations between local firms and foreign-invested companies, such "breakaway entrepreneurs" do represent a potential source for indigenous technological development. They also serve as a useful mechanism for diffusion of technology and know-how. As Stewart and Nihei (1987, 13) have suggested in their study of Thailand and Indonesia, "the main vehicle of technology transfer is ultimately the turnover of trained and experienced managerial and professional employees from MNEs (multinational enterprises) to domestic firms and other domestic organizations." Unfortunately, in high-technology industries, small firms begun by such industrious businessmen have had a poor survival record. In most cases their failures can be attributed to an inability to stay abreast of the constant changes taking place in the technology associated with a particular product or manufacturing process (Simon 1987).

Another problem involves the existence of numerous underground factories. These small, low-capital operations are notorious for pirating foreign products and manufacturing substandard items. One source has suggested that nearly 60 percent of the pirated goods in the world come from Taiwan (*Business Week* 16 December 1985). In one case, uncovered in the late 1970s, several underground factories were manufacturing circuit fuse breakers with forged Mitsubishi and Westinghouse labels. Some of the circuit breakers had no fuses inside, while others used inferior materials. When Mitsubishi brought the case before the Taiwan authorities, the local firms were fined a mere U.S. $600. Westinghouse did not pursue the claim because it feared that the publicity would case doubts on the reliability of its own circuit breakers. Both firms strongly criticized the Taiwan government for what they claimed was inadequate monitoring and enforcement procedures. While publicly government officials denied that the problem was severe, privately they pointed to the political considerations that made shutting down these factories difficult, if not impossible.

More recently, however, in recognition of the severity of the pirating problem, the government has taken major steps to curtail the problem (*Free China Journal* 7 April 1986). Crackdowns have occurred in a great many industries, and on products ranging from microcomputers to denim jeans. A special government committee has been created to oversee the problem. In addition, Taiwan customs officials have been admonished to pay closer attention to the problem of counterfeit products that are being exported. Although the initial crackdown may only produce limited results, the explicit reversal in government policy is sure to make foreign suppliers of technology—both actual and potential—somewhat less apprehensive about transferring advanced technology to Taiwan.

Internal Public Actors

The state has been a major promoter of technology transfer to Taiwan. It has provided a set of attractive incentives that are spelled out in the Statute for the Encouragement of Technical Cooperation. The statute was first issued in 1962. Technology cooperation agreements arranged before this time mainly consisted of machinery purchases accompanied by technical assistance or consultation provided to the purchaser. After 1962, the requirements for such agreements were more clearly spelled out, more thoroughly evaluated for their overall impact, and better controlled for duplication. In 1964 the law was further revised to make such agreements more attractive to foreign companies. According to the 1964 statute, an agreement for the purchase of a product or process technology can be made only if one of these conditions are met: (1) the agreement involves the production of a new product; (2) the new technology will increase the volume of production, improve quality, or reduce production costs; or (3) the new technology will lead to improvements in management or operation efficiency.

The government's technology cooperation approval policies have closely followed its overall economic policies, especially at critical points of economic transition. For example, between 1974 and 1977, the government denied several applications for cooperation because they included the manufacture of highly labor-intensive products. In the mid–1970s, royalty rates were lowered for most projects and the time limits on agreements were reduced to five years or less. These changes were made to reduce the costs to the local firm, in terms of both time and money, for engaging in an agreement designed to upgrade domestic technological capabilities. In the early 1980s, new incentives were introduced to attract so-called high-technology firms.

Although the Taiwan government has consistently tried to promote technology cooperation agreements, its policies have not always been clearly articulated. Confusion over government policies has been reflected in taxation policies regarding royalty payments and technical assistance fees (Kwoh 1978). In the late 1960s and early 1970s, government policies allowed an income tax exemption on royalty payments and technical assistance fees except on licensing or technical assistance paid to a parent firm that owned 80 percent or more equity in its subsidiary. This policy was effective because it discouraged an extensive outflow of funds through intrafirm transfers. In 1977, however, the government decided to revise the income tax laws and deleted the entire exemption for all items, regardless of ownership. In addition, in 1976 the Ministry of Finance issued a regulation stating that all technology-related royalty payments were subject to the Taiwan gross business tax. All companies supplying technology either through license or arrangements with their parent firms were required to pay this tax. With the real transaction costs of managing technology transfers increasing, this law actually discouraged foreign firms from entering into cooperation agreements with local companies. In 1978, the regulation once again was revised to make only those payments and technical fees arranged before 1976 exempt from taxation. This "revision" was curious because it did nothing to increase the overall attractiveness of Taiwan; it merely reduced protests from technology suppliers already on the island. While the goal of this latter policy was to encourage more joint ventures and higher equity participation by local firms (*Economic News* 31 October 1978), its real effect, at least in the short term, was to discourage foreign firms from bringing new technology to the island.

Another source of problems has been the often distant relations between the government and the private local producer. Even though the government approves all technology cooperation agreements, it does not oversee their eventual implementation. Nor are local firms required to report the upgrading of a product from first to second generation. This has two important effects. First, the government is not fully aware of the activities of many local producers and thus may duplicate agreements. Second, the government can never be certain that if and when a second generation technology becomes available, it is transferred to Taiwan. Both of these difficulties impede comprehensive planning by the government involving local technology needs. Since local companies do not engage in this type of forecasting or planning either, Taiwan firms have a difficult time keeping abreast of ongoing technological changes. Moreover, except in the case of state-owned firms, there are no feedback requirements regarding the performance of foreign suppliers.

In spite of the problems associated with technology cooperation agreements, the Taiwan government has remained committed to employing foreign technology to upgrade the island's technology base. This commitment is best exemplified in the decision to establish the Hsinchu Science and Industry Park in the late 1970s. This park constitutes a second generation of foreign investment, where production technologies are characterized by their technical complexity and sophistication rather than their labor intensity. The development of the park has been conceived in three stages. During each successive stage, the government's aim is increasingly to involve the local private sector and to use links with foreign firms as a means to stimulate indigenous technical advancement. Ultimately, the government hopes that local firms will be able to establish independent operations in the park and gradually to decrease reliance on foreign technology suppliers. As of 1986, there were over fifty companies operating in the park, most involved in high-technology areas such as microelectronics, computers, and precision instruments.

To attract foreign firms in such high-technology fields, the government has offered incentives that in many cases equal or exceed those available to other foreign investors (Hsinchu Science and Industry Park Administration 1985). In addition, tax rates and duties have been adjusted to accord with the requirements for establishing a high-technology industry (*Business Asia* 1979). To qualify, firms must not only offer a competitive and sophisticated technology with a stable and possibly growing international market; they also must indicate how they will contribute to the local economy through sourcing practices, worker training, or development of research facilities on Taiwan. Thus, the state has used a variety of means to ensure that the process and nature of technology transfer in the park will accord with its own objectives for future development of the island.

Other activities of the state to improve the technological environment include development of a strategic plan for the creation of a viable informatics industry on Taiwan. Grants have been made to create the Computer Industry Development Center, and funding has been provided for the establishment of an Institute of Information Industry (*Taiwan Industrial Panorama* August 1979; November 1979). Both of these organizations are designed to facilitate the development and application of computers and information systems among public and private sectors firms (Simon and Schive 1986). An Industrial Technology Transfer Corporation was formed in 1979 with government assistance as a complement to these other programs. The firm is a joint venture, with 60 percent of its capital coming from the Industrial Technology Research Institute, a government-sponsored R&D organization, and 40 percent from the private sector. More recently, the government has also been the driving force behind the creation of a U.S. $106 million project to establish a VLSI (very large-scale integrated circuit) company that will manufacture foreign-designed, "application-specific" ICs as well as some of the more general types of chips (*Free China Journal* 3 February 1986). The project represents the largest investment ever made in the domestic electronics industry. This project will be complemented by the establishment of a national laboratory at National Chiao T'ung University dedicated to the development of submicron integrated circuit technology (*Free China Journal* 9 February 1987).

The major force behind all of these efforts has been Li Kuo-ting, minister without portfolio for science and technology applications under the Executive Yuan. Minister Li often has been cited as a principal architect of Taiwan's rapid economic growth. According to Minister Li, the success of these programs in conjunction with the Hsinchu Park will be vital to Taiwan's future economic prosperity, and, perhaps, political survival.

These recent efforts by the state are characterized by three features: extensive government planning and investment; foreign technology as a catalyst for government efforts; and closer cooperation between the government or government-sponsored organizations and local firms. Such activities promise to have important implications for the island's political and technological future. Heavy government intervention will mean not only greater government oversight, but also more extensive relations between the government and local Taiwanese companies, especially as the government seeks more local private investment in these projects. Since the government will play the role of partner, buyer, and possibly licensor, this many mean more direct state control. Nonetheless, even though greater government involvement may be poorly received by the island's large Taiwanese business class, it also may stimulate closer relations between the two groups as they increasingly come to perceive mutual gain in greater cooperation. As the experience of the early 1980s has indicated, however, this will be a gradual process at best. If it does proceed as desired, this cooperation will help improve the bargaining leverage of both local and state firms vis à vis foreign companies, especially in those cases where access to the Taiwan economy and labor force becomes important for particular foreign firms (Haskell 1980). This could be especially true in the high-priority electronics industry because Taiwan's labor force and technical capabilities make it a very attractive site for high-technology foreign investment and technology transfer agreements.

Conclusion

This analysis has suggested that in the mid–1980s, the majority of Taiwan's firms were in the later stages of technology acquisition. As a result of the government's efforts to upgrade Taiwan's technological level, however, local and state-owned firms gradually were acquiring the skills and R&D facilities necessary for technological adaptation and innovation. What factors have been most important in determining the nature and pace of technology absorption on Taiwan?

The initial efforts of external public actors—the Japanese colonial government (1895–1945) and then U.S. AID (1951–1965)—played a critical role in laying the infrastructure necessary for successful technology absorption. Key elements of this infrastructure included a basic education system, transportation links, and an energy network that covered the island. The presence of these factors helped to facilitate the onset of the next stage in Taiwan's technological development.

When AID left in 1965, its role as a supplier of advanced technology was taken over by external private actors, the multinational firms. Although technology transfer has been hampered by tie-in agreements and the occasional transfer of obsolete technology, overall, foreign companies have promoted Taiwan's technological development. Technology cooperation agreements have enabled entrepreneurs gradually to improve product quality, lower production costs, expand local content, and produce more sophisticated products.

On the whole, internal private factors have tended to retard technological advancement on Taiwan. This is not to suggest that Taiwan's private sector is not dynamic (see chapter 11), but only to indicate that there are certain structural limits to technological aggressiveness among a large percentage of firms within Taiwan's business community. Furthermore, many top managers tend to have short-term outlooks that are inimical to investment in rapid and sustained technical advance. Most Taiwan firms remain small- or middle-sized, and lack the capital to invest in R&D facilities and programs. Commercial spying and theft also have discouraged some foreign firms from training local personnel or bringing advanced technology to the island, while underground factories have made several foreign firms cautious about sharing technology with local companies. These problems are particularly difficult to erase, for relations between the government and the private sector are distant, and the government considers it politically infeasible to control all the illegal activities of the private sector.

If technological learning has taken place, it is largely because the internal public actor, the state, has taken an active role in developing incentives to attract foreign firms to Taiwan. Unlike some Third World governments, the Taiwan government has had a good deal of control over the nature of investments and technology cooperation agreements. In many ways, through the upgrading of its own technological base, it has enhanced its bargaining position vis à vis potential foreign investors and technology suppliers. Though the effects of its policies have not always been in line with its goals—as in the case of some tax laws—in general, the government has managed to ensure that the types of investment and technology coming to the island are those that advance its overall development objectives. In the mid–1960s, these objectives were to foster labor-intensive industrialization. By the mid–1970s, government goals had shifted to promoting capital-intensive and then skill-intensive industries. To achieve these objectives, which remain central in the mid- to late–1980s, the government has established several key organizations designed to upgrade R&D capabilities and increase the inflow of complex technologies.

Since the large-scale infusion of foreign technology began in the 1960s, there have been three actors involved in technology transfers: the Taiwan government, foreign corporations, and local entrepreneurs. Of these, the government has had the most control over the process of technology transfer. Foreign firms, of course, have made demands and advanced their interests, but in most cases their activities have been channeled by the government into desired areas. And whereas they always have the option of selecting an alternative site to Taiwan to make their investment or transfer their technology, the fact remains that a sort of interdependence exists, manifested in the stable investment climate and strong technical assets that Taiwan continues to offer. The weakest actor has been the small- and medium-scale local entrepreneur who, because of size constraints and lack of support from larger institutions, has often resorted to illegal methods or short-term approaches to achieve his objectives.

What are the theoretical implications of these findings? The Taiwan case suggests that the radical dependency perspective overstates the strength of external actors relative to internal factors. And it overemphasizes the negative effects while ignoring the positive effects that both foreign firms and the state can have on technological development in the periphery and semiperiphery of the world system. The Taiwan case also supports the hypothesis of Lall and others that in countries where technological learning is initially protected from external influences, there is a greater scope for indigenous technology development. On Taiwan, this protection was afforded not so much to the private sector as it was to the state and state-owned firms. In particular, the assistance supplied by AID during the 1951–1965 period provided the state with the infrastructure and political-military support it needed so the country could compete successfully when it entered the world system as a relatively independent actor in the mid–1960s. Without this period of U.S. support and internal strengthening, it is doubtful that the Nationalist state could have entered the world economy as such a strong actor and remained so up to the present time.

The case of technology transfer highlights some crucial differences between East Asia and other regions of the world system. There is no doubt that the geographic proximity (which means low transport costs) and sociocultural affinities between Taiwan and Japan facilitated the entry of Japanese capital into Taiwan. But what are the implications of the predominance of Japanese linkages for Taiwan's technological development? Although the large number of Japanese investments and technology cooperation agreements has resulted in a large number of local Taiwan businessmen with access to foreign technology, Japanese investments (compared to U.S. and European investments) have been in lower technology sectors, have more tie-in provisions, and more often have served to facilitate the sale of Japanese goods and components rather than to improve the technical capabilities of the local producer. Thus, while transferring relatively simple technological skills to a broad base of entrepreneurs, given present trends, Japanese technology transfer is not likely to meet the needs of Taiwan's increasingly complex industrial structure. Things could change, however, particularly if a sharp appreciation of the yen were to occur, making it necessary for Japanese firms to situate some of their more advanced facilities in places such as Taiwan.

Finally, the Taiwan case shows that, given certain conditions, it is possible for a nation to move up in the world economic system. Building on the achievements of others, the Nationalist state has begun to engineer a gradual transition from technology importation to technology production and innovation. One measure of this success has been the growth of overseas investment from Taiwan by both private and state-owned firms since the early 1970s. By the end of 1985, for example, Taiwan firms had invested over U.S. $117 million in the United States. As suggested, this will be a difficult transition, but it has already begun. The competitive dynamics of the international marketplace will be the final judge of the success of this effort.

Progress toward greater technological sophistication has been promising, but how much room does Taiwan have for maneuver in the future? A small island with few natural resources, Taiwan is dependent on the outside world for raw materials and markets. A semiperipheral area of the world system, Taiwan still is highly dependent on the industrialized world for much of its technology. Thus, only by offering advantages to core investors can Taiwan turn its technological potential into technological success. Whereas the interest of U.S. investors in high-technology industries remains high (as indicted, for example, by the Hewlett Packard-Formosa Plastics agreement announced in 1986 for researching and developing applications software), the interest of at least some Japanese investors in similar industries has seemingly moved across the Taiwan Straits.

Eventually, Taiwan's technological future may come to be more closely linked with that of the China mainland. Technology transfers from Taiwan to China could prove mutually beneficial, and could avoid at least some of the problems of structural inequality and cultural dissonance that accompany technology transfers from core to peripheral areas of the world system. At the same time, Taiwan's political leaders and corporate decision makers will undoubtedly choose to stay strongly tied into the capitalist world system. After all, as liberal theorists maintain, it is the dynamism of this system that has provided Taiwan with the resources and opportunities to establish a new niche for itself in the evolving international division of labor.

Note

1. This chapter is based on field research conducted on Taiwan in 1977–78 and 1984–86. Special thanks go to the National Science Foundation, the East-West Center, and the Pacific Cultural Foundation for financial support.

11

Susan Greenhalgh

FAMILIES AND NETWORKS IN TAIWAN'S ECONOMIC DEVELOPMENT

Although historians of East Asia have long debated the role of Chinese culture in the region's pattern of economic change, social and cultural factors are conspicuously absent from both liberal and radical theories of contemporary Chinese development.

Liberal interpretations of Taiwan's development and distribution assume that familial institutions are Westernizing rapidly, and in any case are largely irrelevant to macroeconomic outcomes (e.g., Fei, Ranis, and Kuo 1979; Galenson 1979).[1] Radical accounts recognize a role for "mesolevel" social forces such as social classes, but few assign an active role to microlevel social institutions such as families and social networks.

Yet research on Taiwan's business enterprises, reviewed in this chapter, makes it clear that such microlevel institutions as families and social networks are critically important for macrotheory. The families at the cores of Taiwan's firms help to shape the way the country is linked to the world economy, and they mediate the effects of the global system on domestic society and economy. Microsocial institutions are also important for comparative theory. Because they vary from society to society, these institutions help produce interregional variations in external ties and internal structures.

Of the three broad perspectives, only conservative theories recognize an important role for historically developed microsocial institutions in East Asian economic development. In a well-known study of world economic development Kahn (1979, 121) argues that the neo-Confucian cultures of East Asia are superior to Western cultures in the pursuit of industrialization, affluence, and modernization. Their superiority stems from their ability to create educated and hardworking individuals, and their capacity for purposive and efficient organizational activity (pp. 121-213). While Kahn assigns a critical role to the culture's capacity to create effective microsocial organizations, oddly, he excludes the family from the list of beneficial institutions. Family loyalty is said to be inimical to development because it promotes corruption and nepotism (p. 381, n. 51). Within the literature on Taiwan, Myers (1984, esp. pp. 515, 527–28) has argued that the dynamic entrepreneurship of small-scale enterprises in particular, and traditional neo-Confucian values in general, have been a motive force for flexible change and rapid growth of manufacturing and services on the island.

Although these conservative accounts contain intriguing ideas, they do not provide a sound starting point for an exploration of microsocial factors in economic development. They treat social and cultural institutions in only a general way, failing to specify which sociocultural institutions are important and neglecting to link these institutions to specific economic outcomes. A second problem involves the issue of culture change and its causes. Kahn argues that although traditionally Chinese culture inhibited development, currently the cultural legacy is positive because most of those cultural elements that restricted growth have eroded. However, Kahn does not provide an adequate explanation for why detrimental characteristics were eliminated while advantageous ones were retained. For this, one needs to move back to the macroeconomic and political context within which social and cultural change occurs.

What this discussion suggests is that fully to understand the role of social institutions in the modern world system, it is necessary to synthesize elements of the radical and conservative approaches. Such a synthesis should recognize the dialectical nature of the contemporary world, in which global and national political and economic forces shape local society (the radical insight), while at the same time local, historically developed social institutions also shape national and global political-economic outcomes (the conservative contribution). This radical-conservative view of microsocial actors can supplement liberal approaches to development and distribution. Liberal accounts provide sound analysis of the market structure of the game, but fail to characterize all the players.

In this chapter I sketch in some elements of such a synthesis for Taiwan. Beginning with general theories of development, the first section reviews historical and anthropological research suggesting the need to incorporate conservative elements into radical-globalist theories. The following three sections discuss the role of two microsocial institutions—families and networks—in Taiwan's macroeconomic performance. The first introduces the family enterprise, the predominant form of business organization on the island. The second explains why family enterprises promote rapid growth and integration into the global economy, and the third presents empirical evidence of these positive developmental roles. A conclusion spells out the implications for theory and outlines areas for future research.

Microsocial Institutions and Radical-Globalist Theories

Radical-globalist theories differ in many respects, but they share the basic assumption that the economic development and global integration of peripheral areas are determined largely by global and national political and economic forces. Peripheral society and culture are largely absent from most of these theories. In accounts that assign them a role they are conceived as dependent or, at best, weak intermediate variables. In such theories the evolution of the global capitalist system is often seen as splintering the dependent society and economy into increasingly unequal regions (Frank 1969b), classes (Evans 1979), sectors (transnational/peripheral [Sunkel 1973] or formal/informal [Portes and Walton 1981]), modes of production (Amin 1976), consumption groups (Kumar 1980), and so forth. Disarticulation of the society in turn exacerbates problems of underdevelopment, unfavorable terms of integration into the world economy, and unequal distribution of income and wealth.

Although forms of disarticulation and underdevelopment have been documented in many areas of Latin America, peripheral regions of East Asia (in particular Taiwan, Korea, and Hong Kong) show much less evidence of these processes. Where are the gaps in these theories?

Macroeconomic Roles of Microsocial Institutions: Families and Networks

One of the earliest critiques of radical-globalist theories stressed their overemphasis on capitalism, transnational corporations, and other global forces as explanatory factors. In neglecting the indigenous social structure of the periphery, radical-globalist theorists implicitly assumed that microsocial structures were passive, even powerless, victims of outside forces. Peripheral society was so weak that it literally fell apart, disintegrating into disparate sectors, regions, and classes, when struck by global capitalism and its agents.

As a solution to the overemphasis on macrolevel structures, few critics have called for increased attention to microsocial institutions. Most fault global theory for ignoring such factors as the peripheral state, local class affiliations and modes of production, ethnic relations, and the like (see, for example, Evans, Rueschemeyer, and Skocpol 1985; Mintz 1977; Smith 1984; Wolf 1982). Yet historical and anthropological research has shown that elements that are still more "micro"—families and networks—play important roles in determining how societies become linked to the world economy and how the global economy affects the development of the global periphery. Ironically, much of this evidence comes from Latin America, the prime empirical arena for radical-globalist theorizing. In an important study of family networks in the eighteenth and nineteenth centuries, Balmori, Voss, and Wortman (1984) showed how the strategies of elite families enabled them both to dominate the economic and political structure of Latin America, and to shape the region's growing links to the European-centered world system (see also Kicza 1983; Plummer 1980). In her study of the nineteenth-century Brazilian northeast, Lewin (1979) showed how features of the elite kinship system—especially its form of descent and preferred form of marriage—worked to keep power within the elite and perpetuate inequality from one generation to the next. A close look at traditional Chinese social structure reveals remarkably strong familial institutions that dominated nearly every feature of social, economic, political and cultural life in the centuries before large-scale contacts with the West (Rozman 1981). Whatever the nature of the capitalist intrusion, it is inconceivable that this family system did not play a central role in determining the manner in which capitalism was absorbed and the character of the resulting patterns of development.

Social Structure of Business Firms and Groups

Most dependency and world system accounts ignore the social structure of not only noncapitalist units such as families and networks, but also capitalist entities such as business firms. The underlying assumption seems to be either that once firms are capitalist they are all the same and their internal organization can be ignored, or that even if their internal structures are different, internal organization does not significantly affect the firms' operation. Both assumptions are challenged by the work of economic historians and social anthropologists on cultural factors in entrepreneurship. This research shows that the nature of business organization and entrepreneurship varies to some extent by the culture in which actors are embedded, and that firm organization critically affects firm operation (e.g., Fruin 1980; Greenfield, Strickon, and Aubey 1979; Nakagawa 1977; Tripathi 1981).

While this body of research focuses largely on the global periphery, the work of radical sociologists on core societies suggests that, even at the centers of global power, many large corporations are embedded in larger financial-industrial interest, or interlock, groups that are held together by familial and other social ties (e.g., Allen 1978; Burch 1972; Fennema 1982; Norich 1980; Solef 1980; related work on the periphery is Zeitlin 1974; Zeitlin, Ewen, and Ratcliff 1974; this point also emerges from histories of great industrial families, e.g., Davis 1978; Koskoff 1978). The sociological work indicates that attention to the social structure underlying business firms and economic groups is likely to provide important clues to patterns of firm operation. This suggestion is clearly relevant to Taiwan. The Tenth Credit Cooperative scandal that erupted in Taipei in early 1985 provides indisputable evidence that the social, in this case familial, character of business organization on the island has a crucial impact on corporate strategies of capital acquisition, investment, and disaster relief (*AWSJ* 20 May 1985; *FEER* 7 March 1985).

These bodies of research and related findings have important implications for world system theories. Since firms are the basic units mediating the integration of peripheral societies into the global economy, firm social structure should affect aspects of integration such as the extent and type of links to other entities in the world system. And if the social organization of firms varies from society to society, this factor should provide a partial explanation for the differing patterns of integration into the global economy.

Thus, a closer look at microsocial structure should provide important clues to why subglobal regions differ in their manner of integration into the world economy and, in particular, why the East Asian region does not fit the conventional stereotype of distorted development and unfavorable terms of global integration. The following sections explore the role of microsocial institutions in Taiwan's economic development and global integration. The underlying argument is that East Asian outcomes are different in part because East Asia's social structure is different.

Social Factors in Taiwan's Development: The Family Enterprise

As documented throughout this volume, Taiwan has avoided most of the problems of underdevelopment and dependent development emphasized by radical-globalist theories. With the exception of a few brief recessions, since the early 1960s Taiwan has enjoyed rapid and increasingly diversified industrial development based on penetration of global markets. Although development has been achieved in part by the use of foreign capital and technology, absorption of foreign resources has not resulted in the displacement of native capitalists. Throughout this period Chinese capitalists have dominated the Taiwan economy and Chinese investment has made up the great bulk—about 95–97 percent—of gross domestic capital formation.[2]

One largely neglected and poorly understood source of the economy's dynamism lies in the nature of the society, in particular, in the vitality of indigenous entrepreneurship and family firms. There is wide consensus that most firms on the island are family enterprises, but there is little agreement on whether these firms facilitate or impede economic advance. On the one hand, many government planners, academics, and foreign businessmen on Taiwan believe that small, family-run firms inhibit the island's development. During the recessions of 1974–75 and 1981–82 these groups voiced their hope that economic downturn would streamline the economy by eliminating small, inefficient, and ill-managed family firms (e.g., *FEER* 27 December 1974). Such hopes, however, failed to materialize. In the mid-1980s these criticisms reemerged in the context of a serious slowdown in export-led growth. The slowdown was considered a result not only of external difficulties such as protectionism, but also of internal structural problems, in particular an archaic banking system and an economy dominated by small family firms. Because of their parochial management, incoherent marketing strategies, concern with short-term profits, and lack of resources, family businesses were considered incapable of upgrading their technology, let alone developing the research and development (R&D) necessary to move Taiwan into the technology-intensive sectors the government considers essential to the future prosperity of the island (*FEER* 22 March 1984; 25 July 1985; 26 September

1985). These arguments about the disadvantages of the family firm are supported by a few studies showing that small firms have higher costs than large firms.[3] Most of the supporting evidence, however, appears to be anecdotal.

In contrast to the dominant view that family firms are a drag on development, a few, mostly Western scholars have hinted at the possibility that these same firms might have contributed to Taiwan's development. This has been suggested by conservative economists such as Myers as well as by anthropological research (Greenhalgh 1984). To date, however, none of these writers has explained how the family firm has facilitated Taiwan's growth or conclusively demonstrated its positive role. Some of the strongest empirical evidence supporting this argument is contained in an article by Y. M. Ho (1980). Using a two-digit industrial breakdown, Ho demonstrated that the rapid growth of manufacturing in the 1960s was characterized by the active participation of small firms throughout the sector. More surprising is the finding that small- and medium-sized firms were technically more efficient than large firms in all but one of the fastest growing manufacturing industries (textiles, wood, paper, basic metals, metal products, and miscellaneous manufactures, but not chemicals). Furthermore, increasing returns to scale, an argument often used against family firms, which are considered too small to realize them, turned out to be unimportant in five of the nine manufacturing industries. Ho's work thus suggests that small, family-run businesses may have made a positive contribution to Taiwan's export-oriented growth, especially in the 1960s, when labor-intensive industries dominated the growth process. This hypothesis gains additional support from the work of Samuel P. S. Ho (1978b), whose study of small-scale enterprises (those with fewer than 100 workers) in Taiwan and South Korea shows that in many industries small establishments were as productive or more productive, in terms of total factor productivity, than large establishments. Small plants were particularly productive in simple assembly and mixing and finishing industries (e.g., textiles) and, increasingly over time, in separable manufacturing operations (e.g., metalworking).

In the following section I develop this argument, suggesting that the Chinese family firm on Taiwan has certain advantages that enabled it to promote rapid growth and integration into the global economy in the 1960s and 1970s. Its disadvantages have become increasingly obvious in the 1980s, but the family enterprise is likely to continue to play important and beneficial roles even as the economy shifts toward more technology- and capital-intensive industries.

Why Family Enterprises Promote Growth and Integration

Although there are many studies of the effects of family enterprises on firm growth and national economic development, none of this literature is directly relevant to the present study. The received wisdom on Chinese family enterprises, which holds that they obstruct economic growth (e.g., Feuerwerker 1958; Levy 1949), is based on earlier historical periods, when the opportunities of the global market were not widely available. (However, recent research on Hong Kong has begun to revise this view, arguing, much as I argue here, that Chinese family firms may facilitate economic growth under contemporary conditions [Wong 1985; 1986].) Most of the studies of family firms in other societies stress the influence of these firms on the local economy, ignoring their impact on the pattern and rate of the country's integration into the world economy (e.g., Benedict 1968; Fruin 1980; Singer 1968; Strachan 1976; Tripathi 1981; White 1974). Furthermore, although family firms in different societies have some features in common, given cross-societal differences in family organization one must be cautious in generalizing from one country to another. Finally, in most of the societies that have been studied (e.g., Japan, Mexico, Nicaragua), family entrepreneurship has declined in importance as industrialization has proceeded (Fruin 1980; Lomnitz and Lizaur 1978; Strachan 1976). On Taiwan, despite rapid industrialization, there are no signs—at least not yet—that families have relinquished their control over the island's economy (supporting data are presented just below). In this section I suggest some of the reasons why this is so. Since there is not space to elaborate all organizational features of Chinese family firms on Taiwan, I propose a set of hypotheses about the key characteristics that have enabled them to promote rapid growth and integration into the global economy.

The family enterprise is a business firm, or group of related firms (*chi-t'uan*, described below), whose major decision-making positions are occupied by individuals related by blood, marriage, or adoption. The family enterprise grows in stages that are linked in part to the development of the family at its core. Although no two families develop in exactly the same way, an ideal or maximal developmental progression would proceed as follows. It would begin with a "nuclear" stage, comprising a married couple and any unmarried children. When the first son (or, much less often, daughter) marries,[4] the firm family develops into a "stem" form (married couple, one married child with his spouse, any unmarried children), and thence into "joint" form (married couple, two or more married children with their spouses, any unmarried children; or married couple, one or more married brothers and their spouses, any unmarried children). The most complex form can be called the "extended" firm family, and comprises either a family that is joint (i.e., contains two or more married couples in the same generation) in both senior and junior generations, or two joint families linked by marriage.

While firm families of all sizes and stages have certain growth-promoting features, nuclear and stem families are often too small to foster rapid economic growth and diversification. In general, it is only extended families that offer the full range of advantages described below. Nuclear, stem, and joint families might best be considered stages on the way to the development of the extended firm family.

The Chinese family enterprise is a highly effective form of organization that promotes internal economic growth and external integration into the global economy. The advantages of the Taiwan family firm stem in large part from four features of its organization, two of which are aspects of its internal structure, and two features of its relation to the environment:[5]

Organization

1. Use of family members to staff key positions and alignment of these positions with members' age, sex, and generation.

2. Package of individual incentives and group risk insurance.

Environment

3. Use of networks of kin and friends to recruit labor, capital, and information.

4. Strategies of spatial dispersal and economic diversification.

The hypotheses developed below are based on my reading of the literature on family economy on Taiwan, as well as study of the organization and operation of the island's largest business groups (discussed below). My understanding of the island's family firms was greatly enriched by interviews, conducted in 1978–1980, with twenty-five business executives (here called "informants"), of whom twenty-four ran family businesses. With the exception of Mark's intensive study of a handful of family enterprises (1972), to my knowledge these are the only interviews with Taiwan's entrepreneurs that focus on the familial organization of their companies.

Personnel

The first factor behind the success of the family enterprise is reliance on family members to fill key roles and alignment of these roles with position in the kinship system. In all the family firms I studied, the top managerial positions were held by core family members. Allocation of these positions among family members was guided in large part by age, sex, and generation (see table 11.1). In large firms and multicompany business groups, senior generation males (informants and brothers in table 11.1) generally filled the top positions of president and board chairman. If they worked, older generation females (especially wives and sisters-in-law of the informants) usually served as financial manager or worked in sales or production. Junior generation males were likely to work as factory manager of a large enterprise, or as president of a small company within a business group. Younger generation females (daughters or daughters-in-law of informants), when they worked, generally held positions of little responsibility such as accountant, clerk, or even production worker. In small enterprises there was considerable role overlap, but this hierarchy of responsibility by position in the kinship system was still very evident. In this sample the sex and generation hierarchies are particularly striking. Eighty-eight percent of all men held managerial positions, while only 14 percent of women were managers. Similarly, 77

Table 11.1

Work Positions of Family Members, 24 Family Firms, 1979

Positions within family firm[a]	Men					Women					
	Informant	Brother	Son	Son-in-law	All men	Wife	Mother, sister	Sister-in-law	Daughter	Daughter-in-law	All women
Managerial positions											
Chairman/president	24	5	3	—	32	2	—	—	—	—	2
General manager	—	2	8	—	10	—	—	—	—	—	—
Financial manager	—	1	1	—	2	2	—	—	—	—	2
Factory manager	—	2	3	—	5	—	—	—	—	—	—
Other manager	—	6	11	—	17	—	—	—	1	—	1
Assistant manager	—	—	3	—	3	—	—	—	—	—	—
Foreman	—	2	—	—	2	—	—	—	—	—	—
Total	24	18	29	0	71	4	0	0	1	0	5
Nonmanagerial positions											
Sales	—	—	3	—	3	4	1	—	1	—	6
Accountant	—	—	—	—	—	—	1	1	2	1	5
Clerical	—	—	—	—	—	—	—	—	3	1	4
Laborer	—	—	6	1	7	1	—	—	—	—	1
Miscellaneous and/or part-time work	—	—	—	—	—	2	—	4	2	7	15
Total	0	0	9	1	10	7	2	5	8	9	31

Note: a. Where individuals hold more than one position, table records only the best (i.e., most responsible) position.

percent of the senior generation but only 53 percent of the junior generation worked in a managerial capacity.

Use of family members to fill key positions is critical to the operation of the family enterprise because it ensures a core of dedicated and trustworthy managers and workers, who will not abandon the enterprise when the going gets rough or brighter opportunities appear elsewhere (for an account of the labor turnover problem see DeGlopper 1979). This is particularly critical on Taiwan, where the desire to be boss (*tang lao-pan*) is extremely strong (DeGlopper 1979; Stites 1982b), and workers who are not personally committed to a firm through familial obligations often depart to set up their own companies, taking with them important technical information and managerial experience (see also chapter 10). Having a group of individuals committed to stay with the firm through strong familial obligations gives the family business important advantages over other firms. Not only can it maintain greater secrecy about its operations—a critical asset in Taiwan's hypercompetitive environment (DeGlopper 1972; Mark 1972; Stites 1982b)—but it also enjoys greater continuity over time in management and operation.

The alignment of business responsibilities with kinship position also gives important advantages to the family enterprise. The correspondence between position within the firm and position within the family lowers transaction costs among key decision-making personnel and ensures a relatively smooth flow of authority from the president/father on down. Because lines of authority are clearly established and culturally sanctioned by widely accepted notions about proper family relationships, family firms are able to respond rapidly to changes in the environment in which they operate.

Incentives

Far from being a communal, group-dominated organization, the Taiwan family enterprise embodies a balance of group and individual benefits that provide strong incentives for sons, the key younger generation members, to remain in the firm. Property acquired by the father (or jointly by the father and one or more sons) is generally held in the father's name to be distributed equally among sons at the time of family partition. However, sons who work full-time in the firm are usually paid salaries, which they may invest in individual assets such as new enterprises or shares in other companies. Thus, even while they are working for the family as a whole, sons are accumulating private assets that will form the core of their personal property after family division. Furthermore, working within the family context provides an important additional benefit not available to the individual entrepreneur: substantial protection against failure. Since a family's capital is usually spread across a number of enterprises, when one company fails, its head can borrow assets from the other companies to start a new venture.

This package of individual incentives and group insurance promotes the emergence of highly motivated, risk-taking entrepreneurs. The capacity to take risks is particularly advantageous where economic activities are exceedingly complex, involving actors in many different countries, and information is highly imperfect. In such circumstances, common throughout the Third World, those able to seize opportunities on limited information are likely to make extremely large profits.

Networks

The Taiwan family enterprise relies extensively on networks of kin and friends for strategic resources such as labor, capital, and information (see, e.g., DeGlopper 1972; 1979; Hu 1983; Mark 1972; Stites 1982b). In my sample of twenty-four familial entrepreneurs, all had relied on family resources for at least a portion of their start-up capital, and many had expanded their capital networks to distant relatives and friends by selling shares in their corporations. In 1979, decades after their formation, these firms still relied heavily on family capital. Two huge business groups—Hsin Yen Textile Group and Kung Hsueh She Group—were almost wholly family-financed. Family firms also used trusted family members to fill their most important managerial positions. In all the firms studied in depth the presidents were family members. In twelve of the thirteen firms for which information is available, distant relatives (i.e., those outside the immediate family) were hired to work in some capacity. Anecdotal evidence suggests that family firms also rely heavily on social networks for information on new products and technology, market trends, and the like. Many entrepreneurs I interviewed seemed to put most trust in information that came from family members and sent key members, usually sons, abroad to gather such information firsthand. (This practice is also reported among plant exporters; see Amsden 1984, 503, n. 8.)

Reliance on social networks for strategic resources facilitates enterprise growth and flexibility in many ways. Use of social networks for labor and capital lowers the cost of these resources because family members will work for less and friends may accept lower wages in exchange for more freedom in when and where they work (Stites 1982b). In an environment in which bank loans are very difficult for small firms to obtain, use of social networks ensures access to much more capital than would otherwise be available.[6]

It also allows the firm greater flexibility in the allocation of these resources: verbal agreements among friends are more easily made and unmade than are formal contracts among strangers (e.g., Hu 1983, 85). The flow of business information through informal channels ensures the rapid transmission of information on changes in technology, markets, and the like. Because social networks provide ready access both to new information and to abundant, flexible, low-cost resources, their use ensures flexibility in the face of change and rapid response to new opportunities. Networks are thus particularly advantageous in peripheral and semiperipheral regions of the world economy, where capital and technology are scarce and where flexibility is the key to successful utilization of world market opportunities.

Use of personal ties to do business also facilitates the creation of new linkages, both within the local economy and between local and foreign firms. My interviews revealed that within the Taiwan economy, center/satellite firm relations are often established when technical or managerial employees of an older firm leave to set up their own factories, which then supply goods to their former employer's company (see also *FEER* 21 July 1983). Similarly, personal connections often underlie joint venture, subcontracting, and technical assistance relations between local and foreign firms, thus shaping the nature of Taiwan's connections to the global economy. In the Taiwan cultural context, the use of personal networks to make international business connections means that many such ties will be with ethnic Chinese and other East Asians. The apparent ease with which Chinese from Taiwan communicate with other East Asians has speeded the movement of Taiwan's companies into areas of the world where other East Asians live. For example, the existence of Chinese computer specialists in California's Silicon Valley has encouraged Taiwan computer companies to establish R&D facilities there (*FEER* 7 March 1985). The linguistic and other cultural similarities between Taiwanese and Chinese from Fukien province have facilitated the investment of Taiwanese firms in the Xiamen (Amoy) Special Economic Zone (*FEER* 9 May 1985).

Strategies

Another source of the family enterprise's competitiveness is its use of spatial dispersal and economic (product or industry) diversification as basic strategies of expansion and consolidation, or risk spreading (for ethnographic descriptions of these strategies see DeGlopper 1972; Mark 1972). Although these are common strategies among all business firms, they are likely to be more prevalent in the family company because they are built into the social structure of the firm. Diversification satisfies the needs of sons to achieve a measure of independence and creativity within the context of the larger father-dominated enterprise. This, in fact, is a primary aim of "joint investment, separate management," a strategy most businessmen consider ideal (Mark 1972). Similarly, dispersal allows sons and their wives to move out of the parental household, thus easing mother-in-law/daughter-in-law tensions that often contribute to the early division of the family, and thus of the family firm. For the family firm, then, these strategies serve a dual function, promoting both economic goals and social cohesion.

Diversification and dispersal strategies are particularly advantageous to firms in the periphery and semiperiphery of the world economy. Given the rapid change of consumer tastes in core markets and the rapid advance of technology, diversification makes firms more likely to survive downturns in core markets and to benefit from the development of new technologies. The advantages of diversification stem in part from the associated small scale of production in each unit: the small subfirms that result do not tie up all the parent firm's resources in the production of one good and can easily shift technology or even product in response to changes in global economic conditions. (Examples of such shifts abounded in my sample; see also DeGlopper 1979; Stites 1982b.) Dispersal also greatly benefits firms outside the core. Given the constant change in factor costs in different parts of the world and the increase in barriers to core markets, firms that move sales outlets or production facilities to other locations are better able to survive and prosper.

Disadvantages of Family Enterprises

Although the family enterprise offers a number of advantages, it also has certain disadvantages, which its critics have duly noted. Perhaps the major disadvantage of the family business is the flip side of its propensity to diversify into relatively small-scale units: because it disperses capital rather than concentrating it, the family firm has relatively few resources to invest in upgrading its technology or in R&D of new technology (see chapter 10). Nor can it easily achieve the economies of scale that reduce unit production costs in large firms (but see Y. M. Ho's finding, noted above, that scale economies are unimportant in many industries). A second set of problems stems from its short lifespan: because its outlook is short-term, geared to the life of its individual members, the family enterprise tends to concentrate on short-term profits. General lack of concern with long-term profitability and business reputation, coupled with the security cushion provided by the family group, encourage the kinds of malpractices for which Taiwan's firms have unfortunately become famous: counterfeiting of products, fabrication of accounts, and other illegal practices such as the use of bank loans to speculate in real estate (*FEER* 21 April 1983; 26 April 1984; 11 April 1985; 23 May 1985).

Given these advantages and disadvantages, Taiwan's family firms probably made their most important contributions to the island's development in earlier stages of that process, the 1960s and early 1970s, when the government sought rapid industrialization via utilization of global capital, technology, and markets. Since the mid–1970s, when the island began to move into industries that are technology, skill, and capital intensive, the family firm may have become less central to Taiwan's development, and may even retard the type of growth the island needs to maintain its position in the world economy. However, even if it relinquishes a leading role in economic development, the family enterprise will continue to play important roles, fostering flexibility, rapid response to new opportunities, and continued participation in global networks of technology, capital, and trade. Amsden's (1984) work on plant exports illustrates the kinds of contributions small firms can make in the 1980s and 1990s. Her research shows that firms engaged in plant exports—the principal form of technology exports in the late 1970s—were mostly small in scale, had quality control and design departments staffed by highly skilled workers, and innovated their technology to a surprising extent.

Prevalence, Structural Complexity, and Scale of Operations

In the absence of aggregate, nationwide data on family firms, the arguments developed above have been based largely on anthropological fieldwork and economic journalism. In this section I present some larger-scale data confirming that Taiwan's family enterprises have facilitated the island's rapid economic growth and global integration. These data show, first, that most of Taiwan's firms are family run, and second, that family enterprises perform better than nonfamily businesses in growth and access to global resources.

Prevalence of Family Enterprises

How numerically important is the family firm in the modern or industrial sector of Taiwan's economy? Throughout the 1970s and early 1980s, the family firm was the predominant form of business organization, and it extended across all scales of organization. According to the 1971 Industrial and Commercial Census, 64.1 percent of manufacturing enterprises employed 1–9 workers, 23.6 percent employed 10–29 workers, while only 4.3 percent employed 100 or more workers (Committee on Industrial and Commercial Censuses 1971). My interviews with presidents of firms in all size classes suggest that the capital and managerial requirements of the 92.1 percent of firms in the 1–50 worker range are within the capability of one family to provide. Although quantitative evidence of the organizational form of small-scale firms is lacking, most observers agree that the vast majority of small firms are family firms (e.g., *FEER*, 25 July 1985).

Data on Taiwan's largest business groups (*chi-t'uan*)—groups of three or more companies interrelated by managerial, capital, and/or production linkages[7]—indicate that the largest firms on the island are also mostly family firms. Using biographical information on leading individuals in these groups, I developed two measures of the extent of familial control: an index of the familial "structure" of the core executive group, and a measure of the extent of familial penetration of management and shareholding.

The "leadership core" includes those executive and management personnel listed in the standard directory to these groups (CCIS 1978, 1983/84), usually chairman of the board and general manager. Examination of the social ties among the individuals holding these positions showed that in 1983/84, sixty-two of the one hundred economic groups had familial groups at their core. Seventeen other groups can be said to be run by individuals. In these groups the executive positions were concentrated in the hands of one individual, while the management positions were dispersed among a number of persons, none related to the

---

Table 11.2

Extent of Familial Penetration, 79 Family-Based Economic Groups, 1983–84

	Close relatives	Same surname
	(percent of total)	
Executive and managerial positions		
Executive positions	80.4	82.8
Managerial positions	37.6	45.1
All executive and managerial positions	59.9	64.8
Stocks		
Large share blocs	39.4	61.4

Note: Includes some groups whose executive cores are individuals but whose shareholders include relatives of these individuals.

---

executive, and none holding more than two positions. Nineteen executive cores included two or more people related by ties of locality (seven),[8] school background (one), shared professional interest (five), or ties of some other sort (six). Thus, most of the groups not run by families were run either by individuals, or by several individuals connected by other forms of network ties.

The data in table 11.2 suggest that among the groups with familial units at their core, familial penetration was deep, and that the more important the executive/managerial position, the more likely it was to be held by a member of the dominant kin group. Whereas kin group members kept the vast majority—about 80–85 percent—of the executive positions for themselves, they were much more likely to allow outsiders to serve as general managers. Only 38 percent of the managerial positions were filled by identifiable relatives, while 45 percent were filled by people with the same surname. (Because information on kin relationships was incomplete it was necessary to distinguish two levels of relatedness: identifiable relatives, those whose kin ties were explicitly mentioned in the text; and individuals with the same surname as the dominant family group. Those with the same surname are likely to be related to the dominant kin group, but a relationship cannot be firmly established without more information.)

Data on shareholding also suggest substantial familial penetration of economic groups and their component companies. Of the blocs of shares held by individuals (as opposed to corporations, which control a small number of share blocs), 39 percent were held by identifiable relatives, while 61 percent were held by those with the same surname. Thus, while more distant kin were rarely brought into management, it appears they were often invited to buy shares.

Putting all this evidence together, one can determine how many firms are familial in form. If a minimum of 62 percent of firms with fifty or more workers are familial (as indicated by the number of business groups with families at their core), and all firms with fewer than fifty workers are family run (as indicated by anthropological and other research), then roughly 97.4 percent of all Chinese business firms on Taiwan are family firms.

Complexity of Family and Scale of Operations

Does familial organization contribute to enterprise development and thus national economic growth? Some suggestive answers can be found by examining the relationship between business group performance and the degree of structural complexity of the familial units at their core. Assuming that all executives and managers are married, the sixty-four family-based groups can be classified as follows: eighteen were either nuclear units of husband and wife (five) or stem units of father and one son or, less frequently, son-in-law (thirteen); twenty-eight were joint units containing two or more nuclear units in either the senior or the junior generation; twelve were extended units, either containing two or more nuclear units in both generations (nine), or containing two joint families joined by marriage (three). (Here I use the 1978 data on these groups, which are more complete for this purpose.)

Table 11.3 shows that as the executive core of family business groups becomes more complex, virtually all aspects of group size and economic strength increase. Moreover, extended familial groups are economically much better off than nonfamilial groups (those with individuals or friends in their executive cores) or all groups. The "leadership network" (those holding executive and managerial positions) of the extended familial group is 2.1 times as large as that of all groups, while the "capital network" (those holding major share blocs in any company in the group) is 1.7 times larger. Greater familial complexity also brings more companies and employees under group control. Extended familial groups control 1.9 times as many companies and employ 2.2 times as many workers as all groups. Greater familial complexity also brings increased assets and sales. Assets per group are 2.5 times higher in extended family groups than in all groups, while sales are 1.8 times higher.

Extended family firms also promote integration into global resource networks. Table 11.4 shows the advantages of extended family firms in obtaining foreign managerial expertise, investment, and technology. Relative to all economic groups, in 1978 extended family economic groups were 3.0 times more successful in bringing foreign management into their executive core, 1.9 times more successful in obtaining foreign investment, and 1.4 times more successful in obtaining technology cooperation agreements with foreign firms. These measures of scale and global resource acquisition are likely to be affected by the economic sector in which groups operate. Unfortunately the small number of groups of each type in each sector makes it difficult to control for sector. However, use of several measures of these outcomes presumably has somewhat reduced the effect of

Table 11.3

Group Type and Group Size, 100 Economic Groups, 1978

Type of economic group (based on structure of executive core)	Size of leadership network (persons)	Size of capital network (persons)	Number of companies	Number of employees	Assets	Sales	Number of groups
Individual[a]	4.2	15.7	4.7	2,150	1,761	1,499	18
Friends	7.2	20.2	5.7	2,436	2,761	2,171	17
Familial							
Nuclear and stem[b]	6.0	14.1	6.2	2,631	1,822	1,715	18
Joint[c]	5.8	17.3	5.8	3,028	3,025	2,764	28
Extended[d]	14.2	33.0	12.5	6,547	7,292	4,288	12
All familial[e]	7.6	19.7	7.3	3,425	3,364	2,681	64
All groups[f]	6.8	19.0	6.5	3,019	2,958	2,375	100
Extended: All groups	2.1X	1.7X	1.9X	2.2X	2.5X	1.8X	—

[a]Includes groups whose executive cores are individuals but whose shareholders include relatives of these individuals.
[b]Executive core includes husband and wife or father and son.
[c]Executive core includes father and two or more sons or two or more brothers.
[d]Executive core is extended in both senior and junior generations or comprises two familial groups joined by marriage.
[e]Includes six "other" types of familial groups.
[f]Includes one group not elsewhere classified.

Table 11.4

Group Type and Foreign Connections, 100 Economic Groups, 1978

Type of economic group (based on structure of executive core)	Foreign executive	Foreign investment	Foreign technology[g]	Number of groups
		(percent of total)		
Individual[a]	11	28	39	18
Friends	6	47	59	17
Familial				
Nuclear and stem[b]	6	28	39	18
Joint[c]	7	29	36	28
Extended[d]	33	75	67	12
All familial[e]	13	34	45	64
All groups[f]	11	40	47	100
Extended: All groups	3.0X	1.9X	1.4X	—

[a]Includes groups whose executive cores are individuals but whose shareholders include relatives of these individuals.
[b]Executive core includes husband and wife or father and son.
[c]Executive core includes father and two or more sons or two or more brothers.
[d]Executive core is extended in both senior and junior generations or comprises two familial groups joined by marriage.
[e]Includes six "other" types of familial groups.
[f]Includes one group not elsewhere classified.
[g]Has signed technology cooperation agreement with foreign firm.

possible sectoral bias. The age of the group does not appear to be a confounding factor. Although extended familial groups were founded slightly earlier than other groups, when age is controlled, extended family groups still performed considerably better than other types of groups. Despite limitations, these data suggest that family enterprise organization contributes to the growth and global integration of enterprises and, by extension, to the growth and global integration of the economy as a whole.

Conclusion

Though of limited quantity and varying quality, the data presented here suggest that microsocial institutions can help to shape a society's pattern of economic growth and participation in the world economy. On Taiwan microsocial effects appear to have been extraordinarily beneficial, promoting rapid growth and effective external ties.

This conclusion challenges a basic assumption of both radical and liberal theories about the balance of power among constituent elements of the world system. These theories assume that microsocial institutions are weak entities, passive elements in processes that are dominated largely by macroeconomic and macropolitical forces. A close look at Taiwan suggests a very different balance of power, one in which microsocial forces not only shape larger outcomes, but also constrain the actions of the state and multinationals.

The power of microsocial institutions such as family enterprises to defy states and foreign corporations has been quite apparent since the early to mid–1970s, when the government began devising means to reduce the influence of family-run firms. Because of intensifying competition from less developed countries, rising wages, and hardening barriers to core country markets, around 1970 the government started to encourage the development of more capital- and technology-intensive industries. These developments threatened the family firm, which often tends to disperse capital, and thus lacks the resources to support capital-intensive methods or develop advanced technology. During the 1970s and 1980s relations between the government and the families operating these firms have at times resembled an outright struggle, in which the state has attempted to encourage mergers and eliminate unprofitable firms (through incentives, making credit contingent on merging, etc.), while family enterprises have sought to retain their independence by refusing to merge, employing illegal means to maintain profits (going underground, evading taxes, using loans to speculate in the real estate market) and moving transactions through informal (network) channels to avoid government scrutiny (*FEER*, 14 October 1977; Stites 1982b, 167–70). This struggle has taken place in a great many arenas. In the mid–1980s issues of contention included the use of the unorganized money market, control of counterfeiting, inclusion of financial institutions within industrial business groups, reform of accounting practices, and the 1984 Labor Standards Law, in particular its provisions on overtime work and pensions (*FEER* 26 April 1984, 6 September 1984, 11 April 1985, 23 May 1985). Although the state has the advantage in legal and financial resources, the slowness of progress in resolving these issues is a clear sign that family enterprises have other sources of strength, some of which have been described above, that they use to protect and advance their interests.

Taiwan's family enterprises have also been successful in pursuing their interests in dealings with foreign companies and banks. Although foreign corporations often call the shots in deals concerning technology, trade, and joint ventures,[9] Chinese entrepreneurs have controlled, manipulated, or sabotaged interactions with foreigners in other ways. Chinese managers hired by multinational companies frequently jump ship and set up rival firms, taking with them valuable contacts, training, and technical information (Simon 1987). More notorious is the practice of counterfeiting. Ingenious Chinese entrepreneurs have devised such good imitations of foreign products—everything from Levi's jeans to Apple II computers—that Taiwan has gained the dubious distinction of being the world's foremost producer of fake goods.[10] Chinese businessmen have also outmaneuvered foreign banks. In mid–1985, 18 percent of the total assets of foreign banks on Taiwan were tied up in uncollectable loans. Many of these loans were given on the basis of unreliable financial statements submitted by Chinese firms (*FEER*, 25 April 1985).

Indeed, it could be said that, although Taiwan's development is not distorted in the ways radical theories predict, it is distorted, or at least shaped, by the excessive influence of family enterprises and network strategies. Many critics have argued that Taiwan's firms are too small, too undercapitalized, and too prone to illegal activity. As has been seen, all these characteristics flow directly or indirectly from the familial nature of the island's businesses and the stronghold that enterprise families have gained in the economy. Although Taiwan may be an extreme case in which society has an exceptionally strong impact on the economy, it suggests that both radical and liberal theorists need to adopt more conservative assumptions about the balance of power between levels in the world economy. In all regions, but especially in East Asia, they need to give microsocial forces a larger share.

The Taiwan material also calls for a "radicalizing" and perhaps also "liberalizing" of conservative theories. Conservative theorists generally recognize a role for microsocial forces in macroeconomic development, but they tend to assume that traditional social and cultural forms simply persist from the past into the present. Although this study has not explored how microsocial institutions got to be how they are, it is clear that contemporary Taiwan families and firms are not mere replications of traditional Chinese families and firms. Anthropological work suggests that they are organized along similar principles, but these units are larger and structurally more complex than they were in the past (e.g., Gallin and Gallin 1982; Greenhalgh 1988). How did this increase in scale come about? With respect to families, I argue elsewhere (1988) that certain political-economic developments both enabled and forced families to grow in size and complexity. Most critical were the land reform, the switch to export-oriented industrialization at the time of a huge boom in the world economy, the nature of the foreign-domestic division of labor, and certain implicit policies of the government toward the family. Macroeconomic and political forces also lay behind the proliferation of family enterprises. Throughout the postwar period the lack of access to bank capital has forced would-be entrepreneurs to rely on families and friends for capital. My interviews showed clearly that in the 1970s the rising costs of labor and capital forced small enterprises to depend increasingly on family resources. Thus, the apparent persistence of apparently traditional social forms obscures the active and continuous adaptation of microsocial institutions to the market forces emphasized by liberal thinkers and the macropolitical and economic processes stressed by radical theorists.

If microsocial forces do play important political-economic roles, then regional differences in microsocial organization should account for some of the differences between subglobal regions in patterns of development, distribution, and global integration. A central theme of this chapter is that Taiwan (and, by implication, the rest of East Asia) is different in part because its microsocial structure is different. Although demonstration of this argument requires cross-national comparisons of a sort I have not attempted, the data presented here make a good prima facie case for it, suggesting that it is worth further investigation.

If Taiwan's microsocial institutions are stronger and more facilitative of development than those elsewhere, why should this be so? They may be stronger both because traditional Chinese familial institutions were extremely strong and cohesive, and because certain aspects of postwar political economy, described above, worked to promote strong families. Because they developed in a traditional economy that shared certain features in common with capitalism—e.g., high degrees of commercialization and monetization, private ownership of property, profit orientation—one might say they were partly "preadapted" to capitalism. This facility for operating in a market economy may lie behind the ease with which Taiwan's families shifted from agriculture to industry and from domestic to internationally oriented economic activity in the postwar period. These ideas, however, are speculative. More research needs to be done to determine the extent to which East Asian microsocial structures are in fact different from those elsewhere, and the degree to which regional differences in social structure lie behind regional differences in economic growth and global integration.

Notes

1. Fei, Ranis, and Kuo (1979) recognize that family influence and rules of family formation have an effect on income distribution, but they leave these effects for others to measure. Similarly, Kuznets (1979) notes the impact of household size and life cycle position on inequality but does not attempt to assess these impacts.

2. Arrived foreign investment as a share of gross domestic private capital formation averaged 5.2 percent in the 1960s and 2.8 percent in the 1970s (Ranis and Schive 1985, 95).

3. For example, in the automobile parts industry, the products of small manufacturers are estimated to cost 20–60 percent more than similar goods produced in the United States or Japan (*FEER*, 27 September 1984). A Ministry of Economic Affairs study in 1974 showed that in a number of manufacturing sectors, production costs of small firms were 10 percent higher than those of large firms. The expenses of small companies were higher because they had higher rates of labor turnover and ordered raw materials in smaller quantities (*FEER*, 18 July 1975).

4. Taiwan is a patrilineal society in which a daughter usually joins her husband's kin group at marriage.

5. Other features of the family firm that contribute to its effectiveness are discussed in the works noted above and in a stimulating article by Lipton (1984). My discussion of Taiwan family firms is based largely on my own fieldwork, conducted in 1978–1980, but also draws on the work of DeGlopper (1972, 1979), Hu (1983), Mark (1972), and Stites (1982).

6. Small manufacturing firms pay wages that are about 15–40 percent lower than those of large firms (Ho 1980, 340). Studies show that up to 40 percent of the capital requirements of private companies are met by loans from the unorganized money market (*FEER*, 25 April 1985). This figure would no doubt approach 100 percent if only the smallest firms were included.

7. The China Credit Information Service, whose materials I used here, defines *chi-*

t'uan as groups of three or more companies whose core company is Chinese, assets and sales both exceed NT $200 million, and members all acknowledge relatedness to the core company (CCIS 1978, 4, 12).

8. Six of the seven groups bound by common locality ties were formed by mainlanders. Four were from Shantung, and one each was from Fukien and Hopei.

9. On Japanese reluctance to transfer advanced technology see chapter 10. Japanese trading companies are believed to control 50–60 percent of Taiwan's trade. Foreign corporations have also been known to pull out of joint ventures (e.g., in petrochemicals and automobiles), leaving their local counterparts in the lurch (see, for example, *FEER*, 6 August 1982, 27 September 1984).

10. A 1982 study conducted by the U.S. International Trade Commission showed that 60 percent of the world's counterfeited goods came from Taiwan. The Taiwan government has taken tough measures against counterfeiters, imposing stiffer penalties for offences and convicting growing numbers of offenders (*FEER*, 23 May 1985).

CONCLUSION

12

Bruce Cumings

WORLD SYSTEM AND AUTHORITARIAN REGIMES IN KOREA, 1948–1984

Theories of the world system and of bureaucratic-authoritarian states in Latin America emerged about a decade ago in American scholarship, the key works being those by Immanuel Wallerstein (1974) and Guillermo O'Donnell (1973). With a few exceptions (e.g., Moulder 1977), little work has been done to see how East Asian development looks through the lenses of either theory. In this essay I wish to make some overarching comments on the theories themselves, and suggest ways in which East Asian development in general and Korean development in particular may help inform the theories and may be explained by them, at least in part.

Grand Theories: Function versus Interest

The two bodies of radical theory are not contradictory. Bureaucratic-authoritarian (BA) models give us the trajectories of individual political economies as they industrialize; the emphasis, somewhat as in modernization theory, is on particular nation-states usually considered apart from each other, or compared with each other on the basis of distinct, if still comparable, developmental trajectories. World system (WS) theory seeks to analyze the totality of global interaction over time. Its tendency is to downplay or even neglect particularities of national and class development; it favors the whole over the parts (for elaboration see chapter 1). Thus a combination of the two bodies of theory should be fruitful.

Yet there remain problems with the two theories. The central statement of BA theory is in a volume rife with controversy about whether the theory applies to any Latin American state save Argentina, and indeed over whether the theory has much utility at all (Collier 1979). Where the BA model is strong in looking at the developmental trajectories of particular societies, WS theory too often tends to see particular national societies as putty to be shaped by external forces. This will not do in Northeast Asia, where one finds similar developmental trajectories but with very different societies and social reactions in Taiwan, South Korea, and Japan. WS theory tends also to treat state power as mostly derivative of class and national conflict, or of position in the world system; BA theory views the state as a resultant of particular industrialization strategies. Both theories tend to deny an autonomous role to the state, and indeed to politics in general. Yet in the East Asian cases of Taiwan, South Korea and Japan, much of the literature dwells upon what is usually called the relative autonomy of the state, and economic development under strong state auspices is common to all of them. At the same time, the best literature on the more or less autonomous role that states play in development has its own explicit or implicit biases against an interest-based analysis, such as that represented by BA and WS theory. This literature also has a tendency toward static or "conjunctural" analysis that is, in my view, less preferable than the emphasis on explaining change over time, and indeed the effects of timing itself ("late" and "late-late" development), that one derives from BA and WS theory (see Cumings 1981). Is there a way to reconcile the strengths and weakness of the two theories and arrive at a superior synthesis?

Perhaps yes, but only at the cost of parsimonious theory. A book that satisfies the demand for comprehensiveness in analysis, but at the cost of parsimonious explanation, is Polanyi's *The Great Transformation* (1944). This is the central "missing link" between Marx, Hobson, and Lenin, on the one hand, and Wallerstein, on the other, in spite of (or perhaps because of) Polanyi's not being a Marxist. Like Wallerstein, Polanyi in effect defines capitalism as production for profit in a world market, rather than linking it to a particular mode of production or social formation. Unlike Wallerstein in theory but like Wallerstein in practice, Polanyi tends to underplay or even deny that social classes and their conflictual interests are motive forces in development. Rather than being class-based, his conception of society is associated metaphorically with a human web that reacts in different but always critically important ways to capitalism and industrial development. So, we might adopt this conception of society embracing Polanyi's human web notion, along with the conventional view of a system structured by groups and classes to fill a critical gap in WS theory.

Polanyi also understands that the functioning of the world system requires a hegemon, a political force capable of looking after the whole and of regulating economic exchange at the most fundamental level. Thus, in the beginning of his book, Polanyi provides a powerful explanation for the nineteenth-century world system, in the form of British hegemony and the gold standard rather than the usual formulations about the balance of power. Elsewhere I have argued that a hegemonic system has been necessary for the functioning of the Northeast Asian political economy (Cumings 1984). Polanyi also has a subtle and therefore often overlooked conception of the timing of industrialization: it makes a difference if you are the only industrializer, such as England, or a "late" industrializer, like Germany or Japan. Gerschenkron (1962), Kurth (1979a), Hirschman (1971), and O'Donnell (1973) have filled out this crucial question of timing.

Still, Polanyi's analysis lacks the predictive and explanatory utility of an interest-based theory. Perhaps none of us likes to live in a world where tough, concrete calculations of interest are the rule, but that is the essence of a capitalist world-economy, accepted by its major theorists from Adam Smith to Karl Marx. They differ only on whether the calculation of interest resides at the individual or the collective level.[1]

Theories of interest that take the individual as the unit of analysis (e.g., rational actor models, "public choice" political economy) may have heuristic utility in model-building, axiomatic theory, and the like.[2] They are not likely, however, to tell one much about East Asian development, which is perhaps the leading example in the world of state-fostered industrialization, as opposed to entrepreneurial, private-sector industrialization.

Wallerstein and O'Donnell both use class-based theories of interest, explicitly or implicitly. O'Donnell explains much about Latin American development in contrasting the interests of national and international bourgeoisies, analyzing inclusionary versus exclusionary coalitions in regard to the working class, and dwelling on the role of transnational elites, particularly technocrats and experts who are "carriers" of core ideologies in developing countries. Wallerstein, like Polanyi, views the transnational bourgeoisie as the human and class equivalent of the world market idea, knowing itself as the only "universal" class, supremely conscious of its interests, the only true class-for-itself in the world system. Polanyi aphoristically reduces this critically important conception to the Rothschild family, carrier and exemplar of the internationalist essence of a world-ranging capitalist class. All other classes, including other types of capitalists, are national and tend more or less to be classes-in-themselves, not classes-for-themselves. If they are the latter, nonetheless their interests often express purely local or national concerns; they lack a conception of the world economy, because they lack world-ranging interests.

Wallerstein expands this idea into a conception of a hierarchy of classes—core, semiperiphery, periphery—that play out upon the world the function of social stratification in particular societies: that is, the middle level disciplines the lower, provides stability to the system and avoids its polarization into two camps, and enables upward and downward mobility. These "classes" often materialize as "nations" in the world system, and indeed conflict within the system is fought out in multiple forms (the state, the class, the nation, the organization, as with multinational corporations) and in multiple ways (mercantilism, socialist withdrawal and self-reliance, the product cycle, wars). The great strength of the theory is its long view, its suppleness, its complexity, its equanimity about politics in the "short run," its dialectics which are necessary to capture a mode of production that, as Schumpeter put it, moves forth in waves of creation and destruction. Its weakness is its lack of parsimonious explanation, its tendency to explain everything and therefore nothing, its bias toward external structuring at the expense of internal dynamics in particular societies. The latter is particularly evident in the major Wallersteinian account of East Asian development, which collapses the agrarian societies of Japan and China together, the strained argument being that the similarities are more compelling than the differences (Moulder 1977, 27–45). Wallerstein thus provides an analysis that casts the debate at the proper level, that of the world system, but like Polanyi ends up with a diffuse menu of explanations for particular events, even for long eras if not for whole epochs of history.

Middle-Range Theories: Region, Product Cycle, Sector

There are some middle-range possibilities that could link the different levels of analysis found in BA and WS theory and preserve the analytical benefits of each while avoiding some of the costs. The first would be to isolate particular regions in the globe for analysis, not necessarily for any theoretical reason (although one disaggregates a welter of experience this way), but at least in the East Asian case, as will be seen, for very good historical reasons. The second would be to isolate particular theories or conceptions of change within the world system and see how much they can explain, such as the theory of the product cycle, which is compatible with both liberal modernization and radical world system analysis. The third and most important middle-range possibility is sectoral analysis. Sectoral analysis holds great potential in East Asia, and thus deserves further elaboration.

For Marx, Polanyi, Wallerstein, and I think also O'Donnell, although he is not explicit on this point, the capitalist world economy does not achieve its maturity or its expansive dynamism until the advent of industry. For Marx and Polanyi the early, textile phase of industrialization in England is critically important to their analyses; for Marxist and non-Marxist analysts such as Hobsbawm and Gerschenkron the next phase, heavy industrialization in steel, railroads, chemicals, and so forth, is perhaps the key determinant of mid- and late-nineteenth-century national rivalries, the relevant state/market mixes and forms peculiar to national industrialization strategies, and the timing of the onset of such strategies. Industrial capitalism may be on everyone's agenda, but no two industrializations are alike (Hobsbawm 1968, 109–33; Gerschenkron 1962).

In contemporary analysis James Kurth, Susan Strange, Thomas Ferguson, and others have focused on industrial sectors as key linkages and structures within the world economy. Some industries tend to be organized nationally (steel, railroads), while others tend to be organized internationally (banks, petroleum). Some have massed laborers and are "labor-intensive" (textiles); others are almost bereft of laborers and therefore labor problems (oil). Some have high start-up costs and others low, making some mobile within the world economy and others less mobile, or some easy to enter and others difficult. Some have simple technologies and therefore rapid product cycles in the world economy (textiles, light consumer electronics); others have complex technologies that can be husbanded and sheltered to keep out competitors (offshore oil).

This list of possibilities could go on, for there are rich rewards from a sectoral approach. An example would be Blair's *Control of Oil* (1978), a lesson in using the typical characteristics of a given industry to help explain the world oil regime, its origins, the great multinationals that dominated the regime, and the slow unravelling of it in the last two decades.

It may be the case that there is an identifiable sectoral interest that would characterize production, the work force, technology transfers, and the organization of bureaucracies regardless of whether it exists in a capitalist or socialist system. Thus, steel production would seem to be rather similar in Japan, South Korea, and China today, the differences varying far more with levels of technology than with social and political organization. The state tends to be more involved in steel than in textiles in all forms of "late" and "late-late" development. The role of multinational corporations seems to vary significantly from sector to sector. Product cycles are quicker in some industries than in others. Finally, it is clear that dependency, or the obstacles to upward mobility in the world system, differ according to sectoral mixes. Primary commodity production in general produces dependency relations that are more or less abject: witness Central America. Yet if the commodity is oil, one finds abject dependency in one era (the Middle East until the 1960s) and rapid upward mobility and a significant transfer of power to the Third World in another (the 1970s). Heavy industries are everywhere seen as necessary to any adequate self-reliance and independence within the system, by socialists like Kim Il Sung and capitalists like Park Chung Hee. "Knowledge industries" such as computers are the contemporary sectors without which core power is unattainable. Yet they seem to have far faster product cycles and technological dispersion, lower start-up costs, and thus greater world system mobility when compared to older heavy industries. Such an approach can explain much about Northeast Asian development, where the "natural" workings of sectoral interest, product cycles, and the like have been guided at least since the 1930s by the planned administrative hand of Japan.[3]

East Asian development also suggests that the relationship between industrialization strategies and BA regimes is anything but simple. In South Korea, as will be seen, a sharp turn toward authoritarianism in 1971–72 coincided with a pronounced "deepening" in the economy as the regime pushed for steel mills, petrochemical complexes, shipbuilding facilities, and auto factories. Yet this was long after the end of the import-substitution phase that is so important for O'Donnell, and after a decade of export-led development. Indeed, the "deepening" was itself a form of import substitution. The export-led program was also in jeopardy in 1971. This was the year in which the first mild downturn occurred in the ROK's rapid growth rates, and the year of the introduction of Nixon's New Economic Policy, which foreshadowed ever-increasing protectionism in the core countries. So, the Korean case seems to support Hirschman's (1979, 75) argument that export-led development may reinforce authoritarian tendencies, because of the necessity to repress interests associated with an earlier import-substitution phase, the difficulties in legitimating "orthodox" economics and exporting, the need to keep labor costs low for comparative advantage, and the like. Yet the Korean case unquestionably suggests a connection between deepening industrialization and authoritarianism as well (see fig. 12.1). What it does not suggest is any linear progression from one industrialization strategy to another, with a corresponding regime change. A dialectical conception on change seems to be more fruitful here.

In the cases of Taiwan and Japan, a preexisting strong state seems simply to have added on or changed functions as industrialization proceeded. Although Japan cannot be called a BA regime in the postwar period, it certainly was in the 1930s an archetype of what I have called a "bureaucratic-authoritarian industrializing regime" or BAIR, and in the postwar period the state bureaucracy was if anything more autonomous in directing the economy and pursuing "administrative guidance" (Cumings 1984, 26–35).The Nationalist state on Taiwan, once strong for promising to retake the mainland and maintaining mainlander power vis à vis Taiwanese natives, has for two decades been "strong" in directing industrial development. The role of the state in Japan has provided a model for planners in both Taiwan and Korea, and indeed, during the colonial period Japan trained state cadres who later rose to important positions in the postwar bureaucracies of both countries. But there is little question that the prior existence of strong states in Japan and Taiwan suggests that causal relations between economics and politics may reverse those of the BA theory: we may need a political explanation of industrial strategies in these two countries (see Hirschman 1979, 81).

Levels of Analysis: The World System

I have made some suggestions for how WS and BA theory might be improved, and some preliminary attempts to show how the Northeast Asian experience helps to inform both theories. The great strength of both theories, but especially WS theory, is their level of analysis. Both treat position in the world system as critical to particular industrialization strategies and roles for the state. It cannot be emphasized enough that WS theory takes the modern world as its subject and global interaction as its level of analysis. Using WS and BA theory as research tools thus imposes a heavy burden. One must seek to understand the totality of relationships affecting the development of, say, Taiwan and its dialectical interaction with the world system. Knowing Taiwan is not enough; knowing the world system is not enough.

The WS level of analysis is holistic and organic; it wars against all disaggregation and empiricism that looks at the parts and forgets the whole. Here is its basic fealty to Marx, and not by accident: both seek to understand a system that by virtue of being capitalist seeks to spread everywhere, to occupy the globe,

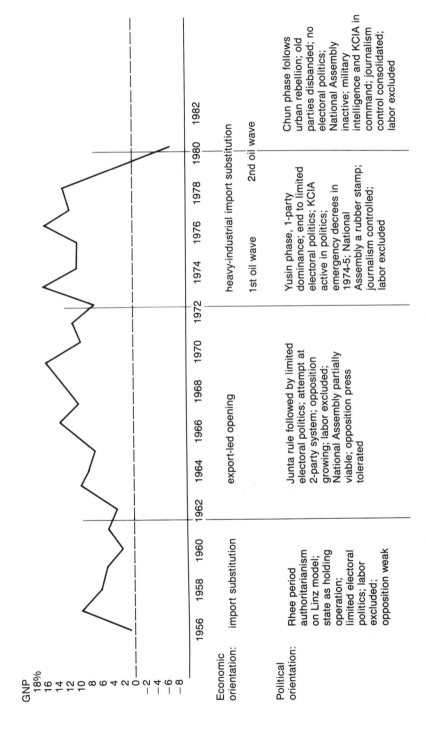

Figure 12.1 GNP Growth, Economic Orientation, and Deepening Authoritarianism.

oblivious to national boundaries, cultural systems, alternative world views. In so doing the system turns nations into sectors in a world-ranging division of labor, stratified entities in a world conceived as an integrated social system. The radical WS theory also respects history and has a basic indeterminacy in the "short run." Here is its superiority to liberal modernization theory, which tends to be ahistorical, to treat all developmental sequences as basically alike, and to possess a truly astonishing determinism at the core of its assumptions about human behavior: that is, all humans are rational actors, acting according to calculations of cost and benefit. Wallerstein and other sociologists like Charles Tilly and Theda Skocpol have made history important to an entire new generation of sociologists, which is no mean feat and something to be deeply grateful for. Far from being "determinist," WS theory posits a determinacy only for the long run: world socialist government one or two centuries hence. In the meantime the world system surprises us with stunning advances and reversals (for example, the opposite trajectories of Taiwan and Brazil in the past few years). In the short run the theory posits no inherent determinacy, so the analyst is left alone with an indeterminate conception and the facts of real people acting in history, if in circumstances not of their choosing. All this is a vast improvement over the modernization literature, and over the earlier dependency literature, carrying with it a strong determinism, not to mention a shriek of protest against capitalism.

The level of analysis of WS theory is so hard to grasp because it so deeply violates the fault lines that we usually pay attention to, regardless of political or analytical preferences. It violates the compartmentalized distinctions between academic disciplines, which fragment knowledge; it violates the presumed organization of the modern world, that is, a world of nation-states. It often violates accepted distinctions between "capitalist" and "socialist" nations, seeing both as particular forms of state and society within the broader capitalist world system. And it violates the regional distinctions so dear to the heart of area specialists. Let us turn now from theory to the regional context of Taiwan's and Korea's development.

The Regional Context: The Centrality of Japan

For the past century, East Asian history has been structured in great measure by Japan's competition with core powers in the world system, which has in turn deeply affected the history of Korea, Taiwan, and China in the same period. In other words, two factors can give us a parsimonious account and a necessary (if not sufficient) explanation of Japan's behavior since 1868: position in the world system and the temporal dimension of industrialization phases. Japan emerged as a modern nation late in world time, and in one of the few remaining interstices in the late nineteenth-century system. The onset and phasing of industrialization can explain the role of the state within Japan,[4] and why Japan has been the virtual originator of the classic product cycle, marked by strong state protection for nascent industries, adoption of foreign technologies, comparative advantage in world markets deriving first from cheap labor cost and later from technical virtuosity, finally a bursting forth into world markets that, at different stages, always struck foreign observers as abrupt and unexpected, thus inspiring (as today) awe and admiration, fear and loathing. It was Professor Akamatsu's "flying geese" pattern of product cycling in industrial development that best captured Japan's virtuosity (and predated Raymond Vernon's work on the subject by two decades) (Cumings 1984, 6–15). Akamatsu showed on graphs time-series curves for textiles, steel, autos, and so forth that depicted the rise and demise of such industries, and that when put together resembled a flock of flying geese. The point was always to decide at what place on the curve to jump off textiles to steel or autos, or electronics, and then farm those declining industries out to places like Taiwan or Korea (Cumings 1984). Of course, in doing this and other things Japan has gotten into a lot of trouble: its history of striving toward core status in the world economy reminds one less of flying geese than of moths toward a flame.

Competition with the core countries also led Japan into imperial ventures, leading to the annexation of Taiwan in 1895 and Korea in 1910, then to Manchuria in 1931; these countries then became the location of heavy industries in the 1930s as Japan—in unprecedented fashion compared with other imperial powers—brought factories to the labor and raw materials rather than vice-versa. Japan also located strong colonial state administrations in the colonies, not to mention social overhead infrastructures that make the traveler, even today, aware of striking similarities in the architectural physiognomy of Taiwan, Korea, and Manchuria. (The railway stations in Taipei, Seoul, and Harbin are good examples.)

Today Japan is far more involved in the economies of Taiwan, Korea, and China than is the United States. South Korea and Taiwan are the location of small and declining Japanese textile producers, light electronics firms, and, in recent years, heavy industries that have usually been built with varying degrees of Japanese ownership, technology, and skills, producing with Taiwanese and Korean labor for preexisting Japanese markets. In the 1980s Japan has embarked on an enhanced military role in the region as well, including joint planning and joint war games with the United States and South Korea. All in all, one can look back on the past century and see only one period, 1945–1960, when Japan was not the key nation-state in structuring East Asian economic interaction, and this period looks increasingly short, like the exception that proved the rule of East Asian development.

It is therefore interesting that some of the chapters in this volume present the benign image of Japan that seems to characterize for so many the Japan-Taiwan interaction since 1895. In the chapters dealing with the colonial period the emphasis is on how Japan developed Taiwan (but see chapters 3 and 5). Nor is there much sense of Japanese exploitation of Taiwan or Taiwanese in the chapters covering contemporary affairs (except chapter 10). All this may be true, but if so, it is only true for Taiwan, and there is the problem. Taiwan was but one part—and not the most important part—of Japan's imperial sphere, and today it is one part in an increasingly far-flung Japanese enterprise. Much of Taiwan's history does, in this volume, seem to confirm conventional theories of development and disprove the dependency or WS approach. But if Korea and Manchuria are added to the account, it is very different. Colonial Korea did have many of the features associated with core-periphery relationships (see Cumings 1981b, ch. 1), and few Koreans would recognize the Japan they knew in the accounts of Taiwan's development. In other words, because of the existence of Korea and subsequently Manchuria, Taiwan got some breathing space within the Japanese empire. Since 1945, of course, Japan, Taiwan, and South Korea have had a unique, artificial, and perhaps temporary breathing space in the world because of American hegemony throughout the period since 1945. Thus Taiwan's development to 1945, and the development of these three since 1960, is put in a different light by focusing on the whole rather than on the parts. Examining Taiwan's development apart from Japan's role, and Japan apart from its competition with and mobility within the global system, can only give a partial answer. This is not to say that emphasis on the system alone will give a completely full answer, either.

Remembering Japan's influence throughout the past century and joint American-Japanese influence since 1945 must be the first step in answering why Korea and Taiwan have had such similar trajectories in the twentieth century. As someone who knows Korea better than Taiwan, I was amazed to see how much similarity there was, even to the very year when critical economic changes began. One could substitute South Korea for Taiwan in Gold's chapter on postwar development (chapter 9) and get about the same phasing, the same timing, and the same policies in the period 1950–1980. After the regrouping of the immediate postwar era, the reverse course in Japan, beginning in 1948, spells out (sooner or later) a reintroduction of Japanese influence in Korea, Manchuria, and Taiwan. This is something George Kennan understood immediately, and indeed in 1949 he remarked, "The day will come, and possibly sooner than we think, when realism will call upon us not to oppose re-entry of Japanese influence and activity into Korea and Manchuria. This is, in fact, the only realistic prospect for countering and moderating Soviet influence in that area" (Kennan 1949). Kennan was a key architect of the reverse course; although his conception was of an appropriate balance of power in Northeast Asia, other officials at the time understood that Japan would reintroduce economic influence again as well, and many thought that rump economies like those in South Korea and Taiwan could not survive without it. This policy was consummated in the early 1960s, in Korea with the normalization of relations in 1965. In the 1950s both Taiwan and South Korea were sustained by direct American aid and military protection, while pursuing domestic strategies of import substitution. In the early 1960s the Kennedy administration, containing many liberal internationalists and free traders, put great pressure on both economies to open up, welcome back Japanese influence, and begin an export-promoting growth strategy. This strategy achieved fruition in the mid–1960s and thereafter, and then in the early 1970s both Taiwan and South Korea once again began import-substituting in producer goods and heavy industry: steel mills, petrochemical refining, automobile factories, and so on. The late 1970s and early 1980s witness the beginning of an attempt by both countries to change their structural position in the world economy, moving from comparative advantage in low labor cost to technological advantages over other Third World producers, beginning multinationalization as Taiwanese and Korean firms move abroad in search of cheap labor, and continuing to provide platforms for the receipt of declining Japanese industries. In this last phase Taiwan seems to have been more successful than South Korea, leading to an economic slide in the latter that, in my view, has detonated much of the political disorder of the past few years.

In any case, what explains this parallelism best? Would it be "conservative" factors such as common cultural background? Some common tradition, such as Confucianism? "Liberal" factors such as a highly educated population? Diffusion of modernizing values? Or would the parallelism be better explained by radical factors such as common position in the world system, the workings of the product cycle, and the dominant influence of Japan and the United States?

The BA model, with its emphasis on the role of state power in varying industrialization strategies, also provides a useful framework for comparing Japan, Taiwan, and Korea. In each country a strong state has guided economic development—in Japan since the early Meiji period, in Korea and Taiwan during the colonial period, and in all three countries since the 1950s. Japan located strong, autonomous, highly penetrating state systems in both colonies, and when Japan retreated abruptly in 1945 it bequeathed the strong states to the Nationalists on Taiwan and the conservative elements clustered around Syngman Rhee in South Korea. The colonial state in Taiwan continued to have a decided autonomy, as colonial officials who had served Japan persisted in office through the transition,[5] and as Nationalist officials, that is, mainlanders, filtered into the commanding heights. The state was not highly interpenetrated with Taiwan society, when compared to other developing countries. In South Korea the postwar situation was different. As in Taiwan, virtually the entire colonial apparatus (south of the thirty-eight parallel, to be sure, but here the colonial state had its capital) was taken over by the American occupation, and then quickly transferred to Korean colonial bureaucrats with conservatives, especially landlords, holding the commanding heights. With the rupture of Korea's national economy making South Korea temporarily inviable, these Korean elements returned the state to its traditional function, that is, as a coercive force designed to protect privilege (meaning mostly landed privilege) (Cumings 1981b, ch. 5). The state did little to stimulate economic growth throughout the Rhee period until 1960. In comparison to Taiwan's state it was much more interpenetrated with society. Whereas in Taiwan the state eliminated the landlords and functioned to preserve Nationalist rather than native Taiwanese interests, in Korea the state preserved native Korean interests, including those of landlords.

In Japan, too, a strong and autonomous state persisted after 1945. Virtually the first act of Douglas MacArthur was to order the continuation of the central bureaucracy, through which the American occupation governed for six years. At the same time the occupation smashed Japan's military, police, landlords, and zaibatsu concentrations through thorough reforms. Foreign economic interests in Japan were not particularly strong, although externally Japan was quickly meshed into the postwar oil regime, with an Occupation Petroleum Board deeply influenced by American multinational oil firms. The United States immediately integrated Japan with the American security structure in the Pacific, and subsequently encouraged a revived and reinvigorated Japanese economy as part of its general cold war strategy. The result was that, from the early 1950s until the early 1970s, Japan had considerable state and economic autonomy, with the United States maintaining a loose and benign grip on Japan's resource and military jugular. This was not a bureaucratic-authoritarian system, since basic democratic freedoms were guaranteed and labor was included rather than excluded. But the state's role bulked very large in the economy. Since Nixon's New Economic Policy was introduced in 1971 the U.S. role has been less benign, seeking in some ways to inhibit Japanese economic dynamism through tough trade negotiations and demands that Japan provide more of its own defense. In the 1980s the relationship has become more tense. But the fact remains that the postwar settlement in East Asia and the American role have provided Japan and Taiwan with autonomous states that have aided economic growth in a variety of ways. In Korea, to which I now turn, the same has been true since 1961.

State and Economy in Park's Korea

Historically Koreans had experience with two state structures, both authoritarian but nevertheless quite different from each other: the traditional Yi state and the modern Japanese state. The Yi had an ostensibly strong, central cast to it, but it was in fact a weak state, competing with and hamstrung by a strong landed aristocracy. The aristocracy used state power to preserve and perpetuate privilege over time. It was this state tradition that most characterized the Rhee regime (1948–1960) and that helped to account for the revolutionary ferment of the early postwar period, as the landed elite sought to maintain its control of land and its access to bureaucratic power. The great weakness of the Rhee regime, which so clearly distinguishes it from the succeeding Park regime, was its inability to conceive of using the state to stimulate the economy in the interests of national wealth and power. It was really the Japanese colonial regime, which did understand the role of the state in economic development, that provided a model for the post–1960, developmental phase in the ROK.

The Park period (1961–1979) saw a very different type of authoritarianism from that of the Rhee period. Gone was the worker and peasant protest of the early

Rhee years, gone was the spectacle of youth groups marching and fighting in the streets, gone was the weak and brittle structure of the Rhee state, and gone was the stagnant economy. Park's Korea may have had a deadly politics, but it had a vibrant economics. Rhee was a traditional dictator, interested in power. His regime resembled that diffuse authoritarianism, with a limited form of pluralism, that Juan Linz (1964) found in late-Franco Spain. Park was a modern leader, interested in power, of course, but also wealth. He was an industrial sovereign: such people, as Hirschman (1977) observed, are too busy keeping time to the fine ticking of an economic watch to be much concerned with the give-and-take of politics. In other words, instead of the ROK having a politics that its people deserve, it got the politics that its economy deserved.

The ROK state did not reach its full, formal, and substantive authoritarian breadth until the Yusin reforms of 1971–72. But the Korean Central Intelligence Agency (KCIA) was organized during the early days after the military coup in 1961, and the Economic Planning Board (EPB) began playing the "MITI function" of administrative guidance of the economy from the mid–1960s onward. The Korean BAIR is closely comparable to the BA regimes of Argentina and Brazil, but its real model is, as suggested earlier, the 1930s' Japanese state. It has considerable autonomy from society and is the prime organizer of economic growth through continuous interventions in the form of long-range plans, provision of capital (mostly from foreign loans), building of transport and communications infrastructures, and suppressing all threats to the existing order whether they come from students, laborers, a middle class wanting representation in the political system, or small firms with national rather than transnational interests. During the Park period the stymied, stalemated, truncated condition of South Korea that characterized the Rhee years was utterly overcome. This portion of Korea is once again, as in the colonial period, integrated with a transnational system, but it is the world market system with several metropoles instead of the colonial one with the metropole in Tokyo.

The assumption of power by the Park junta coincided with the termination of a program of import-substitution industrialization (ISI) that had been fitful and not very successful, but nonetheless comparable to the Taiwan and Latin American cases of the 1950s. A very neat parallelism between economics and politics emerges in South Korea in 1961 in that ISI came acropper at the same time that a relatively democratic regime—the Chang Myon government from 1960 to 1961—was replaced by a military coup. The "easy" phase of ISI was over, but the need then to begin substitutions for durable consumer goods and machinery ran up against the distinct limitations of the Korean economy, such as the small domestic market, limited resource endowments, and large capital requirements for a new import-substitution phase. Furthermore, a more capital-intensive phase would simply exacerbate a prime structural problem in the economy, surplus but relatively well-educated and skilled labor (Kuznets 1977, 151–52; Kim 1975, 20, 25–26). The United States under the Kennedy administration, which believed deeply in the liberal vision of a world-ranging division of labor and the pursuit of comparative advantage (Calleo 1982, 9–24), was hostile to a continuing and deepening import-substitution, and had the muscle to make its viewpoint stick in the ROK, since U.S. grant aid had accounted for something like five-sixths of ROK imports in the late 1950s. In fact the United States cut its direct grant aid drastically at the end of the ISI phase; it hit an all-time low during the Chang Myon regime, amid continuing economic stagnation, inflation, unemployment, and low investor confidence (Han 1974, 208–13). Can one therefore find economic factors behind the Park coup of May 16, 1961?

No doubt economics—especially the lack of investor confidence—played a role in the coup, but it is unlikely that the failure in ISI and the economy was high in the minds of General Park and his allies. More important were generational strains within the military, a developing threat from the Left within South Korea, and the ineptitude of the Chang government. The new regime did not abruptly change the Rhee-Chang economic policies, and the economy continued to stagnate through 1962. Instead of a "deepening" industrialization, the ROK, like Taiwan, pursued in the 1960s an export-led program emphasizing light industries. Instead of the erection of a BAIR, the ROK in 1963 held a relatively free election and developed a constitution that sought to disperse power rather than concentrate it. A formal democratic system masked the reality of authoritarian power held by the military, but the holding of elections in 1963, 1967, and 1971 and the relatively free press of the period are two reasons why the Park state from 1963 to 1971 cannot be called a BAIR. So, the O'Donnell sequential phasing argument does not hold in Korea; a period of export-led development in light industry coincided with an authoritarian regime of limited electoral pluralism, after the ISI period ended.

Yet the sequential argument does not really hold in Latin America, either. Hirschman (1979, 68–71) has argued that O'Donnell interpreted too literally his argument that the move from ISI to another phase of industrialization was "a highly sequential, or tightly staged, affair," and that political changes followed neatly upon economic changes. Problems and potentials of economic development never present themselves clearly and neatly to the actual participants. Just as there are lags and discontinuities as one industrialization scheme gives way to another, so there are gaps and lags in perception of what sort of politics may be required.

What we need is a dialectical, back-and-forth conception of the interaction of politics and economics, of how decisions to push an economy in a certain direction raise new problems and possibilities in politics; and how political changes occasion new problems and potentials in the economy. Each economic shift sets up a new dynamic and gives rise to a proliferation of new interests, which acquire a stake in the existing arrangements. The same is true for the political sphere. When all is said and done, in the 1980s one can look back on the previous two decades of South Korean history and see vast change everywhere: in politics, a strong state that is highly organized and articulated, which penetrates to the lowest levels of Korean society (like the colonial state before it), and which is formidable in a way Rhee's state never was; in society, a millennial change from a condition where peasants constituted the vast majority—65 to 70 percent— of the producing population, to one where agricultural production occupies less than 30 percent of the population, with an associated vast shifting of population to the cities; in the economy, a vast array of light industries producing for export and a new heavy industrial infrastructure that no Korean could have imagined in the 1950s. But how things got that way is quite another question, and there does not seem to be a clear sequencing between economic changes and political changes until the 1970s.

One might argue that the accumulation of state power that grew out of the military coup, combined with the formidable bureaucratic combination that the Japanese had bequeathed, was the necessary condition for the turn from ISI to export-led development in the early 1960s. Indeed, this transition was accomplished by force, quickly, whereas it occurred with great pulling and hauling in several Latin American countries. The junta forced ISI capitalists who had profited through close connections with the Rhee regime to march through the streets, bearing signboards confessing their "corruption." But that would not explain why the junta dismantled itself, so to speak, and ran Park for election in 1963. What does explain both the economic and political sequence is external pressure.

The impetus for the ROK's turn outward in the early 1960s came largely from without: from the United States, the International Monetary Fund and the World Bank, and from Japan. Park Chung Hee might, as a nationalist, have preferred a deepening ISI program, but the Kennedy administration wanted export-led development and it wanted liberalized domestic regimes: thus its human rights pressure on Park to go civilian. It also, as argued earlier, wanted to reintroduce Japanese economic influence. At the same time, Kennedy administration planners partook of—and in the form of W. W. Rostow helped to create—a zeitgeist that favored an open world economy and looked askance at ISI programs. This is clearly marked in two major studies from the period, one of them commissioned by the World Bank (Balassa et al. 1971; Little, Scitovsky, and Scott 1970).[6] Countries like Korea and Taiwan would be the lower rungs of an international division of labor, leading from their comparative advantage in low labor cost, and climbing up the ladder through the "natural" workings of the product cycle. It is this external pressure that, combined with the exhaustion of the "easy" ISI phase, helps to explain why both South Korea and Taiwan began export-led programs in the early 1960s, and why Japanese influence returned to these two former colonies at about the same time.[7]

As I have argued elsewhere (Cumings 1984), Korean society has reacted more strongly to the colonial impact and industrialization than has Taiwan's, and thus in the mid–1960s the normalization of relations with Japan and the subsequent heavy influx of Japanese capital had to be rammed down the throats of tens of thousands of protestors, both in the National Assembly and on university campuses. The opposition feared an increasing dependency on Japan and drew upon wellsprings of anti-Japanese sentiment going back to the colonial period. As Cole and Lyman (1971, 99) put it, the turn toward Japan "ran like a thread through all political and economic events from 1961 to 1965."

With the development of the Second Five-Year Plan in 1965, foreign input in the Korean planning process was pronounced. The failures of the First Five-Year Plan led to the exit from government of many Korean planners; the U.S. aid mission, the World Bank, and German advisers stepped in and largely rewrote and recast the Second Five-Year Plan (Cole and Lyman 1971, 205). A type of transnational planning, one could call it, and the point was to direct South Korea more firmly onto the export-promotion, open-door path. The carrot was the promised benefits that would accrue to the economy; the stick was the refusal of both AID and the World Bank to accept the earlier Korean planning as a basis for determining appropriate levels of outside assistance (ibid., 208).

Transnational involvement in and planning of South Korea's turn outward had an interesting political counterpart as well. The mid-1960s' concern for planned economic development quickly spawned a corollary concern for planned political development. This is best exemplified in the influential work of Samuel Huntington, which provides a stark counterpoint to the sort of political recommendations Koreans and other peoples were used to hearing from Americans. Up until the mid-1960s, Americans generally counseled the successive Korean regimes to limit power, provide checks and balances through various democratic procedures, hold periodic elections, and codify these procedural values in a written constitution. Such advice grew out of the dominant pluralist current in American politics, which saw the government or state as simply one more actor in a myriad of competing groups, parties, and other intermediate forces. Of course, there were always Americans who were willing to justify the violations and end runs around the procedures that characterized the Rhee regime and the early Park years. But the typical advice Koreans received was exemplified by the Kennedy administration's pressure to go civilian in 1963, and by advice of liberal scholars such as Rupert Emerson, who counseled Mr. Park to abide by the constitution, foster a two-party system, and so on.

Huntington had a different perspective, a concern for political stability that transcended liberal categories. "The problem," he wrote, "is not to hold elections but to create organizations." Americans may know how to constrain power, but they do not know how to create it. The lack of viable organization was the prime pathology of political development in the "new" states. Especially there, he argued, "the public interest . . . is whatever strengthens governmental institutions." He lauded the South Korean regime in the 1960s for developing stable institutions (Huntington 1968, 7, 25, 258–61).

This was possibly the first piece of political advice from an American that did not fall on deaf ears in South Korea. Although I have no evidence that Huntington actually advised the Park regime, his book was one of the few in American comparative politics to be translated into Korean, and in any case his ideas expressed a dominant trend in comparative politics in the late 1960s. The Park regime seemed to be on a distinctly Huntingtonian path with the organization and development of the Democratic Republican party (DRP), for it was through parties, Huntington said, that political stability could be created. The DRP was, like the Chinese Kuomintang, organized frankly according to Leninist principles of centralism, hierarchy, and discipline (Kim 1971). Although its role fluctuated during the 1960s, for a time it bid fair to create the first true, modern, Korean political party (leaving aside, of course, the Communist party).

The logic of Huntington's analysis did not stop with the creation of viable parties, however. It could be extended by others to a sophisticated argument on behalf of strong state power, which would control, channel, and mold the highly mobilized forces let loose when a nation industrializes rapidly. This is the meaning of political stability in the midst of millennial economic and social transformation. This is what South Korea largely lacked, or possessed only weakly, until 1961. Whether via Huntington, or via the political logic of economic planning, or simply through the mediation of Park Chung Hee and his allies, this is what Korea has today; it is the great cost of Korean development. It is also an example of how external, international, and transnational economic and political forces can affect or even shape the domestic politics of given countries (on this point in general see Gourevitch 1978).

In the 1971–72 period, the Park regime erected a formal authoritarian state that bears close comparison to the BA model. The Korean Central Intelligence Agency was the key organ of this comprehensive, ubiquitous, penetrating state. It posted agents at every level of government, in the factories, universities, and media offices. It censored the press, broke up political demonstrations, strikes, and the like. It monitored peoples' thoughts, and even at times put an end to the highly political tearoom chatter that so characterizes Seoul. Each successive director of the KCIA rivaled Park Chung Hee's power, until finally one of them, Kim Jae Kyu, shot Park to death over dinner one night in November 1979. Most of this is familiar. The question is, how are we to explain the timing of the emergence of the Yusin state? Why 1971–72 and not 1963, or 1965, or 1969?

The potential for such a state was latent in the ROK from the late 1940s on. Koreans by then controlled the ubiquitous colonial state and used it to eliminate the great internal threat posed by worker and peasant disorders. A corporatist integration of workers under state control occurred then; in other words, the ROK never went through the Latin American phasing of a period of labor inclusion followed by its exclusion as the ISI phase ended. This Korean reality can be viewed in the bland and complacent observation by Cole and Lyman (1971, 235) that there is in South Korea "no political party of consequence . . . that made its appeal openly to workers, small farmers, or others who might be separated out as underprivileged." That is, workers and peasants are simply outside the political system in the ROK; whatever participation they may be involved in is with top-down, centrally controlled organizations and movements like the New Village Movement. If there was an inclusionary phase in the 1950s and 1960s, it meant that there was political participation by students, intellectuals, the urban upper and middle classes (both exceedingly small before the 1970s). The fragmented opposition parties tended to be made up of intellectuals, professional politicians, and superannuated landlords.

By the early 1970s, however, a potential mass base for the opposition had come into being, embracing the growing working and middle classes in the cities, national business interests that had been hurt by the export-led program, and regions like the Southwest that had been left out of much of the development of the 1960s. It was from this region, and with this base, that Kim Dae Jung emerged and mounted a strong challenge to Park's rule. He nearly won the 1971 election, garnering 46 percent of the vote in spite of regime manipulation. His speeches criticized the export-led policies and especially the newly developing dependency on Japan. The election coincided with the first year of weak growth in the economy, thus calling into question the legitimacy of the new program. Still, this electoral challenge cannot explain Yusin. It might be necessary to an explanation, but it is not sufficient. After all, Park was able to kidnap and manhandle Kim Dae Jung in 1973 with little obvious disorder in the polity.

Instead, I think the best explanation of the timing of Yusin would combine the dependency relations engendered by the export-led phase with the "deepening" industrialization program of the Third Five-Year Plan, drafted by economic nationalists who made an end run around "orthodox" economists, both Korean and American, and taking as its goal an enhanced Korean self-reliance within the world system. More broadly, this was a Korean response to the stunning departures of the Nixon years, the two most important for Korea being the 1971 New Economic Policy, heralding core-country protectionism, and the opening to China, which saw the United States deal with the ROK's deadly adversary.

The economic relationships that the export-led phase fostered between Korea and the core economies are not equal, and they cannot be for a long time. As a "late-late" developer, the ROK lacked domestic capital, had a very small domestic market, a stark technological dependency, and had to sell in foreign markets held mostly by multinational corporations. Thus it relied heavily on foreign loans, foreign markets, and simple technologies. A careful study of the ROK economy likened its dependence on Japanese credits and financing to that "characteristic of Korea's earlier satellite role within the Yen Bloc" (Kuznets 1977, 85), meaning of course when Korea was Japan's colony. The ROK's lack of oil left it open to devastating price hikes; it rode out the 1973–74 crisis rather well but suffered badly in the "second oil wave" of 1979. Recessions in the United States and Japan retard the ROK's growth, especially in exports, and as exports fall, fears are raised about Korea's ability to service its growing external debt (1974 and 1981–83 saw flurries of bankers' doubts).

The ROK sought to escape such dependency for the first time in the early 1970s, using its strong state to provision credit to heavy industries, to foster concentration and economies of scale, to build the social overhead infrastructure necessary to accommodate the growing economy, and to repress any objections to "deepening." These developments came only a few years after the institution of the export-led program, which itself necessitated measures to control unions, hold down wages and consumption, and ignore rural interests, measures that could only be accomplished, according to Kuznets (1977, 50, 85, 105), by "a strong government," an "authoritarian regime." In 1971 the growth rate fell for the first time since 1965, from 9.8 percent to 7.3 percent; the balance of payments suffered and inflation went up. All this could only call into question the wisdom of the export-led program featuring light industries and linked almost entirely to Japanese and American credits and markets.

The strengthening of the state in the early 1970s was not required by the exporting program, however, which had been successfully instituted in the mid–1960s by a mixed, weaker authoritarian system. Nor was the Kim Dae Jung challenge enough to explain the timing. The 1960s' ROK state was also strong enough to manage, in Huntingtonian fashion, the rapid political and social changes spawned by economic development. The Yusin system was necessary because it simultaneously pushed the ROK into a heavy industrialization program and did this over the opposition of American planners who argued that the program would violate an international division of labor, would lead to problems of surplus capacity, and rested upon a small domestic market that could never take up the slack that would occur if the world economy went into recession or if protectionist measures began to close off Korean exports. At the same time, a new American administration for the first time since the Korean War withdrew a division of American troops, pursued neomercantile instead of liberal trade policies, and called into question the position of both South Korea and Taiwan within the hegemonic American security system in Northeast Asia. (The ROK then reacted by opening high-level talks with North Korea, for the first time ever, leading to the watershed joint communique of 4 July 1972, pledging both halves of Korea to peaceful reunification. Although this effort went nowhere in the end, it remains true that reunification is another possible means of breaking out of dependency relations for both Koreas.)

The ISI phase in heavy industry in the 1970s was part of Korea's export-led development: steel, autos, ships, and synthetic textiles from the petrochemical industry were mostly for export. The difference was that the new program enhanced self-reliance rather than deepening dependency as the light-industrial export program of the 1960s had done. Indeed, during this period Park borrowed North Korea's *juche* (self-reliance) language, wrote pithy slogans saying "steel equals national power," and called his Yusin system "Korean-style democracy." The Korean BAIR was anything but democratic, but by using this slogan Park distinguished his system from the earlier attempts at dispersal of power and formal democracy, conducted under continuing U.S. pressures, and thus Park seemed to be more nationalistic at the precise time that he was being more undemocratic.

This deepening development, in the context of the removal or threatened removal of U.S. security guarantees and the increasing dependency relationships spawned by light-industrial exporting, is, I believe, the best explanation of the timing of Yusin. It explains more of the variance than other arguments, such as the threat from Kim Dae Jung. An accumulation of state power was necessary both to manage the industrialization program and to enhance ROK power vis à vis more advanced countries, the United States and Japan in particular. Both Korea and Taiwan have been bases for receiving declining industries in Japan; in the textile sector this meant mostly small and unproductive firms moving off to Japan's near hinterland. But with steel, autos, and shipbuilding—using Japanese technologies and usually with plants installed by Japanese technicians—not only were the requirements for state power enhanced, as O'Donnell's argument would suggest, but the ROK state now was taking on powerful interests in Japan and the United States (or seeking to play powerful interests off against each other—MITI versus Japanese steel, or U.S. steel and Congress versus American bankers who helped fund Korean industrialization). With such big goals on his agenda, Park could not be troubled by domestic opposition to his policies, which he crushed ruthlessly in the period 1971–74. But no conceivable enhancement of state power could alter fundamentally Korea's position in the world economy in a short time period, and thus in the late 1970s the second oil shock, problems of surplus capacity in the new heavy industries, increasing protectionism, and rising debts combined to detonate a political crisis that destroyed the Park regime and brought the export-led program to a creaking halt for three years.[8]

Conclusions

The Korean experience suggests the following tentative generalizations. First, today, just as in the colonial period, Korea and Taiwan differ: Taiwan's relatively smooth political economy of growth is matched by Korea's rough-and-tumble ups and downs; Korean society strongly resists its transformation by the economy, and the state must manage both. Second, the striking parallelism in the developmental trajectories of South Korea and Taiwan—import-substitution giving way to export-led development followed by substitution in heavy industrial imports—highlights the importance of world system forces rather than domestic forces in the transformation of both countries. Position in the world system and what Wallerstein calls "development by invitation" (the United States doing the inviting) account for much of this parallelism, both in industrial strategies and in the timing of new phases.

Third, the bureaucratic-authoritarian model fits South Korea (and, I think, Taiwan) only when a dialectical rather than a linear conception of the relationship between economics and politics is followed. In neither nation do changes in the role of the state follow neatly upon changes in industrial strategies; yet in retrospect the relative autonomy and strength of both the Korean and Taiwan states seem essential to direct and manage their paths of development.

Finally, although both Korea and Taiwan in my view are quite sensitive to changes in the world system and have highly exposed positions, both economically and strategically, their states are so strong, their capacities to respond and maneuver in the face of difficulties in the world economy are relatively so great, that the experience of both should force revisions in world system theory. That is, if states are weaker in the semiperiphery and periphery, how does one explain South Korea and Taiwan? It is true that both states are weak relationally to the United States and Japan, and that the United States, at least in the South Korean case, exercises remarkable prerogatives, such as direct command of the ROK military. But the controls that the United States has on Taiwan and Korea are similar to those it has on Japan: outer limit controls in the form of defense, resource, and food dependencies. The outer limits cannot be invoked to keep allies in line without destroying alliance relationships. So, in the meantime—which is most of the time—the domestic strength of the Korean and Taiwan states is far more important than their relational weakness to core states; indeed, the states' relative autonomy is in many ways stronger than that of the American state.

A proper explanation of this relative strength would have to go back to the first half of the twentieth century, where strong colonial states administratively guided development, where the state structure was bequeathed mostly intact in 1945, and where the particular Japanese model of the state's role in development could be revived and used by both Korea and Taiwan. This interesting and in many ways unique peripheral history may account for much of the relative success of both nations in overcoming backwardness and climbing into the semiperiphery, that is, into the hallowed ground of the chosen few.

Notes

1. A particularly good account of capitalist conceptions of interest and how they evolved is Hirschman (1977).

2. A stimulating book that has prompted a good bit of recent research in this vein is Olson (1965); for a critique of Polanyi from a similar standpoint see Hechter (1981).

3. For further elaboration see Cumings (1984).

4. For a Gerschenkronian analysis of the Japanese state see Landes (1965).

5. This point was made by Myron Cohen at the conference at which most of the papers in this volume were originally presented.

6. These books are good representations of a general opposition to ISI by the mid-1960s; their later publication has to do with the rhythms of academic presses.

7. On the extensive Kennedy administration pressure on the ROK to normalize relations with Japan, see Kim (1971, ch. 3).

8. For an elaboration of the crisis of Korean economic and political development in 1979–1983, see Cumings (1984, 35–38; 1983a).

13

Edwin A. Winckler

GLOBALIST, STATIST, AND NETWORK PARADIGMS IN EAST ASIA

The introduction to this volume sketched the evolution of the radical-globalist and radical-statist literatures whose applicability to East Asia has been examined in the preceding chapters. This chapter summarizes the results of this evaluation and their implications for further research. First it asks what the authors concluded about globalist and statist processes in East Asia, noting both divergences and commonalities between their papers. Then, building on the area of agreement, it highlights some globalist and statist processes that the East Asian cases help elaborate, particularly processes identified by the radical literature from which the discussion began.

Globalism

To recapitulate, globalism shifts the assessment of the causes of national development from the national to the supranational level, emphasizing the strength of worldwide processes and the extent to which they structure national activities and subnational outcomes. In the mid–1980s, radicalism, conservatism, and even liberalism are all contributing to this globalist paradigm, with some convergence between them. However, these orientations remain distinct. Liberalism is the least globalist, emphasizing supranational opportunities rather than constraints. Radicalism is the most globalist, emphasizing the constraints that supranational economic processes place on national and subnational actors. Conservatism falls between, recognizing supranational political and economic constraints, but emphasizing the opportunities for successful national political reactions to them. The chapters in this volume show some of these divergences, falling on a continuum from least globalist to most globalist, in both political and economic processes.

Regarding external political processes, Simon (chapter 7) is least globalist. He concedes that ultimately it was American pressure that forced the Nationalist state first to create a domestic private sector and later to reorient the economy toward export promotion. However, he does not attribute this policy to any global economic or political dynamics of capitalism. Moreover he notes that elements within the Nationalist state actively resisted American pressures, in many cases quite successfully. Barrett (chapter 6) does address the dynamics of both American capitalism and Asian geopolitics, but he finds that both left the American state with several choices in its policy toward Taiwan, at least until 1949–1950. It was defeat by Communists that left the Nationalist state no choice but to go along with reformist American aid officials, and the outbreak of the Korean War that left the American state no choice but to defend Taiwan. Winckler (chapter 3) argues that, on Taiwan, as elsewhere in the periphery, core elites do impose systemic constraints, but peripheral elites still have some political choice. They can cultivate their ties with core elites in order to contain peripheral masses, or they can lessen their dependence on core support by increasing their reliance on peripheral masses. Similarly, Greenhalgh (chapter 4) argues that historically, supranational geopolitical processes (imperialist rivalries, communist threat, American insistence) have played a strong role in constraining first Japanese and later Nationalist peripheral elites to adopt economic policies with some favorable distributional consequences for peripheral masses. Finally, giving strongest emphasis to supranational constraints, Cumings (chapter 12) views postwar Northeast Asia as highly programmed, first by Japanese and later by American policy. Cumings argues that, consequently, it is no coincidence that Taiwan and Korea have similar prewar colonial histories and similar postwar policy histories.

Regarding external economic processes, again least globalist, Simon (chapter 10) views the Nationalist state as successfully struggling to maximize opportunities and minimize constraints. Precisely in response to the dangers of dependence, the Nationalists avoid quantitative dependence on foreign investment and achieve significant progress in upgrading Taiwan's technology. Gold (chapter 9) sees some cooperation among foreign business, Nationalist state, and local business. Somewhat globalist, he sees the external actors as having some leverage over the Nationalist state and even more leverage over local business, through the qualitative importance of external investment and technology. Greenhalgh (chapter 4) examines radical globalist claims about the deleterious distributional effects of external economic transactions such as aid, trade, and investment. She argues that the currently fashionable ''new statist'' reaction to the failure of radical-globalist hypotheses understates the role of external economic (and political) processes, and that a new globalist synthesis is needed fully to explain economic distribution on Taiwan. Again most globalist, Cumings (chapter 12) sees the supranational economic environment as highly programmed by product cycles that highly constrain the economic opportunities presented to Taiwan and Korea.

Authors and readers are free either to maximize or to minimize these differences. The editors are inclined to minimize them. Even at their most distant, the authors are not far apart. Thus, among the most liberal and least globalist authors, Simon stresses the potential for "conservative" statist processes to overcome supranational constraints. However, he does not really deny that "radical" dependency processes pose a challenge to peripheral states and firms. In fact, his chapters on foreign-imposed reforms and foreign-derived technology contain much evidence of both past and present external constraints on Taiwan. Conversely, among the most radical and most globalist authors, Cumings emphasizes the role of external American political policies and external global product cycles in producing parallel developments in Korea and Taiwan. However, far from denying that the Korean and Taiwan states have reacted strongly against these constraints, he insists on it.

Thus, in most of the chapters on most issues, most of these analytical glasses are both half full and half empty, and most of the time the authors themselves call attention to this. Consequently, what impresses the editors is the convergence of all the chapters, taken as whole, toward a synthesis of liberal, radical and conservative analyses of globalism. Accordingly, I now turn to the question of what elements in such a synthesis the East Asian cases can help elaborate, focusing particularly on elements from the radical-globalist models with which our discussion began. I focus on two topics in which radical globalism shows continuing promise, the characterization of subglobal regions and the analysis of semiperipheral zones.

Subglobal Regions

The exploration of the East Asian cases suggests that one of the potentials of world system theory that remains to be fully realized is the use of global processes to identify differences between subglobal regions. As summarized in the introduction, one of the virtues of early world system theory was to put the changing dynamics of the core back into radical-globalist theory. One of the virtues of later world system theory has been to disentangle the geopolitical, political-economic, and sociocultural processes involved. The argument here is that a relatively few of these analytical elements from world system theory go a remarkably long way toward identifying the differences between, say, the Northeast Asian (Japan-Korea-Taiwan) and "southern cone" Latin American (Brazil-Chile-Argentina) subglobal regions, and they should prove equally useful for identifying the distinctive characteristics of other subglobal regions.

The essential elements are a three-zone model (core, semiperiphery, and periphery), distinguishing different processes (geopolitical, political-economic, sociocultural) and applied to both the capitalist and socialist worlds. In Latin America, the exclusive dominance of the United States over its "backyard" led many dependency theorists to portray peripheral countries as in direct interaction with a single major core power, undisturbed by either core rivalries, semiperipheral intermediaries, or peripheral powers. (However, for more complex models, see Frank 1978; 1979; Cardoso and Faletto 1979.) In East Asia, in contrast, a more complex structure has produced more complex dynamics, including more, and more rapidly changing, constraints and opportunities (Hinton 1970; Solomon 1980; Barnett 1977; Zagoria 1982).

Thus, East Asia contains competition between and within zones of the capitalist bloc, competition between and within zones of the socialist bloc, and competition between the capitalist and socialist blocs. These competitions have involved rapid mobility between zones and extensive overlap between regions, particularly the Northeast Asia and Southeast Asia subglobal regions that Taiwan straddles. The biggest difference from Latin America is of course the immediacy of East-West confrontation. Moreover, this East-West confrontation is not restricted to core rivalries (USA-USSR), or to temporary surrogates for core powers. Rather, it has included enduring indigenous rivalries in the semiperipheral and peripheral zones (two Chinas, two Koreas, two Vietnams). Meanwhile, of course, there have been West-West rivalries—within the core (USA-Japan), within the semiperiphery (Korea-Taiwan), and within the periphery (e.g., between ASEAN members), not to mention between these zones. Finally, there are also East-East rivalries both between and within levels (e.g., core USSR versus semiperipheral PRC, both of those versus peripheral North Korea and Vietnam, both of the latter against each other). These multilateral, interrelated contests create both constraints and opportunities for each other.

These East Asian points address a significant issue of theoretical strategy that has emerged from the Latin American literature. Some sophisticated Latin Americans, reacting against the mechanical uniformity in early dependency theory, have advocated a more flexible and differentiating "historical-structural" approach stressing the notion of "conjuncture" (Cardoso and Faletto 1979). Any particular historical episode contains a unique combination of external and internal structural elements. Though it should be possible to identify in advance what, analytically, the most important structural elements are likely to be, probably it is not possible to predict in advance how, historically, they will combine. This approach can be a distinct improvement over an analytical machine that grinds out uniformly grim outcomes for every occasion. It is not an improvement, however, if it becomes an excuse for abandoning systematic analysis and relapsing into mere historical narrative. Of course, what structural elements provide the most useful links between abstract concepts and concrete history will always remain controversial. Nonetheless, the East Asia cases suggest that, fully elaborated, the structural elements being identified by world system theory could go a long way toward connecting theory with fact, at least for distinguishing subglobal regions.

Semiperipheral Zone

The exploration of the East Asian cases also suggests that another element of world system theory with additional potential is Wallerstein's controversial concept of a semiperiphery. As noted in the introduction, some critics have denied its empirical existence, while others have questioned its conceptual fruitfulness. As regards its empirical existence, some sophisticated studies have been unable to identify such a zone, while some common-sense approaches claim to have found it. The two sophisticated studies used relational measures of trade and other flows between nations that provide a good approximation of Wallerstein's structural definition (Snyder and Kick 1979; Breiger 1981).

The common-sense approach relies simply on national product per capita (e.g., Arrighi 1985a) or simply identifies the semiperiphery with ''newly indus-trialized countries'' (e.g., the editors of Evans, Rueschemeyer, and Skocpol 1985). In this volume, Greenhalgh proposes explicit criteria for Taiwan's periph-eral and semiperipheral stages (chapter 4). (Although Taiwan was not included in the 1982 World Bank data that Arrighi used, it falls, along with Korea, squarely into the semiperiphery that Arrighi identifies.)

As regards the conceptual fruitfulness of the notion of a semiperiphery, some sophisticated observers consider Wallerstein's zonal typology to be tautologous, while others find it suggestive. Among critics, Stinchcombe has complained that if zonal position is defined in terms both of external function and internal characteristics, there is nothing left to be independently inferred. Most support-ers of the concept, including Wallerstein himself (1985), employ it mostly as a heuristic device that uses economic position to suggest policy dilemmas and political processes. Typically what this means is that the economic challenge to the semiperiphery of shifting from less profitable peripheral-type economic ac-tivities to more profitable core-type ones requires strong state economic action and a concomitant political authoritarianism. This relationship between globa-lism and statism appears in many of the papers in this volume (particularly chapters 4, 5, 9, and 12). Thus the East Asian cases suggest that Wallerstein's zonal typology is useful, provided one avoids the tautologous reasoning against which critics have rightly warned.

However, the East Asian cases also show that Wallerstein's definition of the semiperiphery requires elaboration. The external political role of the semipe-riphery within the world system as a whole remains vague, despite the clarifica-tion of internal political characteristics of (individual) semiperipheral countries. Both the external economic role and internal economic characteristics of semi-peripheral countries also require further clarification.

Politically, Wallerstein's original definitions stipulated that the distinctive political role of semiperipheral countries was to serve as a buffer between core and periphery. Evidently this could occur either directly or indirectly. Semipe-ripheral countries that were regional powers within their own subglobal regions could act as ''subimperial'' surrogates for core powers, intervening directly in military-political processes (e.g., China on behalf of the Soviet Union in the Korean War). Or, semiperipheral countries could act as intermediaries in exploi-tative economic transactions between core and periphery (e.g., Taiwan vis à vis Southeast Asia, on behalf of Japanese or American firms). Evidently Wallerstein's implicit assumption was that these semiperipheral political roles normally correspond to semiperipheral economic capabilities.

The East Asian cases suggest the need to elaborate these concepts. Since, except in the long run, economic capacity and political role may not correspond, the economic and political components of semiperipherality should be assessed separately. Moreover, the different kinds of political roles, and the circumstances under which they are likely to be played, need to be further specified. Japan, for example, has become economically core but remains politically at most semiperipheral, since it still lacks even the capacity for self-defense. Taiwan and Korea have become economically semiperipheral but remain politically peripheral. They have lost their natural political hinterlands to mainland Communist states and have become militarily dependent on the United States.

Economically, Wallerstein's original definitions stipulated that there are no distinctively semiperipheral economic activities, only a mix of core-type and peripheral-type economic activities. This notion of a "product mix" may still apply to Taiwan and South Korea, since capital-intensive and labor-intensive manufactures remain distinct in terms of both origin (male versus female workers) and destination (periphery versus core). However the notion of a "product cycle" suggests that the semiperiphery can have a distinctive role, that of economic intermediary between core and periphery. At least one distinctively semiperipheral economic activity is to accept industries that have run into diminishing returns in the core, first adapting them to the more labor-intensive factor mix available in the semiperiphery, and later further adapting them to the still more labor-intensive factor mix in the periphery.

The notion of a "product cycle" also provides leverage over another problem in analyzing the semiperiphery, namely, how to tell when absolute growth of national product also constitutes relative mobility of national position within or between zones. Clearly, the function of the core is innovating the new package of "leading sector" industries, the function of the semiperiphery is mass producing them once they become standardized, and the function of the periphery is squeezing the last profit out of industries that have already been abandoned by the two higher zones. Equally clearly, countries achieve mobility only to the extent that they advance in the product cycle from imitation toward innovation of products and processes. Of course, one might still wish to supplement these technological criteria with others reflecting ownership of assets, position in markets, and even sheer scale of production.

Statism

Again to recapitulate, statism shifts the explanation of the causes of national development from the supranational to the national level. Statism emphasizes the autonomy and activism of state institutions and the extent to which they influence socioeconomic processes. In the mid–1980s radicalism, conservatism, and even liberalism are all contributing to this statist paradigm, with some convergence between them. Here too, however, these orientations remain distinct. Liberalism is the least statist, emphasizing the separateness of states and markets, and the opportunities rather than constraints that they place on masses. Radicalism is unstatist in emphasizing the constraints that markets place on states, but statist in emphasizing the constraints that states place on masses. Conservativism is the most statist in emphasizing the autonomy of states from markets and in arguing that national development requires state intervention in both market processes and mass mobilization. Again, the chapters in this volume show some of these divergences, falling on a continuum from least statist to most statist, in both economic and political processes.

About the relationship between states and markets on Taiwan, the chapters show some minor differences in emphasis. Simon (chapter 7) emphasizes the extent to which the Nationalists have constrained the role of the state and expanded the role of the market. In his description of the 1950s, this constraint came at American insistence. Gold's chapter about prewar family firms (chapter 5) describes how the colonial state determined development, leaving little scope for "liberal" markets. Gold focuses more on the "conservative" pattern of family economic organization and the "radical" mix of collaboration and conflict between Japanese colonial authorities and Taiwanese economic elite. Gold's second chapter (chapter 9) argues that the Nationalist state has been quite successful at managing markets, and emphasizes that crucial to its success have been the economic leverage that the state sector has maintained over the economy and the political autonomy that the state has maintained over society. Greenhalgh's chapter on postwar family firms (chapter 11) synthesizes processes from all three orientations. "Liberal" markets provide the opportunities to which "conservative" families respond, but their strategies are conditioned by "radical" struggles for capital and labor between state and society.

About the political relationship between state and masses on Taiwan, too, there are minor differences in emphasis between chapters. Again, Simon and Barrett (chapters 6, 7, and 10) make the least point of "radical" conflicts of interests between the political-economic establishment and the general public. Gold (chapter 9) notes that by recruiting external economic and political support the Nationalist state was long able to constrain internal strikes or dissent. He also notes, however, that these constraints have been somewhat relaxed in the 1970s and 1980s. Winckler and Cumings most emphasize "radical" constraints of states on masses. Chapter 3 also stresses the external bases of the Nationalist state's internal political autonomy, and the strong constraints on mass participation this autonomy involves. Winckler sees these constraints as basically continuing, however, despite some shift toward more sophisticated methods of control. Winckler's chapter on postwar elites (chapter 8) also finds little scope for "liberal" political competition and focuses on the "conservative" pattern of network political organization that creates what "radicals" would describe as a mix of collaboration and conflict between the Nationalist political elite and Taiwanese economic elite. Cumings (chapter 12) sees the Korean state as trying to escape the choice between external and internal support. Its ''conservative'' response to a decline in American support was not to recruit internal political support. Rather it accelerated industrial development and suppressed any resulting internal political dissent, provoking a ''radical'' mass response.

Again, authors and readers can make much or little of these differences of emphasis. Again, however, the editors are inclined to minimize them. Even the authors describing reactions against statism nevertheless continue to find a high degree of statism on Taiwan. Greenhalgh (chapter 4), while arguing that current scholarship overemphasizes the distributional role of the Nationalist state, nevertheless recognizes its important impact on inequality. Simon (chapter 10) makes the Nationalist state the most active agent of such transfer by the 1970s and 1980s. Conversely, even the authors describing the persistence, and in the case of Korea the intensification, of statism concede the limitations on the state's role.

Economically, all the chapters agree that, during both the Japanese and Nationalist eras, the state has been the leading entrepreneur of economic development, and the state has played the key role in linking domestic business and labor with foreign capital markets. Moreover, virtually all of the papers agree that both Japanese and Nationalist states have supplemented state firms with private business and market processes, without losing much control over either businessmen or the economy as a result. Politically, all the authors assume an authoritarian prewar legacy, and all agree on the basically authoritarian nature of the resulting postwar regime. All the authors agree that despite tendencies to shift toward greater representative democracy, a strong component of authoritarianism remains and will persist in tension with those liberalizing trends for a long time to come.

Consequently, again what impresses the editors is the convergence of all the chapters, taken as a whole, toward a synthesis of liberal, radical, and conservative analyses of statism. Accordingly, again I turn to the question of what elements of such a synthesis the East Asian cases can help elaborate, focusing again particularly on elements from the radical-statist models with which the discussion began. I focus on two areas of weakness in radical statist literature: global influences and state institutions.

Global Influences

A serious theoretical weakness in the radical-statist literature has been a failure to posit an explicit conception of the supranational environment of state institutions and to specify the mechanisms, both economic and political, connecting it to the national level. O'Donnell's initial version (1973) of the ''bureaucratic-authoritarian'' model was anything but globalist. ''Modernization'' arrived from outside; after that domestic processes took over. This internal focus persists even in later Latin American versions of the "bureaucratic-authoritarian" model, even when foreign corporations are included as domestic political actors, and even when transitions from internal to export orientations are mentioned as domestic political problems (e.g., Collier 1979). No explicit model of the changing supranational environment, particularly of its geopolitical as opposed to political-economic components, was involved.

Such an internal and economic focus is of course more difficult to maintain in East Asia where external military threats are more dire, where many political institutions have recently been imposed from without, and where much manufacturing is not only by foreign firms but also for foreign markets. Accordingly, one of the main contributions of this volume is to place the shifting tensions between autonomy and constraint within authoritarian regimes squarely in the context of a changing world system. East Asia's strong states emerge from global competition—between states rather than between firms. They evolve in response to pressures from the world system that are geopolitical before they are developmental. The intensifying international demand that each state exercise unambiguous sovereignty over its territory has placed particular strain on divided states like Korea and Taiwan (Meyer and Hannan 1979). The rise and decline of the United States as global hegemon has placed particular strain on its client states, particularly Korea and Taiwan (Gilpin 1981; Cumings 1983b). Preoccupation of Asian client states with American opinion has made Washington as crucial a forum for even domestic political struggles as Taipei or Seoul. Sojourning and migration have given Asians a foothold within America itself.

The difficulties that Taiwan has experienced in securing foreign military support, maintaining foreign diplomatic recognition, and retaining supranational organizational memberships illustrate the external political mechanisms involved and their effects on domestic political development. Of these external mechanisms, obviously the most powerful are the threats of war, blockade, sabotage, and subversion. These external threats to national security have blocked any transition from authoritarianism to democracy in these East Asian nations in a way that overrides external economic or internal political and economic processes.

As regards the impact of external economic processes on state institutions, Evans's 1979 monograph on the triangular relations among multinational, state, and domestic corporations in the Brazilian petrochemical industry inaugurated a more comprehensive exploration of external-internal linkages. Most recently Evans (1985) has provided a thoughtful examination of the positive and negative influence of specific supranational economic processes (trade, investment, and loans) on national political development. The chapters in this volume provide further grist for this mill, particularly Greenhalgh's careful discussion of different external economic processes (trade, aid, investment, and technology) (chapter 4), and Simon's detailed study of technology transfer (chapter 10).

State Institutions

Another serious theoretical weakness of the radical statist literature has been a failure to posit an explicit conception of state institutions and to assess the mutual impact of these institutions on each other's development. This is not just a question of advancing beyond a generalized theoretical conception of "the state" to the historical reality of particular "states," but also one of advancing beyond dealing with states as wholes to the practical reality that they are composed of competing institutions. The state is constrained and propelled by its supranational and subnational environments, but its own internal dynamics can provide much of both the impulse and impediment to political development. An injunction to inspect these institutional details has recently been issued by authors synthesizing radical with liberal and conservative models of the state (Evans 1985). However, institutional analysis has long been a strong point of liberal and conservative political science, particularly in studies of authoritarian regimes.

Thus, both of the two major theorists of authoritarianism, the (liberal) Juan Linz (1975) and the (conservative) Amos Perlmutter (1981), placed state institutions and their struggles with each other at the center of their analyses. There is a general tension between formal constitutional ideals and practical institutional realities. There are characteristic tensions between the institutional sectors through which states seek autonomy—legitimation, development and repression. And there is tension between alternative social mechanisms for performing these political functions—political bureaucracies, economic markets, and social networks.

The East Asian cases illustrate all three of these institutional tensions. The tension between formal constitutional ideals and practical institutional realities is sharp, because Western democratic ideals have been grafted onto Eastern authoritarian legacies. Nevertheless, formal constitutional guarantees have so far provided the only legal basis for political opposition to the ruling Nationalist party, though culminating in the upsurge and suppression of dissident activity in the late 1970s. And formal constitutional institutions are playing a crucial role in the development of these regimes, as in the recent transitions from authoritarianism to democracy in Latin Europe analyzed by Juan Linz, and in Latin America.

Conflict between functional institutional sectors—security, development, and legitimation—has also been chronic, though more flamboyant in Korea than on Taiwan. There have also been characteristic tensions within functional sectors—between external military and internal policy, between constitutional and extra-constitutional agencies, and between dominant party and dominated representative and cultural institutions. Unlike the Latin American cases, however, a personal leader has dominated all three sectors. The leader's dominance has derived from military factionalism and has been exercised through internal security institutions that have remained behind the scenes, leaving the party and government out front (Winckler 1984; chapter 3 this volume). As Barrett (chapter 6) shows, sectoral tensions within the American state have also had their impact on Taiwan.

Finally, there is the tension between alternative social mechanisms. Real state institutions do not consist exclusively of bureaucratic processes, but include elements of market and network mechanisms as well. Evans has recently pointed to the presence of "nonbureaucratic" processes in the state and to the tensions they create, using as his example the presence of market processes in state firms. The interplay of bureaucratic and market processes is, of course, present in East Asian states too. But the East Asian cases emphasize the importance of another "nonbureaucratic" mechanism, namely, social networks. Another of the main contributions of this volume is to place the shifting tensions between autonomy and constraint within authoritarian regimes squarely in the context of complex domestic societies. Most of the authors insist that, in East Asia at least, personal networks are central to how global markets and state institutions actually work.

Moreover, the editors would argue, East Asian social networks are more sophisticated than those documented from most other parts of the world. With a thousand years or more of continuous experience at dealing with states and markets, East Asian social networks are preadapted to coping with these rival political-economic forms, and quite effective at prevailing against them. This is, in fact, a point that the radical-statist literature ought to ponder. Many current radical authors are concerned that the role of subnational masses in modifying elite institutions at the national and supranational levels should not be neglected. Evidently what they have in mind are the popular electoral representation or collective mass mobilization typical of Western publics. However, the cumulative impact of private representations through social networks may achieve many of the same effects.

Envoi

In conclusion, we return to where we began in the introduction, with a note on method and purpose. This volume has largely been the theoretically informed exploration of a single "case," Taiwan, with enough reflections from a nearby case, Korea, to highlight some of Taiwan's distinctive features. We argued at the outset that the road to responsible comparison lies through an adequate tour of each of the countries being compared and that, despite rising interest in Taiwan, so far the literature has lacked guides to many avenues of its rather tortuous development. Some of the chapters have surveyed what they regarded as theoretically significant terrain, while others have detailed what they regarded as theoretically significant landmarks. However, no one is more conscious than the authors that there remain large uncharted areas, even in Taiwan's small experience.

Consequently, no summary of tasks for future research can omit the arduous work of continuing to probe the past, present, and future of such geographically distant, linguistically awkward, and politically inconvenient cases as Taiwan and Korea. From the past, there remains the theoretical settlement of the imperial period, and the theoretical colonization of the Japanese period. In the present there is the need to elaborate our still crude maps of multilateral supranational transactions, multifarious national machinations, and multitudinous subnational initiatives. For the future there is the accelerating pace of change that makes scholarly studies and academic concepts out of date before they are off the press.

In sum, the East Asian cases are far from exhausted for comparative-theoretical purposes. This is all the more so because, as the best book on comparative methodology has argued, in fact there is no such thing as comparing countries, only the comparison of how the relationship between particular theoretical variables differs in different systemic contexts (Przeworksi and Teune 1970/1982). So each East Asian country, with its complex history under varied supranational regimes and national regimes, is not a single case but a cornucopia of cases, even for a single theoretical proposition. In this volume, we have plotted the theoretical bearings of dozens of propositions about East Asia, and have still hardly begun.

For travelers merely wishing to confirm their stereotypes of Asian civilization, more than a day or two in Taipei or Seoul may be too much. But those of us who have had the privilege of staying on to meet the people, of getting out to see the country, and of digging in to find the facts know that in such sophisticated societies, nothing is ever merely what it seems, and that the varieties of experience are truly inexhaustible. We only hope that we have managed to convey some of the tentativeness and complexity that our Asian interlocuters have taught us, and enough of the excitement of these places that others will continue the journey.

REFERENCES CITED

Adelman, Irma, and Cynthia Taft Morris. 1973. *Economic Growth and Social Equity in Developing Countries*. Stanford: Stanford University Press.

Adelman, Irma. 1985. "A Poverty-focused Approach to Development Policy." In *Development Strategies Reconsidered*, ed. John P. Lewis and Valeriana Kallab. New Brunswick: Transaction, pp. 49–65.

Ahern, Emily M. 1973. *The Cult of the Dead in a Chinese Village*. Stanford: Stanford University Press.

Ahern, Emily Martin, and Hill Gates, eds. 1981. *The Anthropology of Taiwanese Society*. Stanford: Stanford University Press.

Akita, George. 1967. *Foundations of Constitutional Government in Modern Japan, 1868–1900*. Cambridge: Harvard University Press.

Alford, Robert R., and Roger Friedland. 1985. *Powers of Theory: Capitalism, the State, and Democracy*. Cambridge: Cambridge University Press.

Allen, Michael Patrick. 1978. "Economic Interest Groups and the Corporate Elite Structure." *Social Science Quarterly* 58,4:597–615.

Amin, Samir. 1976. *Unequal Development: An Essay on the Social Formations of Peripheral Capitalism*. New York: Monthly Review.

Amsden, Alice H. 1979. "Taiwan's Economic History: A Case of Etatisme and a Challenge to Dependency Theory." *Modern China* 5,3 (July):341–79.

———. 1981. "Technology Exports from Taiwan," ms.

———. 1984. "Taiwan." *World Development* 12, 5/6 (May/June):491–503.

———. 1985. "The State and Taiwan's Economic Development." In *Bringing the State Back In*, ed. Peter B. Evans, Dietrich Rueschemeyer, and Theda Skocpol. Chicago: University of Chicago Press, pp. 78–106.

Anderson, Perry. 1974. *Lineages of the Absolutist State*. London: New Left Books.

Andreski, Stanislav. 1968 (orig. 1954). *Military Organization and Society*. Berkeley: University of California Press.

Apthorpe, Raymond. 1979. "The Burden of Land Reform in Taiwan: An Asian Model Land Reform Re-analysed." *World Development* 7, 4/5 (April/May):519–30.

Aron, Raymond. 1966. *Peace and War—A Theory of International Relations*. New York: Doubleday.

Arrighi, Giovanni. 1985a. "Introduction." In *Semiperipheral Development*, ed. Giovanni Arrighi. Beverly Hills: Sage, pp. 11–27.

———, ed. 1985b. *Semiperipheral Development: The Politics of Southern Europe in the Twentieth Century*. Beverly Hills: Sage.

Arrigo, Linda Gail. 1980. "The Industrial Work Force of Young Women in Taiwan." *Bulletin of Concerned Asian Scholars* 12,2:25-38.

Asia Research Bulletin. 1977. 6, 9, section 3 (28 February).

Asian Wall Street Journal Weekly (AWSJ). 20 May 1985. "Taiwanese Family Struggles to Contain Fallout from Cathay Plastic Group's Financial Debacle." By Maria Shao, p. 4.

Bachrach, Peter, and Morton Baratz. 1962. "The Two Faces of Power." *American Political Science Review* 56:947-52.

Bagchi, Amiya K. 1982. *The Political Economy of Underdevelopment*. New York: Cambridge University Press.

Balassa, Bela. 1964. *Trade Prospects for Developing Countries*. Homewood, Il.: Irwin.

————. 1967. *Trade Liberalization among Industrial Countries: Objectives and Alternatives*. New York: McGraw-Hill.

————. 1981. *The Newly Industrialized Countries in the World Economy*. Elmsford, N.Y.: Pergamon.

————. 1982. *Development Strategies in Semi-Industrial Economies*. Baltimore: Johns Hopkins University Press.

Balassa, Bela, et al. 1971. *The Structure of Protection in Developing Countries*. Baltimore: Johns Hopkins University Press.

Balmori, Diana, Stuart F. Voss, and Miles Wortman. 1984. *Notable Family Networks in Latin America*. Chicago: University of Chicago Press.

Baran, Paul. 1957. *The Political Economy of Growth*. New York: Monthly Review.

Barclay, George W. 1954. *Colonial Development and Population in Taiwan*. Princeton: Princeton University Press.

Barnett, A. Doak. 1977. *China and the Major Powers in East Asia*. Washington, D.C.: Brookings Institution.

Barrett, Richard E., and Martin K. Whyte. 1982. "Dependency Theory and Taiwan: Analysis of a Deviant Case." *American Journal of Sociology* 87,5 (March):1064-89.

Basu, Dilip K. 1977. "The Opium War and the World Trade System." *Ch'ing Studies* 7, supplement 1:47-62.

————. 1979. "The Peripheralization of China: Notes on the Opium Connection." In *The World System of Capitalism*, ed. Walter Goldfrank. Beverly Hills: Sage, pp. 171-85.

Beckmann, George. 1973. "Brief Episodes: Dutch and Spanish Rule." In *Taiwan in Modern Times*, ed. Paul K. T. Sih. New York: St. John's University Press, pp. 31-58.

Bendix, Reinhard. 1977 (orig. 1964). *Nation-Building and Citizenship*. Enl. ed. Berkeley: University of California Press.

Benedict, Burton. 1968. "Family Firms and Economic Development." *Southwestern Journal of Anthropology* 24,1:1-19.

Bergesen, Albert, ed. 1980. *Studies of the Modern World-System*. New York: Academic.

————, ed. 1983. *Crises of the World System*. Beverly Hills: Sage.

Bergesen, Albert, and Ronald Schoenberg. 1980. "Long Waves of Colonial Expansion and Contraction, 1415-1969." In *Studies of the Modern World-System*, ed. Albert Bergesen. New York: Academic, pp. 231-77.

Black, Cyril E. 1966. *Dynamics of Modernization*. New York: Harper and Row.

Blair, John M. 1978. *The Control of Oil*. New York: Pantheon.

Boli-Bennet, John. 1979. "The Ideology of Expanding State Authority in National Constitutions, 1870-1970." In *National Development and the World System*, ed. John W. Meyer and Michael T. Hannan. Chicago: University of Chicago Press, pp. 222-37.

————. 1980. "Global Integration and the Universal Increase of State Dominance, 1910-70." In *Studies of the Modern World-System*, ed. Albert Bergesen. New York: Academic, pp. 77-108.

Bollen, Kenneth A. 1979. "Political Democracy and the Timing of Development." *American Sociological Review* 44,4 (August):572–87.

————. 1980. "Issues in the Comparative Measurement of Political Democracy." *American Sociological Review* 45,3 (June):370–90.

Bonilla, Frank, and Robert Girling, eds. 1973. *Structures of Dependency*. Stanford: Institute of Political Studies, Stanford University.

Boorman, Scott A., and Harrison C. White. 1976. "Social Structure from Multiple Networks. II. Role Structures." *American Journal of Sociology* 81,6 (May):1384–1446.

Borg, Dorothy, and Waldo Heinrichs, eds. 1980. *Uncertain Years: Chinese-American Relations, 1947–50*. New York: Columbia University Press.

Bornschier, Volker. 1983. "World Economy, Level Development and Income Distribution: An Integration of Different Approaches to the Explanation of Income Inequality." *World Development* 11,1 (January):11–20.

Bornschier, Volker, Christopher Chase-Dunn, and Richard Rubinson. 1978. "Cross-National Evidence of the Effects of Foreign Investment and Aid on Economic Growth and Inequality: A Survey of Findings and a Reanalysis." *American Journal of Sociology* 84,3 (November):651–83.

Bornschier, Volker, and T. H. Ballmer-Cao. 1979. "Income Inequality: A Cross-National Study." *American Sociological Review* 44,3 (June):487–503.

Bousquet, Nicole. 1980. "From Hegemony to Competition: Cycles of the Core?" In *Processes of the World System*, ed. Terence K. Hopkins and Immanuel Wallerstein. Beverly Hills: Sage, pp. 46–83.

Bozeman, Adda B. 1960. *Politics and Culture in International History*. Princeton: Princeton University Press.

Breiger, Ronald L. 1981. "Structures of Economic Interdependence among Nations." In *Continuities in Structural Inquiry*, ed. Peter M. Blau, and Robert K. Merton. Beverly Hills: Sage, pp. 353–80.

Burch, Philip H., Jr. 1972. *The Managerial Revolution Reassessed: Family Control in America's Large Corporations*. Lexington: Lexington Books.

Burt, Ronald. 1982. *Toward a Structural Theory of Action: Network Models of Social Structure, Perception and Action*. New York: Academic.

————. 1983. *Corporate Profits and Cooptation: Networks of Market Constraints and Directorate Ties in the American Economy*. New York: Academic.

Business Asia. 1979. (December).

Business Week. 16 December 1985. "Counterfeit Goods."

Calleo, David P. 1982. *The Imperious Economy*. Cambridge: Harvard University Press.

Campbell, Angus, et al. 1980. *The American Voter*. New York: Wiley.

Caporaso, James A. 1978. "Dependence, Dependency, and Power in the Global System: A Structural and Behavioral Analysis." *International Organization* 32,1:13–43.

Cardoso, Fernando H. 1972. "Dependency and Development in Latin America." *New Left Review* 74 (August):83–95.

————. 1973. "Associated-Dependent Development: Theoretical and Practical Implications." In *Authoritarian Brazil*, ed. Alfred Stepan. New Haven: Yale University Press, pp. 142–76.

————. 1977. "The Consumption of Dependency Theory in the United States." *Latin American Research Review* 12,3:7–24.

Cardoso, Fernando H., and Enzo Faletto. 1979. *Dependency and Development in Latin America*. Berkeley: University of California Press.

Carrington, George Williams. 1977. *Foreigners in Formosa, 1841–74*. San Francisco: Chinese Materials Center.

Cavendish, Patrick. 1969. "The 'New China' of the Kuomintang." In *Modern China's Search for a Political Form*, ed. Jack Gray. London: Oxford University Press, pp. 138–86.

Chang, Han-yu. 1955. "Evolution of Taiwan's Economy During the Period of Japanese Rule." In *Collection of Writings on Taiwan's Economic History*, no. 2. Taipei: Bank of Taiwan, pp. 74–128 (in Chinese).

————. 1969. "A Study of the Living Condition of Farmers in Taiwan, 1931–50." *Developing Economics* 7:35–62.

Chang, Han-yu, and Ramon H. Myers. 1963. "Japanese Colonial Development Policy in Taiwan, 1895–1906: A Case of Bureaucratic Entrepreneurship." *Journal of Asian Studies* 22,4 (August):433–49.

Chang, Kowie. 1968. *Economic Development in Taiwan*. Taipei: Chung Cheng Book Company.

Chang, P'eng-yuan. 1968. "The Constitutionalists." In *China in Revolution*, ed. Mary C. Wright. New Haven: Yale University Press, pp. 143–83.

————. 1970. "Political Participation and Political Elites in Early Republican China: The Parliament of 1913–14." *Journal of Asian Studies* 37,2 (February):293–313.

Chang, Parris H. 1973. "Cheng Ch'eng-kung (Koxinga): A Patriot, Nationalist and Nation-Builder." In *Taiwan in Modern Times*, ed. Paul K. T. Sih. New York: St. John's University Press, pp. 59–86.

Chang, Tsung-han. 1980. *Preretrocession Industrialization in Taiwan*. Taipei: Lien-ching (in Chinese).

Chang, Tzu-hui, ed. 1947. *Taiwan Who's Who*. Taipei: Kuo-kuang (in Chinese).

Chase-Dunn, Christopher. 1979. "The Effects of International Economic Dependence on Development and Inequality." In *National Development and the World System*, ed. John W. Meyer and Michael T. Hannan. Chicago: University of Chicago Press, pp. 131–51.

————. 1980. "The Development of Core Capitalism in the Antebellum United States: Tariff Politics and Class Struggle in an Upwardly Mobile Semi-periphery." In *Studies of the Modern World-System*, ed. Albert Bergesen. New York: Academic, pp. 189–229.

Chaudhuri, K. N. 1978. *The Trading World of Asia and the English East India Company, 1660–1760*. New York: Cambridge University Press.

Ch'en, Ch'eng. 1961. *Land Reform in Taiwan*. Taipei: China Publishing Company.

Ch'en, Chi-lu. 1968. *The Material Culture of the Formosan Aborigines*. Taipei: Taiwan Museum.

Ch'en, Ching-chih. 1973. "Japanese Sociopolitical Control in Taiwan, 1895–1945." Ph.D. dissertation, Harvard University.

————. 1975. "The Japanese Adaptation of the Pao-Chia System in Taiwan, 1895–1945." *Journal of Asian Studies* 34,2:391–416.

————. 1984. "Police and Community Control Systems in the Empire." In *The Japanese Colonial Empire*, ed. Ramon H. Myers and Mark R. Peattie. Princeton: Princeton University Press, pp. 213–39.

Ch'en, Edward I-te. 1968. "Japanese Colonialism in Korea and Formosa." Ph.D. dissertation, University of Pennsylvania.

————. 1970. "Japanese Colonialism in Korea and Formosa: A Comparison of the Systems of Political Control." *Harvard Journal of Asiatic Studies* 30:126–58.

————. 1972. "Formosan Political Movements under Japanese Colonial Rule, 1914–37." *Journal of Asian Studies* 31,3 (May):483–89.

————. 1977. "Japan's Decision to Annex Taiwan." *Journal of Asian Studies* 37,1 (November):61–72.

————. "The Attempt to Integrate the Empire: Legal Perspectives." In *The Japanese*

Colonial Empire, ed. Ramon H. Myers and Mark R. Peattie. Princeton: Princeton University Press, pp. 240–74.

Ch'en, Guu-ying. 1982. "Reform Movement among Intellectuals in Taiwan since 1970." *Bulletin of Concerned Asian Scholars* 14,3 (July-September):32–47.

Ch'en, Hsien-hui, comp. 1957. *Essentials of Industry in Free China*. Taipei: Asia Economic (in Chinese).

Ch'en, Shan-mei. 1978. "The Development of Taiwan's Petrochemicals Industry." *Bank of Taiwan Quarterly* (September):263–320 (in Chinese).

Ch'en, Ta-tuan. 1968. "Investiture of Liu-ch'iu Kings in the Ch'ing Period." In *The Chinese World Order*, ed. John K. Fairbank. Cambridge: Harvard University Press, pp. 135–64.

Ch'en, Ting-gou. 1975. *An Analysis of Industrial and Technology Development in Taiwan's Precision Industries*. Taipei: ITRI (in Chinese).

Ch'en, Yang-te. 1981. *Changes in Locally-Elected Leaders on Taiwan*. Taipei: Four Seasons (in Chinese).

Ch'en, Ching-chih. 1974. "Taiwanese Elites Under Japanese Colonial Rule." Paper prepared for 26th Annual Meeting of the Association for Asian Studies, Boston, Ma.

Chenery, Hollis, et al. 1974. *Redistribution with Growth*. London: Oxford University Press.

Cheng, Tun-jen, and Stephan Haggard. 1987. *Newly Industrializing Asia in Transition*. Berkeley: Institute of International Studies.

Chi, Hsi-sheng. 1976. *Warlord Politics in China, 1916–28*. Stanford: Stanford University Press.

————. 1982. *Nationalist China at War: Military Defeats and Political Collapse, 1937–45*. Ann Arbor: University of Michigan Press.

Ch'ien, Tuan-sheng. 1961. *The Government and Politics of China*. Cambridge: Harvard University Press.

China Credit Information Service (CCIS). 1966. *Namelist of Public and Private Sector Companies on Taiwan*. Taipei: China Credit Information Service (in Chinese).

————. 1973. *Business Who's Who in the Republic of China*. Taipei: China Credit Information Service (in Chinese).

————. 1978. *Who's Who of Outstanding Young Entrepreneurs*. Taipei: China Credit Information Service (in Chinese).

————. Various years. *Business Groups in Taiwan*. Taipei: China Credit Information Service (in Chinese).

China Industry Publishers. 1953. *Who's Who of Famous Industrialists in the Republic of China*. Taipei: China Industry (in Chinese).

China Institute of Engineers. 1958. *History of the Reconstruction of Industry on Taiwan*. Taipei: China Institute of Engineers.

China Science Company. 1953. *Who's Who of the Republic of China*. Taipei: China Science Company.

Chirot, Daniel. 1977. *Social Change in the Twentieth Century*. New York: Harcourt, Brace, Jovanovich.

Chiu, Hungdah. 1973a. "China, the United States, and the Question of Taiwan." In *China and the Question of Taiwan*, ed. Hungdah Chiu. New York: Praeger, pp. 112–91.

————, ed. 1973b. *China and the Question of Taiwan: Documents and Analysis*. New York: Praeger.

————, ed. 1979. *China and the Taiwan Issue*. New York: Praeger.

Chomsky, Noam, and Edward S. Herman. 1979. *The Washington Connection and Third World Fascism*. 2 vols. Boston: South End.

Clough, Ralph N. 1978. *Island China*. Cambridge: Harvard University Press.

Cnudde, Charles F., and Deane E. Neubauer, eds. 1969. *Empirical Democratic Theory*.

Chicago: Markham.

Coble, Parks. 1980. *The Shanghai Capitalists*. Cambridge: Harvard University Press.

Cohen, Jerome A., ed. 1970. *The Dynamics of China's Foreign Relations*. Cambridge: Harvard University Press.

Cohen, Myron L. 1976. *House United, House Divided: The Chinese Family in Taiwan*. New York: Columbia University Press.

Cohen, Paul A. 1970. "Ch'ing China: Confrontation With the West, 1850-1900." In *Modern East Asia*, ed. James B. Crowley. New York: Harcourt, Brace and World, pp. 235-64.

Cohen, Paul, and John Schrecker, eds. 1976. *Reform in Nineteenth Century China*. Cambridge: Harvard University Press.

Cohen, Warren I. 1980. "Acheson, His Advisors and China, 1949-50." In *Uncertain Years*, ed. Dorothy Borg and Waldo Heinrichs. New York: Columbia University Press, pp. 13-52.

Cole, Allan B. 1967. "Political Roles of Taiwanese Enterprisers." *Asian Survey* 7,9:645-54.

Cole, David C., and Princeton N. Lyman. 1971. *Korean Development: The Interplay of Politics and Economics*. Cambridge: Harvard University Press.

Collier, David, ed. 1979. *The New Authoritarianism in Latin America*. Princeton: Princeton University Press.

Committee on Industrial and Commercial Censuses. 1971. *The Report of 1971 Industrial and Commercial Censuses of Taiwan-Fukien District of the Republic of China*. Taipei: Committee on Industrial and Commercial Censuses.

Commonwealth Magazine. 1981-84. *Top 500 Companies in the Republic of China*. *Commonwealth Magazine* (September issues).

Conroy, Hillary. 1960. *The Japanese Seizure of Korea*. Philadelphia: University of Pennsylvania Press.

Coombs, Lolagene C., and Te-hsiung Sun. 1981. "Familial Values in a Developing Society: A Decade of Change in Taiwan." *Social Forces* 59,3 (March):1229-55.

Copper, John F. 1979. "Political Development in Taiwan." In *China and the Taiwan Issue*, ed. Hungdah Chiu. New York: Praeger, pp. 37-76.

Copper, John F., with George P. Ch'en. 1984. *Taiwan's Elections: Political Development and Democratization in the Republic of China*. Baltimore: School of Law, University of Maryland.

Council for Economic Planning and Development (CEPD). 1979. *Taiwan Economic Statistics, 1979*. Taipei: CEPD.

————. Various years. *Taiwan Statistical Data Book*. Taipei: CEPD.

Crane, George T. 1982. "The Taiwanese Ascent: System, State and Movement in the World Economy." In *Ascent and Decline in the World-System*, ed. Edward Friedman. Beverly Hills: Sage, pp. 93-113.

Croizier, Ralph C. 1977. *Koxinga and Chinese Nationalism: History, Myth and the Hero*. Cambridge: Harvard University Press.

Crowley, James B. 1966. *Japan's Quest for Autonomy: National Security and Foreign Policy, 1930-38*. Princeton: Princeton University Press.

————, ed. 1970a. *Modern East Asia: Essays in Interpretation*. New York: Harcourt, Brace and World.

————. 1970b. "A New Deal for Japan and Asia: One Road to Pearl Harbor." In *Modern East Asia*, ed. James B. Crowley. New York: Harcourt, Brace and World, pp. 235-64.

Cumings, Bruce. 1981a. "Interest and Ideology in the Study of Agrarian Politics." *Politics and Society* 10,4:467-95.

————. 1981b. *The Origins of the Korean War: Liberation and the Emergence of*

Separate Regimes, 1945–1947. Princeton: Princeton University Press.
———. 1983a. "South Korea in Crisis: Danger or Opportunity." *SAID Review* 3,2 (Summer-Fall):71–86.
———, ed. 1983b. *Child of Conflict: The Korean-American Relationship, 1945–53.* Seattle: University of Washington Press.
———. 1984. "The Origins and Development of the Northeast Asian Political Economy: Industrial Sectors, Product Cycles, and Political Consequences." *International Organization* 38,1 (Winter):1–40.
Dahl, Robert A., and Charles E. Lindblom. 1953. *Politics, Economics and Welfare.* New York: Harper and Row.
Davidson, James W. 1903. *The Island of Formosa.* New York: Macmillan.
Davis, John H. 1978. *The Guggenheims: An American Epic.* New York: William Morrow.
DeGlopper, Donald R. 1972. "Doing Business in Lukang." In *Economic Organization in Chinese Society*, ed. W. E. Willmott. Stanford: Stanford University Press, pp. 297–326.
———. 1979. "Artisan Work and Life in Taiwan." *Modern China* 5,3:283–316.
Delacroix, Jacques. 1977. "The Export of Raw Materials and Economic Growth: A Cross-National Study." *American Sociological Review* 42,5 (October):795–808.
Deyo, Frederic C. 1987a. "Coalitions, Institutions, and Linkage Sequencing—Toward a Strategic Capacity Model of East Asian Development." In *The Political Economy of the New Asian Industrialism*, ed. Frederic C. Deyo. Ithaca: Cornell University Press, pp. 227–47.
———. 1987b. *The Political Economy of the New Asian Industrialism.* Ithaca: Cornell University Press.
Diamond, Norma. 1979. "Women and Industry in Taiwan." *Modern China* 5,3:317–40.
Directorate-General of Budget, Accounting and Statistics (DGBAS), Executive Yuan. Various years. *Report on the Survey of Personal Income Distribution in Taiwan Area, Republic of China.* Taipei: DGBAS.
Dirlik, Arif. 1975. "The Ideological Foundations of the New Life Movement: A Study in Counter-Revolution." *Journal of Asian Studies* 34,3 (August):945–80.
Dong, Yu-ching. 1985. "Industries in ROC Enter New Era in Investments Abroad." *Free China Journal* (27 January).
Dos Santos, Theotonio. 1970. "The Structure of Dependence." *American Economic Review* 60,2 (May):231–36.
Durdin, Tillman. 1975a. "Chiang Ching-kuo and Taiwan: A Profile." *Orbis* 18:1023–42.
———. 1975b. "Chiang Ching-kuo's Taiwan." *Pacific Community* 7:92–117.
Duus, Peter. 1968. *Party Rivalry and Political Change in Taisho Japan.* Cambridge: Harvard University Press.
———. 1970. "The Era of Party Rule: Japan, 1905–32." In *Modern East Asia*, ed. James B. Crowley. New York: Harcourt, Brace and World, pp. 180–206.
———. 1984. "Economic Dimensions of Meiji Imperialism: The Case of Korea, 1895–1910." In *The Japanese Colonial Empire*, ed. Ramon H. Myers and Mark R. Peattie. Princeton: Princeton University Press, pp. 125–71.
Eastman, Lloyd E. 1967. *Thrones and Mandarins: China's Search for a Policy During the Sino-French Controversy, 1880–85.* Cambridge: Harvard University Press.
———. 1974. *The Abortive Revolution: China under Nationalist Rule, 1927–37.* Cambridge: Harvard University Press.
Economic Cooperation Agency (ECA). 1950. *TOECA 673* (18 September).
Economic News (Taipei). 31 October 1974; 2 February 1978; 14 April 1978; 20 June 1978; 31 October 1978 (in Chinese).
Edwardes, Michael. 1967. *The West in Asia, 1850–1914.* London: Botsford.
Ellsberg, Daniel. 1972. *Papers on the War.* New York: Pocketbooks.

Emerson, Rupert. 1960. *From Empire to Nation*. Cambridge: Harvard University Press.
Eto, Shinkichi. 1963. "An Outline of Formosan History." In *Formosa Today*, ed. Mark Mancall. New York: Praeger, pp. 43–58.
Evans, Peter B. 1979. *Dependent Development: The Alliance of Multinational, State and Local Capital in Brazil*. Princeton: Princeton University Press.
————. 1985. "Transnational Linkages and the Economic Role of the State: An Analysis of Developing and Industrialized Nations in the Post-World War II Period." In *Bringing the State Back In*, ed. Peter B. Evans, Dietrich Rueschemeyer, and Theda Skocpol. Chicago: University of Chicago Press, pp. 192–226.
————. 1987. "Class, State, and Dependence in East Asia: Lessons for Latin Americanists." In *The Political Economy of the New Asian Industrialism*, ed. Frederic C. Deyo. Ithaca: Cornell University Press, pp. 203–26.
Evans, Peter B., Dietrich Rueschemeyer, and Theda Skocpol, eds. 1985. *Bringing the State Back In*. Chicago: University of Chicago Press.
Evans, Peter B., and Michael Timberlake. 1980. "Dependence, Inequality, and the Growth of the Tertiary: A Comparative Analysis of Less Developed Countries." *American Sociological Review* 45,4 (August):531–52.
Fairbank, John K. 1953. *Trade and Diplomacy on the China Coast: The Opening of the Treaty Ports, 1842–1854*. Cambridge: Harvard University Press.
————. 1968a. "A Preliminary Framework." In *The Chinese World Order*, ed. John K. Fairbank. Cambridge: Harvard University Press, pp. 1–19.
————, ed. 1968b. *The Chinese World Order*. Cambridge: Harvard University Press.
————. 1974. "Introduction: Varieties of the Chinese Military Experience." In *Chinese Ways in Warfare*, ed. Frank A. Kierman, Jr. and John K. Fairbank. Cambridge: Harvard University Press, pp. 1–26.
————. ed. 1978. *The Cambridge History of China*. Volume 10: *Late Ch'ing, 1800–1911, Part One*. New York: Cambridge University Press.
Fairbank John K., and Kwang-ch'ing Liu, eds. 1980. *The Cambridge History of China*. Volume 11: *Late Ch'ing, 1800–1911, Part Two*. New York: Cambridge University Press.
Fairbank, John K., Edwin O. Reischauer, and Albert M. Craig. 1965. *East Asia: The Modern Transformation*. Boston: Houghton Mifflin.
Far Eastern Economic Review (FEER). 27 December 1974. "Taiwan's Bid to Beat the Trade Slide." By Susumu Awanohara, pp. 44–47.
————. 18 July 1975. "Throwing Caution to the Winds in Taiwan." By Andrew Davenport, pp. 47–50.
————. 14 October 1977. "Textile Revamp in Taiwan." By Melinda Liu, pp. 49–51.
————. 6 August 1982. "A Painful Parting." By Andrew Tanzer, pp. 62–63.
————. 21 April 1983. "Taiwan's Fiscal Caution." By A. Tanzer, pp. 74–76.
————. 21 July 1983. "Asia Plugs into the Computer." By A. Tanzer, pp. 59–65.
————. 22 March 1984. "The Big Bounce Back." By A. Tanzer, pp. 59–65.
————. 26 April 1984. "Trying to Grow Something Out of a Desert." By A. Tanzer, pp. 90–93.
————. 6 September 1984. "Reforms Belaboured." By Carl Goldstein, pp. 109–10.
————. 27 September 1984. "The Road-Show Is Off." By C. Goldstein, p. 165.
————. 7 March 1985. "An Outward Push." By C. Goldstein, p. 64.
————. 7 March 1985. "Running to the Bank." By C. Goldstein, pp. 50–51.
————. 11 April 1985. "Discredited Policies." By C. Goldstein, pp. 90–91.
————. 25 April 1985. "A Series of Shocks Rocks an Archaic System." By C. Goldstein, pp. 73–74.
————. 9 May 1985. "A Boom on the Quiet." By C. Goldstein, p. 79.
————. 23 May 1985. "More Like the Real Thing." By C. Goldstein, p. 85.

————. 25 July 1985. "After the Boom is Over." By C. Goldstein, p. 51.

————. 26 September 1985. "Export-led Slowdown." By Philip Bowring et al., pp. 99–106

Fei, John C. H., Gustav Ranis, and Shirley W. Y. Kuo. 1979. *Growth with Equity: The Taiwan Case*. New York: Oxford University Press.

Fennema, M. 1982. *International Networks of Banks and Industry*. The Hague: Martinus Nijhoff.

Ferrell, Raleigh. 1969. *Taiwan Aboriginal Groups: Problems in Cultural and Linguistic Classification*. Taipei: Institute of Ethnology, Academica Sinica.

Feuchtwang, Stephan. 1974. "City Temples in Taipei under Three Regimes." In *The Chinese City Between Two Worlds*, ed. Mark Elvin and G. William Skinner. Stanford: Stanford University Press, pp. 263–301.

Feuerwerker, Albert. 1958. *China's Early Industrialization: Sheng Hsuan-huai (1844–1916) and Mandarin Enterprise*. Cambridge: Harvard University Press.

Fiala, Robert. 1983. "Inequality and the Service Sector in Less Developed Countries." *American Sociological Review* 48,3 (June):421–28.

Fieldhouse, David K. 1966. *The Colonial Empires*. New York: Dell.

————. 1973. *Economics and Empire, 1820–1914*. Ithaca: Cornell University Press.

Fields, Gary S. 1984. "Employment, Income Distribution and Economic Growth in Seven Small Open Economies." *The Economic Journal* 94,373 (March):74–83.

Fincher, John. 1968. "Political Provincialism and the National Revolution." In *China in Revolution*, ed. Mary C. Wright. New Haven: Yale University Press, pp. 185–226.

————. 1981. *Chinese Democracy*. Canberra: Australian National University Press.

Finer, Samuel E. 1975. "State- and Nation-Building in Europe: The Role of the Military." In *The Formation of National States in Western Europe*, ed. Charles Tilly. Princeton: Princeton University Press, pp. 84–163.

Foster-Carter, Aidan. 1978. "The Modes of Production Controversy." *New Left Review* 107 (January-February):47–77.

Frank, Andre Gunder. 1969a. "The Development of Underdevelopment." In *Latin America: Underdevelopment or Revolution*, ed. Andre Gunder Frank. New York: Monthly Review, pp. 3–17.

————. 1969b. *Capitalism and Underdevelopment in Latin America: Historical Studies of Chile and Brazil*. New York: Monthly Review.

————, ed. 1969c. *Latin America: Underdevelopment or Revolution*. New York: Monthly Review.

————. 1972. *Lumpenbourgeoisie: Lumpendevelopment: Dependence, Class, and Politics in Latin America*. New York: Monthly Review.

————. 1978. *World Accumulation, 1492–1789*. New York: Monthly Review.

————. 1979. *Dependent Accumulation and Underdevelopment*. New York: Monthly Review.

Fransman, Martin. 1986. *Technology and Economic Development*. Boulder: Westview.

Fransman, Martin, and Kenneth King, eds. 1984. *Technological Capability in the Third World*. London: Macmillan.

Free China Journal. 3 February 1986. "VLSI: A Booster to Information Industry," p. 4.

————. 7 April 1986. "ROC Counterfeiting Cases in Dramatic Drop Since 1983," p. 4.

————. 9 February 1987. "Sub-Microns Large Item in ROC Plans for a National Lab," p. 4.

Freedman, Ronald, and John B. Casterline. 1982. "Nuptiality and Fertility in Taiwan." In *Nuptiality and Fertility: Proceedings of a Seminar Held in Bruges, Belgium, 8–11 January 1979*, ed. L. T. Ruzicka. Liege: Ordina, pp. 61–99.

Freedman, Ronald, and John Y. Takeshita. 1969. *Family Planning in Taiwan: An Experi-

ment in Social Change. Princeton: Princeton University Press.

Freeman, John R., and Raymond D. Duvall. 1984. "International Economic Relations and the Entrepreneurial State." *Economic Development and Cultural Change* 33,2 (January):373–400.

Fried, Morton H. 1966. "Some Political Aspects of Clanship in a Modern Chinese City." In *Political Anthropology*, ed. Marc J. Swartz, Victor W. Turner, and Arthur Tuden. Chicago: Aldine, pp. 285–300.

Friedman, Edward, ed. 1982. *Ascent and Decline in the World-System*. Beverly Hills: Sage.

Fruin, W. Mark. 1980. "The Family as a Firm and the Firm as a Family in Japan: The Case of Kikkoman Shoyu Co. Limited." *Journal of Family History* 5,4 (Winter):432–49.

Furber, Holden. 1976. *Rival Empires of Trade in the Orient, 1600–1800*. 2 Vols. Minneapolis: University of Minnesota Press.

Gaddis, John L. 1980. "The Strategic Perspective: The Rise and Fall of the 'Defensive Perimeter' Concept, 1947–51." In *Uncertain Years*, ed. Dorothy Borg and Waldo Heinrichs. New York: Columbia University Press, pp. 61–118.

Galenson, Walter, ed. 1979a. *Economic Growth and Structural Change in Taiwan: The Postwar Experience of the Republic of China*. Ithaca: Cornell University Press.

Galenson, Walter. 1979b. "The Labor Force, Wages, and Living Standards." In *Economic Growth and Structural Change in Taiwan*, ed. Walter Galenson. Ithaca: Cornell University Press, pp. 384–447.

―――――, ed. 1985. *Foreign Trade and Investment: Economic Growth in the Newly Industrializing Asian Countries*. Madison: University of Wisconsin Press.

Gallin, Bernard, and Rita S. Gallin. 1977. "Sociopolitical Power and Sworn Brother Groups in Chinese Society: Taiwanese Case." In *The Anthropology of Power*, ed. Raymond D. Fogelman and Richard N. Adams. New York: Academic, pp. 89–97.

―――――. 1982. "Socioeconomic Life in Rural Taiwan: Twenty Years of Development and Change." *Modern China* 8,2:205–46.

Gallin, Rita S. 1984. "The Entry of Chinese Women into the Rural Labor Force: A Case Study from Taiwan." *Signs: Journal of Women in Culture and Society* 9,3:383–98.

Galtung, Johan. 1971. "A Structural Theory of Imperialism." *Journal of Peace Research* 8,2:81–117.

Gann, Lewis H. 1984. "Western and Japanese Colonialism: Some Preliminary Comparisons." In *The Japanese Colonial Empire*, ed. Ramon H. Myers and Mark R. Peattie. Princeton: Princeton University Press, pp. 497–525.

Gates, Hill. 1979. "Dependency and the Part-Time Proletariat in Taiwan." *Modern China* 5,3 (July):381–408.

―――――. 1981. "Ethnicity and Social Class." In *The Anthropology of Taiwanese Society*, ed. Emily M. Ahern and Hill Gates. Stanford: Stanford University Press, pp. 241–81.

Gereffi, Gary. 1983. *The Pharmaceutical Industry and Dependency in the Third World*. Princeton: Princeton University Press.

Gerschenkron, Alexander. 1962. *Economic Backwardness in Historical Perspective*. Cambridge: Harvard University Press.

Gilpin, Robert G., Jr. 1975. *U.S. Power and the Multinational Corporation: The Political Economy of Direct Foreign Investment*. New York: Basic.

―――――. 1981. *War and Change in World Politics*. Cambridge: Camridge University Press.

Godelier, Maurice. 1978. "The Concept of the 'Asiatic Mode of Production' and Marxist Models of Social Evolution." In *Relations of Production*, ed. David Seddon. London: Frank Cass, pp. 209–57.

Gold, Thomas B. 1981. "Dependent Development in Taiwan." Ph.D. dissertation, Harvard University.

———. 1986a. "Multilateral Lending Agencies in East Asia." In *Pacific-Asian Issues: American and Chinese Views*, ed. Robert A. Scalapino and Ch'en Qimao. Berkeley: Institute of East Asian Studies, pp. 57–84.

———. 1986b. *State and Society in the Taiwan Miracle*. Armonk, N.Y.: M. E. Sharpe.

Goldfrank, Walter, ed. 1979. *The World System of Capitalism*. Beverly Hills: Sage.

Goodman, Grant K., comp. 1967. *Imperial Japan and Asia: A Reassessment*. New York: Columbia University Press.

Gordon, David M. 1980. "Stages of Accumulation and Long Economic Cycles." In *Processes of the World System*, ed. Terence K. Hopkins and Immanuel Wallerstein. Beverly Hills: Sage, pp. 9–45.

Gordon, Leonard H. D., ed. 1970. *Taiwan: Studies in Chinese Local History*. New York: Columbia University Press.

Gough, Ian. 1975. "State Expenditure in Advanced Capitalism." *New Left Review* 91 (July-August):53–92.

Goulet, Denis, and Michael Hudson. 1971. *The Myth of Aid: The Hidden Agenda of the Development Reports*. New York: IDOC.

Gourevitch, Peter. 1978. "The Second Image Reversed: The International Sources of Domestic Politics." *International Organization* 31,4 (Autumn):881–912.

Granovetter, Mark S. 1974. *Getting a Job: A Study of Contacts and Careers*. Cambridge: Harvard University Press.

Gray, Jack, ed. 1969. *Modern China's Search for a Political Form*. London: Oxford University Press.

Greenfield, Sidney M., Arnold Strickon, and Robert T. Aubey, eds. 1979. *Entrepreneurs in Cultural Context*. Albuquerque: University of New Mexico Press.

Greenhalgh, Susan. 1982. "Income Units: The Ethnographic Alternative to Standardization." In *Income Distribution and the Family*, ed. Yoram Ben-Porath. *Population and Development Review*, supplement to vol. 8 (September):70–91.

———. 1984. "Networks and Their Nodes: Urban Society on Taiwan." *The China Quarterly* 99 (September):529–52.

———. 1985. "Sexual Stratification: The Other Side of 'Growth With Equity' in East Asia." *Population and Development Review* 11,2 (June):265–315.

———. 1988. "Social Causes and Consequences of Taiwan's Postwar Economic Development." In *The Anthropology of Taiwan* (tent. title), ed. Arthur P. Wolf and Kwang-chih Chang. Stanford: Stanford University Press.

Gregor, A. James, Maria Hsia Chang, and Andrew B. Zimmerman. 1981. *Ideology and Development: Sun Yat-sen and the Economic History of Taiwan*. Berkeley: University of California, Center for Chinese Studies.

Gregor, A. James, and Maria Hsia Chang. 1982. "The Economic History of Taiwan and the Notion of Imperialist Exploitation." *Jerusalem Journal of International Relations* 6,2:61–87.

Grichting, Wolfgang L. 1970. *The Value System in Taiwan, 1970: A Preliminary Report*. Taipei: Privately published.

Grieco, Joseph. 1984. *Between Dependency and Autonomy: India's Experience with the International Computer Industry*. Berkeley: University of California Press.

Griffin, Keith. 1973. "An Assessment of Development in Taiwan." *World Development* 1,6:31–42.

Griswold, A. Whitney. 1938. *The Far Eastern Policy of the United States*. New York: Harcourt, Brace and World.

Gurtov, Melvin. 1967. "Recent Developments in Formosa." *The China Quarterly* 31 (July-September):59–95.

Haggard, Stephan, and Tun-jen Cheng. 1987. "State and Capital in the East Asian NICs." In *The Political Economy of the New Asian Industrialism*, ed. Frederic C. Deyo. Ithaca: Cornell University Press, pp. 84–135.

Hall, John Whitney. 1970. *Japan From Prehistory to Modern Times*. New York: Dell.

Halliday, Jan. 1975. *A Political History of Japanese Capitalism*. New York: Monthly Review.

————. 1980. "Capitalism and Socialism in East Asia." *New Left Review* 124 (November-December):3–24.

Halliday, Jan, and Gavan McCormack. 1973. *Japanese Imperialism Today*. New York: Monthly Review.

Hamilton, Gary G. 1977. "Chinese Consumption of Foreign Commodities: A Comparative Perspective." *American Sociological Review* 42,6 (December):877–91.

Hammer, Heather Jo. 1984. "Comment on 'Dependency Theory and Taiwan: Analysis of a Deviant Case.'" *American Journal of Sociology* 89,4 (January):932–37.

Han, Sungjoo. 1974. *The Failure of Democracy in Korea*. Berkeley: University of California Press.

Hao, Yen-p'ing, and Erh-min Wang. 1980. "Changing Chinese Views of Western Relations, 1840–95." In *The Cambridge History of China*, ed. John K. Fairbank and Kwang-chih Liu. New York: Cambridge University Press, pp. 142–201.

Harrell, C. Stevan. 1982. *Ploughshare Village: Culture and Context in Taiwan*. Seattle: University of Washington Press.

Hartz, Louis. 1964. *The Founding of New Societies*. New York: Harcourt, Brace and World.

Haskell, Barbara. 1980. "Access to Society: A Neglected Dimension of Power." *International Organization* (Winter):89–120.

Hayter, Teresa. 1971. *Aid as Imperialism*. Middlesex, England: Penguin.

Headrick, Daniel R. 1981. *The Tools of Empire: Technology and European Imperialism in the Nineteenth Century*. New York: Oxford University Press.

Hechter, Michael. 1975. *Internal Colonialism*. Berkeley: University of California Press.

————. 1981. "Karl Polanyi's Social Theory: A Critique." *Politics and Society* 10,4:399–431.

Heinrichs, Waldo. 1980. "Summary of Discussion." In *Uncertain Years: Chinese-American Relations, 1947–50*, ed. Dorothy Borg and Waldo Heinrichs. New York: Columbia University Press, pp. 119–28.

Hermet, Guy, et al., eds. 1978. *Elections Without Choice*. New York: Wiley/Halstead.

Hinton, Harold C. 1970. *China's Turbulent Quest: An Analysis of China's Foreign Relations Since 1949*. New York: Macmillan.

Hintze, Otto. 1975 (orig. 1906). *The Historical Essays of Otto Hintze*. New York: Oxford University Press.

Hirschman, Albert O. 1971. *A Bias for Hope: Essays on Development and Latin America*. New Haven: Yale University Press.

————. 1977. *The Passions and the Interests: Political Arguments for Capitalism Before Its Triumph*. Princeton: Princeton University Press.

————. 1979. "The Turn to Authoritarianism in Latin America and the Search for its Economic Determinants." In *The New Authoritarianism in Latin America*, ed. David Collier. Princeton: Princeton University Press.

Hirschmeier, Johannes. 1964. *The Origins of Entrepreneurship in Meiji Japan*. Cambridge: Harvard University Press.

Ho, Samuel P. S. 1971. "The Development Policy of the Japanese Colonial Government in Taiwan, 1895–1945." In *Government and Economic Development*, ed. Gustav Ranis. New Haven: Yale University Press, pp. 287–328.

————. 1978a. *Economic Development of Taiwan, 1860–1970*. New Haven:

Yale University Press.

————. 1978b. "Small Scale Industries in Two Rapidly Growing Less Developed Countries: Korea and Taiwan—A Study of their Characteristics, Competitive Bases, and Productivity." *Studies in Employment and Rural Development*, no. 53. Washington, D.C.: World Bank.

Ho, Yhi-min. 1980. "The Production Structure of the Manufacturing Sector and Its Distribution Implications." *Economic Development and Cultural Change* 28,2 (January):321–43.

Hobsbawm, Eric. 1968. *Industry and Empire*. London: Penguin.

————. 1985. *Workers: Worlds of Labor*. New York: Pantheon.

Hofheinz, Roy, and Kent Calder. 1982. *The East Asia Edge*. New York: Basic.

Hollist, W. Ladd, and James N. Rosenau, eds. 1981. *World System Structure*. Beverly Hills: Sage.

Holt, Robert T., and John E. Turner. 1966. *The Political Basis of Economic Development: An Exploration in Comparative Political Analysis*. Princeton: D. Van Nostrand.

Hopkins, Terence K., and Immanuel Wallerstein, eds. 1980. *Processes of the World System*. Beverly Hills: Sage.

Hsiao, Frank S. T., and Lawrence R. Sullivan. 1983. "A Political History of the Taiwanese Communist Party, 1928–31." *Journal of Asian Studies* 42,2 (February):269–89.

Hsiao, Hsin-huang Michael. 1981. *Government Agricultural Strategies in Taiwan and South Korea: A Macrosocial Perspective*. Taipei: Institute of Ethnology, Academia Sinica.

Hsinchu Science and Industry Park Administration. 1985. *Hsinchu Science and Industry Park: An Overview*. Taipei.

Hsing, Mo-huan. 1971. *Taiwan: Industrialization and Trade Policies*. London: Oxford University Press.

Hsiung, Tun-sheng. 1978. *Who's Who in the Republic of China*. 3 vols. Taipei: Chunghuo.

Hsu, Immanuel C. Y. 1960. *China's Entry into the Family of Nations: The Diplomatic Phase, 1858–80*. Cambridge: Harvard University Press.

————. 1980. "Late Ch'ing Foreign Relations, 1866–1905." In *The Cambridge History of China*, ed. John K. Fairbank and Kwang-chih Liu. New York: Cambridge University Press, pp. 70–141.

Hsu, Shih-k'ai. 1972. *Taiwan under Japanese Rule*. Tokyo: Tokyo University Press (in Japanese).

Hsu, Wen-hsiung. 1980a. "From Aboriginal Island to Chinese Frontier: The Development of Taiwan Before 1683." In *China's Island Frontier*, ed. Ronald G. Knapp. Honolulu: University Press of Hawaii, pp. 3–30.

————. 1980b. "Frontier Social Organization and Social Disorder in Ch'ing Taiwan." In *China's Island Frontier*, ed. Ronald G. Knapp. Honolulu: University Press of Hawaii, pp. 87–106.

Hu, Tai-li. 1983. "My Mother-In-Law's Village: Rural Industrialization and Change in Taiwan." Ph.D. dissertation, City University of New York.

Huang, Mab. 1975. *Intellectual Ferment for Political Reforms in Taiwan, 1971–73*. Ann Arbor: Center for Chinese Studies, University of Michigan.

Huang, Shu-min. 1981. *Agricultural Degradation: Changing Community Systems in Rural Taiwan*. Washington, D.C.: University Press of America.

Huang, T'ien-chung. 1971. "A Study of the Voting Behavior of the Residents of Taipei City." M.A. thesis, National Chengchi University (in Chinese).

Huntington, Samuel P. 1968. *Political Order in Changing Societies*. New Haven: Yale University Press.

Huntington, Samuel P., and Joan M. Nelson. 1976. *No Easy Choice: Political Participation in Developing Countries*. Cambridge: Harvard University Press.

Huntington, Samuel P., and Clement Moore, eds. 1970. *Authoritarian Politics in Modern Society*. New York: Basic.

Hveem, Helge. 1983. "Selective Dissociation in the Technology Sector." In *The Antinomies of Interdependence: National Welfare and the International Division of Labor*, ed. J. G. Ruggie. New York: Columbia University Press, pp. 273–316.

Ichiko, Chuzo. 1980. "Political and Institutional Reform, 1901–11." In *The Cambridge History of China*, ed. John K. Fairbank and Kwang-chih Liu. New York: Cambridge University Press, pp. 375–415.

Industry of Free China. 1954. "Forum on Industrial Management: The Transfer of the Four Public Enterprises to Private Ownership," *Industry of Free China* (February):27–33.

Inkeles, Alex. 1975. "The Emerging Social Structure of the World." *World Politics* 27 (July):467–95.

Inkeles, Alex, and David H. Smith. 1974. *Becoming Modern: Individual Change in Six Developing Countries*. Cambridge: Harvard University Press.

Investment Commission. 1979. "The Operating Situation Within Technology Cooperation Firms and Taiwan's Economic Climate: An Investigative Report." Taipei: Ministry of Economic Affairs (in Chinese).

———. 1985. "Statistics on Foreign Investment and Technology Cooperation in Taiwan, 1952–84." Taipei: Ministry of Economic Affairs (in Chinese).

Iriye, Akira. 1965. *After Imperialism: The Search for a New Order in the Far East, 1921–31*. Cambridge: Harvard University Press.

———. 1970. "Imperialism in East Asia." In *Modern East Asia*, ed. James B. Crowley. New York: Harcourt, Brace and World, pp. 122–50.

———. 1972. *Pacific Estrangement: Japanese and American Expansion, 1897–1911*. Cambridge: Harvard University Press.

Israel, John. 1963. "Politics on Formosa." In *Formosa Today*, ed. Mark Mancall. *The China Quarterly*, pp. 59–67.

Iwasaki, Ketsuji. 1903. *Who's Who In Taiwan Business*. Taihoku: Taiwan Zasshisha (in Japanese).

Jacobs, J. Bruce. 1971. "Recent Leadership and Political Trends in Taiwan." *The China Quarterly* 45 (January-March):129–54.

———. 1976. "The Cultural Bases of Factional Alignment and Division in a Rural Taiwanese Township." *Journal of Asian Studies* 36,1 (November):79–97.

———. 1979. "A Preliminary Model of Particularistic Ties in Chinese Political Alliances." *The China Quarterly* 78 (June):237–73.

———. 1980. *Local Politics in a Rural Chinese Cultural Setting*. Canberra: Contemporary China Centre, Research School of Pacific Studies, Australian National University.

———. 1984. "Political Opposition and Taiwan's Political Future." *Australian Journal of Chinese Affairs* 6.

Jacoby, Neil H. 1966. *U.S. Aid to Taiwan: A Study of Foreign Aid, Self-Help, and Development*. New York: Praeger.

Jansen, Marius B. 1970. "The Meiji State: 1868–1912." In *Modern East Asia*, ed. James B. Crowley. New York: Harcourt, Brace and World, pp. 95–121.

———. 1984. "Japanese Imperialism: Late Meiji Perspectives." In *The Japanese Colonial Empire*, ed. Ramon H. Myers and Mark R. Peattie. Princeton: Princeton University Press, pp. 61–79.

Jo, Yung-hwan, ed. 1974. *Taiwan's Future?* Tenipe: Union Research Institute for Center for Asian Studies, Arizona State University.

Johnson, Chalmers. 1982. *MITI and the Japanese Miracle*. Stanford: Stanford University Press.

————. 1987. "Political Institutions and Economic Performance: The Government-Business Relationship in Japan, South Korea, and Taiwan." In *The Political Economy of the New Asian Industrialism*, ed. Frederic C. Deyo. Ithaca: Cornell University Press, pp. 136–64.

Johnson, Harry G. 1967. *Economic Policies Toward Less Developed Countries*. Washington, D.C.: Brookings Institution.

Joint Commission on Rural Reconstruction (JCRR). 1950. *General Report of the Joint Commission on Rural Reconstruction (October 1, 1948 to February 15, 1950)*. Taipei: JCRR.

————. 1965. *JCRR Annual Reports on Land Reform in the Republic of China: October 1948-June 1964*. Taipei: JCRR.

Jones, Susan Mann, and Philip Kuhn. 1978. "Dynastic Decline and the Roots of Rebellion." In *The Cambridge History of China*, ed. John K. Fairbank. New York: Cambridge University Press.

Journal of Commerce. 2 April 1976.

Kagan, Richard C. 1982. "Martial Law in Taiwan." *Bulletin of Concerned Asian Scholars* 14,3 (July-September):48–54.

Kahn, Herman. 1979. *World Economic Development: 1979 and Beyond*. New York: Morrow Quill.

Kallgren, Joyce K. 1963. "Nationalistic China's Armed Forces." In *Formosa Today*, ed. Mark Mancall. *The China Quarterly*, pp. 91–100.

Kaplan, Barbara Hockey, ed. 1978. *Social Change in the Capitalist World Economy*. Beverly Hills: Sage.

Kaplan, John. 1981. *The Court-Marshal of the Kaohsiung Defendants*. Berkeley: Institute of East Asian Studies, University of California.

Kawata, Tomoyuka. 1917. *Formosa Today*. Osaka: Taikansha.

Keightley, David N., ed. 1983. *The Origins of Chinese Civilization*. Berkeley: University of California Press.

Kennan Memorandum. 1949. "Kennan Memorandum to Dean Rusk." Record Group 59, U.S. National Archives, Policy Planning Staff file, box no. 13.

Keohane, Robert O. 1984. *After Hegemony: Cooperation and Discord in the World Political Economy*. Princeton: Princeton University Press.

Keohane, Robert O., and Joseph S. Nye, eds. 1972. *Transnational Relations and World Politics*. Cambridge: Harvard University Press.

————. 1977. *Power and Interdependence: World Politics in Transition*. Boston: Little, Brown.

Kerr, George. 1965. *Formosa Betrayed*. London: Eyre and Spottiswoode.

————. 1974. *Formosa: Home Rule and Licensed Revolution*. Honolulu: University Press of Hawaii.

Key, V. O., Jr. 1949. *Southern Politics*. New York: Knopf.

Kicza, John E. 1983. *Colonial Entrepreneurs: Families and Business in Bourbon Mexico City*. Albuquerque: University of New Mexico Press.

Kierman, Frank A., Jr., and John K. Fairbank, eds. 1974. *Chinese Ways in Warfare*. Cambridge: Harvard University Press.

Kim, Jai-hyup. 1978. *The Garrison State in Pre-War Japan and Post-War Korea: A Comparative Analysis*. Washington, D.C.: University Press of America.

Kim, Key-Huik. 1980. *The Last Phase of the East Asian World Order: Korea, Japan and the Chinese Empire, 1860–82*. Berkeley: University of California Press.

Kim, Kwan-bong. 1971. *The Korea-Japan Treaty Crisis and the Instability of the Korean Political System*. New York: Praeger.

Kim, Kwang-suk. 1975. "Outward-Looking Industrialization Strategy: The Case of Korea." In *Trade and Development in Korea*, ed. Wontack Hong and Anne O. Krueger.

Seoul: Korea Development Institute.

Kindleberger, Charles P. 1973. *The World in Depression, 1929–39*. Berkeley: University of California Press.

Kirk, William. 1941–42. "Social Change in Formosa." *Sociology and Social Research* 26:18–26.

Knapp, Ronald G., ed. 1980a. *China's Island Frontier*. Honolulu: University Press of Hawaii.

————. 1980b. "Settlement and Frontier Land Tenure." In *China's Island Frontier*, ed. Ronald G. Knapp. Honolulu: University Press of Hawaii, pp. 55–68.

Knight, F. H. 1921. *Risk, Uncertainty and Profit*. Boston: Houghton Mifflin.

Biography of Ku Hsien-jung. 1940. Taihoku (in Japanese).

Koo, Anthony. 1968. *The Role of Land Reform in Economic Development: A Case Study of Taiwan*. New York: Praeger.

Koo, Hagen. 1984. "The Political Economy of Income Distribution in South Korea." *World Development* 12,10 (October):1029–37.

————. 1987. "The Interplay of State, Social Class, and World System in East Asian Development: The Cases of South Korea and Taiwan." In *The Political Economy of the New Asian Industrialism*, ed. Frederic C. Deyo, pp. 165–81.

Koskoff, David E. 1978. *The Mellons: the Chronicle of America's Richest Family*. New York: Thomas Y. Crowell.

Krueger, Anne O. 1983. *Trade and Employment in Developing Countries*. Chicago: University of Chicago Press.

Kublin, Hyman. 1969. "The Evolution of Japanese Colonialism." *Comparative Studies in Society and History* 2:67–84.

————. 1973. "Taiwan's Japanese Interlude, 1895–1945." In *Taiwan in Modern Times*, ed. Paul K. T. Sih. New York: St. John's University Press, pp. 317–58.

Kubota, Akira. 1924. *Short Biography of Yen Yun-nien*. Taihoku: Taiwan Shinminposha (in Japanese).

Kuhn, Philip. 1970. *Rebellion and Its Enemies in Late Imperial China*. Cambridge: Harvard University Press.

Kumar, Krishna, ed. 1980. "Social and Cultural Impact of Transnational Enterprise: An Overview." In *Transnational Enterprises: Their Impact on Third World Societies and Cultures*, ed. Krishna Kumar. Boulder: Westview, pp. 1–43.

Kung, Lydia. 1983. *Factory Women in Taiwan*. Ann Arbor: UMI Research Press.

Kuo, Shirley W. Y. 1983. *The Taiwan Economy in Transition*. Boulder: Westview.

Kuo, Shirley W. Y., Gustav Ranis, and John C. H. Fei. 1981. *The Taiwan Success Story: Rapid Growth with Improved Distribution in the Republic of China, 1952–79*. Boulder: Westview.

Kuo, Ting-yee. 1973a. "Early Stages of Sinicization of Taiwan, 230–1683." In *Taiwan in Modern Times*, ed. Paul K. T. Sih. New York: St. John's University Press, pp. 21–30.

————. 1973b. "History of Taiwan." In *China and the Question of Taiwan*, ed. Hungdah Chiu. New York: Praeger, pp. 3–27.

————. 1973c. "The Internal Development and Modernization of Taiwan, 1683–1874." In *Taiwan in Modern Times*, ed. Paul K. T. Sih. New York: St. John's University Press, pp. 171–240.

Kuo Wan-yong. 1975. "Income Distribution by Size in Taiwan Area: Changes and Causes." In *Income Distribution, Employment, and Economic Development in Southeast and East Asia*, ed. H. T. Oshima and S. Ishikawa. Tokyo: Japan Economic Research Center, pp. 80–153.

Kurth, James. 1979a. "Industrial Change and Political Change: A European Perspective." In *The New Authoritarianism in Latin America*, ed. David Collier. Princeton: Princeton University Press, pp. 319–62.

————. 1979b. "The Political Consequences of the Product Cycle: Industrial History and Political Outcomes." *International Organization* 33,1 (Winter):1–34.

Kuznets, Paul W. 1977. *Economic Growth and Structural Change in the Republic of Korea*. New Haven: Yale University Press.

Kuznets, Simon. 1955. "Economic Growth and Income Inequality." *The American Economic Review* 45,1:1–28.

————. 1976. "Demographic Aspects of the Size Distribution of Income: An Exploratory Essay." *Economic Development and Cultural Change* 25,1 (October): 1–94.

————. 1979. "Growth and Structural Shifts." In *Economic Growth and Structural Change in Taiwan*, ed. Walter Galenson. Ithaca: Cornell University Press, pp. 15–131.

Kwoh, Vicky. 1978. "Taxation on Royalty Fees and Technical Assistance Fees." *Lee and Li Bulletin* (Taipei) (March).

Ladejinsky, Wolf I. 1977. *Land Reform as Unfinished Business: The Selected Papers of Wolf Ladejinsky*. New York: Oxford University Press.

Lall, Sanjaya. 1979. "Developing Countries and the Emerging International Technological Order." *Journal of International Affairs* (Spring/Summer):77–88.

Lamley, Harry. 1964. "The Taiwan Literati and Early Japanese Rule, 1895–1915." Ph.D. dissertation, University of Washington.

————. 1968. "The 1895 Taiwan Republic." *Journal of Asian Studies* 27,4 (August):789–862.

————. 1970. "The 1895 Taiwan War of Resistance: Local Chinese Efforts against a Foreign Power." In *Taiwan*, ed. Leonard H. D. Gordon. New York: Columbia University Press, pp. 23–77.

————. 1970–71. "Assimilation Efforts in Colonial Taiwan: The Fate of the 1914 Movement." *Monumentica Serica* 29:496–520.

————. 1973. "A Short-Lived Republic and War, 1895: Taiwan's Resistance Against Japan." In *Taiwan in Modern Times*, ed. Paul K. T. Sih. New York: St. John's University Press, pp. 241–316.

————. 1977. "Hsieh-tou: The Pathology of Violence in Southeastern China." *Ch'ing Studies* 3,7 (November):1–39.

————. 1981. "Subethnic Rivalry in the Ch'ing Period." In *The Anthropology of Taiwanese Society*, ed. Emily. M. Ahern and Hill Gates. Stanford: Stanford University Press, pp. 282–318.

Landes, David S. 1965. "Japan and Europe: Contrasts in Industrialization." In *The State and Economic Enterprise in Japan*, ed. William W. Lockwood. Princeton: Princeton University Press, pp. 93–182.

Langer, William. 1935. *The Diplomacy of Imperialism*. New York: Knopf.

Lasswell, Harold D. 1937. "Sino-Japanese Crisis: The Garrison State vs. The Civilian State." *The China Quarterly* 11:643–49.

————. 1941. "The Garrison State." *American Journal of Sociology* 46,4 (January):455–68.

Lebra, Joyce C. 1975. *Japan's East Asia Co-Prosperity Sphere in World War II: Selected Readings and Documents*. New York: Oxford University Press.

Lee, Kuo-wei. 1972. "A Study of Social Background and Recruitment Process of Local Political Decision-Makers in Taiwan." *Indian Journal of Public Administration* 18:227–44.

Lenin, V. I. 1939. *Imperialism, the Highest Stage of Capitalism*. New York: International.

————. 1972 (orig. 1896). *Collected Works*. Vol. 3: *The Development of Capitalism in Russia*. Moscow: Progress.

Leonard, Jane Kate. 1984. *Wei Yuan and China's Rediscovery of the Maritime World.* Cambridge: Harvard University Press.

Lerman, Arthur. 1977. "National Elite and Local Politicians in Taiwan." *American Political Science Review* 71:1406–22.

————. 1978. *Taiwan's Politics: The Provincial Assemblyman's World.* Washington, D.C.: University Press of America.

Lerner, Daniel. 1958. *The Passing of Traditional Society: Modernizing the Middle East.* Glencoe, Il.: Free Press.

Lerner, Daniel, and Wilbur Schram, eds. 1967. *Communications and Change in the Developing Countries.* Honolulu: East-West Center Press.

————, eds. 1976. *Communications and Change, The Last Ten Years—and the Next.* Honolulu: East-West Center Press.

Levy, Marion J., Jr. 1949. *The Family Revolution in Modern China.* Cambridge: Harvard University Press.

————. 1953. "Contrasting Factors in the Modernization of China and Japan." *Economic Development and Cultural Change* 2,3 (October):161–97.

————. 1966. *Modernization and the Structure of Societies: A Setting for International Affairs.* 2 vols. Princeton: Princeton University Press.

Lewin, Linda. 1979. "Some Historical Implications of Kinship Organization for Family-Based Politics in the Brazilian Northeast." *Comparative Studies in Society and History* 21,2 (April):262–92.

Leys, Colin. 1974. *Underdevelopment in Kenya: The Political Economy of Neo-Colonialism, 1964–71.* Berkeley: University of California Press.

————. 1978. "Capital Accumulation, Class Formation and Dependency: The Significance of the Kenyan Case." *Socialist Register*, pp. 241–66.

Li, K. T. 1976. *The Experience of Dynamic Growth on Taiwan.* Taipei: Meiya.

Lichtheim, George. 1971. *Imperialism.* London: Penguin.

Lien, Chan. 1973. "Taiwan in China's External Relations, 1683–1874." In *Taiwan in Modern Times*, ed. Paul K. T. Sih. New York: St. John's University Press, pp. 87–170.

Lien, Ya-tang. 1920–21. *A History of Taiwan.* Taihoku: Taiwan History Press (in Chinese).

Lin, Cheng-chieh. 1981. *The Enjoyable Design of Elections.* Taipei: Roots Magazine (in Chinese).

Lin, Ching-yuan. 1973. *Industrialization in Taiwan, 1946–72: Trade and Import-Substitution Policies for Developing Countries.* New York: Praeger.

Lin, Man-hung. 1979. "Trade and Socioeconomic Change in Late Ch'ing Taiwan". *Shih-huo yue-k'an* 9,4 (20 July):146–60 (in Chinese).

Lin, Po-shou. 1975. *Family History of the Lins of Pan-ch'iao.* Taipei: K'un-chi Printers (in Chinese).

Linck-Kesting, Gudula. 1979. *Ein Kapitel Chinesischer Grenzgeschichte: Han und Nicht Han im Taiwan der Qing Zeuit, 1883–95.* Wiesbaden: Fran Steiner Verlag.

Lindblom, Charles, E. 1977. *Politics and Markets.* New York: Basic.

Linz, Juan. 1964. "An Authoritarian Regime: Spain." In *Cleavages, Ideologies and Party Systems*, ed. Erik Allardt and Yrjo Littunen. Helsinki: Academic Bookstore, pp. 291–341.

————. 1975. "Totalitarian and authoritarian regimes." In *Handbook of Political Science.* Vol. 3: *Macropolitical Theory*, ed. Fred I. Greenstein and Nelson W. Polsby. Reading: Addison-Wesley, pp. 175–411.

————. 1978. "Non-Competitive Elections in Europe." In *Elections Without Choice*, ed. G. Hermet et al. New York: Wiley/Halstead, pp. 36–65.

Lipset, Seymour M. 1981 (orig. 1960). *Political Man: The Social Bases of Politics.*

Baltimore: Johns Hopkins University Press.

Lipton, Michael. 1984. "Family, Fungibility and Formality: Rural Advantages of Informal Non-Farm Enterprise Versus the Urban-Formal State." In *Human Resources, Employment and Development*. Vol. 5: *Developing Countries*, ed. Samir Amin. New York: St. Martins, pp. 189–242.

Little, Arthur D. 1973. *A National Industrial Development Overview: Guidelines and Strategy for Taiwan*. Taipei.

Little, Ian M. D. 1979. "An Economic Reconnaissance." In *Economic Growth and Structural Change in Taiwan*, ed. Walter Galenson. Ithaca: Cornell University Press, pp. 448–507.

Little, Ian, Tibor Scitovsky, and Maurice Scott. 1970. *Industry and Trade in Developing Countries: A Comparative Study*. London: Oxford University Press.

Liu, Chin-ch'ing. 1975. *Analysis of Taiwan's Postwar Economy*. Tokyo: Tokyo University Press (in Japanese).

Liu, F. F. 1956. *A Military History of Modern China, 1924–49*. Princeton: Princeton University Press.

Liu, Henry (Chiang-nan). 1984. *Biography of Chiang Ching-kuo*. Los Angeles: American Tribune (in Chinese).

Liu, Kwang-chih, and Richard J. Smith. 1980. "The Military Challenge: The Northwest and the Coast." In *The Cambridge History of China*, ed. John K. Fairbank and Kwang-chih Liu. New York: Cambridge University Press, pp. 202–73.

Liu, Paul K. C. 1983. "The Role of Education in Fertility Transition in Taiwan." Taipei, Academia Sinica, *Institute of Economics Discussion Paper* no. 8302 (January).

Livingston, Jon, et al., eds. 1973. *The Japan Reader: Imperial Japan, 1800–1945*. New York: Pantheon.

Lomnitz, Larissa Adler, and Marisol Perez Lizaur. 1978. "The History of a Mexican Urban Family." *Journal of Family History* 3,4 (Winter):392–409.

Lowi, Theodore J. 1979. *The End of Liberalism: The Second Republic of the United States*. 2d ed. New York: Norton.

Lowy, Michael. 1981. *The Politics of Combined and Uneven Development*. London: Verso Editions and New Left Books.

Lundberg, Erik. 1979. "Fiscal and Monetary Policies." In *Economic Growth and Structural Change in Taiwan*, ed. Walter Galenson. Ithaca: Cornell University Press, pp. 263–307.

MacKay, George Leslie. 1895. *Far from Formosa*. New York: Revell.

McNeill, William. 1979 (orig. 1965). *A World History*, 3d ed. New York: Oxford University Press.

————. 1982. *The Pursuit of Power*. Chicago: University of Chicago Press.

Mahler, Vincent A. 1980. *Dependency Approaches to International Political Economy: A Cross-National Study*. New York: Columbia University Press.

Mancall, Mark., ed. 1963a. *Formosa Today*. Special issue of *The China Quarterly* 15 (July-September).

————. 1963b. "Introduction." In *Formosa Today*, ed. Mark Mancall. *The China Quarterly*, pp. 1–42.

————. 1964a. "Succession and Myth in Taiwan." *Journal of International Affairs* 18:12–20.

————, ed. 1964b. *Formosa Today*. New York: Praeger.

Mark, Lindy Li. 1972. "Taiwanese Lineage Enterprises: A Study of Familial Entrepreneurship." Ph.D. dissertation, University of California, Berkeley.

Marshall, T. H. 1964. *Class, Citizenship and Social Development*. Garden City, N.Y.: Anchor.

Marton, Katherine. 1987. *Multinationals, Technology and Industrialization: Implications and Impact in Third World Countries*. Lexington: Lexington Books.

May, Ernest R., and James C. Thompson. 1972. *American-East Asian Relations: A Survey*. Cambridge: Harvard University Press.

Meier, Gerald M. 1964. *Leading Issues in Development Economics: Selected Materials and Commentary*. New York: Oxford University Press.

Meisner, Maurice. 1963. "The Development of Formosan Nationalism." In *Formosa Today*, ed. Mark Mancall. *The China Quarterly*, pp. 147–62.

Mendel, Douglas. 1970. *The Politics of Formosan Nationalism*. Berkeley: University of California Press.

Meskill, Johanna. 1979. *A Chinese Pioneer Family: The Lins of Wufeng, Taiwan, 1729–1895*. Princeton: Princeton University Press.

Metzger, Thomas A. 1977. *Escape from Predicament*. New York: Columbia University Press.

Meyer, John W. 1980. "The World Polity and the Authority of the Nation-State." In *Studies of the Modern World-System*, ed. Albert Bergesen. New York: Academic, pp. 109–38.

Meyer, John W., and Michael T. Hannan, eds. 1979. *National Development and the World System*. Chicago: University of Chicago Press.

Miliband, Ralph. 1969. *The State in Capitalist Society: An Analysis of the Western System of Power*. New York: Basic.

————. 1973. "Poulantzas and the Capitalist State." *New Left Review* 82 (November/December):83–92.

Mintz, Sidney W. 1977. "The So-Called World System: Local Initiative and Local Response." *Dialectical Anthropology* 2,4:253–70.

Miyagawa, Jiro. 1926. *People of New Taiwan*. Tokyo: Takushoku Tsushinsha (in Japanese).

Miyazaki, Kenzo. 1932. *Biography of Mr. Ch'en Chung-ho*. Taihoku: Taiwan Nichinichi Shinposa (in Japanese).

Modelski, George. 1978. "The Long Cycle of Global Politics and the Nation-State." *Comparative Studies in Society and History* 20,2 (April):214–35.

Mommsen, Wolfgang J. 1982. *Theories of Imperialism*. Chicago: University of Chicago Press.

Moore, Barrington. 1966. *Social Origins of Dictatorship and Democracy: Lord and Peasant in the Making of the Modern World*. Boston: Beacon.

Moulder, Frances V. 1977. *Japan, China and the Modern World Economy*. New York: Cambridge University Press.

Murphy, Rhoads. 1974. "The Treaty Ports and China's Modernization." In *The Chinese City Between Two Worlds*, ed. Mark Elvin and G. William Skinner. Stanford: Stanford University Press, pp. 17–71.

Mutual Security Agency (MSA). 1952. *TOMUS/D-9* (28 January)

————. 1953a. *TOMUS/D-215* (12 June)

————. 1953b. *TOMUS/D-6* (20 July)

————. 1953c. *TOMUS/D-16* (27 July)

————. 1953d. *TOMUS/D-54* (6 August)

————. 1953e. *TOMUS/D-74* (28 October)

Mutual Security Mission. 1953. "Fundamental Conclusions as a Result of Study and Close Association with Conditions of the Industrial Society." (11 December, unpubl. internal document).

Myers, Ramon H. 1972a. "Taiwan Under Ch'ing Imperial Rule, 1684–1895: The Traditional Economy." *Journal of the Insitute of Chinese Studies of The Chinese University of Hong Kong* 5,2:373–409.

————. 1972b. "Taiwan Under Ch'ing Imperial Rule, 1684–1895: The Traditional

Society." *Journal of the Institute of Chinese Studies of The Chinese University of Hong Kong* 5,2:413–51.

————. 1973. "Taiwan as an Imperial Colony of Japan: 1895–1945." *Journal of the Institute of Chinese Studies of the Chinese University of Hong Kong* 6:425–53.

————. 1974. "Taiwan's Agrarian Economy Under Japanese Rule." *Journal of the Institute of Chinese Studies of The Chinese University of Hong Kong* 7,2:451–74.

————. 1984. "The Economic Transformation of the Republic of China on Taiwan." *The China Quarterly* 99 (September):500–28.

Myers, Ramon H., and Mark R. Peattie, eds. 1984. *The Japanese Colonial Empire, 1895–1945*. Princeton: Princeton University Press.

Nadel, Siegfried Frederick. 1957. *Theory of Social Structure*. Glencoe, Il.: Free Press.

Nagai, Yonosuke, and Akira Iriye, eds. 1977. *The Origins of the Cold War in Asia*. New York: Columbia University Press.

Najita, Tekuo. 1967. *Hara Kei in the Politics of Compromise, 1905–1915*. Cambridge: Harvard University Press.

Nakagawa, Keiichiro, ed. 1977. *Social Order and Entrepreneurship*. Tokyo: University of Tokyo Press.

Nakamura, Takafusa. 1981. *The Postwar Japanese Economy: Its Development and Structure*. Tokyo: University of Tokyo Press.

————. 1983. *Economic Growth in Prewar Japan*. New Haven: Yale University Press.

Nathan, Andrew J. 1976. *Peking Politics, 1918–23: Factionalism and the Failure of Constitutionalism*. Berkeley: University of California Press.

————. 1985. *Chinese Democracy*. New York: Knopf.

Nie, Norman H., et al. 1979. *The Changing American Voter*. Cambridge: Harvard University Press.

Nish, Ian H. 1966. *The Anglo-Japanese Alliance*. London: Athlone.

Nolan, Peter D. 1983. "Status in the World System, Income Inequality, and Economic Growth." *American Journal of Sociology* 89,2 (September):410–19.

Nordlinger, Eric A. 1981. *On the Autonomy of the Democratic State*. Cambridge: Harvard University Press.

Norman, E. Herbert. 1940. *Japan's Emergence as a Modern State*. New York: Institute of Pacific Relations.

————. 1975 (orig. 1940). *Origins of the Modern Japanese State*. New York: Pantheon.

Norich, Samuel. 1980. "Interlocking Directorates, the Control of Large Corporations, and Patterns of Accumulation in the Capitalist Class." In *Classes, Class Conflict, and the State: Empirical Studies in Class Analysis*, ed. Maurice Zeitlin. Cambridge: Winthrop, pp. 83–106.

Numazaki, Ichiro. 1986. "Networks of Taiwanese Big Business." *Modern China* 12,4 (October):487–534.

O'Donnell, Guillermo A. 1973. *Modernization and Bureaucratic-Authoritarianism: Studies in South American Politics*. Berkeley: Institute of International Studies, University of California.

Olson, Mancur. 1965. *The Logic of Collective Action*. Cambridge: Harvard University Press.

Organization for Economic Cooperation and Development (OECD). Various years. *Development Cooperation: Efforts and Policies of the Members of the Development Assistance Committee*. Paris: OECD.

Overseas Development Council (ODC). 1979. *The United States and World Development: Agenda 1979*. New York: Praeger.

Owen, Roger, and Bob Sutcliffe, eds. 1977. *Studies in the Theory of Imperialism*. London: Longman.

Ozawa, Terutomo. 1979. *Multinationalism, Japanese Style: The Political Economy of Outward Dependency*. Princeton: Princeton University Press.

Ozono, Ichizo. 1916. *Records of Taiwanese*. Taihoku: Iwahasi (in Japanese).

————. 1921. *The Devil Ku Hsien-jung*. Taihoku: Taiwan Bunji KK (in Japanese).

————. 1931a. *The Times and the Men*. Taihoku: Nippon Shokuminchi Hihansha (in Japanese).

————. 1931b. *Enterprises and Men*. Taihoku: Nippon Shokuminchi Hihansha (in Japanese).

————. 1931c. *Pan-ch'iao and the House of Lin Pen-yuan*. Taihoku: Nippon Shokuminchi Hihansha (in Japanese).

Packenham, Robert A. 1973. *Liberal America and the Third World*. Princeton: Princeton University Press.

Paine, Edward (with Ai Chih Tsai). 1946. *Formosa Weekly Report for Office of the Economic and Financial Advisor, United Nations Relief and Rehabilitation Administration, Taipei*. Taipei: Report 1–20, 26 May–6 October.

Palma, Gabriel. 1978. "Dependency: A Formal Theory of Underdevelopment of a Methodology for the Analysis of Concrete Situations of Underdevelopment?" *World Development* 6, 7/8 (July/August):881–924.

Parish, William L. 1970. "Kinship and Modernization in Taiwan." Ph.D. dissertation, Cornell University.

Pasternak, Burton. 1969. "The Role of the Frontier in Chinese Lineage Development." *Journal of Asian Studies* 28,3:551–61.

————. 1972. *Kinship and Community in Two Taiwanese Villages*. Stanford: Stanford University Press.

Patnaik, Prabhat. 1972. "Imperialism and the Growth of Indian Capitalism." In *Studies in the Theory of Imperialism*, ed. Roger Owen and Bob Sutcliffe. London: Longman, pp. 210–29.

Patrick, Hugh, ed. 1987. *Japan's High Technology Industries: Lessons and Limitations of Industrial Policy*. Seattle: University of Washington Press.

Paukert, Felix. 1973. "Income Distribution at Different Levels of Development: A Survey of Evidence." *International Labour Review* 108, 2–3:97–125.

Peattie, Mark R. 1984. "Japanese Attitudes Toward Colonialism, 1895–1945." In *The Japanese Colonial Empire*, ed. Ramon H. Myers and Mark R. Peattie. Princeton: Princeton University Press, pp. 80–127.

Peck, James. 1976. "Revolution versus Modernization and Revisionism." In *China's Uninterrupted Revolution*, ed. Victor Nee and James Peck. New York: Pantheon, pp. 57–217.

P'eng, Ming-min. 1971. "Political Offenses on Taiwan: Laws and Problems." *The China Quarterly* 47:471–93.

————. 1972. *A Taste of Freedom*. New York: Holt, Rinehart and Winston.

Pepper, Suzanne. 1978. *Civil War in China: The Political Struggle, 1945–49*. Berkeley: University of California Press.

Perkins, Dwight H., ed. 1975. *China's Modern Economy in Historical Perspective*. Stanford: Stanford University Press.

Perlmutter, Amos. 1981. *Authoritarianism: A Comparative Institutional Analysis*. New Haven: Yale University Press.

Perry, Elizabeth J. 1980. "Review of States and Revolutions." *Journal of Asian Studies* 39,3 (May):533–35.

Plummer, Brenda Gayle. 1980. "The Metropolitan Connection: Foreign and Semiforeign Elites in Haiti, 1900–15." *Latin American Research Review*: 119–42.

Polachek, James. 1976. "Literati Groups and Literati Politics in Early Nineteenth Century China." Ph.D. dissertation, University of California, Berkeley.

————. "The Inner Opium War." Typescript.
Polanyi, Karl. 1967 (orig. 1944). *The Great Transformation*. New York: Beacon.
Pollack, Jonathan. 1986. "The Military Balance in the Taiwan Strait and the Implications of China's Military Modernization." *AEI Foreign and Defense Review* 6,3:35–41.
Portes, Alejandro, and John Walton. 1981. *Labor, Class, and the International System*. New York: Academic.
Poulantzas, Nicos. 1973. *Classes in Contemporary Capitalism*. London: Verso.
Przeworksi, Adam, and Henry Teune. 1982 (orig. 1970). *Logic of Comparative Social Inquiry*. Melbourne, Fl.: Krieger.
Pu, Yu-fu. 1965. *Who's Who of Outstanding Personages on Taiwan*. Taipei: Newsworld (in Chinese).
Pye, Lucian W., ed. 1963. *Communications and Political Development*. Princeton: Princeton University Press.
————. 1971. *Warlord Politics*. New York: Praeger.
Pye, Lucian W., and Sidney Verba, eds. 1965. *Political Culture and Political Development*. Princeton: Princeton University Press.
Quester, George. 1977. *Offense and Defense*. New York: Wiley.
Ramirez, Francisco O., and Jane Weiss. 1979. "The Political Incorporation of Women." In *National Development and the World System*, ed. John W. Meyer and Michael T. Hannan. Chicago: University of Chicago Press, pp. 238–49.
Ramirez, Francisco O., and Richard Rubinson. 1979. "Creating Members: The Political Incorporation and Expansion of Public Education." In *National Development and the World System*, ed. John W. Meyer and Michael T. Hannan. Chicago: University of Chicago Press, pp. 72–82.
Ranis, Gustav, ed. 1971. *Government and Economic Development*. New Haven: Yale University Press.
————. 1974. "Taiwan." In *Redistribution with Growth*, ed. Hollis Chenery et al. London: Oxford University Press, pp. 285–90.
————. 1979. "Industrial Development." In *Economic Growth and Structural Change in Taiwan*, ed. Walter Galenson. Ithaca: Cornell University Press, pp. 206–62.
Ranis, Gustav, and Chi Schive. 1985. "Direct Foreign Investment in Taiwan's Development." In *Foreign Trade and Investment*, ed. Walter Galenson. Madison: University of Wisconsin Press, pp. 85–137.
Rankin, Karl J. 1964. *China Assignment*. Seattle: University of Washington Press.
Ransom, Harry H. 1963. *Can American Democracy Survive the Cold War?* New York: Doubleday.
Reischauer, Edwin O., and John K. Fairbank. 1960. *East Asia: The Great Tradition*. Boston: Houghton Mifflin.
Republic of China, Chamber of Industry and Commerce. 1955, 1963, 1970. *Who's Who of Industry and Commerce in the Republic of China*. Taipei: Chamber of Industry and Commerce.
Republic of China, Government Information Office. Various years. *China Yearbook*. Taipei: Government Information Office.
Riggs, Fred W. 1952. *Formosa Under Chinese Nationalist Rule*. New York: Macmillan.
Robinson, Ronald. 1977. "Non-European Foundations of European Imperialism: Sketch for a Theory of Collaboration." In *Studies in the Theory of Imperialism*, ed. Robert Owen and Bob Sutcliffe. London: Longmans, pp. 117–42.
Rohsenow, Hill Gates. 1973. "Prosperity Settlement: The Politics of Paipai in Taipei, Taiwan." Ph.D. dissertation, University of Michigan.
Rokkan, Stein, et al. 1970. *Citizens, Elections, Parties*. New York: David McKay.
Rosenau, James N., ed. 1967. *Domestic Sources of Foreign Policy*. New York: Free Press.

—————, ed. 1969. *International Politics and Foreign Policy*. 2d ed. New York: Free Press.

Rozman, Gilbert, ed. 1981. *The Modernization of China*. New York: Free Press.

Rubinson, Richard. 1976. "The World-Economy and the Distribution of Income Within States: A Cross-National Study." *American Sociological Review* 41,4 (August):638–59.

—————. 1978. "Political Transformation in Germany and the United States." In *Social Change in the Capitalist World Economy*, ed. Barbara Hockey Kaplan. Beverly Hills: Sage, pp. 39–74.

—————, ed. 1981. *Dynamics of World Development*. Beverly Hills: Sage.

Rubinson, Richard, and Dan Quinlan. 1977. "Democracy and Social Inequality: A Reanalysis." *American Sociological Review* 42,4 (August):611–23.

Ruggie, John, ed., 1983. *The Antinomies of Interdependence: National Welfare and the International Division of Labor*. New York: Columbia University Press.

Rushing, Francis, and Carole G. Brown. 1986. *National Policies for Developing High Technology Industries*. Boulder: Westview.

Rustow, Dankwart A. 1967. *A World of Nations*. Washington, D.C.: Brookings Inst.

Sakai, Robert K. 1968. "The Ryukyu (Liu-ch'iu) Islands as a Fief of Satsuma." In *The Chinese World Order*, ed. John K. Fairbank. Cambridge: Harvard University Press, pp. 112–34.

Sando, Ruth Ann E. 1981. "The Meaning of Development For Rural Areas: Depopulation in a Taiwanese Farming Community." Ph.D. dissertation, University of Hawaii.

Sangren, Paul Steven. 1980. "A Chinese Marketing Community: An Historical Ethnography of Ta-ch'i, Taiwan." Ph.D. dissertation, Stanford University.

—————. 1984. "Traditional Chinese Corporations: Beyond Kinship." *Journal of Asian Studies* 43,3 (May):391–415.

Scalapino, Robert A. 1953. *Democracy and the Party Movement in Prewar Japan*. Berkeley: University of California Press.

Schaller, Michael. 1979. *The U.S. Crusade in China, 1938–45*. New York: Columbia University Press.

Schreiber, Jordan C. 1970. *U.S. Corporate Investment in Taiwan*. New York: Dunellen.

Schurmann, Franz. 1973. *The Logic of World Power*. New York: Pantheon.

Scott, Maurice. 1979. "Foreign Trade." In *Economic Growth and Structural Change in Taiwan*, ed. Walter Galenson. Ithaca: Cornell University Press, pp. 308–83.

Seers, Dudley. 1983. *The Political Economy of Nationalism*. New York: Oxford University Press.

Shaw, Yu-ming. 1979. "Modern History of Taiwan: An Interpretive Account." In *China and the Taiwan Issue*, ed. Hungdah Chiu. New York: Praeger, pp. 7–36.

Shen, T. H. 1970. *The Sino-American Joint Commission on Rural Reconstruction*. Ithaca: Cornell University Press.

Shepherd, John Robert. 1981. "Plains Aborigines and Chinese Settlers on the Taiwan Frontier in the Seventeenth and Eighteenth Centuries." Ph.D. dissertation, Stanford University.

Shih, Ming. 1962. *Four Hundred Years of Taiwan History*. Tokyo: Otoba Shobo (in Japanese).

—————. 1980. *Four Hundred Year History of the Taiwanese People*. San Jose: P'eng-tao Culture Co. (in Chinese).

Sih, Paul K.T., ed. 1973. *Taiwan in Modern Times*. New York: St. John's University Press.

Sih, Paul K.T. 1970. *The Strenuous Decade: China's Nation-Building Efforts, 1927–37*. New York: St. John's University Press.

Silin, Robert H. 1976. *Leadership and Values: The Organization of Large-Scale Taiwanese Enterprises*. Cambridge: Harvard University Press.

Simon, Denis Fred. 1980. "Taiwan, Technology Transfer and Transnationalism: The Political Management of Dependency." Ph.D. dissertation, University of California, Berkeley.

———. 1986. "Taiwan's Political Economy and the Evolving Links Between the PRC, HK and Taiwan." *AEI Foreign Policy and Defense Review* 6,3:42–51.

———. 1987. *Taiwan, Technology Transfer and Transnationalism*. Boulder: Westview.

Simon, Denis Fred, and Chi Schive. 1986. "Taiwan." In *National Policies for Developing High Technology Industries*, ed. Francis Rushing and Carole G. Brown. Boulder: Westview, pp. 201–26.

Singer, Milton. 1968. "The Indian Joint Family in Modern Industry." In *Structure and Change in Indian Society*, ed. Milton Singer and Bernard S. Cohen. Chicago: Aldine, pp. 423–52.

Skinner, G. William. 1977a. "Cities and the Hierarchy of Local Systems." In *The City in Late Imperial China*, ed. G. William Skinner. Stanford: Stanford University Press, pp. 275–353.

———, ed. 1977b. *The City in Late Imperial China*. Stanford: Stanford University Press.

Skocpol, Theda. 1979. *States and Revolutions: A Comparative Analysis of France, Russia and China*. New York: Cambridge University Press.

Smith, Carol A. 1984. "Local History in Global Context: Social and Economic Transitions in Western Guatemala." *Comparative Studies in Society and History*, 26,2 (April):193–228.

Smith, Tony. 1979. "The Underdevelopment of Development Literature: The Case of Dependency Theory." *World Politics* (January).

———. 1981. *The Pattern of Imperialism*. New York: Cambridge University Press.

Snyder, David, and Edward L. Kick. 1979. "Structural Position in the World System and Economic Growth, 1955–70: A Multiple-Network Analysis of Transnational Interactions." *American Journal of Sociology* 84,5 (March):1096–1126.

So, Kwan-wai. 1975. *Japanese Piracy in Ming China during the 16th Century*. East Lansing: Michigan State University Press.

Solef, Michael. 1980. "The Finance Capitalists." In *Classes, Class Conflict, and the State: Empirical Studies in Class Analysis*, ed. Maurice Zeitlin. Cambridge: Winthrop, pp. 62–82.

Solomon, Richard H., ed. 1980. *Asian Security in the 1980s: Problems and Policies for a Time of Transition*. Boston: Oelgeschlager.

Speare, Alden, Jr. 1969. "The Determinants of Rural to Urban Migration in Taiwan." Ph.D. dissertation, University of Michigan.

Speidel, William M. 1967. "Liu Ming-ch'uan in Taiwan, 1884–1891." Ph.D. dissertation, Yale University.

———. 1974. "Elite Response to Modernization in Late Ch'ing Taiwan." Paper prepared for 26th Annual Meeting of the Association for Asian Studies, Boston, Ma.

———. 1976. "The Administrative and Fiscal Reforms of Liu Ming-ch'uan in Taiwan, 1884–91." *Journal of Asian Studies* 35,3 (May):441–59.

Spence, Jonathan D., and John E. Wills, Jr., eds. 1979. *From Ming to Ch'ing*. New Haven: Yale University Press.

Spencer, Daniel, and Alexander Worniak, eds. 1967. *The Transfer of Technology to Developing Countries*. New York: Praeger.

Stavis, Benedict. 1974. *Rural Local Governance and Agricultural Development in Taiwan*. Ithaca: Rural Development Committee, Cornell University.

Stepan, Alfred. 1978. *State and Society: Peru in Comparative Perspective*. Princeton: Princeton University Press.

Stewart, Charles, and Yasumitsu Nihei. 1987. *Technology Transfer and Human Factors*. Lexington: Lexington Books.

Stewart, Frances. 1977. *Technology and Underdevelopment*. London: Macmillan.

Stinchcombe, Arthur. 1982. "The Growth of the World System." *American Journal of Sociology* 87,6 (May):1389–95.

Stites, Richard. 1982a. "Small-Scale Industry in Yingge, Taiwan." *Modern China* (April):247–79.

————. 1982b. "Small-Scale Industry in Yingge, Taiwan." Ph.D. dissertation, University of Washington.

Stockholm International Peace Research Institute (SIPRI). 1975, 1978. *World Armaments and Disarmament Yearbook*. Cambridge: M.I.T. Press.

Strachan, Harry W. 1976. *Family and Other Business Groups in Economic Development: The Case of Nicaragua*. New York: Praeger.

Strange, Susan, and Roger Tooze, eds. 1981. *The International Politics of Surplus Capacity: Competition for Market Shares in the World Recession*. Winchester, Ma.: Allen Unwin.

Street, James, and Dilmus James, eds. 1979. *Technological Progress in Latin America: The Prospects for Overcoming Dependency*. Boulder: Westview.

Stueck, William W., Jr. 1981. *The Road to Confrontation: American Policy Towards China and Korea, 1947–50*. Chapel Hill: University of North Carolina Press.

Sun, Chia-ch'i. 1961a. *How Chiang Ching-kuo Stole the Country*. Hong Kong: Independent (in Chinese).

————. 1961b. *Why I Left the Nationalist Party*. Hong Kong: Independent (in Chinese).

Sunkel, Osvaldo. 1973. "Transnational Capitalism and National Disintegration in Latin America." *Social and Economic Studies* 22:132–76.

Swartz, Marc J., Victor W. Turner, and Arthur Tuden, eds. 1966. *Political Anthropology*. Chicago: Aldine.

Swidler, Ann. 1986. "Culture in Action." *American Sociological Review* 51,2 (April):273–86.

Szymanski, Albert. 1981. *The Logic of Imperialism*. New York: Praeger.

————. 1983. "Comment on Bornschier, Chase-Dunn, and Rubinson." *American Journal of Sociology* 89,3 (November):690–94.

Tai, Hung-chao. 1970. "The Kuomintang and Modernization in Taiwan." In *Authoritarian Politics in Modern Society*, ed. Samuel P. Huntington and Clement Moore. New York: Basic, pp. 406–36.

————. 1974. *Land Reform and Politics: A Comparative Analysis*. Berkeley: University of California Press.

Taipei Consular Files, U.S. Consulate. 1947–50. Washington, D.C.: National Archives.

Taiwan Commercial Who's Who. 1948. Taipei: Kuo-kuang (in Chinese).

Taiwan Factory Namelist. 1968 (in Chinese).

Taiwan Industrial Panorama (Taipei). 1979. Issues 8 and 11.

Taiwan Jinshikan (Who's Who in Taiwan). 1934. Taihoku: Taiwan Shinposha.

Taiwan Kaisha Tekiyo (Outline of Companies in Taiwan). 1924. Taihoku: Taiwan Ginko.

Taiwan Minkan Shokuinroku (Employees of Private Enterprises in Taiwan). 1920. Taihoku: Matsuuraya.

Taiwan Private-Sector Factory Namelist. 1953. 2 vols. Taichung: Taiwan Provincial Government (in Chinese).

Taiwan Research Center. Various years. *Taiwan Yearbook*. Tokyo: Taiwan Research

Center (in Japanese).

Taiwan Shin Min Pao. 1938. *Who's Who of Taiwan*. Taipei: TSMP (in Japanese).

Taiwan Who's Who. 1953 Taipei: New Taiwan (in Chinese).

T'ai-yang K'uang-yeh Kung-ssu Ssu-shih-nien Chih (Fortieth Anniversary of Taiyang Mining Corporation). 1958. Taipei.

Takekoshi, Yosaburo. 1907. *Japanese Rule in Formosa*. New York: Longman's Green.

Tang, Hui-sun. 1954. *Land Reform in Free China*. Taipei: Joint Commission on Rural Reconstruction.

Tang, Mei-chun. 1978. *Urban Chinese Families: An Anthropological Field Study in Taipei City, Taiwan*. Taipei: National Taiwan University.

Taylor, Charles L., and M. C. Hudson. 1972. *World Handbook of Political and Social Indicators*. 2d ed. New Haven: Yale University Press.

Taylor, John G. 1979. *From Modernization to Modes of Production*. London: Macmillan.

Teng, Ssu-yu, and John K. Fairbank, eds. 1954. *China's Response to the West*. Cambridge: Harvard University Press.

Thomas, Clive. 1984. *The Rise of the Authoritarian State in Peripheral Societies*. New York: Monthly Review.

Thomas, George, and John Meyer. 1980. "Regime Changes and State Power in an Intensifying World-State-System." In *Studies of the Modern World-System*, ed. Albert Bergesen. New York: Academic, pp. 139–58.

Thomas, George, et al. 1979. "Maintaining Boundaries in the World System: The Rise of Centralist Regimes." In *National Development and the World System*, ed. John W. Meyer and Michael T. Hannan. Chicago: University of Chicago Press, pp. 187–206.

Thompson, E. P. 1963. *The Making of the English Working Class*. London: Gollancz.

Thompson, William R. 1983. "Succession Crises in the Global Political System: A Test of the Transition Model." In *Crises of the World System*, ed. Albert Bergesen. Beverly Hills: Sage, pp. 93–116.

Tien, Hung-mao. 1972. *Government and Politics in Republican China, 1927-37*. Stanford: Stanford University Press.

―――. 1975. "Taiwan in Transition: Prospects for Sociopolitical Change." *The China Quarterly* 64 (December):615–44.

Tilly, Charles, ed. 1975. *The Formation of National States in Western Europe*. Princeton: Princeton University Press.

―――. 1978. *From Mobilization to Revolution*. Reading: Addison-Wesley.

Trimberger, Ellen Kay. 1973. "A Theory of Elite Revolutions." *Studies in Comparative International Development* 7,3 (Fall):191–207.

―――. 1978. *Revolution from Above*. New Brunswick: Transaction.

Tripathi, Dwijendra. 1981. *The Dynamics of a Tradition: Kasturbhai Lalbhar and His Entrepreneurship*. New Delhi: Manohar.

Ts'ai, P'ei-huo, et al., eds. 1982 (orig. 1971). *A History of the Taiwanese Nationalist Movement*. Taipei: Independent Evening Post (in Chinese).

Tsou, Tang. 1959. *The Embroilment over Quemoy*. Salt Lake City: IIS.

―――. 1963. *America's Failure in China, 1941-50*. Chicago: University of Chicago Press.

Tsurumi, E. Patricia. 1967. "Taiwan Under Kodama Gentaro and Goto Shimpei." In *Papers on Japan* 4, ed. Albert Craig. Cambridge: East Asian Research Center, Harvard University.

―――. 1977. *Japanese Colonial Education in Taiwan, 1895-1945*. Cambridge: Harvard University Press.

―――. 1980. "Mental Captivity and Resistance: Lessons from Taiwanese Anti-Colonialism." *Bulletin of Concerned Asian Scholars* 12,2 (April-June):2–13.

————. 1984. "Colonial Education in Korea and Taiwan." In *The Japanese Colonial Empire*, ed. Ramon H. Myers and Mark R. Peattie. Princeton: Princeton University Press, pp. 275-311.

T'u, Chao-yen. 1975. *Taiwan Under Japanese Imperialism*. Tokyo: Tokyo University Press (in Japanese).

Tuchman, Barbara. 1972. *Stillwell and the American Experience in China, 1911-45*. New York: Macmillan.

Tucker, Nancy Bernkopf. 1983. *Patterns in the Dust*. New York: Columbia University Press.

Tung, William. 1968. *Political Institutions of Modern China*. The Hague: Martinus Nijhoff.

Tylecote, Andrew B., and Marian L. Lonsdale-Brown. 1982. "State Socialism and Development: Why Russian and Chinese Ascent Halted." In *Ascent and Decline in the World-System*, ed. Edward Friedman. Beverly Hills: Sage, pp. 255-87.

United Nations. 1967, 1980. *Statistical Yearbook, 1967, 1979/80*. New York: United Nations.

————. 1979. *U.N. Yearbook of International Trade Statistics*. New York: United Nations.

United States. Agency for International Development (US AID). 1955a. "Memo from R.D. Smith to Arndt, Logan c/o AD/E." (31 March, unpub. memorandum).

————. 1955b. "Memo from Y.M. Lin to R.D. Smith." (18 March, unpub. memorandum).

————. Department of Defense. 1971. *United States-Vietnam Relations, 1945-67*. Washington, D.C.: GPO.

————. Department of State. 1949. *United States Relations with China*. Washington, D.C.: GPO.

Vaitsos, Constantine. 1973. "Bargaining and the Distribution of Returns in Purchase of Technology by Developing Countries." In *Underdevelopment and Development: The Third World Today*, ed. Henry Bernstein. New York: Penguin, pp. 315-22.

Valenzuela, Samuel J., and Arturo Valenzuela. 1978. "Modernization and Dependency: Alternative Perspectives in the Study of Latin American Underdevelopment." *Comparative Politics* 10,4 (July):535-57.

Verba, Sidney, et al. 1978. *Participation and Political Equality: A Seven Nation Comparison*. New York: Cambridge University Press.

Wade, Robert. 1984. "Dirigisme Taiwan-Style." *Institute of Development Studies Bulletin* 15,2 (April):65-70.

————. 1985. "East Asian Financial Systems as a Challenge to Economics: Lessons from Taiwan." *California Management Review* 27,4 (Summer):106-127.

————. 1988. *Governing the Market: Economic Theory and Taiwan's Industrial Policies*. Princeton: Princeton University Press (tent.)

Wakeman, Frederic. 1966. *Strangers at the Gate*. Berkeley: University of California Press.

————. 1970. "High Ch'ing: 1683-1839." In *Modern East Asia*, ed. James B. Crowley. New York: Harcourt, Brace and World, pp. 1-28.

————. 1975. *The Fall of Imperial China*. New York: Free Press.

————. 1977. "Rebellion and Revolution: The Study of Popular Movements in Chinese History." *Journal of Asian Studies* 36,2 (February):201-38.

Wakeman, Frederic, and Carolyn Grant, eds. 1975. *Conflict and Control in Late Imperial China*. Berkeley: University of California Press.

Walker, Richard. 1973. "Taiwan's Movement into Political Modernity, 1945-72." In *Taiwan in Modern Times*, ed. Paul K. T. Sih. New York: St. John's University

Press, pp. 359–96.

Wallerstein, Immanuel. 1974. *The Modern World-System: Capitalist Agriculture and the Origins of the European World-Economy in the Sixteenth Century*. New York: Academic.

————. 1976. "The State and Social Transformation: Will and Possibility." In *Underdevelopment and Development: The Third World Today*, ed. Henry Bernstein. New York: Penguin, pp. 277–83.

————. 1979. *The Capitalist World-Economy*. New York: Cambridge University Press.

————. 1980. *The Modern World-System II: Mercantilism and the Consolidation of the European World-Economy*. New York: Academic.

————. 1983. *Historical Capitalism*. New York: Schocken.

————. 1985. "The Relevance of the Concept of Semiperiphery to Southern Europe." In *Semiperipheral Development*, ed. Giovanni Arrighi. Beverly Hills: Sage, pp. 31–39.

Walton, John. 1966. "Substance and Artifact: The Current Status of Research on Community Power Structure." *American Journal of Sociology* 71, 4 (January):430–38.

————. 1971. "A Methodology for the Comparative Study of Power: Some Conceptual and Procedural Applications." *Social Science Quarterly* 52 (January):39–60.

————. 1984. *Reluctant Rebels*. New York: Columbia University Press.

Waltz, Kenneth N. 1979. *The Theory of International Politics*. Reading: Addison-Wesley.

Wang, Hung-yue. 1976–77. "Carry Forward the Seventy-five-Year Record." *Shih-ye Shih-chieh* 128–36 (November-July) (in Chinese).

Wang, I-shou. 1980. "Cultural Contact and the Migration of Taiwan's Aborigines: A Historical Perspective." In *China's Island Frontier*, ed. Ronald G. Knapp. Honolulu: University Press of Hawaii, pp. 31–54.

Ward, Michael Don. 1978. *The Political Economy of Distribution: Equality versus Inequality*. New York: Elsevier.

Ward, Robert, ed. 1968. *Political Development in Modern Japan*. Princeton: Princeton University Press.

Weber, Max. 1968 (orig. 1925). *Economy and Society*. 3 vols. New York: Bedminster.

Wei, Yung. 1973. "Political Development in the Republic of China on Taiwan." In *China and the Question of Taiwan*, ed. Hungdah Chiu. New York: Praeger, pp. 74–111.

White, Harrison C. 1970. *Chains of Opportunity: System Models of Mobility in Organizations*. Cambridge: Harvard University Press.

White, Harrison C., Scott A. Boorman, and Ronald L. Breiger. 1976. "Social Structure from Multiple Networks. I. Blockmodels of Roles and Positions." *American Journal of Sociology* 81,4 (January):730–80.

White, Lawrence J. 1974. *Industrial Concentration and Economic Concentration in Pakistan*. Princeton: Princeton University Press.

Whyte, Martin K., and William L. Parish. 1984. *Urban Life in Contemporary China*. Chicago: University of Chicago Press.

Wickberg, Edgar B. 1970. "Late Nineteenth Century Land Tenure in North Taiwan." In *Taiwan*, ed. Leonard H. D. Gordon. New York: Columbia University Press, pp. 78–92.

————. 1981. "Continuities in Land Tenure, 1900–1940." In *The Anthropology of Taiwanese Society*, ed. Emily Martin Ahern and Hill Gates. Stanford: Stanford University Press, pp. 212–38.

Wilber, Charles, ed. 1979. *The Political Economy of Development and Underdevelopment*. New York: Random House.

Williams, Jack F. 1980. "Sugar: The Sweetener in Taiwan's Development." In *China's*

Island Frontier, ed. Ronald G. Knapp. Honolulu: University Press of Hawaii, pp. 219–51.

―――, ed. 1976. *The Taiwan Issue*. East Lansing: Asian Studies Center, Michigan State University.

Wills, John E., Jr. 1968. "Ch'ing Relations with the Dutch, 1662–90." In *The Chinese World Order*, ed. John K. Fairbank. Cambridge: Harvard University Press, pp. 225–56.

―――. 1974. *Pepper, Guns and Parleys: The Dutch East India Company and China, 1662–81*. Cambridge: Harvard University Press.

―――. 1979. "Maritime China from Wang Chih to Shih Lang: Themes in Peripheral History." In *From Ming to Ch'ing*, ed. Jonathan D. Spence and John E. Wills. New Haven: Yale University Press, pp. 201–38.

Wilson, Richard W. 1970. *Learning to Be Chinese*. Cambridge: M.I.T Press.

Winckler, Edwin A. 1979. "China's World-System: Social Theory and Political Practice in the 1970s." In *The World System of Capitalism*, ed. Walter Goldfrank. Beverly Hills: Sage, pp. 53–69.

―――. 1981. "Roles Linking State and Society." In *The Anthropology of Taiwanese Society*, ed. Emily M. Ahern and Hill Gates. Stanford: Stanford University Press, pp. 13–37.

―――. 1984. "Institutionalization and Participation on Taiwan: From Hard to Soft Authoritarianism?" *The China Quarterly* 99 (September):481–99.

―――. 1987. "Statism and Familism on Taiwan." In *Ideology and National Competitiveness: An Analysis of Nine Countries*, ed. George Lodge and Ezra Vogel. Boston: Harvard Business School Press.

Wolf, Eric R. 1982. *Europe and the People Without History*. Berkeley: University of California Press.

Wong, Chun-Kit Joseph. 1981. *The Changing Chinese Family Pattern in Taiwan*. Taipei: Southern Materials Center.

Wong Siu-lun. 1985. "The Chinese Family Firm: A Model." *The British Journal of Sociology* 36,1:58–72.

―――. 1986. "Modernization and Chinese Culture in Hong Kong." *The China Quarterly* 106 (June):306–25.

World Bank. 1980, 1983. *World Tables*. Washington, D.C.: World Bank.

―――. Various years. *World Development Report*. Washington, D.C.: World Bank.

World Culture Service. 1952. *Who's Who of Free China*. Taipei: World Culture Service.

―――. 1957. *Who's Who in Free China*. Vol. 4: *Industrial and Commercial Entrepreneurs*. Taipei: World Culture Service.

Wright, Mary C. 1957. *The Last Stand of Chinese Conservatism*. Stanford: Stanford University Press.

―――, ed. 1968. *China in Revolution: The First Phase, 1900–1913*. New Haven: Yale University Press.

Wu, Tsung-min. 1979. "Study of the Formation of Taiwan Business Groups." M.A. thesis, National Chengchih University (in Chinese).

Wuthnow, Robert. 1980. "World Order and Religious Movements." In *Studies of the Modern World-System*, ed. Albert Bergesen. New York: Academic, pp. 57–76.

―――. 1983. "Cultural Crises." In *Crises in the World System*, ed. Albert Bergesen. Beverly Hills: Sage, pp. 57–71.

Yanaihara, Tadeo. 1956. Orig. 1929. *Taiwan Under Japanese Imperialism*. Taipei: Bank of Taiwan (in Chinese).

Yang, B. L. 1978. *Taiwan Who's Who in Business*. Taipei: Harvard Management Service.

Yang, Martin C. 1970. *Socioeconomic Results of Land Reform in Taiwan*. Honolulu: University of Hawaii Press.

Yen, Sophia S. F. 1965. *Taiwan in China's Foreign Relations, 1836–74.* Hamden, Ct.: Shoe String.

Yi, Hsi. 1955. "The Investment of Japanese Zaibatsu in Taiwan." *Collection of Writings on Taiwan's Economic History*, No. 2. Taipei: Bank of Taiwan, pp. 129–39 (in Chinese).

Yi, Hsi-liang. 1955. "A Retrospective on Economic Development in Taiwan During the Period of Japanese Occupation." *Chu-yi yu Kuo-ts'e* 5:22–28 (in Chinese).

Yin, Alexander Chien-chung. 1975. "Migration and Voluntary Associations in Rural and Urban Taiwan: A Study of Group Adaptive Strategies in Social Change." Ph.D. dissertation, University of Hawaii.

Young, Arthur. 1963. *China and the Helping Hand, 1937–45.* Cambridge: Harvard University Press.

Young, Ernest. 1970. "Nationalism, Reform and Republican Revolution: China in the Early Twentieth Century." In *Modern East Asia*, ed. James B. Crowley. New York: Harcourt, Brace and World, pp. 151–79.

Young, Marilyn B. 1972. "The Quest for Empire." In *American-East Asian Relationships: A Survey*, ed. Ernest May and James C. Thompson. Cambridge: Harvard University Press, pp. 131–42.

Yu, George T. 1966. *Party Politics in Republican China: The Kuomintang, 1912–24.* Berkeley: University of California Press.

Yu, Hsi. 1955. "The Capital Structure of Taiwanese Enterprises in the Period of Japanese Occupation." *Collection of Writings on Taiwan's Economic History*, No. 2. Taipei: Bank of Taiwan, pp. 140–45 (in Chinese).

Zagoria, Donald S., ed. 1982. *Soviet Policy in East Asia.* New Haven: Yale University Press.

Zeitlin, Maurice. 1974. "Corporate Ownership and Control: The Large Corporations and the Capitalist Class." *American Journal of Sociology* 79,5 (March):1073–1119.

Zeitlin, Maurice, Lynda Ann Ewen, and Richard Earl Ratcliff. 1974. "New Princes for Old? The Large Corporation and the Capitalist Class in Chile." *American Journal of Sociology* 80,1 (July):87–123.

Zelin, Madeleine. 1985. *The Magistrate's Tael: Rationalizing Fiscal Reform in Eighteenth Century Ch'ing China.* Berkeley: University of California Press.

INDEX